EMILE DURKHEIM

EMILE DURKHEIM

Le Suicide

One Hundred Years Later

Edited by
David Lester, PhD

The Charles Press, Publishers
Philadelphia

The Charles Press, Publishers
Post Office Box 15715
Philadelphia, PA 19103
(215) 545-8933

Library of Congress Cataloging-in-Publication Data

Emile Durkheim : le suicide one hundred years later / edited by David
  Lester.
       p. cm.
    Includes bibliographical references and index.
    ISBN 0-914783-73-4
    1. Durkheim, Emile, 1858-1917. Le suicide. 2. Suicide-
  Sociological aspects. I. Lester, David, 1942-
  HV6545.E48 1994
    394'.8 – dc20   94-1056
                                                                     CIP

Editor

David Lester, PhD

Professor of Psychology
Richard Stockton State College
Pomona, New Jersey
and
Executive Director
Center for the Study of Suicide
Blackwood, New Jersey

Contributors

G.E. Berrios, MA (Oxon), MD
Consultant and Lecturer in Neuropsychiatry
Department of Psychiatry
University of Cambridge
Cambridge, England

Kevin D. Breault, PhD
Associate Professor of Sociology
Austin Peay State University
Clarksville, Tennessee

Jack P. Gibbs, PhD
Centennial Professor of Sociology, Emeritus
Vanderbilt University
Nashville, Tennessee

Barclay D. Johnson, PhD
Assistant Professor of Sociology
Department of Sociology and Anthropology
Carleton University
Ottawa, Ontario, Canada

Howard I. Kushner, PhD
Director, Master of Arts in Liberal Arts Program
Department of History
San Diego State University
San Diego, California

David Lester, PhD
Executive Director
Center for the Study of Suicide
Blackwood, New Jersey

Sean MacNamara, BA
Department of Sociology
University of California
San Diego, California

Philip A. May, PhD
Director, Center on Alcoholism, Substance
    Abuse, and Addictions
Department of Sociology and Psychiatry
University of New Mexico
Albuquerque, New Mexico

Ferenc Moksony, PhD
Associate Professor of Sociology
Budapest University of Economic Sciences
Budapest, Hungary

Michael A. Overington, PhD
Professor of Sociology
Saint Mary's University
Halifax, Nova Scotia, Canada

Bernice A. Pescosolido, PhD
Associate Professor of Sociology
Indiana University
Bloomington, Indiana

David P. Phillips, PhD
Professor of Sociology
University of California
San Diego, California

Todd E. Ruth, BA
Department of Computer Science
San Diego, California

Steven Stack, PhD
Director, Criminal Justice Program
Wayne State University
Department of Sociology
Detroit, Michigan

Steve Taylor, PhD
Lecturer in Medical Sociology
University of London
London, England

Nancy Westlake Van Winkle, PhD
Assistant Professor of Behavioral Sciences
College of Osteopathic Medicine
Oklahoma State University
Tulsa, Oklahoma

Bijou Yang, PhD
Assistant Professor of Economics
Drexel University
Philadelphia, Pennsylvania

Contents

Preface

David Lester, PhD

Nearly 100 years have passed since the publication of Emile Durkheim's landmark book, *Le Suicide.* The book is frequently described as one of the two or three most important and influential works ever published in the social sciences and is considered the seminal work on suicide. Many other books on suicide were published before *Suicide** and, of course, hundreds since then, but only Durkheim's book has achieved unrivaled, overwhelming prominence. Remarkably, the importance of *Suicide* has not diminished or become lost with time; even today, practically every new book on suicide and self-destruction cites Durkheim's contribution and influence.

How many books in the social sciences (or for that matter, any science) are actively discussed, cited as a reference and still written about 100 years later as the publication of the present volume attests? Just what was Durkheim's contribution to our understanding of suicide? Are his methods and conclusions justifiable? Would Durkheim's work pass muster today? In effect, what was so monumental in Durkheim's work that it left the indelible mark it has on current thinking? Over the years, several scholars have attempted to answer these and similar questions. In light of the leading position Durkheim's views have been accorded, not infrequently these critics seem like lone swimmers bucking the tide of accepted thinking. Could some of Durkheim's views possibly have been wrong?

As we approach the hundredth anniversary of the publication of Durkheim's remarkable book, it seemed valuable and propitious to celebrate this event with this book. To this end, I invited some of the most highly esteemed suicidologists and scholars throughout the world (mainly sociologists, but also those from other academic disciplines) to write essays on their views of Durkheim and the exact nature and quality of his contribution to the study of suicide. This volume presents these essays — some highly critical, some worshipful, and others, using Durkheim's theory as a springboard, have developed new hypotheses; the range

---

* From here on, I have used the anglicized version of the title of Durkheim's book. While most of the contributors have done the same, some have retained the original French title, *Le Suicide.*

of the contributors' interests and subjects varies greatly. Included in the collection is an early paper written by Durkheim on suicide that has been translated into English for the first time. This article permits comparison of Durkheim's early thoughts on suicide with his more mature views described in *Suicide* nine years later. Although many of the contributors express negative views of Durkheim's work, all acknowledge the primacy of his theory. The opinions are fascinating and do much to clarify Durkheim's role. I am very grateful to all of the contributors for their sterling efforts in making this book the successful venture I originally envisioned. Before presenting the essays, it is appropriate to provide a very brief biography of Durkheim's schooling, academic career and role in originating the science of sociology. This information offers a context for judging Durkheim's work.

EMILE DURKHEIM: A BRIEF BIOGRAPHY

David Emile Durkheim was born in France on April 5, 1858 at Epinal in Lorraine. The youngest of four children, he had an older brother and two older sisters. His father, grandfather and great-grandfather had been rabbis and his mother came from a family of merchants. Durkheim grew up in a close-knit orthodox and traditional Jewish family and was destined for the rabbinate, but at an early age he decided not to follow this career. One biographer (Lukes 1972) describes Durkheim as a child who had a serious and austere view of life, who felt remorse whenever he experienced any pleasure.

Schooling

Durkheim went to the local school where he performed well, skipping two grades. Durkheim was 12 years old during the Franco-Prussian war, during which time the Prussians occupied the town of Epinal. The French defeat perhaps contributed to his patriotism and his desire to contribute to the renaissance of France. Durkheim received his *baccalauréats* in letters in 1874 and in sciences in 1875. In 1876, he left for Paris to prepare himself for entrance to the Ecole Normale Supérieure, but it took him three years before he was finally admitted. During these years, not only did he suffer from financial hardship, but he was also burdened by having to study subjects such as Latin and rhetoric in order to master the entrance requirements.

At the Ecole, Durkheim found the academic competition stressful, and he developed a strong fear of failure. Although he obtained his *licence* with maximum honors after his first year (for which he delivered an oral improvisation on the genius of Molière), he remained apprehensive about his ability. The course of study was hard. In fact, the students were essentially locked in for much of the time, allowed outside only on Thursday afternoons and on Sundays. Despite this, the time Durkheim spent at the Ecole was intellectually exhilarating and led to close friendships with the other students. Many students were concerned with social and political issues, and this certainly motivated Durkheim's involvement with these issues. He thought that he would spend the first part of his adulthood in scientific study and the remainder in politics. At that time, his friends described Durkheim's manner as mature and serious, nicknaming him "the Metaphysician." During his years at the Ecole, Durkheim broke his affiliation with Judaism, henceforth regarding religion as a distorted form of morality.

In his second year at the Ecole, Durkheim turned to the study of sociology. Influenced by the philosophers Renouvier and Boutroux, he also espoused the scientific study of morality and rationalism. During his final year, he was seriously ill and this impaired his academic performance, but nevertheless he successfully took his *agrégation* on 1882. He then began teaching philosophy in the lycées, where he did well and was admired and respected by his students. An inspector of the schools described Durkheim as serious, cold in appearance, conscientious, hard-working, well-informed and clever. His teaching was described as exact, precise and clear.

In 1885-86, Durkheim spent a term visiting several German universities, including Berlin and Leipzig, under the sponsorship of the Ministry of Public Instruction. His articles on philosophy and social science while in Germany were well received, and in 1887 he was appointed *chargé de cours* of social science and pedagogy, a position created for him in the Faculty of Letters of the University of Bordeaux, where he stayed until 1902.

In 1887, Durkheim married Louise Dreyfus, whose family was from Alsace and whose father ran a foundry in Paris. Their marriage was happy; Louise helped him in his work, copying manuscripts, correcting proofs and assisting with the work on *Année Sociologique*. They had two children, André and Marie.

The University Teacher

Durkheim spent 15 years at the University of Bordeaux where he prepared several important courses of lectures on topics ranging from the history of pedagogy to criminology. During this time, he also published many major studies including *The Division of Labor*, *The Rules of Sociological Method*, and *Suicide*. He worked long hours on his lectures and scholarly work, and he had several mental breakdowns because he overworked.

The appointment of Durkheim — a social scientist — to the Faculty of Letters was an innovation for there were many critics of the sociological view of phenomena. His appointment was officially in pedagogy, but he was allowed to add sociology to pedagogy on the faculty list only as a special favor. In this way, sociology was first introduced into French universities. The unpopularity of Durkheim's views perhaps prevented him from being offered a professorship in Paris and encouraged his stay in Bordeaux.

Durkheim pursued his intellectual goals by persuading the faculty to include required social science courses in the program for the *agrégations* in philosophy and in law. He gave lectures on education to the school teachers once or twice a week. Both in Bordeaux and later in Paris, he had a tremendous influence on school teachers in France. He took this extracurricular teaching very seriously, but it was a burden to him. On Saturdays he gave public courses on social science, most of which were on difficult topics. He used an entirely new approach that required intensive preparation. In 1896, he and his colleagues established a new journal, *Année Sociologique,* but Durkheim was the major influence at the journal, participating in everything from revising the copy to supervising the setting up of the proofs. In 1893, he presented his doctoral thesis at the Sorbonne, and his doctorate was awarded despite opposition of his examiners to his ideas. He was described at that time as tall, thin and already bald. His voice could be feeble and subdued but it rose and grew animated as he talked.

His work on suicide began with an article in 1888, followed by a public course on this subject (his third) in 1889-90. He then worked on the topic for seven more years before producing his monumental book *Le Suicide,* published in 1897. Interestingly, one of Durkheim's closest friends at the Ecole, Victor Hommay, committed suicide in 1886 while teaching in a provincial lycée.

His ideas on social science continued to arouse controversy and his works were often critically reviewed. He responded with vehement defenses and attacks on others. Politically, Durkheim was a liberal, a socialist and anticlerical. At the time of the famed Dreyfus affair, in which Alfred Dreyfus, an innocent Jewish army officer was convicted of being a traitor, Durkheim became an active member of the *Ligue pour la Défense des Droits de l'Homme,* and he founded an association of university teachers and students at Bordeaux where political and ideological issues were discussed.

Finally, in 1902, Durkheim was appointed as *chargé d'un cours* in the Science of Education at the Sorbonne, and he remained there until his death in 1917. Since his lectures on education were compulsory for all students seeking *agrégations* in sciences and in letters, this new position gave him great influence over the teachers of France in whom he tried to imbue a rational secular morality. He reportedly fell into a depression when he first arrived in Paris, occasioned to some extent by the guilt he felt about leaving his friends and colleagues in Bordeaux.

At the Sorbonne he continued his scholarly studies, but he also assumed administrative duties, another area in which his influence was also felt. His ideas continued to provoke great controversy, partly because he expressed them so pungently and dogmatically and partly because they were so extreme. In particular, many scholars were aroused by his methodological principles, his critique of liberal economics, and his sociological treatment of morality, knowledge and religion.

The War and His Last Years

The advent of the First World War ended Durkheim's intellectual work because he completely immersed himself in the war effort. He continued to teach, of course, though many students were drafted into the military. His chief activities in the war effort were writing and organizing, particularly to counter German propaganda. He was on countless committees despite his ill health.

Durkheim was very devoted to his son André, who shared his father's intellectual interests. André was sent to the Bulgarian front in late 1915 and was declared missing in January 1916. By April, Durkheim realized that André was dead. Adding to this pain, Durkheim was accused twice that year of being a German sympathizer, once in the French Senate.

Durkheim continued his activities despite his grief and his ill health. He became feverish and emaciated and late in 1916 he suffered a stroke. His health never recovered, and on November 15, 1917, he died.

Durkheim was a man who had a considerable presence, dominating every situation in which he found himself. His students became his disciples. Even in his daily life he was serious and forbidding, yet to his friends, he could be warm and loyal. In an era when an intellectual person could have a serious impact on society, Durkheim's influence was profound.

REFERENCES

LaCapra, D. *Emile Durkheim*. Ithaca, NY: Cornell University Press, 1972.
Lukes, S. *Emile Durkheim: His Life and Work*. New York: Harper & Row, 1972.
Taylor, S. *Durkheim and the Study of Suicide*. New York: St. Martin's Press, 1982.

EMILE DURKHEIM

1

Suicide and Social Theory

Steve Taylor, PhD

Durkheim intended *Suicide* to be much more than a book about why people kill themselves. Its more general aim was to demonstrate to a skeptical world the case for an independent academic discipline concerned with the study of society. The purpose of this chapter is to focus on Durkheim's search for a "science of society" and to consider whether or not, a hundred years on, *Suicide* has any continuing relevance for social theory. By social theory I do not mean particular theories of this or that form of behavior, but rather the fundamental philosophical dilemmas that necessarily lie at the core of all social investigation.

Unfortunately, there are many actively engaged in research who mentally "switch off" at the mention of social theory, claiming that they are only interested in "real research" and not abstract theorizing. Such a response is unjustified. Theory and research are not separate activities, but rather inextricably bound together. As Johnson, Dandecker and Ashworth (1984), in their classic text on social theory, rightly observe:

> Sociological analysis...cannot help but bring into play a whole body of theorizing about the nature of society and social action and how sociological knowledge may be generated. The most antitheoretical observer is, in fact, involved in complex forms of theorizing. Thus even to recommend simple data collection...is to theorize the social world as an aggregate of particular items of behavior which are amenable to such forms of investigation (p. 12).

The authors go on to point out that there are two theoretical questions which are unavoidable for social researchers because all social knowledge *assumes* an answer to each. The first question is, what is the nature of social reality? The second is, how can we obtain knowledge of it? In explaining how Durkheim approached these "unavoidable" questions in *Suicide,* I shall first distinguish Durkheim's position from some of the mistaken interpretations of the work that abound in the secondary literature. Second, I shall outline the conception of social reality and the means of understanding it advanced in *Suicide*. Finally, I shall consider the extent to which contemporary social theory can be said to have progressed "beyond Durkheim." In raising these issues I am not implying that "theorizing" is a substitute for, or prior to, empirical research. However, I am suggesting that as "theory" is an inevitable part of "research," more thought should be given to the assumptions underlying the collection and interpretation of data.

THE MYTHOLOGY OF SUICIDE

I have argued elsewhere that it is important to distinguish the theoretical position of *Suicide* from the erroneous accounts of the book that predominate in the secondary texts (Taylor, 1982). These errors have been repeated so often and are now so widely believed that *Suicide* is now interpreted in terms of a series of mythologies. There are two that are particularly important in this context. The first, usually advanced critically by proponents of an interpretive, or subjectivist, approach to social science, claims that *Suicide* was a model for modern positivist sociology. Thus Wacquant (1993) has written:

> *Suicide* [is] arguably the exemplar of French positivism, in which Durkheim shunned the analysis of meaning of suicide in favor of uncovering its social types and causes via a statistical analysis of its group correlates and variations (p. 497).

Positivism is, of course, used in a variety of ways (Giddens, 1977). However, its essential characteristics may be defined as a philosophical position embodying an ontology grounded in nominalism and phenomenalism; an epistemology arguing that the only certain knowledge we can obtain comes from observation or experience and a variety of methodologies based on a belief in the unity of scientific practice. The majority of subsequent studies of suicide rates by sociologists make precisely these assumptions, and there are certainly positivistic elements in Durkheim's work. However, the theoretical position in *Suicide* may be differentiated from positivism in important respects. First, for Durkheim, social facts which allegedly cause suicide were not nominal but holistic, not given by experience but, nonetheless, real. Thus we find Durkheim trying to explain the stable rate between suicide and various forms of external association in terms of (invisible but real) "suicidogenic currents," arising from the moral forces generated by collective life. The causal concepts of egoism, altruism, anomie and fatalism could not be experienced by sensory perception but were only revealed by theoretical analysis. Thus it is surely curious, and it should have struck the many writers who see *Suicide* as the "exemplar" of positivism as curious, that we find there neither the fact-value dichotomy nor the distinction between (fictional) theoretical and (real) observational categories that characterize positivist works. On the other hand, contrary to the claim of Wacquant and so many others, we do find Durkheim trying to explain (in a nonsubjectivist sense) the meaningful states that give rise to suicidal impulses.

A second widespread myth about *Suicide* is that, in trying to explain such an "individual" act in terms of society, Durkheim was arguing the case for a crude, antipsychological sociologism that ignored the individual. This accusation is usually thrown at *Suicide* from psychological and psychiatric students of the problem. Hendin (1978), for example, suggested that Durkheim's aim "was to make the psychology of suicide seem irrelevant." We even find sociologists, who should know better, peddling the same myth. Gibbs (1968) tells us that "Durkheim had an axe to grind. Above all, he was an implacable foe of psychological explanations." Pope (1976) supports this, suggesting that Durkheim was attempting to demonstrate the superiority of sociological explanations over psychological ones.

In fact, Durkheim was opposed to neither psychology nor the study of the individual. He was interested in both. His opposition was to *individualist* explanation. This is not a criticism of studying the individual (i.e. as opposed to the social), it is a criticism of accepting individual consciousness as the basis for explaining people's actions. In the first place, as Durkheim (1952) made clear in his criticism of Tarde:

> ...psychical life, far from being directly cognisable, has on the contrary profound depths inaccessible to ordinary perception, to which we attain only gradually by devious and complicated paths like those employed by the sciences of the external world. The nature of consciousness is therefore far from lacking mystery for the future (p. 311).

Secondly, in his criticism of utilitarianism, Durkheim argued that the very existence of "individuals," and their capacity to form stable relations of exchange and contract, necessarily presupposes the existence of an overriding moral order.

It was the *relationship* between the individual and this moral order that Durkheim sought to explain. At the center of his theory of suicide (and of his sociology generally) was his notion of *homo duplex*. Each person's life has a double center of gravity. On the one hand there is individuality and the body on which it is based; on the other hand, there is all that expresses something other than the self. There is perpetual tension between the two. As Durkheim (1952) explains:

> To be sure in so far as we are solidary with the group and share its life, we are exposed to their influence; but so far as we have a distinct personality of our own we rebel against and try to escape them. Since everyone leads this sort of double existence simultaneously, each of us has a double impulse. We are drawn in a social direction and tend to follow the inclinations of our own natures....Two antagonistic forces confront each other. One, the collective force tries to take possession of the individual, the other, the individual force, repulses it (p. 318).

In Durkheim's theory of suicide the key concept of integration, rather than being some empiricist notion of the amount or strength of the "social support" an individual can draw on (cf. Lin and Ensel, 1989), is the theoretical concept of harmony between the antagonistic poles of human existence. Therefore, the sources of psychological distress that give rise (among other things) to suicide, come either from excessive repression of the individual nature by the social (altruism, fatalism), or from the social nature being eclipsed by the individual (egoism, anomie). In this context, applying Durkheim's theory of suicide to health generally, Taylor and Ashworth (1987) have observed:

> From this [Durkheimian] point of view it is not a question of whether [or not] particular social situations, or given events, are necessarily stressors, but rather how we are to explain a process that upsets the balance between the individual and social components of human nature (p. 47).

Thus, in contrast to much recent sociology, which tends to work with a mechanical and materialist model of social causation, Durkheim's work *retains* the individual and seeks to explain suicide in terms of series of *meaningful* states. While society "exists in" and inevitably influences all people, it does not and can never "take them over" (conquest by socialization) in the manner assumed by much sociological theory. Contrary to the myth, it is not Durkheim, but many of his "successors" in sociology (in particular) who have created the division between supposedly "external" and "internal" explanations, by employing a crude social determinism where "factors" literally external to passive individuals "push" them toward suicide, crime, disease or whatever. In using abstract theoretical structures to try and explain human actions in terms of the tensions arising from the precarious relationship between the animal and social beings in all persons, Durkheim has far more in common with Freud than with most of the sociologists allegedly following in his tradition.

THE REALITY OF SOCIETY

If, as I have suggested above, *Suicide* is not the classic example of a positivist social determinism, in what ways is the work of interest to contemporary social theory? My answer to this would be that, as *social* scientists, our concern is to try to produce explanations and relatively objective data about the relationship between collective life and individual actions of one sort or another. I have already observed that this necessarily involves certain unavoidable theoretical tensions. I would further argue that Durkheim's work is of particular relevance in this context because he set out more clearly and coherently than any other major social theorist the problems created by the *idea* of a science of society and, in *Suicide,* we see perhaps his most spectacular attempt to overcome these problems.

What characterized Durkheimian sociology, and distinguished it from empiricism and idealism, is the insistence that there can be no social science without the recognition and demonstration that society is an irreducible reality.

> If there is such a science as sociology, it can only be the study of a world hitherto unknown, different from those explored by the other sciences. This world is nothing if not a system of realities (Durkheim, 1952, p. 310).

In this sense Durkheim's view can be further differentiated from the functionalism of Parsons (1968) and others. While the functionalist examines the relations between the observable components of the "social system," Durkheim was concerned with the theoretical analysis of the hidden structures that generate these observable phenomena. Durkheim set out to show that societies were *really* more than the sum of their parts and generated a collective consciousness, a kind of group mind. Many secondary commentators from Parsons onwards, broadly sympathetic to Durkheim, have sought to defend him by explaining away this "metaphysical oversight." Lukes (1975), in his acclaimed academic biography of Durkheim, has suggested that the description of "forces" and "currents" acting on individuals and inclining them to suicide was "distinctly inappropriate analogical language...at odds with the central social psychological theory advanced in *Suicide*" (p. 216). Cresswell (1974) has argued that Durkheim's concept of the collective consciousness could now be supplanted and that "later writers had considerable justification in ignoring [Durkheim's] philosophical realism" (p. 143).

However, given Durkheim's intentions, as opposed to the empiricists who followed him, the language was completely appropriate. His concepts, he insisted over and over again, were not fictions, but social realities. Thus explaining the relationship between the collective consciousness and suicide, he argued that:

> It is not a mere metaphor to say of each human society that it has a greater or lesser aptitude for suicide; the expression is based on the nature of things. Each social group really has a collective inclination for the act, quite its own, and the source of all inclination rather than their result (Durkheim, 1952, p. 299).

It is important to distinguish between two responses to Durkheim's realism. It is one thing to question, as many critics have legitimately done, Durkheim's *particular* interpretation and alleged demonstration of social reality in terms of a collective consciousness arising from the moral forces of social life. However, it is much harder to dismiss the more general point Durkheim makes time and again in *Suicide* that, without *some* irreducible reality to study, there can be no science of society. Durkheim warned that those who try to build explanations on the shifting sands of empirical associations, or on states of individual consciousness are, in fact, robbing sociology "of the only object proper to it" (Durkheim, 1952, p. 38).

However, this is precisely what generations of social scientists have tended to do, including those claiming to be developing Durkheim's theory of suicide (Taylor, 1982). The general association of social research with empiricism of one sort or another has meant that most work is restricted either to subjectively perceived empirical associations, or to interpretive accounts of "real world" situations. Thus the popular view of social science, that it is, at best, a more systematic account of the lay person's view of the world is, apparently, one most social scientists are content to embrace. The search for the generative mechanisms that might give rise to various empirical associations has been ruled out of court by most social researchers and, whatever the value of their work in descriptive terms, it makes no sense to talk about it as "social science."

Durkheim was aware of the limitations of such approaches, even in his day, and sought to avoid them by trying to establish a definite object of inquiry, a social reality which exists over and above individuals considered singly and constrains their activities. But how are we to interpret this reality and *demonstrate* its effects on individual action? Durkheim was clear in *Suicide* that we cannot resort to experience:

> If we really had only to open our eyes and take a good look to perceive at once the laws of the social world, sociology would useless or at least very simple (Durkheim, 1952, p. 311).

The nature of social reality, then, is not "given" to us by our mere participation in society; it is only to be revealed by abstract theoretical analysis. However, Durkheim was quite clear that demonstration of its effects must transcend the logic of rationalist argument and that sociology "must become more than a new sort of philosophical literature" (Durkheim, 1952, p. 36).

This was the problem Durkheim tried to resolve most dramatically in *Suicide,* arguing that the regularity of the suicide rates can be explained in terms of differing currents of egoism, anomie, altruism and fatalism. However, in attempting such an exercise, Durkheim tried to get the best of two contradictory theoretical worlds. Without appearing to relinquish his realism, he still maintained that we know social reality exists by experiencing its effects. At times, he went as far as claiming that the variation and stability of the rates in themselves *proved* that such an apparently individual act as suicide is constrained to a greater or lesser degree by the moral forces of social life:

> But it hardly seems possible to use that there will not emerge...from every page of this book, so to speak, the impression that the individual is dominated by a moral reality greater than himself: namely collective reality. When each people is seen to have its own suicide-rate, more constant than that of the general mortality...and that marriage, divorce, the family, religious society, the army, etc., affect it in accordance with definite laws, some of which may even be numerically expressed—these states and institutions will no longer simply be regarded as characterless, ineffective ideological arrangements. Rather they will be felt to be real, living, active forces which, because of the way they determine

the individual, prove their independence of him....Thus it will appear more clearly why sociology can and must be objective, since it deals with realities as definite and substantial as those of the psychologist or biologist (Durkheim, 1952, p. 38).

This assertion is clearly at odds with the central theoretical position of *Suicide*. If, as Durkheim tells us, the relationships between suicide and various rates of external association are merely manifestations of social reality, then they cannot be used (as they legitimately can in empiricism) to establish causality. Durkheim's explanation of the comparatively low suicide rates of Jews is often cited in this context. Although education was associated with comparatively high suicide rates, this did not apply to Jews who tended to be well educated and yet well protected from suicide. Durkheim explained this by observing that education tended to have a different meaning for Jews. It did not undermine, but rather was superimposed on, their collective social values.

While this explanation is quite consistent with the general social-psychological theory of *Suicide,* which sees suicidal actions as the product of certain meaningful states and does not assume a necessary order at the nominal and phenomenal level, it is totally *inconsistent* with Durkheim's claim that his theory is both derived from and confirmed by the data. Durkheim's more sophisticated empiricist critics, such as Gibbs and Martin (1964) and Douglas (1967), have homed in on this. They argue that the theory is not really scientific at all because, in the final analysis, it refuses to submit itself to the empirical world for validation or refutation. In contrast, analysis of *Suicide* from a realist position suggests more or less the opposite view of an essentially scientific theory welded to a crude empiricist epistemology (Taylor, 1982). However, both critiques demonstrate the inconsistencies and contradictions in *Suicide* in terms of *Durkheim's* own criteria for establishing a science of society. Rather than going beyond the limits of rationalism and empiricism, as he clearly intended to do, Durkheim vacillated between the two epistemological positions he had previously identified as false, in the sense of being "nonscientific."

When we inquire further into the origins of Durkheim's causal concepts—his collective representations—we also find him less than consistent. He was clear that they were more than material factors (positivism), or underlying material structures (Marxism). Thus he did not attribute the "social causes" of suicide to "factors" in the material or social environment. However, he was equally clear that society is not reducible to structures of thought (idealism). Thus he was not, and would not be, interested in (interpretive) sociological explanations of suicide based on individual experiences of suicidal situations (cf. Baechler, 1979), or the (social constructionist) problem of how certain deaths came to be seen, or labeled, as "suicides" (cf. Atkinson, 1979). Again, Durkheim had good reasons for wanting sociological explanations to avoid being *either* materialist *or* idealist. Indeed, it is not difficult to develop a compelling Durkheimian critique of these positions as they apply to the sociology of suicide (Taylor, 1990). However, looking at Durkheim's own position, we are entitled to conclude that, if the origins of his causal concepts are to be found in neither matter nor in mind, their ontological status is, to say the least, ambiguous. The irony is that we are tempted to "read" Durkheim's concept of society as a fiction, a description of something more "real." This was the last thing he intended. In fact, all his sociological work was directed to demonstrating precisely the opposite.

BEYOND DURKHEIM?

Given the ambiguities and failings of *Suicide* in terms of Durkheim's own aims, are we therefore justified (as most social theorists seem to feel we are) in granting the book an honored, but essentially historical, role in the development of social science? Have we subsequently resolved the problems the book poses for social theory, or rendered them irrelevant? I am not optimistic. It seems to me that social science's response to the problems raised by Durkheim has been to retreat into schools of thought that cluster around one or other of the poles of the realist-nominalist, materialist-idealist dilemmas he tried to synthesize. For example, in my own field—the sociology of health—the two dominant paradigms are a positivist sociology looking for the influence of "social" (i.e., material) variables on the origins of disease, and a variety of interpretive perspectives trying to understand varying conceptions, and experiences, of health and illness (Gerhardt, 1989).

Both these approaches, however, share the positivist view of science (the debate being whether or not it is applicable to the study of society) and a commitment to empiricism of one sort or another. In philosophy and in social theory in the 1970s and 1980s, an increasingly widespread disillusionment with empiricism, in all its forms, resulted in the theoretical pendulum swinging back toward examining the possibilities of a realist science of society (Harre, 1986; Bhaskar, 1986).

Of course, the adoption of realist theory and the development of realist strategies for research (Pawson, 1989) hardly represents a solution to the Durkheimian problem. While releasing the researcher from the straitjacket of empiricism, it directs attention back toward the problem of establishing, in order for social science to exist, properties of social life that are irreducible to their effects. From this position, social science involves the theoretical exercise of uncovering the generative structures that produce observable effects. However, having made this ontological leap, we are back with the epistemological problem of demonstrating the relationship between structure and effects. While the natural scientist (working with closed systems) is usually able to predict outcomes, the social scientist (invariably working with open systems (is denied decisive test situations. Thus, as Bhaskar (1979) rightly observes, social science has to be explanatory and nonpredictive. The realist is thus left to fall back upon rationalist justifications of theory. Now it may well be that rationalism as an epistemology is preferable to empiricism, and certainly the example of linguistics would suggest that this is so. However, Durkheim was clear a social *science* should provide more than a rationalist explanation of its theories, and it was this realization that dragged him back in the direction of empiricism. I have already discussed the specific contradictions this produced in *Suicide,* but the problems that gave rise to them are fundamental to all social science.

The more the social scientist tries to use effects to demonstrate the existence of generative structures, then the more these structures are diluted until they become mere descriptions of the empirical world. We can observe this in many post-Durkheimian sociological works on suicide, for example, where concepts such as egoism, integration or anomie have become descriptions for processes such as urbanization, industrialization, decline in religion and so on. Alternatively, the more structures and effects are kept conceptually distinct, in best rationalist tradition, then the more the material world dissolves into a mere representation of the logical, deductive powers of the human mind. This can be seen in Taylor's (1982) rationalist attempt to adapt Durkheim's theoretical model to a variety of suicidal actions illustrated by case studies. In the final analysis, it is only reason (i.e., as opposed to empirical "proof") that links the explanatory structure to the real world.

Durkheim's desire to avoid both these positions in *Suicide* led to the vacillation and contradiction outlined above. However, the tendency of approaches in contemporary social science to run up one or other of the nonproductive cul-de-sacs he identified and sought to avoid hardly represents progress.

CONCLUSION

Natural science is neither the ordering of experience nor the mind understanding itself, yet it is difficult for the social scientist to avoid one or other of these positions. Few have been more aware of this than Durkheim and perhaps nowhere are the resulting tension and the brilliant attempt to resolve them more evident than in *Suicide.* This is one of the reasons why this incredible book should be read with more care by more people. With social science in something of a "crisis"—both theoretically and methodologically—perhaps *Suicide* is even more important today than it was in 1897.

REFERENCES

Atkinson, J. *Discovering Suicide.* London: Macmillan, 1978.
Baechler, J. *Suicides.* Oxford: Blackwell, 1979.
Bhaskar, R. *The Possibility of Naturalism.* Brighton: Harvester, 1979.
Bhaskar, R. *Scientific Realism and Human Emancipation.* London: Verso, 1986.

Cresswell, P. Suicide: The stable rates argument. *Journal of Biosocial Science,* 1974, 6, 133-145.

Douglas, J. *The Social Meanings of Suicide.* Princeton, NJ: Princeton University Press, 1967.

Durkheim, E. *Suicide: A Study in Sociology.* London: Routledge, 1952.

Gerhardt, U. *Ideas About Illness.* London: Macmillan, 1989.

Gibbs, J. (ed.). *Suicide.* New York: Harper & Row, 1968.

Gibbs, J., and Martin, W. *Status Integration and Suicide.* Eugene: University of Oregon Press, 1964.

Giddens A. *Studies in Social and Political Theory.* London: Hutchinson, 1977.

Harre, R. *Varieties of Realism.* Oxford: Blackwell, 1986.

Hendin, H. Suicide: The psychosocial dimension. *Suicide and Life-Threatening Behavior,* 1968, 8, 115-123.

Johnson, T., Dandeker, C., and Ashworth, C. *The Structure of Social Theory.* London: Macmillan, 1984.

Lin, N., and Ensel, W. Life stress and health: stressors and resources. *American Sociological Review,* 1989, 54, 382-399.

Lukes, S. *Emile Durkheim: His Life and Work: An Historical and Critical Study.* London: Peregrine, 1975.

Parsons, T. *The Structure of Social Action.* Glencoe, IL: Free Press, 1968.

Pawson, R. *A Measure for Measures: A Manifesto for Empirical Sociology.* London: Routledge, 1989.

Pope, W. *Durkheim's Suicide: A Classic Analyzed.* Chicago: University of Chicago Press, 1976.

Taylor, S. *Durkheim and the Study of Suicide.* London: Macmillan, 1982.

Taylor, S. Suicide, Durkheim and Sociology. In D. Lester (ed.), *Current Concepts of Suicide.* Philadelphia: The Charles Press, 1990.

Taylor, S., and Ashworth, C. Durkheim and Social Realism: An Approach to Health and Illness. In G. Scambler (ed.), *Sociological Theory and Medical Sociology.* London: Tavistock, 1987.

Wacquant, L. Positivism. In W. Outhwaite and T. Bottomore (eds.), *Twentieth-Century Social Thought.* Oxford: Blackwell, 1993.

2

Was Durkheim Right?
A Critical Survey of the Empirical
Literature on *Le Suicide*

K. D. Breault, PhD

> ...the time has come for sociology to spurn popular success...and assume the exacting character befitting every science. It will then gain in dignity and authority what it will perhaps lose in popularity. For as long as it remains involved in partisan struggles...it has no right to speak with a voice that would silence passions and prejudices (Durkheim, *The Rules of Sociological Method,* 1895: 1964, concluding remarks).

As the 100th anniversary of the publication of *Le Suicide* approaches, it is only appropriate that we ask the question, was Durkheim right? The present chapter attempts to answer that question with a critical tour of the empirical literature on suicide in sociology. Readers interested in more in-depth or comprehensive reports are directed to Breault (1986), Lester (1972, 1983), McIntosh (1985), and Stack (1982).

FOUR CAUSES OF SUICIDE

If we put aside the thorny issue of the separability of Durkheim's main explanatory concepts, social integration and social regulation, Durkheim's "theory" is composed of four theories of suicide.[1] For Durkheim, social integration and social regulation are two different continua, at the ends of which are located the four independent theories of suicide. Durkheim identifies the four types as altruistic, fatalistic, anomic and egoistic. When social integration is at a high level in society, Durkheim argues altruistic suicide occurs; when social regulation is high, fatalistic suicide results; when social regulation is low, anomic suicide occurs; and when social integration is low, egoistic suicide results. Additionally, Durkheim makes a distinction between

11

modern and premodern suicide, altruistic and fatalistic suicide generally falling into the latter category, anomic and egoistic suicide in the former.

Putative support for Durkheim's theory of altruistic suicide abounds. In the absence of overt force, altruistic suicides sacrifice themselves for group interests. The Masada story and the more recent mass suicide in Jonestown, Guyana, are often mentioned. While these and similar examples are cited as support for Durkheim's theory (despite theoretical difficulties), virtually no research has been done on altruistic suicide. Perhaps, as in many ways, Durkheim set the standard here. His own cursory discussion of altruistic suicide leaves much to be desired. My impression is that today, the collective sentiment favors altruistic suicide. Many seem prepared to support the hypothesis that high social integration causes some people in special circumstances to commit suicide out of social obligation. But citing examples is not satisfactory. Without research to test the hypothesis that high social integration is the cause of suicide we cannot begin to answer the question of whether Durkheim was right about altruistic suicide. Are there, or have there been, circumstances under which high social integration is *not* associated with "obligatory, optional or acute" suicide? We do not know.[2]

Durkheim spent little time on fatalistic suicide except to provide the examples of slaves in historical times and very young husbands and childless married women today. In the modern era, American slaves may have had substantially *lower* suicide rates than whites (Fogel and Engerman, 1974). As for very young husbands, marriage today is much less regulatory, and males of all ages have rather less drastic alternatives. Empirically, young husbands have low suicide rates, yet young widowers have very high rates (Smith, et al., 1988). While childless married women may have elevated suicide rates (Danigelis and Pope, 1979), their mortality (to say nothing of morbidity) may be better understood as a lack of social integration (see egoistic suicide below) than, as Durkheim put it, "...futures pitilessly blocked and passions violently restrained by oppressive discipline."

Prior to 1970, much research was devoted to anomic suicide, the type Durkheim says occurs in modern society when social regulation is low. It is not entirely clear to me why this literature is now extinct, but on that score we can perhaps all agree—there has been little research on anomic suicide in the last 20 years or so.[3] Possible causes for the demise of this literature would include: no consensus on how to measure anomie or test the theory; the view that Durkheim's *Le Suicide* was methodologically prescientific and, therefore, useless at a time when methodological techniques suggested to some that physics, chemistry and sociology could be mentioned in the same breath; and the related view that, for theoretical reasons, *Le Suicide* was so hopelessly confused that our energies would be better spent if we rewrote the book with our new scientific toolbox in hand.[4] It seems that the interest in anomic suicide was in the wrong place at the wrong time. As a casualty of passing methodological and theoretical prescriptions for how sociology should be conducted, perhaps Durkheim's anomic suicide deserves another look, although we must again conclude that we do not know if Durkheim was right. In summary, if empirical research is our judge, there is scant evidence that Durkheim's theories of altruistic, fatalistic and anomic suicide are correct.

EGOISTIC SUICIDE

A renaissance in Durkheim studies occurred in the 1970s, the focus of which continues to be egoistic suicide. Today, neither empirical research nor evidence supporting Durkheim are lacking. As we shall see, the issue is whether the research and evidence are meaningful.

There can be little doubt that Durkheim's egoistic suicide has received the most attention. Whether it is research in sociology, psychology, psychiatry or general medicine, if Durkheim's work is being tested (and, of course, often it is not indicated as such), it is likely to be the egoistic theory. Perhaps Durkheim would not be overly disappointed by the neglect shown his other theories of suicide. To me, *Le Suicide,* and much of Durkheim's later work, revolves around the egoistic theory. Rather than merely adding the fatalistic theory for "completeness sake," it is my impression that altruistic suicide and the social regulation theories were included for completeness. Durkheim makes the fewest errors, is the least ambiguous and develops the most original and extensive theory when he discusses egoistic suicide. Note that egoistic suicide is the first theory discussed in *Le Suicide,* and it takes up more space than the other three theories combined.

Durkheim argues that the lack or loss of social integration in modern society causes some vulnerable people to commit suicide. Despite difficulties some interpreters have had with social integration, Durkheim plainly means the degree to which people are attached, bonded or connected to each other. Durkheim is talking about social and emotional ties and the amount and intensity of such bonds.

Durkheim focuses on the family, religion and politics. With regard to the family, Durkheim predicts that unmarried persons have higher suicide rates than married persons, singles have higher rates than the widowed, and married persons without children have higher rates than the married with children. With few exceptions, researchers have focused on divorce rates.

It is well known that Durkheim predicts Protestants have higher suicide rates than Catholics, and Catholics higher rates than Jews. Less well known is Durkheim's (1908) reversal of this ordering, in which Jews are seen as having the highest suicide rates while Catholics have the lowest. It is now perhaps generally understood that Durkheim's denominational propositions were an attempt on his part to test the fundamental issue that religious commitment in general has important integrative effects. Accordingly, Durkheim argues that religion is protective of suicide because religious adherents enjoy the social integration that group membership provides. Researchers have focused on both issues, denominational effects and those of religious participation across denomination.

Less explored than his propositions about religion and the family, Durkheim's theory concerning political and social integration involves political upheavals, election crises and wars. Durkheim predicts that, during such events, suicide rates decline as people are more closely bound together.

THE EVIDENCE

Perhaps the strongest evidence in support of Durkheim's egoistic theory is found in the area of the family. Over a large group of studies, divorce rates or nonmarried status have been shown to be positively correlated with suicide rates (e.g., Breault, 1986, 1988; Breault and Barkey, 1982; Danigelis and Pope, 1979; Girard, 1988; Gove, 1973; Kobrin and Hendershot, 1977; Kowalski, et al., 1987; Lester, 1993; Pescosolido and Mendelsohn, 1986; Stack, 1980b, 1981, 1984; Trovato, 1987; Wasserman, 1984). However, there have been several exceptions (e.g., Rico-Velasco and Mynko, 1973; Vigderhous and Fishman, 1978).

Impressive as such a list is, one of the most enduring themes in the literature is that of methodological criticism, and quite serious flaws, many of which are associated with aggregate analyses, are readily identified: unrepresentative samples (Breault, 1986; Rico-Velasco and Mynko, 1973), too few observations (Girard, 1988; Lester, 1993; Stack, 1981, 1984; Trovato, 1987; Vigderhous and Fishman, 1978), high levels of aggregation, (Girard, 1988; Lester, 1993; Stack, 1980b, 1981, 1984; Trovato, 1987; Vigderhous and Fishman, 1978; Wasserman, 1984), the failure to control for important variables (Breault and Barkey, 1982, 1986; Girard, 1988; Kowalski, et al., 1987; Stack, 1980b, 1981, 1984; Trovato, 1987; Vigderhous and Fishman, 1978; Wasserman, 1984), misspecification (the use of confounding variables, e.g., Girard, 1988), monotonically invariant variables in time-series analysis (e.g., Stack, 1981), analysis restricted to one year (e.g., Breault and Barkey, 1982), variables that are not comparable across units of analysis as in cross-national research (e.g., Breault and Barkey, 1982), the failure to use stable suicide rates with very small units of analysis (e.g., Kowalski, et al., 1987), and likely multicollinearity in small samples composed of high level aggregates. As these are not insignificant problems, they jeopardize the results of much of the literature.[5]

Recent attempts to find denominational differences in suicide rates have produced mixed results. Because denominational categories such as Catholic and Protestant are today so heterogenous—they include members with widely varying degrees of religious commitment—there is every reason to believe that Durkheim's denominational propositions will *not* be supported. While at least one study (Templer and Veleber, 1980) sustained Durkheim on the basis of state-level data—a level of aggregation that seems much too high for the purpose—I was surprised to find that in a sample which included the largest

414 counties in the U.S. (those with 1980 populations greater than 100,000), Catholics had significantly lower suicide rates than Protestants (Breault, 1986). In that paper, I was quick to focus on some of the methodological shortcomings of studies that found no denominational differences (e.g., Bainbridge and Stark, 1981; Bankston, et al., 1983; Pope and Danigelis, 1981; Stack, 1980a). However, when I analyzed the full set of American counties (Breault, 1988), and thus corrected one of the errors of my earlier study, I too failed to find significant Catholic-Protestant differences. That seemed to be the end of the story until a draft of Pescosolido and Georgianna's (1989) study landed on my desk. Unsatisfied with the crude Catholic-Protestant dichotomy, they looked at a large group of Protestant denominations and discovered that liberal denominations tended to have the highest suicide rates while conservative ones had low rates. Pescosolido and Georgianna's research appears to confirm Durkheim's theory of the integrative effects of religious denomination on suicide and represents an important advance in the literature.

Greater consensus has been reached on the fundamental proposition that in general religious adherence reduces suicide. Bainbridge and Stark (1981), Breault (1986, 1988), Breault and Barkey (1982), Lester (1993), Martin (1984), Stack (1983, 1985) and Stark, Doyle and Rushing (1983) have shown that measures of religion adherence, such as church membership rates, are negatively related to suicide.[6] One exception to this pattern is a study by Bainbridge (1989) in which significant negative effects for church membership evaporated once controls were introduced. The sample used by Bainbridge consisted of the largest 75 metropolitan areas in the United States, and for that reason suffers from the same flaw that, for example, characterizes some of my 1986 analyses, specifically the use of nonrepresentative units of analysis and a high level of aggregation. When small, representative units at lower levels of aggregation are analyzed, as is the case with all American counties, church membership is the *strongest* determinant of suicide rates (Breault, 1988).

Durkheim's hypotheses about politics have been the least studied and supported. Among recent studies that favor Durkheim are Boor (1981, 1982), Lester (1978) and Phillips and Feldman (1973). Marshall (1981), Stack (1985) and Wasserman (1983) found no support. The mixed results offer no simple explanation and many of the studies suffer from the above methodological limitations.

NEW RULES OF SOCIOLOGICAL METHOD?

Where does this brief survey leave us? Despite the many problems in the literature, it appears that two parts of Durkheim's egoistic theory are confirmed, the hypotheses concerning the family and religion. This preliminary conclusion is justified because, as the literature has improved in quality, Durkheim's hypotheses continue to receive support—perhaps even greater support. At the same time, the methodological challenges posed by the literature provide us with our first set of requirements concerning how, in the sociological tradition, we should study suicide in the future. The research most vulnerable to criticism is that which is characterized by the following: small samples (this applies to most time-series analyses), unrepresentative samples, high-level units of analysis such as countries, states and SMSAs (a problem in most time-series research), and the failure to control for variables previously shown to be correlates of suicide. Such a list *precludes* aggregate time-series and cross-national research and much of the existing aggregate cross-sectional literature. In addition, while the above problems are quite serious by themselves, much of the research is characterized by more than one flaw. Undoubtedly, it is just a matter of time before we will see cross-national research based on a small, unrepresentative sample of countries for which a limited set of variables are available—but it will not come from my hands (with the exception from my days as a graduate student: Breault and Barkey, 1982).

DURKHEIM, PSYCHOLOGY AND QUANTITATIVE METHODOLOGY

Sociologists have neglected a key part of *Le Suicide's* argument. Durkheim was not primarily interested in why people kill themselves. He seized on the topic of suicide because it provided him the opportunity to show that sociological explanation was superior to psychological explanation—to show that sociology also deserved a place in the university curriculum. The first two chapters of his book contain Durkheim's answer to the psychology of his time. Do we have a legitimate answer today?

In the research that I have cited up to this point, investigators have controlled for such variables as age, sex, race/ethnicity, demographic variables (e.g., population size, migration), economic variables (e.g., unemployment, female labor force participation), socioeconomic variables (e.g., education, occupational status), but not a single psychological variable. Today, Durkheim's arguments against psychological explanations would be considered primitive. Needless to say, psychology is not the field it was in 1897. And gone are the not so distant days when psychiatrists could report on the handful of suicides they had seen over a lifetime of practice. Today, the great majority of suicide investigators are research psychologists and psychiatrists. In the course of considerable research, they have discovered factors that are consistently related to suicide: affective disorders, schizophrenia, inherited predisposition to affective illness, substance abuse, low levels in cerebrospinal fluid of 5-hydroxyindoleacetic and homovanillic acids, homosexuality, previous suicidal behavior, impulsiveness and aggressiveness. The most important of these are affective disorders, namely depression. What is the relationship between social integration and suicide controlling for depression? Can we be confident that marital status and religious commitment have significant effects on suicide without controlling for psychological variables such as clinical depression?

Ever since *Le Suicide* was published, readers have been misled by Durkheim's highly sociologistic language—language he used primarily as a way of "selling" and establishing sociology. It is true that Durkheim scholarship has remarkably improved but even recent scholars have erred. Durkheim was not as neglectful of psychology as some have suggested. He rejects psychological explanations in part because he was not convinced that there were psychological regularities in suicide, and in his day the field of psychology had not yet identified consistent suicide correlates. One of the explanations Durkheim rejects is alcoholism. Does he reject alcoholism because it is an individual level or psychological cause, that is, for philosophical/sociologistic reasons? On the contrary, Durkheim rejects alcoholism for empirical reasons. He presents tables and shows that there is no correlation between suicide rates, rates of alcohol consumption and rates of alcohol-related illness. Similarly, when Durkheim rejects neurasthenia as a cause of suicide, he does so only after consulting the relevant data available to him. He produces six tables, three of which compare the rate of suicide with the rate of insanity.

Today, Durkheim would not be satisfied with our failure to control for empirically supported psychological variables. Even though he advocated a sharp division between sociology and psychology, his methodological approach would have precluded the exclusion of psychological explanations if such explanations had been empirically demonstrated. The strong quantitative strategy Durkheim initiated, that which he helped convince the rest of us to adopt, demands that we consider all factors that are possible determinants of suicide. To do the job Durkheim originally intended, to show that sociological explanation is viable, we must include psychological variables. We have no choice, just as Durkheim would have no choice today. Of course, there is always hubris.

BEYOND SUICIDE

In this light, the results for egoistic suicide look much less impressive. Marital status and religious adherence are strong suicide correlates when placed alongside economic and other variables, but that may be because psychological factors have been omitted. If we must now have less confidence in mainly sociological studies that have neglected psychological variables, are there individual level studies that have employed both sociological and psychological variables?

On occasion, psychologists and psychiatrists have tested Durkheimian variables at the individual level. Much of this research is of limited value because it is in the same shape as the sociological studies discussed above— some of the very same methodological mistakes have been made.[7] However, there is a high-quality literature to which sociologists, epidemiologists, psychologists and others have contributed that is of considerable interest (e.g, Berkman and Breslow, 1983; Berkman and Syme, 1979; Blazer, 1982; Bruhn and Stewart, 1977; Colantonio, et al., 1992; Hanson, et al., 1989; House, et al., 1982; Schoenbach, et al., 1983).[8] Here, the findings indicate that marital status, church attendance and membership, interactions with friends and relatives, membership in voluntary organizations and participation in social leisure activities—all Durkheimian social integration variables—are significant determinants of mortality after a battery of controls are employed, including mental and physical health. And the rather surprising fact is that in these studies the dependent variables have not been limited to suicide but have included other causes of death, total mortality and morbidity. This research satisfies the above rules in that large samples were used (often thousands of people), samples were randomly selected from disparate communities (e.g., Alameda County, California; Durham County, North Carolina; and Tecumseh, Michigan), the studies were at the individual level (level of aggregation was not an issue), and a long list of variables was controlled.[9]

As an example, Berkman and Syme (1979) found that for male church members aged 60 to 69, the death rate (all causes) was 21.6 percent, while the rate for male nonchurch members the same age was 30.3 percent. The advantage church members enjoyed also applied to men and women of other age categories. The most protected group were female church members aged 30 to 49 who were 2.8 times more likely to survive than female nonchurch members of the same age. (Most recently, Colantonio and coworkers [1992] were able to link church attendance with protection from stroke.)

For Durkheim, this line of research would represent a most extraordinary extension of his theory. Since most people during Durkheim's time died of infectious diseases, which presumably are resistant to the effects of social integration, it may not have occurred to him that the egoistic theory could be generalized to cover mortality from diseases such as heart disease, cancer and stroke.

THE GEOGRAPHY OF MORTALITY

When I first became aware that social integration had been related to causes of mortality other than suicide, I did what any self-respecting aggregationist would do—I attempted to replicate the findings at the aggregate level. I began this work by selecting the universe of American counties, a relatively low level unit of analysis and a very large, representative "sample." While I could not test psychological factors, I had a large set of variables that previously had been used with suicide (Breault, 1988). The dependent variables were the more than 160 causes of death tracked by the American government. A summary of this study has been prepared for another publication, but I can report the striking finding that, with the exception of suicide and several other causes of death, social integration was generally *not* related to mortality in the expected negative direction, and that in several important cases a significant *positive* relationship was found—the higher the social integration, the higher the mortality rate.

For many months, I tried to explain away these results through the use of every methodological procedure I could think of. In the end, our toolbox was empty, and Durkheim's theory was not supported—the notable exception being suicide. What should we make of these results? Either the aggregate or individual level results are correct. Since there is no apparent reason to doubt the individual level research, suspicion must fall on the aggregate results. I was stumped until, with some reluctance, I reconsidered the exception—the ecological results for suicide. The conclusion I have come to is that the relationship across American aggregates between suicide and social integration, specifically divorce and church membership rates, is a fortuitous one.

When we do correlational studies, we give lip service to the notion that our results may not indicate causality. I submit that research on suicide done with American aggregates, such as states, SMSAs, cities and counties, will inevitably produce results for divorce, church membership and related variables that are more a function of the geographic distribution of these variables than a causal relationship. What I am saying is that much of the sociological literature on egoistic suicide is based on a coincidence of geography and that social integration and suicide coincide geographically at the aggregate level. I believe there is a causal relationship between social integration and suicide, one that has been demonstrated at the individual level, but the aggregate association of these variables is without substantive meaning or has a meaning that is unrelated to the individual level causal relationship.

The geography of suicide mortality in the United States is, with some important exceptions (e.g., Florida and Hawaii), characterized by a sharp east-west divide. In my 1986 study of suicide, where the largest 216 counties in the country were investigated, 22 of the 35 highest-ranking counties on suicide, were located in the 13 most western states (Alaska, Arizona, California, Colorado, Hawaii, Idaho, Montana, Nevada, New Mexico, Oregon, Utah, Washington and Wyoming). Of the 35 lowest ranking counties on suicide, none were located in the West. In my 1988 study, based on the full set of counties, 92 (46 percent) of the 200 highest ranking counties on suicide were located in the West. This is remarkable because western counties make up only 13.4 percent of the total. Of the 200 lowest ranking counties on suicide, only 17 (8.5 percent) were in the West. Overall, 75.2 percent of western counties have suicide rates that are higher than the mean for the country (12.2 per 100,000). The mean suicide rate for western counties is 16.3 per 100,000, compared to 11.5 for nonwestern counties.

The same pattern holds for divorce and church membership. Divorce rates tend to be high in the West and low in the rest of the country.[10] Similarly, church membership rates are low in the West (with the exception of Utah) but generally high elsewhere. The mean church membership rate for western counties is 42.6 percent, while the rate for the rest of the country is 59.5 percent. The divorce rate for western counties is 7.0 per 1000, while it is 4.2 for nonwestern counties.

Geographical patterns such as these do not, of course, preclude causality, but without the east-west division in suicide and social integration there is little relationship between the variables. For present purposes, let us examine the county level relationship between church membership, divorce and suicide for each of the 50 states. Recall that church membership was the strongest determinant of suicide in the full set of counties, while divorce was a very strong factor significant at the .001 level. Table 1 presents the Pearson correlation coefficients and significance levels for the relationship between suicide rates and church membership and divorce rates for each of the 50 states with counties as the unit of analysis.[11]

The results show that in only nine states (Arkansas, California, Indiana, Iowa, New Jersey, North Carolina, Tennessee, Washington and Wisconsin) is there a significant negative relationship between church membership and suicide. In two states (Kentucky and Virginia), a significant positive relationship is indicated. Note that for the entire data set of 3055 counties, the correlation between suicide and church membership is a highly significant -.272.

Similar results were obtained for divorce. In eight states, the expected positive relationship is found (Alabama, Iowa, Massachusetts, New Jersey, New York, South Carolina, South Dakota and Washington). Alaska shows a significant negative relationship. The correlation between suicide and divorce in the full set of counties is .201 (p =.001). In summary, only 17 of these 100 tests of Durkheim's theory are supportive, and only three states show both a church membership and divorce effect (Iowa, New Jersey and Washington).

To further indicate the influence of the east-west geographic pattern, Table 2 presents Pearson correlation coefficients for combinations of western and nonwestern states.

In other words, Pearson's *r* was determined for the combined county groups of selected western and nonwestern states. Colorado and Oregon were chosen because they are disparate western states with numerous counties and, by themselves, each has an insignificant relationship between suicide and church membership. The nonwestern states were chosen arbitrarily with the consideration that they too could not have a significant relationship between suicide and church membership (see Table 1). In the case of every combination, a significant relationship was found, one that was highly significant with a relatively large correlation. For example, by themselves neither Colorado or Illinois shows a significant relationship between suicide and church membership (Pearson *r*'s = -.133 and -.175, respectively). When the counties for the two states are combined, the relationship is highly significant (-.384).

Similarly, different combinations of western and nonwestern states were chosen for the relationship between suicide and divorce. For example, Wyoming and Connecticut each show a nonsignificant relationship between suicide

Table 1.

Pearson's Correlation Coefficients and Significance Levels for Suicide and Social Integration Variables with Counties as the Unit of Analysis

Church Membership			Divorce		Church Membership			Divorce	
Alabama	-.101	NS	.326	.05	Montana	.014	NS	.090	NS
Alaska	.671	NS	-.910	.001	Nebraska	-.127	NS	.001	NS
Arizona	-.469	NS	-.134	NS	Nevada	-.359	NS	.221	NS
AR	-.364	.01	-.037	NS	NH	-.088	NS	-.378	NS
CA	-.403	.01	.012	NS	N. Jersey	-.626	.01	.441	.05
Colorado	-.133	NS	-.071	NS	NM	.065	NS	-.189	NS
CT	.209	NS	-.484	NS	New York	-.145	NS	.376	.01
Delaware	.497	NS	-.754	NS	NC	-.240	.05	.088	NS
Florida	-.098	NS	-.021	NS	N. Dakota	.090	NS	.070	NS
Georgia	-.078	NS	.035	NS	Ohio	-.052	NS	.072	NS
Hawaii	-.574	NS	-.092	NS	Oklahoma	.110	NS	.045	NS
Idaho	-.094	NS	-.093	NS	Oregon	.023	NS	.172	NS
Illinois	-.175	NS	.159	NS	PA	-.020	NS	.087	NS
Indiana	-.227	.05	.158	NS	R. Island	-.362	NS	.753	NS
Iowa	-.518	.001	.386	.001	SC	-.141	NS	.319	.05
Kansas	-.114	NS	.028	NS	S. Dakota	-.212	NS	.254	.05
Kentucky	.275	.01	.108	NS	Tennessee	-.248	.05	-.095	NS
Louisiana	.080	NS	.040	NS	Texas	.000	NS	.083	NS
Maine	-.110	NS	-.284	NS	Utah	-.129	NS	.257	NS
Maryland	.316	NS	-.004	NS	Vermont	-.488	NS	.351	NS
MA	-.279	NS	.755	.001	Virginia	.199	.05	-.046	NS
Michigan	.048	NS	-.196	NS	WA	-.368	.05	.347	.05
MI	-.076	NS	.189	NS	WV	.125	NS	-.100	NS
MS	.112	NS	.072	NS	WI	-.287	.05	.126	NS
Missouri	-.089	NS	.009	NS	Wyoming	-.319	NS	.296	NS

Table 2.

Pearson's Correlation Coefficients and Significance Levels for Suicide
and Social Integration Variables for Combined Western and
Nonwestern States with Counties as the Unit of Analysis

Church Membership		
Colorado & Illinois	-.384	.001
Colorado & Louisiana	-.343	.001
Colorado & Massachusetts	-.248	.05
Colorado & Minnesota	-.497	.001
Colorado & Ohio	-.169	.05
Oregon & Alabama	-.487	.001
Oregon & New York	-.428	.001
Oregon & Pennsylvania	-.356	.001
Oregon & South Carolina	-.548	.001
Oregon & South Dakota	-.355	.001

Divorce		
California & Indiana	.160	.05
California & Kansas	.321	.001
California & North Dakota	.570	.001
California & Wisconsin	.552	.001
California & Virginia	.207	.01
Wyoming & Connecticut	.515	.01
Wyoming & Maryland	.565	.001
Wyoming & Michigan	.281	.01
Wyoming & Rhode Island	.582	.01
Wyoming & Vermont	.387	.05

and divorce (Pearson r's = .071 and .296, respectively). When combined, the relationship becomes much stronger and is significant (.515, p>.01).

Findings such as these demonstrate that aggregate results based on U.S. units of analysis which are supportive of Durkheim's theory are mainly an artifact of the geography of suicide and social integration.[12] This also applies to Canada which similarly shows an east-west divide in suicide and social integration. Therefore, in addition to avoiding small samples, unrepresentative ones, high levels of aggregation, aggregate time-series and cross-national analyses, we must also refrain from doing cross-sectional research based on American and Canadian aggregates. And who said social science was easy?

ONE MORE VERY SMALL PROBLEM

Not long ago, preparing to teach a course on crime and delinquency, one of my other interests, I read a report which analyzed infanticide across a sample of industrialized nations. Homicide in general is roughly comparable to suicide in frequency. For the last 15 years of so the national homicide rate has fluctuated between 8 and 10 per 100,000 population. By contrast, in developed countries infanticide is much rarer, between 10 and 50 times rarer than the overall rate of homicide. Increasingly, I have come to think that this is a problem.

The reason why I and a number of others have been able to do aggregate studies of suicide is because the ecological fallacy has been "refuted." Bogue and Bogue (1976) and others have shown that when a rigorous set of standards are adhered to, aggregate analyses provide reliable predictions about individual level behavior.[13] What has never been shown is that aggregate level data can be used to make predictions about very rare events such as infanticide. Indeed, the evidence suggests that the rarer the event, the more likely unreliable estimates will be produced. There is no consensus on how rare is rare, but the most reliable individual level predictions are found when a substantial proportion of the population engages in the behavior being studied. Bogue and Bogue (1976) suggested a mean of 50 percent participation rule and made this comment, "Extreme caution is advised when the dependent variable comprises less than 2 percent...of the population." Clearly, infanticide falls into this category, but of course so do suicide and homicide. The county mean for suicide as expressed as a percentage is .00122 or roughly 1,650 times smaller than 2 percent. The highest county suicide rate in the 1970s (Kobuk, Alaska, with 57.3 per 100,000), is one that is about 350 times less than the 2 percent minimum. Of course, we may wish to disregard the Bogues' rule, but the simple fact is that there is no scientific evidence that reliable group level estimates of individual behavior can be made for rare phenomena. In the absence of such evidence, the ecological study of suicide cannot be justified. And because psychological variables are not available at the aggregate level, there can be little doubt that additional ecological research would be without merit. Therefore, to our new rules of sociological method, let us add: no more aggregate studies.[14]

WAS DURKHEIM RIGHT?

As discussed in this chapter, there is good evidence that Durkheim's theory of egoistic suicide is correct and that it can be extended to include various forms of morbidity and mortality. The ecological study of suicide may be at an end, but the research horizon has never been so broad. Let me suggest three avenues of research.

First, we need to know more about the relative contributions of social integration and psychological variables such as depression. While research has consistently shown that depressives are much more likely to commit suicide, investigators familiar with clinical populations have observed that among those who have either made serious suicide attempts or who have succeeded, the lack or loss of social integration is a very common feature.[15] High-quality research is needed in this area. Psychologists, psychiatrists and medical researchers who disregard Durkheim's social integration variables are making the same mistake sociologists have made. Sociologists have a wonderful opportunity to step into this area and make lasting contributions.

Second, while there now exists convincing evidence of a strong negative relationship between social integration and mortality, much more research is needed on the benefits of social integration with regard to morbidity.

Third, what are the mechanisms by which social integration is protective of health? Various explanations, most of which have focused on social supports (e.g., Umberson, 1987), have been advanced but none seem entirely satisfactory. And much more research is needed on the relative roles of formal versus informal social supports (see Litwak, et al., 1989). Perhaps one of the most understudied areas is that of physiology, for example, the relationship between social integration and immune system function. My feeling is that formal and informal supports are inadequate to explain many of the findings: social integration must directly affect people on the inside.

Almost 100 years after its publication, the ideas in *Le Suicide* continue to remain at the forefront of scientific investigation. It is no accident. Durkheim wished to show that the social bonds forged by humans are sustaining of life. Is that not sociology's "one law," and is not Durkheim's *Le Suicide* sociology's greatest contribution?

NOTES

1. To my mind, the issue has not been productive. It concerns whether Durkheim conflated social integration with social regulation. Johnson (1965) and Pope (1976) suggested that Durkheim had made this error. I think that, unlike Weber, who laboriously (some would say, painfully) constructed his theoretical structures from the bottom up, Durkheim was more concerned about where he was going

and not always clear or consistent about how to get there. Durkheim scholars who focus on his theoretical minutia may come to any number of conclusions that will have little bearing on what he intended. Durkheim's attitude toward theory, facts and theory construction was opportunistic and instrumental. What mattered for him was the larger picture, the overarching theoretical framework. While we have a duty to point out where Durkheim falls short of our standards, we have no less an obligation to portray his views as he intended. Of course, finding out what Durkheim intended is not always an easy task.

2. For a recent fan of altruistic suicide, see Huffine (1989). For a study of suicide in primitive societies, see Smith and Hackathorn (1982).

3. One notable paper was Abrahamson (1980).

4. Perhaps, the best attempt to rewrite Durkheim's book was that of Gibbs and Martin (1964), although in retrospect status integration theory was quite capable of standing alone. In addition, I suspect that had these authors not labored on a theme related to Durkheim during a time of little interest in his work, the recent Durkheim revival might have been postponed.

5. Many of the same problems have plagued the homicide literature. Yet, until recently, the homicide research evidenced little agreement. At this point, the reader may be tempted to think that either Durkheim was very lucky or that his theory is very robust.

6. It should be noted that these studies present just as many methodological distractions as the research on marital status.

7. For a brief overview of the literature on youth suicide, see Pfeffer (1989). For some other recent papers, see Adam, et al. (1982), Goldney (1981), Humphrey (1977), Isherwood, et al. (1982), Murphy, et al. (1979) and Slater and Depue (1981).

8. For other interesting work in this literature, see Berkman (1982), Cassel (1976), Cobb (1976), Moen, et al. (1989) and Seeman, et al. (1987). For reviews of the general literature and a bibliography, see Berkman (1985), House and Kahn (1985) and Bruhn, et al. (1987). For work on the relationship between social support and depression, see Andrews, et al. (1978), Flaherty, et al. (1983), Kaplan, et al. (1987), Monroe, et al. (1986) and Oxman, et al. (1992).

9. One weakness in some of these studies is that too few variables, especially psychological ones, have been included.

10. For a large county level study of divorce which discusses the east-west divide in divorce, see Breault and Kposowa (1987).

11. The results are based on the BGCODA 70-9 data set discussed in Breault (1988). The set includes 3,055 counties for which complete data were available and permits cross-sectional analyses of ten years of averaged data, 1970-1979. Averaging insured stable rates for the smallest counties, 261 of which had populations less than 5,000 in 1980. In all, BGCODA comprises 285,000 suicides for the decade of the 1970s.

12. The implication is that suicide rates are high in the west for reasons other than divorce or church membership rates. While the attempt to discover the causes of aggregate level suicide may appear to be unproductive, one important variable immediately comes to mind. On average, western states have large populations of native Americans, and while they make up only a small proportion of the entire population, suicide is rare enough that high rates of suicide for small segments of the population may have considerable impact on the overall rates. Do native Americans commit suicide for lack or loss of social integration? Explaining low church membership and high divorce in the West is another matter. Perhaps the West is characterized by cultural themes that produce low social integration, that is, a rejection of traditional forms of religious organization and an emphasis on

self-reliance. Note that the West has the highest rate of cult membership (Stark, et al., 1979).

13. See also Firebaugh (1978), Gove and Hughes (1980), Hammond (1973), Hannan and Burstein (1974), and Hanushek, et al. (1974).

14. Some may argue that sociology's focus should be on suicide rates and not on how individuals behave. It seems to me that today this most radical of views would rob suicide research of meaning. If we are not interested in why people kill themselves, how do we defend the research? What is the point if we find that a variable is the cause of suicide rates, but we know that for methodological reasons we cannot impute it to individuals? Consider another issue. In merely explaining rates, we may find ourselves in the same boat as homicide researchers who have different causes of homicide depending on the type of rate. In aggregate cross-national research, economic inequality is a major factor, but in American work, poverty and social integration (specifically, family dissolution) are now viewed as the main causal determinants. From a theoretical point of view, how do we explain these results? Does it make sense to have different theories of homicide for different types of homicide rates?

15. Fellow aggregationists may find Robins' (1981) book interesting. Robins presents detailed information on 134 suicides that took place in one year in St. Louis, Missouri. While affective disorders were found in nearly half the group, social integration deficits are clearly suggested in more than 75 percent.

REFERENCES

Abrahamson, M. Sudden wealth, gratification and attainment. *American Sociological Review*, 1980, 45, 49-57.

Adam, K. S., Bouckoms, A., and Streiner, D. Parental loss and family stability in attempted suicide. *Archives of General Psychiatry*, 1982, 39, 1081-1085.

Andrews, G., Tennant, C., Hewson, D., and Schonell, M. The relation of social factors to physical and psychiatric illness. *American Journal of Epidemiology*, 1978, 108, 27-35.

Bainbridge, W. S. The religious ecology of deviance. *American Sociological Review*, 1989, 54, 288-295.

Bainbridge, W. S., and Stark, S. Suicide, homicide and religion. *Annual Review of the Social Sciences of Religion*, 1981, 5, 33-56.

Bankston, W. B., Allen, H. D., and Cunningham, D. Religion and suicide. *Social Forces*, 1983, 65, 521-528.

Berkman, L. F. Social network analysis and coronary heart disease. *Advances in Cardiology*, 1982, 29, 37-49.

Berkman, L. F. The relationship of social networks and social support to morbidity and mortality. In S. Cohen and S.L. Syme (eds.), *Social Support and Health*. New York: Academic Press, 1985.

Berkman, L. F., and Breslow, L. *Health and Ways of Living*. New York: Oxford University Press, 1983.

Berkman, L. F., and Syme, L. S. Social networks, host resistance, and mortality. *American Journal of Epidemiology*, 1979, 109, 186-204.

Blazer, D. G. Social support and mortality in an elderly community population. *American Journal of Epidemiology*, 1982, 115, 684-694.

Bogue, D. J., and Bogue, E. J. Ecological correlation reexamined. In D. J. Bogue and E. J. Bogue (eds.), *Essays in Human Ecology*. Chicago: University of Chicago Press, 1976.

Boor, M. Effects of United States Presidential elections on suicide and other causes of death. *American Sociological Review*, 1981, 46, 616-618.

Boor, M. Reduction in deaths by suicide, accidents, and homicide prior to United States Presidential elections. *Journal of Social Psychology,* 1982, 118, 135-136.

Breault, K. D. Suicide in America. *American Journal of Sociology,* 1986, 92, 628-656.

Breault, K. D. Beyond the quick and dirty. *American Journal of Sociology,* 1988, 93, 1479-1486.

Breault, K. D., and Barkey, K. A comparative analysis of Durkheim's theory of egoistic suicide. *Sociological Quarterly,* 1982, 23, 629-632.

Breault, K. D., and Kposowa, A. J. Explaining divorce in America. *Journal of Marriage and the Family,* 1987, 49, 549-558.

Bruhn, J. G., and Wolf, S. *The Roseto Story.* Norman, OK: University of Oklahoma Press, 1979.

Bruhn, J. G., Philips, B. U., Levine, P. L., and Mendes de Leon, C. F. *Social Support and Health.* New York: Garland, 1987.

Cassel, J. The contribution of the social environment to host resistance. *American Journal of Epidemiology,* 1976, 104, 107-123.

Cobb, S. Social support as a moderator of life stress. *Journal of Psychosomatic Medicine,* 1976, 38, 300-314.

Colantonio, A., Kasl, S. V., and Ostfeld, A. M. Depressive symptoms and other psychosocial factors as predictors of stroke in the elderly. *American Journal of Epidemiology,* 1992, 136, 884-894.

Danigelis, N., and Pope, W. Durkheim's theory of suicide as applied to the family: An empirical test. *Social Forces,* 1979, 57, 1081-1106.

Durkheim, E. *The Rules of Sociological Method.* New York: Free Press, 1964 (originally published 1895).

Durkheim, E. *Le Suicide.* Paris: Presses Universitaires de France, 1930 (originally published 1897).

Durkheim, E. *Suicide.* Glencoe, IL: Free Press, 1966 (1897).

Durkheim, E. Review of H. A. Krose, *Die Ursachen der Selbstmordhaufigkeit. Année Sociologique,* 1908, 11, 511-515.

Firebaugh, G. A rule for inferring individual level relationships from aggregate data. *American Sociological Review,* 1978, 43, 557-572.

Flaherty, J. A., Gaviria, F. M., Black, E. M., Altman, E., and Mitchell, T. The role of social support in the function of patients with unipolar depression. *American Journal of Epidemiology,* 1983, 140, 473-476.

Fogel, R. W., and Engerman, S. L. *Time on the Cross.* Boston: Little, Brown, 1974.

Girard, C. Church membership and suicide reconsidered. *American Journal of Sociology,* 1988, 93, 1471-1478.

Goldney, R. D. Parental loss and reported childhood status in young women who attempt suicide. *Acta Psychiatrica Scandinavica,* 1981, 64, 34-47.

Gove, W. Sex, marital status and mortality. *American Journal of Sociology,* 1973, 79, 45-68.

Gove, W., and Hughes, M. Re-examining the ecological fallacy. *Social Forces,* 1980, 58, 1157-1177.

Hammond, J. L. Two sources of error in ecological correlations. *American Sociological Review,* 1973, 39, 764-777.

Hannan, M. T., and Burstein, L. Estimation from grouped observations. *American Sociological Review,* 1974, 39, 374-392.

Hanson, B. S., Isacsson, S. O., Janzon, L., and Lindell, S. E. Social network and social support influence mortality in elderly men. *American Journal of Epidemiology,* 1989, 130, 100-111.

Hanushek, E. A., Jackson, J. E., and Kahn, J. Model specification, use of aggregate data, and the ecological correlation fallacy. *Political Methodology,* 1974, 1, 89-107.

House, J. S., and Kahn, R. L. Measures and concepts of social support. In S. Cohen and S. L. Syme (eds.), *Social Support and Health*. New York: Oxford University Press, 1985.

House, J. S., Robbins, C. A., and Metzner, H. L. The association of social relationships and activities with mortality. *American Journal of Epidemiology*, 1982, 116, 123-140.

Huffine, C. L. Social and cultural risk factors for youth suicide. In *Report of the Secretary's Task Force on Youth Suicide. Volume 2: Risk Factors for Youth Suicide*. Washington, DC: U.S. Government Printing Office, 1989.

Humphrey, J. A. Social loss. *Diseases of the Nervous System*, 1989, 38, 157-160.

Isherwood, J., Adam, K. S., and Hornblow, A. R. Life event stress, psychological factors, suicide attempts and auto-accident proclivity. *Journal of Psychosomatic Research*, 1982, 26, 391-383.

Johnson, B. D. Durkheim's one cause of suicide. *American Sociological Review*, 1965, 30, 875-886.

Kaplan, G. A., Roberts, R. E., Camacho, T. C., and Coyne, J. C. Psychological predictors of depression. *American Journal of Epidemiology*, 1987, 124, 206-220.

Kobrin, F. E., and Hendershot, G. E. Do family ties reduce mortality? *Journal of Marriage and the Family*, 1977, 39, 737-745.

Kowalski, G. S., Faupel, C. E., and Starr, P. D. Urbanism and suicide. *Social Forces*, 1987, 66, 85-101.

Lester, D. Internal conflict and personal violence. *International Journal of Group Tensions*, 1978, 8(3/4), 68-70.

Lester, D. *Why People Kill Themselves*. Springfield, IL: Charles C Thomas, 1992.

Lester, D. *Patterns of Suicide and Homicide in America*. Commack, NY: Nova Science Publishers, 1993.

Marshall, J. Political integration and the effect of war on suicide. *Social Forces*, 1981, 59, 771-785.

Martin, W. T. Religiosity and United States suicide rates, 1972-1978. *Journal of Clinical Psychology*, 1984, 40, 1166-1169.

McIntosh, J. L. *Research on Suicide*. Westport, CT: Greenwood, 1985.

Moen, P., Dempster-McClain, D., and Williams, R. M. Social integration and longevity. *American Sociological Review*, 1989, 54, 635-647.

Monroe, S. M., Bromet, E. J., Connell, M. M., and Steiner, S. C. Social support, life events and depressive symptoms. *American Journal of Epidemiology*, 1986, 54, 424-431.

Murphy, G. E., Armstrong, J. W., Hermele, S. L., Fisher, J. R., and Clendenin, W. W. Suicide and alcoholism. *Archives of General Psychiatry*, 1979, 36, 65-69.

Oxman, T. E., Berkman, L., Kasl, S., Freeman, D. H., and Barrett, J. Social support and depressive symptoms in the elderly. *American Journal of Epidemiology*, 1992, 135, 356-368.

Pescosolido, B. A., and Mendelsohn, R. Social causation or social construction of suicide? *American Sociological Review*, 1986, 51, 80-101.

Pescosolido, B. A., and Georgianna, S. Durkheim, suicide, and religion. *American Journal of Sociology*, 1989, 54, 33-48.

Pfeffer, C. R. Family characteristics and support systems as risk factors for youth suicidal behavior. In *Report of the Secretary's Task Force on Youth Suicide. Volume 2: Risk Factors for Youth Suicide*. Washington, DC: U.S. Government Printing Office, 1989.

Phillips, D. P., and Feldman, K. A dip in deaths before ceremonial occasions. *American Sociological Review*, 1973, 38, 678-696.

Pope, W. *Durkheim's Suicide*. Chicago: University of Chicago Press, 1976.

Pope, W., and Danigelis, N. Sociology's 'One Law.' *Social Forces*, 1981, 60, 495-516.

Rico-Velasco, J., and Mynko, L. Suicide and marital status. *Journal of Marriage and the Family*, 1973, 35, 239-244.

Robins, E. *The Final Months*. New York: Oxford University Press, 1981.

Schoenbach, V. J., Kaplan, B. H., Fredman, L., and Kleinbaum, D. G. Social ties and mortality in Evans County, Georgia. *American Journal of Epidemiology*, 123, 577-591.

Seeman, T. E., Kaplan, G. A., Knudsen, L., Cohen, R., and Guralnik, J. Social network ties and mortality among the elderly in the Alameda County study. *American Journal of Epidemiology*, 1987, 126, 714-723.

Slater, J., and Depue, R. A. The contribution of environmental events and social support to serious suicide attempts in primary depressive disorder. *Journal of Abnormal Psychology*, 1981, 90, 275-285.

Smith, D. H., and Hackathorn, L. Some social and psychological factors related to suicide in primitive societies. *Suicide and Life-Threatening Behavior*, 1982, 12, 195-211.

Smith, J. C., Mercy, J. A., and Conn, J. M. Marital status and the risk of suicide. *American Journal of Public Health*, 1988, 78, 78-80.

Stack, S. Religion and suicide. *Social Psychiatry*, 1980a, 15, 65-70.

Stack, S. The effects of marital dissolution on suicide. *Journal of Marriage and the Family*, 1980b, 42, 83-92.

Stack, S. Divorce and suicide. *Journal of Family Issues*, 1981, 2, 77-90.

Stack, S. Suicide. *Deviant Behavior*, 1982, 4, 41-66.

Stack, S. The effect of religious commitment on suicide. *Journal of Health and Social Behavior*, 1983, 23, 362-374.

Stack, S. The effect of domestic/religious individualism on suicide, 1954-1978. *Journal of Marriage and the Family*, 1985, 47, 431-447.

Stack, S., and Hass, A. The effect of unemployment duration on national suicide rates. *Sociological Focus*, 1984, 17, 17-29.

Stark, R., Bainbridge, W. S., and Doyle, D. P. Cults of America. *Sociological Analysis*, 1979, 40, 347-359.

Templer, D. I., and Veleber, D. M. Suicide rate and religion within the United States. *Psychological Reports*, 1980, 47, 898.

Umberson, D. Family status and health behaviors. *Journal of Health and Social Behavior*, 1987, 28, 306-319.

Vigderhous, G., and Fishman, G. The impact of unemployment and familial integration on changing suicide rates in the U.S.A., 1920-1969. *Social Psychiatry*, 1978, 13, 239-248.

Wasserman, I. M. Political business cycles, Presidential elections, and suicide and mortality patterns. *American Sociological Review*, 1983, 48, 711-720.

Wasserman, I. M. A longitudinal analysis of the linkage between suicide, unemployment, and marital dissolution. *Journal of Marriage and the Family*, 1984, 46, 853-859.

3

Durkheim's Heavy Hand in the Sociological Study of Suicide

Jack P. Gibbs, PhD

If Whitehead was correct—that remembrance of ancestors dooms a field—further sociological studies of suicide will be unproductive. Emile Durkheim's theory (1951) has dominated those studies for generations, and his disciples rarely note that his great work was published nearly a century ago. Vintage would be irrelevant if sociologists would simply honor Durkheim but go beyond him. Unfortunately, with few exceptions (e.g., Gibbs and Martin, 1964; Johnson, 1965; Martin, 1968; Pope, 1976; and Stark, et al., 1983), sociologists neither grant defects in Durkheim's theory nor give serious attention to contenders, not even those inspired by his work.

Although this chapter emphasizes defects in Durkheim's theory, it is not a belittlement of the man himself. Far from it; without Durkheim there might well have been no "sociology of suicide." Hence, sociologists should rightly proclaim Durkheim to have been a genius, and then *get on with it.*

THE THEORY'S TWO BASIC PREMISES

Some attention is given subsequently to Durkheim's types of suicide, but only because many other expositions treat the types as central. To the contrary, stating Durkheim's theory in terms of suicide types only beguiles or confuses.

Insufficient Integration and Egoistic Suicide

Durkheim's book illustrates how an imaginative data analysis can lead to a

This chapter was completed while the author was a fellow at the Center for Advanced Study in the Behavioral Sciences. I am grateful for financial support provided by the National Science Foundation, Grant No. BNS-8700864.

novel theory. The data consisted primarily of official European suicide statistics over the 1800s. Durkheim marshalled evidence to show that *generally* the suicide rate is: (1) greater for Protestants than for Catholics or Jews; (2) correlated positively among various social units (e.g., Italian provinces) with level of educational attainment; (3) less for the married than the single (never married); (4) less for married individuals who have children than for the childless; (5) correlated negatively among territorial divisions of France with average family size; and (6) declines sharply during great national wars or political upheavals.

Integration as the common denominator

Durkheim arrived at his theory by pursuing this question: what do the populations having relatively high suicide rates share in common that distinguishes them from other populations? Durkheim's partial answer (p. 209; unless indicated otherwise, all page numbers refer to *Suicide*, 1951) is explicit: less social integration. However, Durkheim neither reached that answer nor supported it by using integration measures; rather, he made interpretive use of the integration *notion*. Thus, "the proclivity of Protestantism for suicide must relate to the spirit of free inquiry that animates this religion" (p. 158), and "if Protestantism concedes a greater freedom to individual thought than Catholicism, it is because it has fewer common beliefs and practices" (p. 159). Then there is a similar interpretation of the presumed positive association between education and suicide (p. 168): "this is due...to the weakening of traditional beliefs and to the [resulting] state of moral individualism...."

Both interpretations stress *normative consensus*, but that is not the stress when interpreting the married's lower suicide rate. There Durkheim becomes preoccupied with (1) recognizing the relevance of age and sex when comparing marital statuses, (2) arguing against the "matrimonial selectivity" interpretation, and (3) attempting to ascertain if the lower rate is due to the conjugal relation or to familial relations (children in particular). Because of those preoccupations, Durkheim actually never offered an interpretation of the married's lower rate, even though concluding (p. 198) that "marriage has...a preservative effect of its own against suicide." Be that as it may, the only obvious way that marriage integrates is *relational*, not consensual.

Another interpretation is suggested where Durkheim asserts a negative correlation between the suicide rate and average family size (or "family density"). Here he concludes (p. 202) that "the state of integration of a social aggregate can only reflect the intensity of the collective life circulating in it" and that a social aggregate is "more unified and powerful the more active and constant is the intercourse among its members." So his argument is *behavioral;* an increase in family size furthers integration through greater familial interaction.

Still another interpretation of integration surfaces (p. 208) in Durkheim's observations on the decline in the suicide rate during great wars or political upheavals: "great social disturbances and great popular wars rouse collective sentiments, stimulate partisan spirit and patriotism, political and national faith alike, and concentrating activity toward a single end, at least temporarily cause a stronger integration of society." The statement describes integration in *psychological* terms, one of numerous instances where Durkheim's explanation contradicts his shrill antireductionism, especially in *The Rules of Sociological Method* (1938).

Some implications of the divergent interpretations

Durkheim's theory is not defective because he failed to formulate an integration measure. Instead, he suggested four meanings (consensual, relational, behavioral, and psychological); and there is even a fifth possibility—organizational—in light of this observation (p. 161): "the Anglican clergy is the only Protestant clergy organized in a hierarchy."

The diversity of meanings may well preclude a comprehensible definition of integration, let alone one that promises appreciable empirical applicability.[1] Indeed, if the diversity signifies multiple "dimensions" of integration, the prospects for a measurement procedure are worse. Worst of all, the diverse ways that Durkheim used the term enabled him to indulge in *ad hoc* explanations. Two illustrations must suffice. In commenting on the purported positive association between levels of educational attainment and suicide rates, Durkheim admits (p. 167): "Of all religions, Judaism counts the fewest suicides, yet in none other is education so general." However, he then argues that Jews seek education to further their struggle against prejudice and concludes (p. 168): "So the exception is only apparent; it even confirms the law." Essentially the same conclusion is reached when explaining why England did not have (in the 1800s) a higher suicide rate. In brief, according to Durkheim (pp. 160-161), England was highly integrated, despite being predominantly Protestant, because of *(inter alia)* the number of Anglican clergy and their hierarchical organization (Durkheim ignored the diversity of Protestant denominations in England).

Now contemplate the suicide decline during revolutions, which Durkheim attributed to an *increase* in integration. Suppose that the statistics had indicated greater suicides? What would have prevented Durkheim from attributing the increase to a decline in social integration? The point is that nebulous notions make it possible to interpret virtually any contrast in suicide rates.

Egoistic suicide

The foregoing differs from many expositions of Durkheim's theory in that there is no emphasis on "egoism" as a cause of suicide, nor on egoistic suicides. Durkheim did use such terminology frequently, but it adds nothing to the theory. The reason is suggested by the only passage (p. 209) where Durkheim comes close to an explicit definition: "we may call egoistic the special type of suicide springing from excessive individualism." Given that elsewhere Durkheim attributed excessive individualism to insufficient integration, egoistic suicide is simply the appropriate designation for a suicide *caused* by insufficient integration. That interpretation may appear puzzling because the word "vain" or "arrogant" or "self-centered" comes to mind when thinking about the meaning of egoist; but *Durkheim never made use of anything like those words in his ostensible partial definitions of egoistic suicide.*

Excessive Integration and Altruistic Suicide

Having concluded that insufficient integration causes suicide, Durkheim then argues (pp. 217-240) that *excessive* integration does the same. In defending that argument Durkheim made extensive use of historical and anthropological literature. Because of space limitations, that use must be illustrated by only three summary statements, the first two pertaining to "suicide situations" among nonliterate peoples (e.g., Hawaii in the early 1800s), ancient societies (e.g., Gaul), or non-Western social units (e.g., Bengal). First, men (warriors especially) commonly ended their life rather than die of old age or illness. Second, subordinates (e.g., wives, servants) were expected to commit suicide on the death of their superordinate (e.g., husband, king). Third, in Europe during the 1800s the military suicide rate, of elite units particularly, was much greater than the civilian rate.

Principal doubts, objections, and criticisms

Unless based on a measurement procedure, any statement about the amount of integration in any social unit is conjecture; and all the more when expressing a judgment as to "excessiveness" or "insufficiency." For that matter, only in the military-civilian comparison did Durkheim consider actual suicide rates; and after an extensive analysis of relevant data, Pope (1976: 103-115) has challenged Durkheim's conclusion. Finally, although accounts of ritual suicide suggest that suicide is endemic, no one has demonstrated a connection between *kinds* of suicide and the suicide rate (other than it cannot be zero).

Durkheim's most general claim in connection with excessive integration is that suicide is "surely very common among primitive peoples" (p. 219). That claim is inconsistent with numerous observations by anthropologists that suggest enormous variation in the suicide rate among nonliterate peoples. Four observations (all quoted in Gibbs, 1971: 283) must suffice:

> *The Mohave:* "The conflict between longing for the dead and the impossibility of catching up with them should one live too long after they died leads to an appalling number of suicides."

The Havasupai: "Suicides...are rare....there have been no instances for a generation."

White Mountain Apache: "one or more cases of self-destruction occur every year."

Southern Ute: "No instance of death by suicide was learned of...."

Because Durkheim provided no evidence that *beyond some magnitude* there is a *positive* association among populations between integration measures and suicide rates, his argument about excessive integration is largely conjecture. Moreover, the closest he comes to an explication of the postulated causal connection between excessive integration and suicide is this (p. 219): "when a person kills himself, in all these cases, it is not because he assumes the right to do so but, on the contrary, *because it is his duty.*" Here Durkheim offers a *normative* explanation; but elsewhere (e.g., pp. 156-157, in connection with Catholicism and Protestantism) he denies that social condemnation of suicide influences the rate.

Altruistic suicide

Durkheim *gave the name* "altruistic" to suicides caused by excessive integration. Hence, criticisms in connection with egoistic suicide apply in connection with altruistic suicides. The only exception is that Durkheim came close to an explicit definition of altruism that *appears* logically independent of integration. He describes (p. 221) altruism as a "state" in which "the ego is not its own property, where it is blended with something not itself, where the goal of conduct is exterior to itself, that is, in one of the groups in which it participates." That ostensible definition borders on the incomprehensible;[2] and even if (p. 221) "the suicide caused by intense altruism [is] *altruistic suicide,*" altruistic suicides are simply suicides caused by excessive integration.

Insufficient Regulation and Anomic Suicide

The second key causal variable is "social regulation." Durkheim's argument is that both insufficient regulation and excessive regulation cause suicide, but the argument is not understandable without illustrations of the data that ostensibly shaped his thinking.

Three kinds of associations

Durkheim reached his conclusion about regulation by examining three sets of nineteenth-century European data. Each set supposedly indicates that insufficient regulation causes suicide.

One data set suggests that suicides increase during an economic crisis, but

Durkheim's interpretation is cryptic. He denies that poverty or economic stress itself causes suicide,[3] and in rambling passages he argues that restraints on passions, aspirations, or appetites are needed to avoid pathological consequences. Here Durkheim comes close to suggesting that disappointments, suffering, and frustration enter into the etiology of suicide; but he maintains that economic crises are associated with suicide only because they are indicative of insufficient regulation.

Statistics for populations distinguished by kind of economic activity (e.g., trade, transportation, agriculture) led Durkheim to conclude (pp. 257-258) that certain occupations have relatively high suicide rates because the related activities are largely unregulated. Some occupations entail more speculative activities or risks than do others, and in that sense some occupations are less regulated than others. However, Durkheim used the term "regulation" loosely; and he did not demonstrate the occupational differences in question, let alone show that they are correlated with variation in the suicide rate among occupations or industries.

Of all the contrasts that informed Durkheim, the greater suicide rate of the divorced is the most incontrovertible. Yet Durkheim appears concerned not with explaining the greater rate but, rather, with using it to throw light on the married's low rate. The attempt is confusing because earlier Durkheim had examined the married's rate to support his arguments about integration, not regulation. For that matter, Durkheim appears unconcerned with the possibility that the experience of divorce itself or the social condition of the divorced is conducive to suicide; instead, he makes statements like this (p. 271): "divorce implies a weakening of matrimonial regulation."

Anomic suicide

Durkheim all but admits that by "anomy" he *means* insufficient regulation. He even speaks (p. 253) of the "state of deregulation or anomy" and refers to anomic suicides as resulting (p. 258) from "man's activity's lacking regulation and his consequent suffering." He then says: "By virtue of its origin we shall assign this last variety the name of *anomic suicide.*"

The suggestion that the term "anomie" plays no essential role in Durkheim's theory is controversial, but it will not do for critics to point out that in *The Rules of Sociological Method* (1938) Durkheim equated anomie with normlessness. Although normlessness precludes regulation, sociologists have come to use the term "anomie" so uncritically that Durkheim's meaning is now totally lost.

Excessive Regulation and Fatalistic Suicide

Durkheim designated his fourth type of suicide as "fatalistic" and described its cause in what was for him uncommonly human terms (p. 276): "It is the suicide deriving from excessive regulation, that of persons with futures piti-lessly blocked and passions violently choked by oppressive discipline." While the reference (p. 276) to "suicides of slaves, said to be frequent under certain conditions" furthers plausibility (despite only one citation), the same is not true of the other examples, young husbands and married women without children.

Given that Durkheim relegated the subject to a footnote (p. 276) and characterized it as of "little contemporary importance," it is not surprising that many commentators have ignored his fourth type of suicide.[4] However, if only because Durkheim wrote before twentieth-century totalitarianism, the possi-bility of excessive regulation is more than merely of historical interest. What-ever humanity's fate, the key notion is excessive regulation, and the label "fatalistic suicide" adds nothing. Indeed, it may well be, as Pope suggests (1976: 43), that Durkheim invented the fatalistic type simply because he could not otherwise explain the relatively high suicide rates of young husbands and childless married women.

Statement of the Two Premises

Durkheim's four types add nothing if the theory explains variation in the suicide rate and not individual cases. Although Durkheim was at great pains to identify that variation as posing *the* sociological question, he was a master at rhetoric; and he may have anticipated that many readers would not regard the theory as plausible and interesting if it had no bearing on individual suicides. The types of suicide suggest some bearing, and in the chapter entitled "Individual Forms of the Different Types of Suicide" Durkheim (1951) comes close to more than a suggestion (see, especially, pp. 277-278). Nonetheless, because his suicide typology adds nothing to the theory as it applies to rate variation, no reference is made to the types in stating premises.

Terminological considerations

Each premise in Durkheim's theory commences with the phrase "Among social units or for a unit over time" to signify that the premise extends to the suicide rates of all *social* populations (e.g., countries, occupations, age groups) and temporal variation in the rate. The point is made because Durkheim used the term "society" so frequently and uncritically that he obscured the bearing of his theory on other types of units and trends.

Recall that Durkheim identified four causes of variation in the suicide rate—insufficient integration, excessive integration, insufficient regulation, and excessive regulation. So each premise must recognize not only the insufficient-excessive distinction but also that both integration and regulation are determinants.

The first premise

Durkheim contributed to what has become virtually a maxim for sociologists: In stating a theory, do not make the premises explicit or label them. This version of Durkheim's theory violates that maxim, commencing with Postulate 1: Among social units or for a unit over time, if the influence of variation in regulation is eliminated, an increase in integration beyond some magnitude causes an increase in the suicide rate; and below some magnitude a decrease in integration causes an increase in the suicide rate.

The postulate does not stipulate what would be evidence of causation, and such stipulation is difficult and controversial. However, that problem (see Gibbs, 1982b) is not peculiar to Durkheim's theory, and it must suffice to say that causal evidence requires demonstration of a maximization of correlations when there is a time lag between the alleged causal variable and the effect variable. Durkheim did not even suggest the lag's length; hence, it must be established through induction (i.e., exploratory research). Reliance on induction would not be a special defect of Durkheim's theory, but a particular difficulty makes the theory distinctive. Even if there were measures of integration and regulation, Durkheim never suggested what levels constitute "insufficient" and "excessive." They can be established (if at all) only through attempts to identify the point or range where there is a change in the direction of the association between the measures (integration or regulation) and suicide rates, assuming there is a change.

The second premise

The second major causal variable comes in Postulate 2: Among social units or for a unit over time, if the influence of variation in integration is eliminated, an increase in regulation beyond some magnitude causes an increase in the suicide rate; and below some magnitude a decrease in regulation causes an increase in the suicide rate.

All observations on the *form* of Postulate 1 also apply in this case, but the logical relation between the two postulates should be clarified. The two postulates are logically related only in that the suicide rate is the dependent variable in both. However, even if other generalizations could be deduced from the two postulates, the deductions would not enhance the theory's testability.

Despite the logical independence of the two postulates, Durkheim's theory cannot be understood fully without considering both in conjunction. That conjunction is depicted in Table 1, which is virtually identical to Johnson's tabular summary (1965) of the theory. Even though the table footnotes pertain to the four types of suicide, note again that they are not essential components of the theory.

Table 1.

A Representation of Durkheim's Theory

Degree of Social Regulation	*Degree of Social Integration*		
	high	moderate	low
high	high suicide rate A	moderate suicide rate D	high suicide rate G
moderate	moderate suicide rate B	low suicide rate E	moderate suicide rate H
low	high suicide rate C	moderate suicide rate F	high suicide rate I

Predominant types of suicide:

A = altruistic and fatalistic
B = altruistic
C = altruistic and anomic
D = fatalistic
E = no particular type
F = anomic
G = egoistic and fatalistic
H = egoistic
I = egoistic and anomic

Principal Defects

No extant version of the theory can be tested defensibly, meaning such that independent investigators agree in the choice of procedure and in the findings reported for the same populations. The reason is not just that Durkheim scarcely formulated an explicit definition of integration or regulation; additionally, he used those terms so uncritically and diversely that his statements make their meanings indistinguishable (for elaboration, see Johnson, 1965, and Pope, 1976).

Even if Durkheim had formulated explicit definitions of integration and regulation that make them distinct, he did not stipulate anything like measurement procedures. Nonetheless, numerous sociologists have reported research findings as though they are tests of Durkheim's theory. Such reports ignore Durkheim's exclusive reliance on *inferences* about differences between particular populations as regards integration or regulation. Consider his inference that during the 1800s European Catholics were more integrated than were European Protestants. Regardless of how Durkheim made that inference,[5] it was not based on measures of integration. Further, even if Durkheim had employed a defensible measure and demonstrated that the integration value is greater for Catholics, the percentage Catholic could not be the measure of integration or even a defensible "indicator." Durkheim treated other variables as indicative of integration-marital composition, family density, etc.—and there is no basis to assume that Durkheim identified all manifestations or indicators of integration.

The construct-concept distinction

The suggestion is not that Durkheim could have formulated clear and complete definitions of his two key terms, let alone defensible measurement procedures. Such formulations are not possible in the case of *constructs,* "integration" and "regulation" being instances. When using a construct, unlike a concept, the theorist may leave it undefined. Even when a construct is defined, the theorist does not regard the definition as complete and clear, another contrast with a concept. Finally, again unlike a concept, the theorist does not regard the definition as promising sufficient empirical applicability.

In light of the foregoing, "suicide rate" is a concept. The reliability of official suicide rates is another matter, but theorists should face that issue when stipulating requisite data for tests of their theories. However, even if sufficient reliability is assumed, the two postulates are not systematically testable if only because amount of integration and amount of regulation are constructs. The theory will remain untestable until it encompasses at least two more postulates, one linking integration to some concept and the other linking regulation to another concept.

THEORETICAL DEVELOPMENTS INSPIRED BY DURKHEIM

To his credit, Durkheim's work has inspired several theories. This brief survey is restricted to theories published since mid-century, because earlier ones (e.g., Halbwachs, 1930) currently receive scant attention (but see Travis, 1990).

The Theory of Andrew F. Henry and James F. Short, Jr.

The Henry-Short theory (1954) differs from Durkheim's in four respects. First, Henry and Short made greater use of psychological or psychoanalytical notions, notably the frustration-aggression hypothesis and cathexis. Second, they emphasized status. Third, they were more concerned than was Durkheim with correlates of *change* in suicide rates, especially economic conditions (fluctuations in the business cycle particularly). Fourth, Henry and Short treated both the homicide rate and the suicide rate as dependent variables.

Premises and theorems or conclusions

Even though Henry and Short used the labels postulate, proposition, assumption, definition, and hypothesis, they provide no rationale for using one label rather than another. Indeed, ignoring those labels, the theory is stated in the conventional discursive mode (merely the conventions of a natural language).

The closest that Henry and Short come to explicit premises is where (1954: 75) they state two postulates, as follow:

Postulate 1: "Suicide rates in high status categories are higher than suicide rates in low status categories because high status categories are subject to fewer external constraints than low status categories."

Postulate 2: "The probability of suicide varies inversely with the strength of the relational system because persons with strong relational systems are subjected to greater external restraints than persons with weak relational systems."

The theory's logical structure cannot be clarified without decomposing the two postulates and adding statements that Henry and Short left unlabeled or identified as propositions, hypotheses, or definitions (see, especially, 1954: 16-17 and 74-75).

Premise 1: External restraints over behavior vary directly with the strength of the relational system.

Premise 2: External restraints over behavior vary inversely with the suicide rate.

Premise 3: External restraints over behavior vary directly with the homicide rate.[6]

Premise 4: Status varies inversely with the strength of the relational system.[7]

In accordance with the sign rule (Gibbs, 1985: 30), the four premises imply several theorems; but for reasons indicated subsequently only the three that follow are testable, and even those tests require judgments as to the relative *status* of broad population divisions (e.g., men vs. women).

Theorem 1 (from Premises 1, 2, and 4): Status varies directly with the suicide rate.

Theorem 2 (from Premises 1, 3, and 4): Status varies inversely with the homicide rate.

Theorem 3 (from Premises 2 and 3): The suicide rate varies inversely with the homicide rate.

A diachronic proposition

All previous components of the theory are synchronic generalizations, meaning that they pertain to differences in the suicide rates of populations and not to change in a population's rate. However, the theory can be construed as encompassing this *diachronic* proposition: over time, the correlation between measures of economic prosperity and suicide rates of a high status division of a population is more negative than is the same correlation for a low status division. "Over time" refers to annual trends, and a "population" could be the residents—all status divisions combined—of a country or a smaller territorial unit (e.g., a metropolitan area). The measure of economic prosperity refers to the population as a whole and not to some status division of it.

Although Henry and Short did not formally deduce the diachronic proposition, it appears to stem from two assumptions.[8] First, frustration is the proximate cause of suicide. And, second, a decline in economic prosperity results in more frustration for high status divisions because of relatively greater downward mobility.

The immediate consideration is not the validity of the proposition or the two assumptions. Rather, because the proposition cannot be deduced from the synchronic postulates or premises, it is as though there are two distinct theories; and Henry and Short's concern (1954: 69) about possible confusion does not mitigate. Unless the two kinds of variation in the suicide rate—among populations (synchronic) or over time (diachronic)—have different causes, the two parts of the theory are inconsistent. Specifically, the synchronic generalizations attribute variation in the suicide rate to variation in the strength of the relational system or status, but the arguments underlying the diachronic generalization depict frustration as causal. Moreover, even granting that economic prosperity solely determines the amount of frustration, there is a direct relation between status and economic prosperity (i.e., high status divisions are wealthier). So if status and suicide are positively associated, as Henry and Short assert, then the association between economic prosperity and the suicide rate is *positive* among status divisions but *negative* over time for any status division.

Henry and Short extended their observations on status contrasts to the relation over time between economic prosperity and the homicide rate. Unfortunately, space limitations preclude treating that part of the theory and related findings.

Maris' Theory

After a critique of Durkheim's theory and several contenders, Maris formulated a single postulate (1969: 159 and 177) as a step toward another contender. Maris (1969: 159) characterized the postulate as "explanatory" but stated it this way (1969: 14): "The suicide rate varies inversely with external constraint."

The postulate differs from one of the Henry-Short generalizations only in that the independent variable is *external* constraint rather than external *restraint*. So Maris' theory can be regarded as an advance only in one sense; whereas Henry and Short do not stipulate any procedure for measuring external restraint, Maris attempts such a stipulation in connection with external constraint.

Maris' key statement is (1969: 179): "Integration is the structural aspect and regulation the normative aspect of external constraint." He treats the statement as though it were conceptual, but it is really an untestable assertion of two causes of external constraint—integration and regulation. Moreover, because integration or regulation are no less constructs than is external constraint, Maris' statement does not make his postulate testable. Yet he writes (1969: 180-181) as though integration and regulation are concepts, not constructs. Thus, "a *rough* indication of the social integration of a particular individual could be obtained by simply *counting* the number of direct inter-personal dependency relationships." Maris neither suggests a "counting" procedure nor recognizes the complexity, one illustrated by this question: who has the greatest number of dependency relationships, a widowed father of two children who owns a store with two employees and 2500 regular customers, or a childless married store owner with ten employees and 500 regular customers? In the case of regulation, Maris proposes (1969: 181) that points be assigned "for being a particular sex or age, in a specific social class or occupation" so as to "reflect the amount of dominance exerted on the individual."

The Status Integration Theory

Although inspired by Durkheim, the connection between his theory and the status integration theory (e.g., Gibbs and Martin, 1964; Gibbs, 1982a) is limited to *Postulate 1* of the latter: *The suicide rate of a population varies inversely with the stability and durability of social relationships within that population.* Critics (e.g., Maris, 1969: 50) notwithstanding, the postulate is in no sense an operationalization of Durkheim's social integration; and the only relation between the latter term and status integration is one imagined by critics. Moreover, the postulate implies nothing about regulation, and it has no bearing on Durkheim's claim that *excessive* integration generates suicides. Finally, should a critic demand that the postulate itself be explained, any scientific theory *necessarily* leaves at least one question unanswered: If the premises are true, why?

The real problem is that the postulate cannot be tested, because there is no prospect of an empirically applicable formula (including data instructions) for expressing the durability and stability of social relationships. However, one of Weber's arguments (see Gibbs and Martin, 1964: 17) justifies *Postulate 2: The stability and durability of social relationships within a population vary directly with the extent to which individuals in that population conform to the patterned and socially sanctioned demands and expectations placed upon them by others.*

No one can count violations of or conformity to socially sanctioned demands and expectations in any population over, say, one year; therefore, Postulate 2 is also untestable. But if critics doubt its validity, they should routinely violate social sanctioned demands or expectations and contemplate the consequences.[9] To be sure, an isolated violation may be idiosyncratic and not disrupt a social relationship. Yet *Postulate 3* identifies a condition under which violations would be common and very disruptive: *The extent to which individuals in a population conform to patterned and socially sanctioned demands and expectations placed upon them by others varies inversely with the extent to which individuals in that population are confronted with role conflicts.*

Doubts about role conflict's reality can be allayed by observing the behavior of married merchant seamen or university students employed full-time, but it is difficult to imagine a measurement procedure. Nonetheless, the primary determinant of conflict is the occupancy of incompatible statuses, meaning two or more statuses having conflicting roles (i.e., conformity to one role makes it difficult if not impossible to conform to the other role). So *Postulate 4: The extent to which individuals in a population are confronted with role conflicts varies directly with the extent to which individuals occupy incompatible statuses.*

Postulate 4 is not a tautology. *Intrastatus* role conflict is possible; hence, the postulate implicitly asserts that the paramount locus of role conflict is *interstatus.* But there is no empirically applicable criterion for identifying incompatible statuses, let alone a measure of incompatibility. Instead, there are two crucial assumptions: (1) movement in and out of one achieved status is indicative of the status' compatibility or incompatibility with other statuses (ascribed or achieved) and (2) such movement results in relatively rare simultaneous occupancy of two or more incompatible statuses.

The assumptions are limited to two types of status pairs, ascribed-achieved and achieved-achieved, because putative "voluntary" status changes are limited to achieved statuses; and only such movement is indicative of status compatibility-incompatibility. So if X_1 is a particular status in a particular family of ascribed statuses (e.g., "age 19") and Y_1 is one of a family of achieved statuses (e.g., "banker"), then the proportion of X_1 individuals (i.e., occupants of that status) who are also Y_1 individuals indicates the amount of status compatibility.[10] Simultaneous occupancy of incompatible statuses is infrequent for three reasons: first, the role conflict may be so conspicuous that population members rarely attempt the occupancy, and perhaps it is socially discouraged; second, an occupant may resolve the role conflict by moving out of one or both statuses; or, third, an occupant may be deprived of one status because of role violations.

Each occupancy proportion is a *measure of status integration;* and in a population where status integration is at a maximum, all proportions are either 1.000 or .000. Described still another way, when status integration is at a maximum, knowledge of all but one status of any population member's statuses assures an accurate prediction of that member's unknown status. By contrast, when status integration is at a minimum, correct predictions are due to sheer chance.

Observe that a status integration measure is not a measure of anything else. Nonetheless, the two crucial assumptions are the basis for the last premise, *Postulate 5: The extent to which individuals occupy incompatible statuses varies inversely with the degree of status integration.*

The derivation of a testable theorem

None of the five postulates are testable in any direct sense if only because at least one of each postulate's constituent terms (variables) is a construct. However, in accordance with the "sign rule," the five postulates taken together imply a testable theorem: *The suicide rate of a population varies inversely with the degree of status integration in that population.*

The theorem's derivation is controversial primarily because some sociologists reject the sign rule.[11] Some critics have expressed vague reservations that are later seized upon by others as somehow demonstrating that the rule is invalid.[12] Still other critics appear to argue that the sign rule is logically invalid unless applied to premises that assert causation.[13] All such criticisms play fast and loose with the meaning not just of logically valid but also of logic itself.

In criticizing the theory Maris (1969: 51) made this observation: "The definition of a valid argument is that *if* the *premises* are true, then the conclusion must be true." He never asked: if the premises are known to be true, why assess their empirical validity by deducing conclusions? As for Maris' claim *(ibid.)* that "Proving...the theorem is true...proves nothing about the truth value of any particular premise," he ignored this point: a false theorem is evidence of at least one false premise. That point takes on added significance in light of Popper's dictum that scientific generalizations may be falsified but never verified. Hence, nothing is gained by demanding some deductive procedure that *verifies* the premises.

Maris and other critics are really urging avoidance of the fallacy of affirming the consequent—judging the premises as "true" because the conclusion is true. Such judgment would not be defensible even if it were possible to make a unique derivation, meaning to demonstrate that the conclusion can be derived *only* from the premises in question (i.e., the premises are both necessary and sufficient for the conclusion). A unique derivation cannot be demonstrated; and until Maris and his coworkers come to accept that awful fact, their criticisms of deductive theories will be grossly unrealistic. Scientists in advanced fields have lived with the problem in question for centuries, precisely because it is possible through deductions and tests of conclusions to *falsify* premises about infinite classes.

To be sure, assumptions must be made to justify expectations of accurate predictions in testing theorems. In this case the assumption is that (1) all of the associations asserted in the premises are sufficiently close to justify a prediction of the *sign* of a theorem and/or (2) the error terms (were the variables in the premises mensurable) would not be correlated so highly as to preclude such justification. If critics dismiss the assumption as unrealistic, they should be asked: given that the premises are not testable, what is the basis for dismissing the assumption?

Measurement

The theorem is testable because the constituent variables are concepts.[14] In the case of the suicide rate *(SR)*, there is a conventional formula: $SR = [(Ns/Ny)/P]$, where Ns is the number of members of a designated population (e.g., California residents) who committed suicide during a designated period (e.g., 1989-1991), Ny is the number of years in that period, and P is the number of population members (preferably at the period's midpoint).

Table 2 illustrates status integration measures. The proportions *within* a particular column (elementary measures) would enter into a within-column test, and for each column the prediction (hypothesis) would be a negative coefficient of correlation between the proportions and suicide rates. So within the first column the single should have the lowest suicide rate, the married the next-to-lowest rate, the divorced the next-to-highest rate, and the widowed the highest rate.

The data are arranged so as to take all statuses into account, but the data's adequacy always depends on the number of statuses (e.g., in Table 2 the data would be less than ideal if "religion" were unknown). Also note that within-column tests for some other *family* of achieved statuses (e.g., occupations) would require another table.

The next-to-last row of Table 2 illustrates the "column" measure of status integration. The hypothesis would be a negative correlation *among columns* between the SP^2 values and suicide rates (each rate would pertain to the column as a whole—all marital statuses combined). So the third column should have the highest suicide rate, and the second column the lowest.

Such a *between-columns* test appears to take into account all other statuses, but it does so far less than in a within-column test. The column measures pertain only to the status family in the rows and do not take into account the possibility

Table 2.

Measures of Marital Integration in a Hypothetical Social Unit

	Occupied State Configurations[1]		
	$A_3\text{-}S_1\text{-}E_3$ $O_4\text{-}R_2\text{-}O_2$	$A_4\text{-}S_1\text{-}E_2$ $O_3\text{-}R_1\text{-}P_1$	$A_5\text{-}S_2\text{-}E_2$ $O_1\text{-}R_3\text{-}P_3$
Marital Status	*Col. 1*	*Col. 2*	*Col. 3*
Single	0.912	0.000	0.247
Married	0.063	1.000	0.252
Widowed	0.010	0.000	0.251
Divorced	0.015	0.000	0.250
$\sum P^2_3$	1.000	1.000	1.000
$\sum P^2$	0.836	1.000	0.250
W^4	0.240	0.352	0.408

[1] All possible combinations of occupied statuses in the social unit (a country or a community). In this illustration A signifies age, S sex, E ethnicity-race, O occupation, R religious affiliation, and P parental status. Each number signifies a particular status within a family of statuses (e.g., S_1 would be a male, S_2 a female).
[2] Sum of column proportions.
[3] Measure of marital integration for the status configuration.
[4] Proportion of the social unit's population in the status configuration. The row sum of the W values is 1.000 regardless of the number of columns, but in a real social unit there are likely to be far more than three occupied status configurations.

of column differences as regards dimensions of integration between achieved statuses, such as between religion and occupation. The only solution may be between-columns tests in which all possible combinations of achieved statuses are considered when computing the measure for any particular status family, but such a measure has not been perfected for between-column test.[15] As long as only ascribed statuses are in the column heading and only one family of statuses in the rows, the measurement problem is circumvented; but nothing like a maximum negative correlation would be expected in a between-columns test because the column measures reflect only one dimension of status integration.

Finally, the total measure of marital integration for Table 2 would be the average of the column measures, which is .692 (2.086/3 or [.836 + 1.000 + .250]/3). Any inclusive social unit having a lesser average would be expected to have a higher suicide rate, and any social unit having a greater average would be expected to have a lower rate. However, predictions would be more accurate if based on a *weighted* total: $(SP^2)(W)$, where SP^2 is (as before) the marital integration measure for a particular column and W the proportion of the social unit's total population in that column (the last row of Table 2). Even a weighted measure of marital integration would not permit confident predictions, because it would reflect only one dimension of status integration.

Comparisons of the Theories as Regards Predictive Power

There are two reasons why independent critics are likely to disagree if they assess theories in light of this question: how well does the theory explain what it purports to explain? First, there is little agreement even among philosophers of science as to the nature of explanation. Second, there is even greater dissensus as to criteria of an *adequate* explanation. There is much greater prospect of agreement in independent assessments of a theory if each assessment focuses on this question: what is the theory's predictive power relative to that of contenders?

Predictive power is the criterion for further assessments of the three theories—Durkheim's, Henry-Short, and status integration.[16] However, it may well be that the criterion is rejected by most sociologists. Even before the escalation of antipositivism, most sociologists assessed theories primarily in light of preconceptions, background assumptions, or presuppositions, all of which make personal opinion paramount. Whatever the alternative, sociologists commonly make two mistakes when rejecting the predictive power criterion. First, they ignore the need to consider a theory's predictive power relative to that of contenders, as opposed to some absolute standard. Second, they equate predictive accuracy and predictive power.

Testability

Testability is a dimension of predictive power distinct from predictive accuracy (i.e., from test outcomes), and systematic tests are impossible unless falsifiable predictions can be deduced from the theory. So testability connects Popper's emphasis on falsifiability and the more inclusive notion of predictive power. The point is made because, after decades of shrill criticisms of Popper, antipositivists have yet to provide a coherent alternative (postpositivism, structuralism, deconstructionism, postmodernism, hermeneutics, post-empiricism, etc., notwithstanding).

Only synthetic statements are potentially testable, but an instance is not testable in any direct sense unless its constituent terms are empirically applicable. If a term denotes a quantitative phenomenon, empirical applicability requires an intelligible formula and one that can be applied because acquisition of the requisite data is feasible. Nevertheless, judgments of potential testability are so conjectural that only actual tests inspire confidence. As for Popper's notion of falsifiability, it must pertain not to outcomes of actual tests but, rather, to the requirement that a scientific theory comprise synthetic generalizations that imply testable predictions.

The testability of Durkheim's theory

After nearly a century there is little prospect of a measure of social regulation or social integration, let alone one that is empirically applicable and acceptable to critics. Furthermore, measures by themselves would not make Durkheim's theory testable.[17] Recall that above or below some unspecified level integration or regulation generates suicides, but the level can be established only inductively (if at all).

The foregoing implies a denial of any real prospects for defensible actual tests of Durkheim's theory. As for the numerous purported tests, it is subsequently argued that none of them will bear examination.

The testability of the Henry-Short theory

The theory's premises are not directly testable because the empirical applicability of "strength of the relational system" and "strength of external restraints over behavior" appears negligible. However, three theorems have been deduced from the formal version of the theory. Theorem 3, which asserts an inverse relation between the suicide rate and the homicide rate, is clearly testable if official data can be used; but there are doubts about Henry and Short's reports of tests that bear on Theorems 1 and 2.

Although Henry and Short report numerous findings concerning the relation between status and the suicide rate, Theorem 1 is *systematically* testable only to the extent that trained observers agree in judging the relative status of population divisions (e.g., age groups, race-ethic sectors).[18] Henry and Short leave that contingency implicit, but it is clearly suggested by their test procedure.

Had Henry and Short defined status in terms of income, then perhaps their assumptions about the U.S. population would have been demonstrably warranted; but their status criteria (1954: 24) extend to achievement, possession, authority, and power. If only because those criteria are quantitative and no measure is specified, there are doubts about the Henry-Short test procedure, especially its applicability in other cross-cultural and historical contexts. For that matter, it is debatable whether the status theorem applies to territorial variation in U.S. suicide rates (among states or cities), much less international comparisons.

Because there are conventional measures of economic prosperity, the diachronic generalizations in the Henry-Short theory appear testable. Recall, however, that they are couched in terms of status distinctions (e.g., the correlation between economic prosperity and the suicide rate over time is asserted to be less positive for low status population divisions); hence, their testability is just as questionable as the testability of the synchronic generalizations.

The *potential* for tests of the Henry-Short theory is greater than has been suggested, and clarification of "status" along with an empirically applicable measure would greatly enhance the theory's testability. Again, though, whatever the theory, judgments of testability tend to be debatable.

The testability of the status integration theory

The theory is testable, and the reason is not just the intelligible formulas for the suicide rate and the status integration measures. Application of each formula is feasible because of readily accessible data, incomplete though the status data are.

The rate formula can be applied to published official data (census and vital statistics reports) for various populations throughout the world. To be sure, there are widespread doubts about the reliability of official suicide statistics; but the theory should be construed as assuming that they are *proportionately* reliable to the point that the direction (sign) of the relation between integration measures and suicide rates can be predicted accurately. Yet the theory does not stand or fall on that assumption, and nothing concerning official suicide data is peculiar to the theory.

Published census reports provide data for measures of several status integration dimensions in various populations throughout the world. The problem is that tables in census volumes cross-classify very few statuses (especially the achieved). Thus, in the case of the U.S. census data make it possible to compute measures of *single* integration dimensions, such as marital or occupational, with age, sex, and race; but few census tables cross-classify even two families of achieved statuses, and there are no U.S. census data on religious affiliation. The consequence has been tests based on all too few status families. Fortunately, there is a solution—acquisition of more adequate data through conventional survey procedures.

Approximately 250 tests of the theory have been reported. An exact count is not needed to make an overall comparison: The number is far greater than for the Henry-Short theory, and even greater than *purported* tests of Durkheim's theory.

Predictive Accuracy

There is a logical connection between testability and predictive accuracy in that tests are necessary to assess accuracy. Hence, the predictive accuracy of Durkheim's theory cannot be assessed until restated so as to make it testable.

The predictive accuracy of the Henry-Short theory

By virtue of assuming that in the U.S. status is greater for whites, males, upper income groups, young and middle-aged, and army officers vs. enlisted men,

Henry and Short (1954: 70) then *predicted* higher suicide rates for those divisions. The findings (1954: 71) totally support the race, sex, and military predictions but not those pertaining to age and income. Three totally correct predictions out of five are hardly impressive.[19] Moreover, in explaining the incorrect predictions, Henry and Short (1954: 72) resort to some of Durkheim's arguments and to statistics indicating that the married have a lower suicide rate. By that path they appear to suggest that relational system strength must be taken into account as well as status, but their explication is murky and ignores two crucial considerations. First, Henry and Short clearly imply that status varies inversely with the strength of the relational system (1954: 75); hence, it is not at all clear how both relational system strength and status could decline beyond middle age (1954: 70). For that matter, if relational system strength does decline among the elderly and the decline increases the suicide rate, what of persistent reports (e.g., Gibbs, 1982a) of a decline in the rate of U.S. white females past about age 50? The second consideration pertains to Henry and Short's appeal to the married's lower suicide rate (1954: 73-75) to bolster their claim that the rate varies inversely with relational system strength. The married do have a lower rate when age composition is controlled; but if suicide and status are positively associated, as Henry and Short assert (1954: 17), then the lower rate for the married implies that they have lower status!

So even granting Henry and Short's assumptions about the U.S. status hierarchy, there are doubts about their theorem (suicide and status are positively associated). Those doubts grow on recognition that Henry and Short (1974: 71) relied heavily on Dublin and Bunzel for evidence that "suicide predominates primarily at the top of the socioeconomic scale," but numerous researchers (e.g., Maris, 1969: 117-134) have reported contrary findings.

Henry and Short never explicitly assert an inverse relation between homicide and suicide (Theorem 3), let alone present systematic evidence. Perhaps they refrained in recognition of numerous exceptions (especially, Lester, 1987), one being the gender difference, with females having both the lowest suicide rate and the lowest homicide rate (whether as victims or as slayers).

Henry and Short report four series of tests (U.S. data, circa 1900-1950) that bear on their generalization about differential correlations over time between measures of economic prosperity and suicide rates. All four are interpreted as consistent with the proposition. Specifically, the negative correlation is greater for males, whites, ages 15 to 64, and high-income territorial divisions of Chicago.

The findings are important if only because a *special* theory about temporal variation in the suicide rate could be a strategic step toward a general theory.[20] Nonetheless, recall that the tests stand or fall on the identification of American status differentials. One finding illustrates the issue. The correlation between suicide rates and business fluctuations is more negative for nonwhite females than for nonwhite males, but Henry and Short (1954: 35) argue that the differential is not really a negative finding because black females have higher status than do black males. So their judgments of status differentials appear altered by test findings.

The predictive accuracy of the status integration theory

The initial assessment of predictive accuracy (Gibbs and Martin, 1964: 197-200) focused primarily on the 175 coefficients of correlation between status integration measures and suicide rates. Of that number, 160 (91.4 percent) have the predicted negative sign, and the magnitude of 115 (71.9 percent) of the 160 coefficients exceed .49. A second overall assessment has not been made, but general observations suggest similar outcomes in subsequent tests. However, some *series* of tests have been much more impressive than the summaries indicate. For example, in a series of 60 within-column tests (1960 and 1980 data) pertaining to the integration of marital status with age for U.S. white males and white females (Stafford, et al., 1990: 23), *all* 60 coefficients—one for each of 15 age groups, males and females separately at two time points—are negative as predicted; and 49 (82 percent) of the coefficients exceed .50.

Returning to tests in general, the outcomes become more impressive on recognition that in virtually all tests the integration measures were limited to one family of achieved statuses, predominantly either occupational or marital. Nonetheless, there is not an overwhelming difference between the theory's predictive accuracy and that of the Henry-Short theory.

Scope

Scope refers to the number of dependent variables in the theory and their inclusiveness. So scope is especially relevant in connection with the idea of explanatory power, but its importance depends appreciably on testability. If a theory has enormous scope but is untestable, its scope is less relevant; hence, a distinction between "ostensible scope" and "test scope" should be recognized.

The scope of Durkheim's theory

It is minimal because there is only one dependent variable or *explicandum*—variation in the suicide rate. Should it be argued that there are four dependent variables—a rate for each type of suicide—Durkheim never made reference to such rates; and there is every reason to doubt the empirical applicability of the types when classifying individual cases.

The foregoing assessment pertains to the ostensible scope of Durkheim's theory; but it extends also to test scope, presuming that any of the purported tests are defensible. Such is the case because a theory's test scope cannot exceed its ostensible scope, though the former may be substantially less than the latter.

The scope of the Henry-Short theory

Although the theory's discursive and bifurcated formulation (synchronic vs. diachronic) makes judgments difficult and controversial, its scope appears greater than that of Durkheim's theory. Taking "status" as the independent variable, there are four dependent variables: strength of the relational system, strength of external restraints, suicide rate, and homicide rate.

Because measures of the two "strength" variables did not enter into reported tests of the theory, its ostensible scope exceeds its test scope, four versus two dependent variables. Nonetheless, the test scope of the Henry-Short theory exceeds that of Durkheim's theory, even accepting purported tests of the latter.

The scope of the status integration theory

Taking "occupancy of incompatible statuses" as the primary determinant in the theory, there are five dependent variables: suicide rate, stability and durability of social relationships, conformity to socially sanctioned demands and expectations, amount of role conflict, and degree of status integration. Described otherwise, each of those five variables is a direct or indirect consequence of occupancy of incompatible statuses.

The foregoing pertains exclusively to *ostensible* scope, in light of which the status integration theory exceeds the Henry-Short theory. However, in testing the integration theory predictions are made only about suicide rates; so the theory's *test* scope is less than that of the Henry-Short theory. Because the comparisons are incongruent, there is no clear-cut difference between the theories.

Range

A generalization may be ambiguous unless it includes a unit term (or phrase), meaning a term that denotes a class of things or events, as opposed to properties or characteristics of such things or events. Sociology has an astonishing variety of units—individuals, countries, organizations, age groups, cities, and marital statuses, to mention a few. It is unlikely that any sociological generalization holds for all types of units, let alone equally well; nevertheless, a theory's range is a matter of the number of unit types to which it applies.

There are two ways to avoid minimum scope. First, if a generalization applies to more than type of unit, then there are at least two versions of it in the theory, with the only difference being the unit term or phrase (e.g., "countries" in one version of the generalization but "cities" in another version). Second, each premise and conclusion has the same unit term or phrase, one that *generically* denotes two or more specific types. "Populations" and "territorial units" are instances.

Like scope, range is an important dimension of predictive power because it bears on the idea of explanatory power. Moreover, the distinction between "ostensible" and "test" applies to both range and scope in exactly the same way.

The range of Durkheim's theory

Despite Durkheim's virtually obsessive references to "society," the theory's range is enormous because integration and regulation are properties of virtually any social unit. Even so, range is less than maximum; it is difficult to see how the theory applies to individuals.

Because of doubts about purported tests of Durkheim's theory, its indisputable major merit is its *ostensible* range; and the theory illustrates why all other dimensions of predictive power are secondary to testability and predictive accuracy. Enormous ostensible scope or range is far less a merit if the theory is untestable or if tests have indicated negligible predictive accuracy. However, sterile arguments about the relative importance of the various dimensions of predictive power can be avoided, because the ultimate goal is always a theory that exceeds each contender as regards *all* dimensions.

The range of the Henry-Short theory

Because Henry and Short did not use any particular unit term consistently, their theory's range is not readily ascertainable (a common problem in assessing discursive theories). However, judging from the social units compared in tests—age groups, race, sex, and divisions of the military population—the theory's range appears impressive; but that basis for judgment cannot reveal any gap between ostensible range and test range.

Like Durkheim's theory, even the ostensible range of the Henry-Short theory is less than maximum because it does not extend to individuals; but Durkheim's theory has a greater ostensible range. It is difficult to think of countries, provinces, states, or cities as ordered in some status hierarchy; therefore, the ostensible range of the Henry-Short theory does not extend to various types of territorial units.

The range of the status integration theory

The theory's unit term is "populations," an indication of enormous ostensible range (though it might be desirable to substitute the term "social units" for "populations"). Moreover, the theory's ostensible range and its test range differ little, because numerous types of populations (countries, states, metropolitan areas, cities, age, sex, race, occupations, marital statuses, and parental statuses) have been compared in tests.

Although the status integration theory's ostensible and/or test range exceeds that of contenders, like the contenders it does not extend to individuals. Opponents of reductionism might not view that range limit as a shortcoming, but it is sheer obstinacy to deny the superiority *(ceteris paribus)* of a theory that implies predictions about differences among both social units and individuals.

Parsimony

Suppose that a theory comprises five premises and ten conclusions, while another theory comprises three premises and also three conclusions. Only an obstinate critic would deny that the theory having the conclusions/premises ratio of 3:1 is more parsimonious than is the theory having a ratio of 1:1, and scarcely less obstinate to deny that parsimony is a dimension of predictive power.

Although both are dimensions of predictive power, parsimony is far removed from predictive accuracy; and the contrast illustrates why predictive power should not be equated with predictive accuracy. However, when testability is ignored, the conclusions/premises ratio is only *ostensible* parsimony; and test parsimony excludes untested conclusions.

The parsimony of Durkheim's theory

Until someone restates the theory such that conclusions can be deduced rigorously from the premises, its parsimony cannot be reckoned. That point will be rejected by those who prefer some other criterion of parsimony and are indifferent to the need for agreement in judgments.

A formal restatement of the theory is not needed merely to assess its parsimony. Whatever the dimension of predictive power, appreciable agreement in independent assessments of contending theories is unlikely unless those theories were stated in accordance with some formal mode.

The parsimony of the Henry-Short theory

If the previous formal version is accepted, then the theory's ostensible parsimony is 1.50 (four premises and six conclusions, including Theorems 1, 2, and 3). By contrast, test parsimony is only 0.50 (the same four premises but only Theorems 1 and 2 as conclusions); however, it would be 0.75 if Theorem 3 were treated as a tested conclusion.

The low value for test parsimony suggests a critical need in the development of the theory. One construct, strength of the relational system, is linked with only one concept (status); and its linkage with just one more would increase test parsimony considerably.

The parsimony of the status integration theory

The theory's ostensible parsimony is 1.80 (five premises and nine conclusions, including the previously stated theorem), which is substantially greater than that for the Henry-Short theory. On the other hand, the theory's test parsimony is only 0.20, far less than that for the Henry-Short theory. Given the incongruent comparisons, neither theory is clearly more parsimonious than the other.

The low test parsimony points to a particular need in further development of the theory. Only two of the five constructs are linked with a concept, and just one more link could increase test parsimony from 0.20 to 0.50, thereby equaling the test parsimony of the Henry-Short theory.

Intensity

The notion of causation makes the distinction between a diachronic relation and a synchronic relation crucial, for the common conception has it that causes *precede* their effects. Hence, unless a theory indicates how "lagging" the variables influences their association, the theory has no clear bearing on causation. Yet a "lagged" association is a type of space-time relation, and a theory's intensity is simply the number of types dealt with by the theory. So a theory that asserts only cross-sectional, synchronic relations has minimal intensity.

Because the variety of space-time relations (Gibbs, 1982) exceeds conventional distinctions (e.g., diachronic vs. synchronic, cross-sectional vs. longitudinal), it may appear that no theory can approach maximum intensity. However, if a generalization asserts or implies that a particular type of space-time relation between two constituent variables will be greater (closer) than is any other type *for the same variables,* the generalization actually deals with *all* types of relations. Of course, even if a theory deals with all types one way or another, tests may have been limited to one type (commonly cross-sectional, synchronic). That possibility has to do with the distinction between ostensible intensity and test intensity.

Each contending theory's intensity is so negligible that a detailed examination would serve no purpose. It need only be said that the constituent generalizations about relations between variables evidently apply to both synchronic (cross-sectional) and diachronic (longitudinal) relations. Nevertheless, none of the three theories stipulate the appropriate time lags, nor does any include assertions about different types of space-time relations (i.e., which is closer). It is not just a matter of appreciable ostensible intensity but minimal test intensity; both are minimal.

Despite their similarities, the theories differ sharply as regards prospects for increasing intensity. If generalizations about appropriate time lags or contrasts in different types of space-time relations cannot be deduced from the theories, they can be arrived at (if at all) only through exploratory research. Because the requisite research cannot be undertaken unless the independent variables are mensurable, there is no prospect for increasing the intensity of Durkheim's theory; and without a measure of status, the same is true of the Henry-Short theory. So only the status integration theory is amenable to the requisite kind of exploratory research.

Discriminatory Power

If a theory comprises two or more testable conclusions, it may extend to a generalization about differences between the *magnitudes* of the associations (i.e., one conclusion vs. others). Such generalizations could be based on this principle: the greater the number of intervening variables, the less the association between the two variables in question. In any case, *discriminatory power* is another dimension of predictive power.

The three theories have no discriminatory power. None of them comprise assertions about differential magnitudes of association. Yet the potential is greater for the Henry-Short theory, especially as regards *test* discriminatory power. Such is the case because only that theory comprises at least two testable generalizations (assuming that "status" is an empirically applicable term).

A Brief Overview

Comparisons of the status integration theory and the Henry-Short theory do not permit the conclusion that one substantially exceeds the other as regards predictive power. Therefore, each theory should receive equal attention, at least until advocates of the Henry-Short theory stipulate a measure of status.

By contrast, Durkheim's theory has far less predictive power than does either contender. That conclusion will stand until someone develops a defensible measure of social regulation and social integration or restates the theory formally such that those two terms are linked to concepts other than the suicide rate.

ANOMALIES: ANOTHER BASIS FOR ASSESSING THEORIES

Some suicide rates are anomalies in being extreme exceptions to putative uniformities or patterns. Explanations of those anomalies are secondary to the need for systematic tests of contending theories, but there is merit to this question: to what extent does each contender *predict* what was heretofore an anomaly?

The Myth of the Married's Lowest Rate

One putative uniformity is simple: The married have the lowest suicide rate. But the generalization is false, and there are exceptions even when age composition is controlled. For over a century there have been numerous social units and years in which among ages 15 to 19 (or approximations) single men had the lowest suicide rate.

Durkheim's theory

Durkheim was aware of the anomaly, even elevating it to a "law" (p. 178): "Too early marriages have an aggravating influence on suicide, especially as regards men." Even so, his explanation is merely the attribution of the high rate to fatalism (p. 276).

The point warrants emphasis because Durkheim's defenders *misinterpret* his recognition (pp. 171-202) that the ratio of the married's suicide rate to rates of other marital statuses (Durkheim's famous coefficient of preservation) varies enormously. Far from explaining the variation, Durkheim's related observations border on logomachy. While the *general* challenge is to explain variation in preservation coefficients, there is another marital anomaly that Durkheim failed to explain: instances among elderly females where the widowed's suicide rate is slightly less than the married's.[21] Actually, it is not just a matter of an isolated failure. Durkheim's explanation of variation in the suicide rate among marital statuses is so convoluted and objectionable, particularly in connection with age, sex, and anomie, that only Pope's extensive criticism (1976: 77-92 and 124-141) is complete.

The Henry-Short theory

Until someone perfects a measure of status that applies to marital distinctions, there is no basis for assessing the Henry-Short theory in light of the two anomalies. Surely there is a greater prospect for that measure than for a measure of external restraint or strength of the relational system.

Even if a defensible measure of status should be developed, the Henry-Short theory anticipates two *unlikely* possibilities. First, for age group 15 to 19, status is greater for the married than for the single, especially in the case of males. Second, among very elderly women status is greater for the widowed than for the married.

The status integration theory

The suicide rate of the married exceeds the *single* only among the young, precisely where the integration measure is greater for the single (i.e., the proportion single is greater than the proportion married). Moreover, the gender difference for ages 15 to 19 in the association between marital status and suicide rates poses no puzzle; the contrast between the two proportions (single vs. married) is greater for males.

The decline among the elderly in the married's coefficient of preservation relative to the widowed is consistent with the theory, because past ages 40 to 54 (depending on the social unit and years) the proportion married decreases with age and the proportion widowed increases. As for the gender difference, the increase in the proportion widowed commences earlier for women; and in official statistics only among very elderly women does the proportion come to exceed the proportion married.

Finally, something should be said about status integration and Durkheim's preservation-aggravation coefficients. Although never acknowledged by critics, two series of tests have shown (Gibbs and Martin, 1964: 98-118) that among U.S. age groups there is a *positive* correlation between these two ratios: (1) the status integration measure for the married to the measure for each other marital status (single, widowed, divorced) and (2) the suicide rate of each of the others to the married rate. Separate tests at two time points were conducted for males, females, and both sexes combined; without exception, each correlation is positive.

Age and Suicide

Although suicide rates do vary with age, there is no single pattern. Three illustrations (from Gibbs, 1971: 291; and Tatai, 1983: 26) must suffice: (1) among U.S. white males the suicide rate increases with age up to 85 and over; (2) among U.S. white females the suicide rate increases up to about age 50, then declines regularly; and (3) for both sexes in Japan the rate increases up to about age 25, then declines and remains relatively low until about age 45, when it commences to increase.

Because few official reports on suicide show numbers for regular age groups (e.g., 10-14, 15-19) *beyond age 84,* the male rate appears to increase throughout *all* ages. Yet official U.S. vital statistics publications report suicide by age up to 100 and over, and for several decades the white male rate has declined sharply *past age 89.* Consider the following average annual 1978-82 suicide rates per 100,000 population (data sources: Bureau of the Census 1983: Tables 41 and 43, and National Center for Health Statistics, 1982, 1984, 1985, 1986a, 1986b: Table 7-5 or 8-5) for eight age groups of U.S. white males: ages 65-69, 30.6; ages 70-74, 36.9; ages 75-79, 45.9; ages 80-84, 50.8; ages 85-89, 57.2; ages 90-94, 50.5; ages 95-99, 37.1; and ages over 99, 13.7.

Should it be argued that white males over age 89 are too feeble to commit suicide, there is no supporting evidence; and the argument is an *ad hoc* explanation of variation in the suicide rate, meaning without regard to variation in general. The point is that the dramatic decline poses a real challenge for contending theories, and the same is true of the extremely low rate for ages less than 15.

Durkheim's theory

As for variation in the suicide rate by age, Durkheim's theory is worse than "no explanation" (see Pope, 1976: 143, 147-148). He mistakenly argued (p. 101) that there is something close to a universal pattern—an ever-increasing rate with increasing age.

It is puzzling that Durkheim did not explain what he took to be the predominant age pattern in terms of integration or regulation. In any case, this particular defect in his theory is commonly ignored by commentators (e.g., Maris, 1969).

The Henry-Short theory

A confident assessment of the theory's relevance will require a measure of status that applies to age differentials. However, Henry and Short (1954: 16) stated in connection with U.S. data that "the decline in status in the later years is accompanied by an increase rather than the predicted decrease in suicide." Perhaps their assumption about the U.S. age-status relation was incorrect; but the simple reverse assumption—status increases with age—simply will not do, because there are at least two distinct patterns in the U.S. age-suicide relation.

It is difficult to see how findings concerning the age-suicide relation could support the Henry-Short assertion of a positive association between status and suicide. Thus, in the case of U.S. white males it would have to be assumed that status increases from an extremely low level for children to an extremely high level at about age 90, at which point an enormous decline commences.

The status integration theory

The theory is particularly relevant if only because most tests have had something to do with variation among age groups. Those tests have revealed a substantial *negative* association between integration measures and suicide rates. Yet such correlations are largely peculiar to occupational integration (Stafford and Gibbs, 1988), which suggests (1) contrary to the theory, not all statuses are relevant, let alone equally relevant; *or* (2) the appropriate measure of several dimensions of status integration *simultaneously* has yet to be formulated.

If general observations are credible, the theory's most singular merit is its relevance in explaining the relatively low suicide rate of the very old and of children. Published census data are not available for measures of the various integration dimensions for ages 0-4, 5-9, 10-14, 85-89, 90-94, 95-99, and over 99; but casual observations indicate that marital integration and labor force integration approach the maximum in those age groups. However, even for white males over 99, marital integration is probably substantially less than maximum; but that exception explains why their suicide rate is typically greater than that for ages less than 15.

The Gender Contrast and the Complexity of the Notion of an Anomaly

Only recently have anthropologists (especially Counts, 1990) commenced reporting observations consistent with this generalization: the traditionally greater male suicide rate does not hold among some non-Western social units, tribes or bands in particular. However, it could be argued that those social units are not anomalies; rather, they are only special cases of enormous variation in the ratio of the male rate to the female rate, in one study (Gibbs, 1971: 289) from 1.1 for Luxembourg to 23.0 for Nicaragua. Given such variation, instances of a greater female rate are hardly surprising.

Durkheim's theory

Durkheim's statements about the greater rate for European males are scarcely comprehensible. Consider one of many instances (p. 341): "Woman kills herself less...not because of physiological differences from man but because she does not participate in collective life in the same way."

The statement does not even suggest recognition of the enormous variation in the gender difference; and one must wonder why Durkheim did not employ his usual explanatory notions, such as greater but not excessive regulation of women. In any case, Durkheim offered no coherent explanation of the gender difference (for a more elaborate commentary, see Pope, 1976: 49-52, 142-143, 150-152), and at various places in *Suicide* (pp. 166, 215-216, 272, 299, 385-386) he resorted to biological notions.

The Henry-Short theory

Even accepting the assumption that in the U.S. men have more status, the Henry-Short theory cannot explain variation in the male/female suicide ratio without a measure of status that applies to men and women in various countries. For each country the question is not which sex has the greater status but the amount of the differential.

Even if the status of women varies, it does not appear to exceed that of men in tribes or bands where women evidently have a much higher suicide rate (Counts, 1990). In those social units women are clearly dominated by men and commonly resort to "revenge suicide" *(ibid.)*.

The status integration theory

The gender contrast poses no obvious problem for the theory. It is possible to compute measures of several dimensions of status integration for men and women in various countries. The *expected* finding is that status integration measures are greater for women, and in all tests to date that expectation has been confirmed for occupational integration (especially Gibbs and Martin, 1964; Stafford and Gibbs, 1985, 1988).

The problem is not so much that the gender difference is *far less* consistent with the theory in the case of marital and labor force integration, because the occupational integration contrast is *proportionately* so great as to possibly outweigh other dimensions. More serious, the ratio of the male to the female suicide rate has been taken as the dependent variable in only one line of status integration research, and even in that case (Gibbs and Martin, 1964: 175-186) the proportion of women in the labor force was treated as *indicative* of "less status integration." The finding—a substantial negative correlation among countries between the ratio of the male to the female suicide rate and the proportion of women in the labor force—does suggest support for the theory.[22] Nonetheless, there is an acute need for comparisons of variation in the sex ratio of the suicide rates with variation in the gender difference as regards various dimensions of status integration. Finally, additional special tests of the theory (Gibbs and Martin, 1964: 175-181) should focus on those social units where women have the higher suicide rate.

TWO RETROGRESSIONS

Since Durkheim, most sociological research on suicide has extended his focus on rates. That continuity is now jeopardized, with no prospect of a viable alternative.

Durkheim and Douglas

Durkheim's extreme "sociologism" made his theory controversial from the outset. However, Jack Douglas' critique (1967) of Durkheim's work did more than contribute to the controversy; it challenged an entire tradition.

The reliability of official suicide rates

Because Durkheim's theory is based largely on official suicide statistics, it would be difficult to exaggerate the potentially damaging consequences of Douglas' assertion that these statistics are grossly unreliable. Yet his concern with the subject was entirely proper. Douglas recognized (1967: 163-231) predecessors, and the subject's importance transcends Durkheim. Indeed, the fate of sociological research on suicide largely hinges on the issue. Practical considerations alone virtually dictate exclusive use of official statistics, as they have throughout this chapter.

The objection is to Douglas' method and the sweep of his conclusion. Rather than inspect death records (official or unofficial) in particular social units and compare the ensuing *unofficial* suicide rates with the official rates,[23] Douglas focused primarily on references to two lines of research. The first line (1967: 193) comprises four comparisons of the official number of suicides for a particular social unit (e.g., Saxony) before and after a change in the compilation procedure, and in each instance there was an enormous increase in the annual number. Then Douglas refers (1967: 203-204) to two comparisons of suicide statistics reported for the same social unit by different agencies (e.g., the justice department vs. the interior ministry); but the one case where the difference is described by Douglas (he speaks of one rate as "10 percent to 16 percent higher") is not unusual for social science data.

Douglas dodged this question: how can so few instances justify a conclusion about the reliability of official suicide rates *in general*? The paucity of evidence is not the most important consideration.[24] Instead, it is difficult to imagine evidence that would justify Douglas' sweeping conclusion; and it has been undermined by Pescosolido and Mendelsohn's research (1986) and Kleck's survey of findings (1988), which indicate that, at least in recent years, official U.S. suicide rates have been reliable to the point that their use to test theories would not seriously bias the outcome. Yet those findings scarcely demonstrate that even most official suicide rates are sufficiently reliable; indeed, reliability may vary enormously (in addition to Douglas, 1967; Gibbs, 1971; Pescosolido and Mendelsohn, 1986; and Kleck, 1988, see Clarke-Finnegan and Fahy, 1983; Day, 1987; and Kolmos and Bach, 1987). The problem simply haunts suicide research.

The road to obscurantism

Although Douglas condemns official suicide statistics, he never suggests a procedure for computing unofficial rates; and his solipsism creates doubts about the very idea of computing a rate or even speaking of suicides as real. "Suicides are not something of a set nature waiting to be correctly or incorrectly categorized by officials. The very nature of the 'thing' is itself problematic so that 'suicides' cannot correctly be said to exist (i.e., to be 'things') until a categorization has been made. Moreover, since there exists great disagreement between interested parties in the categorizations of real-world cases, 'suicides' can generally be said to exist and not to exist at the same time, though this might seem a rather incongruous way of putting it" (Douglas, 1967: 196).

Suicides cannot be identified without *inferences,* but the crucial consideration is the amount of agreement among independent investigators in classifying deaths as to cause. Far from offering a methodology to further agreement, Douglas appears indifferent to the subject; and he does not recognize that the foremost issue is *proportionate* reliability (amount of variation among populations in the ratio of actual suicides to the official number) rather than *absolute* reliability.

Douglas' antipositivism is blatant, and he evidently rejects the quest for an explanation of variation in rates. However, insofar as he proposes an alternative, it is no more intelligible than prescribing a concern with the "social meanings" of suicide.[25] Far from posing a potentially answerable question, Douglas does not even indicate how incompatible conclusions about social meanings are to be resolved.

Signs of a Shift in the Focus of
Sociological Studies of Suicide

In the past two decades there have been signs of a shift in the sociological study of suicide away from a concern with rates to individual cases or, ambiguously, "suicide." Even though the major names in the break from Durkheim (Maris, 1981: 307 cites Douglas, Garfinkel, and Goffman) are commonly identified as "interpretive sociologists," it may be a mistake to attribute the change to antipositivism. Thus, the change is clearly manifested in Maris' work (especially 1981). He appears to have grown weary of theories about the suicide rate, but he does not champion the causes of avowed antipositivists (e.g., rejection of quantitative methods, indifference if not hostility to the idea of objectivity, commitment to the "value-laden" view of science).

The immediate interpretation problem is that Maris and his coworkers have not made their rejection of the rate question explicit, let alone the reasons for it. Perhaps it is a reaction against the indifference of sociologists (in keeping with Durkheim) to questions about individual suicides.

Whatever the reason for the shift in focus, the danger is loss of the "rates question" without a coherent alternative (see the "antiquantitative" studies of suicide cited by Maris, 1981: 23). That danger is manifested in Maris' report (1981) of extensive quantitative research on individual cases of suicides, attempted suicides, and "natural" deaths. At some points Maris writes as though he is concerned with suicidal careers, but at others he appears concerned with suicidal behavior. Why not say simply that the goal is a theory that explains why some individuals commit suicide? Granted that the explanation may be furthered by research on attempted or partial suicides, a theory about suicidal behavior in general is best pursued through "special" theories, including at least one about completed suicides.[26] No less serious, although Maris (1981: 287) speaks of moving toward a theory of suicidal careers, that goal is obscure. Consider his summary (1981: 296-318) in the form of 122 conclusions or propositions and a series of axioms. The conclusions are a melange of generalizations, ranging from the cryptic (e.g., "Human life can be divided into different stages, each with its own development tasks.") to barefoot empiricism (e.g., "Birth order is not a factor in either attempted or completed suicide.").[27] As for the axioms (1981: 311-318), they are not directly testable (e.g., "Suicide is inversely related to satisfaction with the human condition."), nor do they imply testable conclusions. Subsequently, Maris (1981: 318-320) suggests that adding "provisional assumptions" permits derivation of his conclusions or propositions, but only to admit (1981: 320) that "the derivation cannot be precise."

So the danger is not just that a theory about suicidal behavior will be untestable. Additionally, whatever a testable theory's subject, sociologists will not assess it by reference to its predictive power.[28] Stating the argument

differently, changing the question for theories will not resolve the epistemological issue.

RESEARCH ON DURKHEIM'S THEORY

Since 1950 there have been four major lines of sociological research on suicide:
first, research bearing on Durkheim's theory; *second,* research bearing on a
contending but Durkheim-inspired theory; *third,* research bearing on the
suggestion-imitation theory;[29] *fourth,* largely descriptive research. Brief observations have been made previously on the second and third lines, and the
fourth does not warrant attention. The research has been atheoretical, largely
descriptions of temporal and geographic (longitude-latitude) variation in the
suicide rate. However, a theory about repetitive temporal variation (seasonal,
monthly, daily, hourly) is a possibility, and the most promising step
(Gabennesch, 1988) is alien to Durkheim's perspective because psychological
considerations are emphasized. Very briefly, suicide reaches its peak when
expected changes for the better are most likely to be perceived as unrealistic,
such as hopes for a "new week" being dashed by Monday's events.

The Two Principal Subtypes of Durkheimian Research

Durkheim's theory is commonly depicted as bearing on societal variation, a
depiction that underestimates two dimensions of the theory's predictive
power-intensity and range. The theory is not limited to territorial variation,
and there is no reason why it cannot explain differences among localities or
intranational political divisions (e.g., cities, provinces).

The theory's intensity is more difficult to describe, largely because the
varieties of temporal variation are far greater than "longitudinal" and "diachronic" suggest. There are at least three forms: *first,* repetitive, such as hourly
suicide trends in Chicago; *second,* historical, such as annual suicide rates of the
U.S. between 1919 and 1940; *third,* episodic or event-related, such as Great
Britain during World War II.

Episodic research bearing on Durkheim's theory

There is no reason why the theory cannot explain at least some forms of
temporal variation, because it is plausible to assume that both integration and
regulation vary over time. However, Durkheim supported his theory primarily
in connection with episodes—major political changes (wars, revolutions,
rebellions) and economic crises.

Research findings are predominantly consistent with one of Durkheim's
generalizations: when a country enters into a war, especially a popular war, its
suicide rate declines. Durkheim attributed the decline to an increase in social
integration; but he did not use an integration measure, nor have subsequent

researchers. However, some of them have doubted Durkheim's interpretation, suspecting that the suicide decline is due to (1) a drop in unemployment rates during wars and (2) a positive association between unemployment rates and suicide rates.[30] Hence, researchers have reported evidence that when changes in the unemployment rate are taken into account, war has no special effects on the suicide rate (see, e.g., Wasserman, 1989, and Marshall, 1981).

Should it be argued that the evidence supports Durkheim's contention that economic crises are manifestations of anomie (insufficient regulation), the argument is contrary to Durkheim's emphasis on the postulated war-integration relation. For that matter, Durkheim's arguments about economic variables and suicide are confusing. Although economic crises are associated with increases in the suicide rate, Durkheim implicitly denies that crisis hardships (e.g., loss of jobs, drastic reduction in standard of living) actually cause suicides. Rather, he suggests that both the crisis and the suicide increase are manifestations of anomie. That suggestion is consistent with his claims (1) that poverty somehow *prevents* suicide and (2) that either sharp increases or sharp decreases in prosperity are conducive to suicide (i.e., it is not the direction of economic change—greater or less prosperity—that is important but the change itself, because change indicates a lack of regulation).

Durkheim presented some evidence to support both claims, but in recent decades numerous researchers have reported a *negative* association among occupational categories between socioeconomic status and the suicide rate (e.g., Lampert's research [1984] on Sacramento County, California), just the reverse of what Durkheim claimed. Moreover, findings indicate that sharp increases in prosperity are not significantly associated with increases in the suicide rate (e.g., Henry and Short, 1954: 42).

The most common evidence that the *direction* of economic change does make a difference (Durkheim notwithstanding) takes the form of a substantial positive association between the unemployment rate and the suicide rate over time (see, especially, Marshall and Hodge, 1981; Platt, 1984; and Diekstra, 1990). Such association holds so consistently that it poses a major challenge for any theory about the suicide rate; and all the more given the enormous body of evidence that a congruent relation holds at the individual level (see citations in Platt, 1984, and Diekstra, 1990), meaning that a disproportionate number of unemployed commit suicide and a disproportionate number of suicide victims were unemployed.

Of the contenders, the status integration theory is the most relevant, because the status "unemployed" always has a low degree of integration (i.e., in the family of labor force statuses, the unemployed are always an extreme minority).[31] The Henry-Short theory is also relevant, but there is an inconsistency. Henry and Short suggest that unemployment rates are positively correlated over time with suicide rates because unemployment reduces the unemployed's status (more so for high status population divisions), but one premise in the theory's "synchronic" part is that status varies *directly* with suicide.

No theory answers all questions about the unemployment-suicide association (see, especially, Platt, 1984). For one, why does it hold much more consistently over time than cross-sectionally (e.g., among cities)?[32] For another, does the association reflect unemployment selectivity or more nearly direct causation?

Durkheim did not examine the unemployment-suicide association; and, as indicated previously, his arguments about suicide and economic conditions are confusing. Less obvious, Durkheim's antireductionism makes his theory irrelevant in contemplating the unemployment-suicide association at the individual level, especially the possibility that mental illness is a selectivity mechanism (see Platt, 1984, and Diekstra, 1990). While the relevance of mental illness in explaining variation in the suicide rate remains debatable, Durkheim created a misleading impression—that at the individual level the association is negligible (for several references to contrary research findings, see Platt, 1984: 108, and Diekstra, 1990).

The near obsession with religion and suicide

For some 30 years sociological research on Durkheim's theory has increasingly focused on the relation between suicide rates and religious variables. That focus stems primarily from Durkheim's assertion that Catholics have a lower suicide rate than Protestants and his attribution of the difference to greater Catholic integration. However, there is now evidence indicating that in numerous populations the rate difference does not hold and/or that there is no significant negative correlation between the percent Catholic and suicide rates (see references in Faupel, 1987: 523). Doubts about Durkheim's arguments grow when rates are computed separately for various Protestant denominations in the same unit (e.g., a country), and Day (1987) has seriously challenged the reliability of the *kind* of suicide data Durkheim used to demonstrate the Catholic-Protestant suicide differential.

Those sociologists who conducted the research in question commendably broke with tradition—praise of Durkheim's theory without even purported tests (for some key references, see Pope, 1976: 2-5)—but they appear insensitive to two questions. First, given that Durkheim merely assumed that Catholics are more integrated than Protestants, why create the impression that his theory stands or falls on the difference between the two suicide rates? Second, even if Durkheim had employed a defensible measure and demonstrated that in nineteenth-century Europe Catholics were more integrated, why assume that the difference holds in all places and times? Pope and Danigelis (1981) have rightly pointed to instances where sociologists have identified the alleged Catholic-Protestant suicide differential as a law, but contrary evidence is not the only consideration. Crude extrapolation is the only basis for identifying Durkheim's statements on the subject as constituting a law.

Doubts about the Catholic-Protestant differential eventually shifted attention to other religious variables, such as church membership rates for U.S. metropolitan areas or states and the volume of religious publications for countries (e.g., Stack, 1983, and Breault, 1986). There are some significant negative associations between those variables and suicide rates, but also several insignificant associations, particularly when other variables (e.g., population mobility, level of economic development) are controlled (e.g., Bainbridge, 1989, and Stack, et al., 1983).

The Great Illusion

Studies of the religion-suicide association illustrate the illusion that defensible tests of Durkheim's theory are possible without a radical restatement of it. Consider reported statistical associations between religious variables and suicide rates. Even if all the associations had been significant, at no point in *Suicide* does Durkheim assert that the variable in question (e.g., church membership rates) is positively correlated with or is a measure of, to use his terminology (1951: 208), the "degree of integration of religious society." To the contrary, Durkheim's nebulous treatment of social integration is well illustrated by his application of that notion to religion.

Despite the foregoing, the search for indicators of religious integration has become a cottage industry, and there are various objections to it.[33] For one, if only because the research is guided more by the availability of published data than by an explicit theoretical rationale, inconsistent findings are inevitable.

Rather than abandon the strategy, sociologists will increasingly attempt to justify particular indicators by arguing that the desired results do obtain in one condition or another. Thus, Simpson and Conklin (1989) report a negative association among countries between the percentage Islamic and the suicide rate, as though it supports Durkheim's theory.[34] There is no departure from Durkheim's evidential methodology; rather, the research merely substituted "Islamic" for "Catholic." Then, Faupel and his coworkers (1987) report a negative association between indicators of religious integration and suicide rates for *urban* populations, without recognizing that Durkheim's assertions about religious integration (p. 208) are not so limited. Worse, like other "searchers for indicators," Faupel and his coworkers do not see that their strategy makes the theory unfalsifiable. If one indicator does not support Durkheim, try another; or if an indicator does support Durkheim but only in the initial tests, then limit the tests to some condition; and if all else fails, resort to a radical reinterpretation of Durkheim's ideas about religion and suicide (e.g., Faupel, et al., 1987; Bankston, et al., 1983; and Pescosolido and Georgianna, 1989). The possibilities are infinite!

Above all, those who search for indicators never recognize that the introduction of any particular indicator in a purported test *transforms* the theory. Hence, they provide no rationale for the indicator, nor confront this question: why select an indicator that is relevant (if at all) only for certain kinds of variation in the suicide rate" Thus, no report of research on church membership rates even recognizes *nonterritorial* variation (e.g., by marital status) in the suicide rate.

The general point is that systematic tests of Durkheim's theory are impossible without a transformation of it, but there is no implied demand for a measure of integration or of regulation. To the contrary, any purported measure is likely to prove indefensible.[35] So integration and regulation must be treated as constructs and linked to concepts, which is precisely what researchers do when they identify such variables as "church membership rate" as an indicator. The term is a concept; but to so identify it would be a tacit admission of transforming Durkheim's theory, and the admission creates the need for a theoretical rationale to justify whatever postulate connects the concept and one of Durkheim's constructs.

Far from recognizing the necessity of transforming Durkheim's theory when attempting to test it, Breault and Barkey (1983) condemn any transformation.[36] They state no rationale for the condemnation, but their pronouncement perpetuates the illusion that defensible tests of Durkheim's theory are possible without restating it.

THE BOTTOM LINE

To repeat, without Durkheim there might well have been no sociology of suicide. Nevertheless, sociologists are inclined to squander legacies, and they have allowed avowed antipositivists to act as eager accessories. Sociologists have given serious attention to Douglas' unwarranted claim that all official suicide rates are grossly unreliable, and their credulity is all the more remarkable because the claim reflects a tacit rejection of the very idea of a suicide rate and a conception of sociology totally alien to conventional science.

Paradoxically, however, the Durkheimian legacy is jeopardized more by veneration of him than by his antipositivist critics. In refusing to transform Durkheim's theory or seriously consider alternatives (even those clearly inspired by Durkheim's work), sociologists have tacitly rejected predictive power as the criterion for assessing theories. So if Whitehead's dictum (to forget an ancestor suggests a denial of genius and ingratitude) is too harsh, it can be rephrased: veneration of an ancestor precludes defensible answers to the scientific questions posed by that ancestor.

NOTES

1. A term or its definition is "empirically applicable" to the extent that independent observers agree in applying the term or definition to identify or describe the same particular events or things. When the term or definition refers to a quantitative

phenomenon, empirical applicability is a matter of the absolute congruence (agreement) or proportionate congruence (correlation) between values computed by independent investigators for two or more entities—populations or individuals—and in either case the same for each investigator. Either congruence will be negligible unless the investigators use the same formula, including instructions as to requisite data and their acquisition. Indeed, without such a formula, investigators are likely to report that they cannot apply the term or definition, in which case empirical applicability is at the absolute minimum. However, that minimum may obtain even if a formula is specified, because investigators may regard it as unintelligible or report that its application is not feasible (the data instructions are alien to the conditions of work in the field, including research resources). So the notion of empirical applicability goes beyond "reliability" in that "intelligibility" and "feasibility" are dimensions distinct from congruence.

2. The statement is all the more difficult to understand because it appears far removed from the conventional meaning of altruism—willingness to sacrifice for the well-being of others.

3. Page 254: "Poverty protects against suicide because it is a restraint in itself."

4. Yet in the most systematic critique of Durkheim's types of suicide, Hynes (1975) devotes considerable attention to the fatalistic type. For that matter, commentators on Durkheim typically devote far more attention to the fatalistic type than did Durkheim himself.

5. No one really knows how Durkheim reached his inference; and if it is justified because Protestants had a higher suicide rate, the argument becomes a grotesque circularity.

6. The key argument in the case of Premises 3 and 4 appears to be this (Henry and Short, 1954: 17): "when external restraints are weak, aggression generated by frustration will be directed against the self and when external restraints are strong, aggression generated by frustration will be directed outwardly against another person."

7. Henry and Short never make this generalization explicit, but their two postulates clearly imply it.

8. Actually, the proposition is a rewording of what Henry and Short (1954: 23) identify as a hypothesis: "the suicide rate of high status groups correlates more highly with the business cycle than does the suicide rate of lower status groups which are subordinate in the social system." The hypothesis was reworded to emphasize its diachronic character, and the term "business cycle" was avoided because it erroneously suggests an exclusive concern with cyclical trends.

9. This challenge illustrates a difference between the theory's terminology and Durkheim's terminology. The meaning of social integration is so vague that it has no bearing on any particular kind of behavior.

10. If two statuses, Y^1 and Z^1, are both achieved (e.g., "married" and "banker"), then their compatibility must be inferred from the greater of the two proportions, the proportion of Y^1 occupants who are also Z^1 occupants and the proportion of Z^1 occupants who are also Y^1 occupants. Examples limited to two statuses simplify matters, but the assumption actually pertains to *inclusive* status configurations. Thus, rather than consider a particular age status and a particular occupation, the question should be: Given an all-inclusive ascribed status configuration (e.g., white, female, age 28, American-born, Hispanic), what proportion of occupants are also married, residential parent of two school-age children, labor force participant, employed, nurse, and practicing Methodist (a particular *inclusive* achieved status configuration). The proportion reflects not just the compatibility between the two configurations but also the compatibility of the achieved statuses.

11. The rule is applied by assigning a plus sign (+) to any premise that asserts a direct relation or positive association between the two variables and by assigning a negative sign (-) to other premises. A theorem deduced from a set of premises has a negative sign if and only if there is an *odd number* of premises that have been "signed" negatively.

12. For a more extensive commentary and key references, see Gibbs, 1985: 31.

13. Such an argument is far from clear as to why causal assertions are the remedy, let alone how causal premises are to be translated into assertions of space-time relations (without which the premises are not testable even indirectly).

14. There are modes of formal theory construction (e.g., Gibbs, 1972) in which the theorem would be identified as an implied proposition.

15. The one attempt by Stafford and Gibbs (1985) resulted in very little support for the theory as regards between-column tests, and that research also served to question an assumption not made explicit previously—that all statuses are equally relevant. The assumption was a necessary simplification, and exploratory work is needed to assess the assumption with a view to formulating an alternative. However, as long as the "equal relevance" assumption is maintained, the most promising column measure will require a computational procedure that cannot be explicated by tabular arrangements of achieved statuses. As the first step in illustrating the alternative measure, recognize that $SP^2 = SX^2/(SX)^2$, where SP^2 is computed as shown in Table 1, and X is the number of individuals in each status of a particular family of achieved statuses (e.g., as shown in Table 2, "single"). Now suppose that there are only three families of achieved statuses (X, Y, and Z) and each family comprises only two statuses. So we have X_a and X_b, Y_a and Y_b, and Z_a and Z_b, with each symbol henceforth designating both the status in question and the number of occupants. As such, the *complex* status integration measure (to differentiate it from that employed by Stafford and Gibbs, 1985) *for a column*—each pertaining to a distinctive combination of ascribed statuses— would be the sum of 16 component values. The following formula for computing the *first* component value, that for the integration of the Z statuses with the ascribed statuses *and* the X_a–Y_a status configuration, illustrates the formula for the other 15 (X_a–Y_b would be the next status configuration in the series of four values for the Z statuses):

$$([Z_a2 + Z_b2] / [Z_a + Z_b]^2) (N / SN)$$

where N is the number of individuals in the X_a–Y_a status configuration and SN is the total number of individuals in the column (the ascribed status configuration in question).

16. Recall that Maris' partial theory is excluded from further consideration because it is only a reduced version of the Henry-Short theory.

17. The term "operationalization" or any related term is avoided because it only obfuscates.

18. All comments made in connection with Theorem 1 apply generally to Theorem 2, which asserts a negative association between status and the homicide rate. However, because of space limitation and the focus on Durkheim, a systematic treatment of Henry and Short's generalizations about homicide is precluded.

19. This brief assessment excludes findings pertaining to homicide. The exclusion reflects not only space limitations but also a concern with comparing the Henry-Short theory with Durkheim's theory.

20. For that matter, the Henry-Short findings (especially 1954: 42) are contrary to Durkheim's assertion that suicide rises during speculative phases of business prosperity.

21. The anomaly is not explained by Durkheim's observations (pp. 185-199) on the lower suicide rate of parents (vs. the childless), but that contrast is entirely consistent with the status integration theory. Excluding the single and the young (say, 15-23), for both sexes the greatest proportion are parents, which is to say greater status integration.

22. A positive association between female labor force participation and the suicide rate (female or total) has been reported by several investigators (e.g., Davis, 1981; Stack, 1987; and Lester, 1988). In some comparisons the association is not significantly positive, but the investigators expressed no awareness that once the proportion of women in the labor force exceeds .50 any further increase is indicative of an *increase* in labor force integration. No less important, in measuring labor force integration there is a need (particularly in the case of females) to compute separate (component) measures for each combination of age, marital, and parental status, and then compute a *composite* measure. Also no less important, the investigators did not acknowledge the need to take other integration dimensions (e.g., occupational) into account.

23. Gibbs (1971: 277-278) reports one such investigation in New Zealand, and the outcome contradicts Douglas.

24. Douglas did nothing to augment the evidence.

25. For that reason, Douglas' work is a retrogression; but the same is not true of all departures from Durkheim. The attention to suicide prevention during recent decades (see Lester's survey, 1990b) has been divorced from Durkheim's theory, perhaps because the theory had no applied value ("testability" is a *necessary* condition for applied value). Similarly, despite mixed findings, recent studies of the media impact on suicide (see Stack's survey, 1990) is not a retrogression, even though many of the findings in that research (pioneered by David Phillips) suggest that Durkheim prematurely dismissed suggestion and imitation as etiological factors.

26. Maris' concern with suicidal careers and suicidal behavior is all the more confusing because he appears to recognize that completed suicides and attempted suicides, partial suicides, or parasuicides, evidently have different etiologies, the once popular belief to the contrary notwithstanding.

27. Worse, some of the generalizations appear contradictory. Thus, Maris (1981: 297) asserts a "positive association between age and the suicide rate" but subsequently recognizes that rates of white females and blacks peak before age 50.

28. For that matter, works like Maris' culminate with such a melange of findings and generalizations that systematic assessments are precluded. Moreover, it is puzzling that Maris did not place much greater emphasis on disruptions in social relations as an etiological factor at the individual's level. Such an emphasis would be compatible with Durkheim's theory, the Henry-Short theory, and the status integration theory, because one way or another those theories emphasize the importance of the strength of social relations. No less important, an emphasis on disruptions in social relations would be compatible with various psychological perspectives (including the psychoanalytic) on suicide (especially Leenaars, 1990). Nonetheless, formulating a theory will be difficult because of the need to recognize anticipation of disruptions, distinctions as to kinds of anticipated or actual disruptions (e.g., those that inevitably follow graduation vs. death of a spouse), and perhaps even the timing of disruptions (e.g., loss of a parent at age 7 vs. age 70).

29. Prior to this line of research and even before 1950, research outside the Durkheim tradition focused primarily on the now largely defunct social disorganization theory. The theory's demise should not be lamented. Purported tests of it were idiosyncratic, and its relevance in explaining nonterritorial variation in the suicide

rate (e.g., by age, sex, or marital status) is questionable at best (for a more extensive commentary, see Gibbs and Martin, 1964: 202-206).

30. Should it be claimed that the unemployment-suicide relation confirms Durkheim's arguments about integration, the claim would only perpetuate Durkheim's loose use of the term. For that matter, prolonged increases in unemployment rates are manifestations of an economic crisis, which Durkheim treated in connection with regulation (i.e., anomie), *not* integration. The reported suicide decline just before a Presidential election appears to be more nearly a pure integration effect, but even in that case critics have attributed the decline to unemployment decreases just before the election. For a related debate see *American Sociological Review,* Vol. 49 (October, 1984), pp. 706-709.

31. However, should the proportion unemployed ever come to reach .50, further increases would not be expected to be associated with *increases* in the suicide rate. Indeed, the theory implies a novel generalization: Among social units or for a social unit over time, when other dimensions of status integration are approximately constant, the greater the unemployment rate, the less the suicide rate *of the unemployed.*

32. Research on the association is a step away from Durkheim's concern with economic causes; but there is a connection between unemployment and economic crises, and a focus on unemployment permits a greater range of research.

33. The entire enterprise is degenerating into debates over the appropriate methodology and the choice of indicators (see, e.g., *American Journal of Sociology,* Vol. 93 [May, 1988], pp. 1471-1486, and *Sociological Quarterly,* Vol. 24 [Autumn, 1983], pp. 625-632).

34. Should it be objected that the implied generalization is not limited to any particular condition, imagine what the finding would be if the correlation were computed for, say, Scandinavian countries or American states.

35. For that matter, the most promising step (Bille-Brahe, 1987) toward a measure of social integration exemplifies a concern with *behavioral* variables, something alien to the common preoccupation of sociologists with *structural* notions.

36. Like many other sociologists, Breault does not recognize that without a transformation of Durkheim's theory the selection of "indicators" to test it can be whimsical. Indeed, in a critique of Breault's 1986 article, Girard (1988: 1477) points out that Breault used the percent divorced as a measure of "family integration," but for Durkheim divorce reflected conjugal anomie.

REFERENCES

Bainbridge, W. S. The religious ecology of deviance. *American Sociological Review,* 1989, 54, 288-295.

Bankston, W. B., Allen, H. D., and Cunningham, D. S. Religion and suicide. *Social Forces,* 1983, 62, 521-528.

Bille-Brahe, U. Suicide and social integration. *Acta Psychiatrica Scandinavica,* 1987, 76 (Supplement 336), 45-62.

Breault, K. D. Suicide in America. *American Journal of Sociology,* 1986, 92, 628-656.

Breault, K. D., and Barkey, K. Reply to Stark. *Sociological Quarterly,* 1983, 24, 629-632.

Bureau of the Census. *1980 Census of Population, Volume 1, Part B.* Washington, DC: U.S. Government Printing Office, 1983.

Clarke-Finnegan, M., and Fahy, T. J. Suicide rates in Ireland. *Psychological Medicine,* 1983, 13, 385-391.

Counts, D. A. Abused women and revenge suicide. In D. Lester (ed.), *Current Concepts of Suicide.* Philadelphia: The Charles Press, 1990.

Davis, R. A. Female labor force integration, status integration and suicide, 1950-1969. *Suicide and Life-Threatening Behavior*, 1981, 11, 111-123.

Day, L. H. Durkheim on religion and suicide. *Sociology*, 1987, 21, 449-461.

Diekstra, R. Suicide, depression, and economic conditions. In D. Lester (ed.), *Current Concepts of Suicide*. Philadelphia: The Charles Press, 1990.

Douglas, J. D. *The Social Meaning of Suicide*. Princeton, NJ: Princeton University Press, 1967.

Durkheim, E. *The Rules of Sociological Method*. Chicago: University of Chicago Press, 1938.

Durkheim, E. *Suicide* (Translated by J. A. Spaulding and G. Simpson). New York: Free Press, 1951.

Faupel, C. E., Kowalski, G. S., and Starr, P. D. Sociology's one law. *Journal for the Scientific Study of Religion*, 1987, 26, 523-534.

Gabennesch, H. When promises fail. *Social Forces*, 1988, 67, 129-145.

Gibbs, J. P. Suicide. In R. K. Merton and R. Nisbet (eds.), *Contemporary Social Problems*. New York: Harcourt Brace Jovanovich, 1971.

Gibbs, J. P. *Sociological Theory Construction*. Hinsdale, IL: Dryden Press, 1972.

Gibbs, J. P. Testing the theory of status integration and suicide rates. *American Sociological Review*, 1982a, 47, 227-237.

Gibbs, J. P. Evidence of causation. *Current Perspectives in Social Theory*, 1982b, 3, 93-127.

Gibbs, J. P. The methodology of theory construction in criminology. In R. F. Meier (ed.), *Theoretical Methods in Criminology*. Beverly Hills, CA: Sage, 1985.

Gibbs, J. P., and Martin, W. T. *Status Integration and Suicide*. Eugene: University of Oregon Press, 1964.

Girard, C. Church membership and suicide reconsidered. *American Journal of Sociology*, 1988, 93, 1471-1479.

Halbwachs, M. *Les Causes du Suicide*. Paris: Felix Alcan, 1930.

Henry, A. F., and Short, J. F. *Suicide and Homicide*. New York: Free Press, 1954.

Hynes, E. Suicide and Homo Duplex. *Sociological Quarterly*, 1975, 16, 87-104.

Johnson, B. D. Durkheim's one cause of suicide. *American Sociological Review*, 1965, 30, 875-886.

Kleck, G. Miscounting suicides. *Suicide and Life-Threatening Behavior*, 1988, 18, 219-236.

Kolmos, L., and Bach, E. Sources of error in registering suicides. *Acta Psychiatrica Scandinavica*, 1987, 76 (Supplement 336), 22-43.

Lampert, D. I. Occupational status and suicide. *Suicide and Life-Threatening Behavior*, 1984, 14, 254269.

Leenaars, A. A. Psychological perspectives on suicide. In D. Lester (ed.), *Current Concepts of Suicide*. Philadelphia: The Charles Press, 1990.

Lester, D. Murders and suicide. *Behavioral Sciences and the Law*, 1987, 5, 49-60.

Lester, D. Economic factors and suicide. *Journal of Social Psychology*, 1988, 128, 245-248.

Lester, D. (ed.), *Current Concepts of Suicide*. Philadelphia: The Charles Press, 1990a.

Lester, D. The prevention of suicide. In D. Lester (ed.), *Current Concepts of Suicide*. Philadelphia: The Charles Press, 1990b.

Maris, R. W. *Social Forces in Urban Suicide*. Homewood, IL: Dorsey Press, 1969.

Maris, R. W. *Pathways to Suicide*. Baltimore: Johns Hopkins University Press, 1981.

Marshall, J. R. Political integration and the effect of war on suicide. *Social Forces*, 1981, 50, 771-785.

Marshall, J. R., and Hodge, R. W. Durkheim and Pierce on suicide and economic change. *Social Science Research*, 1981, 10, 101-114.

Martin, W. T. Theories of variation in the suicide rate. In J. P. Gibbs (ed.), *Suicide.* New York: Harper & Row, 1968.

National Center for Health Statistics. *Vital Statistics of the United States, 1978, or 1979, or 1980, or 1981, or 1982, Vol. II, Part B.* Washington, DC: U.S. Government Printing Office. 1982, 1984, 1985, 1986a, 1986b.

O'Carroll, P. W. A consideration of the validity and reliability of suicide mortality data. *Suicide and Life-Threatening Behavior,* 1989, 19, 1-16.

Pescosolido, B. A., and Georgianna, S. Durkheim, suicide, and religion. *American Sociological Review,* 1989, 54, 33-48.

Pescosolido, B. A., and Mendelsohn, R. Social causation or social construction of suicide? *American Sociological Review,* 1986, 51, 80-100.

Platt, S. Unemployment and suicidal behavior. *Social Science Medicine,* 1984, 19, 93-115.

Pope, W. *Durkheim's Suicide.* Chicago: University of Chicago Press, 1976.

Pope, W., and Danigelis, N. Sociology's 'one law.' *Social Forces,* 1981, 60, 495-516.

Simpson, M. E., and Conklin, G. H. Socioeconomic development, suicide, and religion. *Social Forces,* 1989, 67, 945-964.

Stack, S. A comparative analysis of suicide and religiosity. *Journal of Social Psychology,* 1983, 119, 285-286.

Stack, S. The effect of female participation in the labor force on suicide. *Sociological Forum,* 1987, 2, 257-277.

Stack, S. Media impacts on suicide. In D. Lester (ed.), *Current Concepts of Suicide.* Philadelphia: The Charles Press, 1990.

Stafford, M. C., and Gibbs, J. P. A major problem with the theory of status integration and suicide. *Social Forces,* 1985, 63, 643-660.

Stafford, M. C., and Gibbs, J. P. Change in the relation between marital integration and suicide rates. *Social Forces,* 1988, 66, 1060-1079.

Stafford, M. C., Martin, W. T., and Gibbs, J. P. Marital status and suicide. *Family Perspectives,* 1990, 24, 15-31.

Stark, R., Doyle, D., and Rushing, J. Beyond Durkheim. *Journal for the Scientific Study of Religion,* 1983, 22, 120-131.

Tatai, K. Japan: Part I. In L. A. Headley (ed.), *Suicide in Asia and the Near East.* Berkeley: University of California Press, 1983.

Travis, R. Halbwachs and Durkheim. *British Journal of Sociology,* 1990, 41, 225-243.

Wasserman, I. M. The effect of war and alcohol consumption patterns on suicide. *Social Forces,* 1989, 68, 513-530.

4

Who Committed *Suicide*?

Michael A. Overington, PhD

"Who committed *Suicide*?" What kind of a damned "clever" question is that? Don't such titles often signal that this is another one of those "Let's play around with words and confuse the issue" papers? Yes, I am afraid so. Here, the title intends to signal that Emile Durkheim, the distinguished sociologist, and "Emile Durkheim," the rhetorical *persona* of *Suicide*, are necessarily distinct characters; one is social, the other literary. And that distinction is a key one, for the social construction of scientific knowledge is accomplished in part through the literary conventions of argumentation. In short, I shall argue that it is the rhetorical artifice with which *Suicide* makes its moral case that is a significant part of its survival as a scientific landmark among sociologists.

I come at *Suicide*, then, not as one interested in its theoretical or substantive contributions but as one puzzled at its continuing vitality among sociologists. Indeed, this centennial marker is only further evidence that people are still interested in Durkheim's work and this long after it has been declared variously wanting and defective as a piece of theory or research. In the 1970s a number of works (among these the more general are LaCapra, 1972, Lukes, 1972, and Wallwork, 1972; and Pope, 1976 remains the classic reanalysis of *Suicide*) recognised that the work was conceptually flawed and the presentation of data failed to support his own case. As a scientific landmark they find it wanting in both scientific precision and substantive results: despite this we continue to celebrate *Suicide*.

There are many ways to "read" a text. Sometimes we give it a broad external context, we place it in some interpetation of the historical and intellectual world in which it appeared. Sometimes we give it a narrower external context,

I wish to thank my colleagues Jutta Dayle and Rick Hadden for their careful reading of an earlier draft of this chapter. I was glad to take advantage of their comments. As promised, I have "nicked" Mike Larsen's wonderful expression "narrative and descriptive methodologies" to seize a tradition for this essay.

we place it in the biographical achievements of the author taken as an individual life, as an example of Freud's or Jung's psychological insights, or whatever. Sometimes we read the text internally as a piece of scientific prose in which a substantive claim is made or a conceptual model is clarified. There is, however, no way to "read" without a context of some kind. The question is always in which context, or range of contexts, to place a text. In this essay, I shall give *Suicide* a singular and rhetorical context. I shall read the text of this classic monograph as an argument which is intentionally addressed to an audience; in other words, I shall appreciate the work for the form of reasoning and not criticize it for the substance of conclusions. But what does all this talk about rhetoric mean? What is sociology from a rhetorical point of view?

Even to ask such a question presupposes that one's public be somewhat familiar with and partially sympathetic to changes in our thinking about sociology as a social practice. In particular, this question anticipates that one's public be willing to consider sociological discourses as genres of writing to be analysed as any literary text (cf. Bazerman, 1988; Bazerman and Paradis, 1991). No doubt for some this would be a strikingly odd point of view. Indeed, many well intentioned sociologists still maintain that their investigations of social life eventuate in a rational construction of its empirical character; and moreover, they claim that the adequacy of these constructions can be tested against a reality which is separate from their own formulations. And even this caricature is much removed from earlier more "positive" ways of expressing this viewpoint! However, while this position dominates our introductory textbooks, it is an aging orthodoxy. There already exist a number of competing beliefs which are shared among sociologists and other social scientists. If not, where would be my public?

To grasp the origins of this orthodoxy which afflicts our textbooks, we have to look briefly at twentieth century positivism. Its original ambition was to establish a clear criterion for judging the meaning of statements, to sort out what made sense from what could never make sense. Mostly being scientists or having scientific training, the early positivists were not without their own presumptions about where to look for meaningful statements. Hence, their criterion attempted to show clearly that the rational character of well formed statements was established through their empirical adequacy; and the latter was judged by regular scientific practices. Now, this was all very well and good in the beginning, but attempts at clarity are notoriously controversial. No scholar worth their salt was going to leave this simple solution to an old, old problem without a quick look. The results of such scrutiny have slowly obscured the clarity of the original "verification" theory of meaning as its proponents cast and recast it in their efforts to deal with criticism, both of its logical difficulties and its misrepresentations of regular scientific practice.

The core of these efforts were attempts to give clear philosophic meaning to "empirical" as a standard for the rational character of statements. So we find that from the empirical as "verification," this principle is formed over some decades into talk of "justification," "confirmation," falsification," or "testing." It is keenly pathetic that the notion of "testing," the last and least rigourous, philosophic mould for a criterion of empirical meaning, was broken by its dependence on purely social arrangements. As Herbert Feigl, a staunch advocate of logical positivism, said:

> Since science is, as one might say, by definition, a social enterprise, it must insist on operations which are repeatable not only by one observer but in principle performable by any properly equipped observer. A statement is scientifically meaningful only if it is intersubjectively testable (1945: 257).

In philosophical circles, then, the rigor of this criterion of meaning was seriously undermined more than forty years ago. This, however, has not registered at all well among orthodox social scientists who continue to use the language of "verifying," "falsifying," "testing" and so on, as if these words meant something independent of the practical activities of their own disciplines. It is this rather odd, unsupported talk which constitutes most discussions of the scientific method in our textbooks.

With this loss of philosophic confidence in the simplicity of positivist constructions of science, it is not surprising to find Stephen Toulmin (1977) noting a major shift in the assumptions of philosophers and historians of science in the 1960s and 1970s. Equally unsurprising, this shift was toward an acceptance of the scientific community as a major factor in the creation of scientific knowledge. During this period and more emphatically thereafter, inquiry into the development of scientific knowledge shifted from philosophic reconstructions of the logical rigor of formal reasoning to social and historical investigations of informal, collective standards in scientific practice. Of course, it was recognized that these informal standards would have logical elements and scientific reasoning would resort to logical forms of argument. However, it was also accepted that scientific communities would be the *authorities* for the "logic" of these practices and arguments: no longer would philosophical principles of rational adequacy hold sway as *external* authorities. In a sense, this shift was from a concern for human rationality in its "purest" form to an interest in how community standards could provide for knowledge which was not merely local.

This does not mean that inquiries by historians, philosophers, sociologists and the like assumed a new orthodoxy wherein the scientific community became the sacred guarantor of scientific knowledge. Nor was everyone interested in the centrality of the scientific community in quite the same way. For example, scholars working in the "sociology of scientific knowledge" used this notion to undermine the privileged, uncontested character of science as the essential form of human knowledge (for a classic example of this work, see Knorr-Cetina and Mulkay, 1983). Alternatively, for those with a rhetorical bent, the "scientific community" offered a somewhat different set of possibilities. Most importantly, the rhetorically concerned were able to think of the scientific community as that context in which knowledge, for scientists, could be accomplished. In rhetorical terms, this meant that the "community" became an "audience."

This latter shift is not just a change of words to suit a different scholarly vocabulary: it is a crucial claim about the nature of scientific reasoning. For the many versions of "positivism," the meaningful character of statements depended on both their logical form and their empirical coherence with the "natural" world. Such views implied that statements are both "self-uttering" and "self-evident"; and that was never an understanding which should have sat easily among sociologists. In an important sense, the acknowledgement of an "audience" becomes a recognition that statements are made to "somebody" who has a part to play in creating their meaning. Yes, "meaning" is again the criterion, but not as a standard of testability rather as one of interactive appeal. In this "rhetorical" approach, scientific discourse is created by people and addressed to people; although, obviously, it is not created by just any folk, nor is it addressed to just anybody. However, this newer emphasis on the social in science is far from taking over discussion and debate. The philosopher of science Mario Bunge (1991) recently outlined a range of objections to the socializing of scientific knowledge that attempts to organize this terrain for a new counterattack.

Despite such objections, which often talk past efforts to locate the conceptual in the context of the social, what now appears stunningly obvious to many sociologists is that arguments in sociological discourse are both created by people and read and responded to by people. To make public sense, a reasoning among sociologists has to be commented on by others with similar training. Some poor soul has to read the work and do something about it, if it is to take on any particular social character. Of course, one should recognize that there is much less agreement on the fuller implications of all this; and that would be another essay entirely.

This point of view is recognizably part of the acknowledgments of textuality which get names like "post modernism," "post structuralism," "post positivism," (or are inventively termed "narrative and descriptive methodologies") This is most clearly a turn toward the rhetorical in such recent work as Billig, 1989; Brown, 1987, 1989; Hunter, 1990; and Simons, 1989, 1990 to mention but a few of the volumes and articles which have appeared in the past ten years. Somewhat before this, in my own acknowledgment of the so-called "rhetorical turn"(Overington, 1977), I established a four-part model of the construction of scientific knowledge. As is central to a rhetorical approach, this model gave place to the scientific community as the "audience," those who could possibly respond to some argument. In addition, it featured some familiar and distinctive rhetorical concepts which help understand any kind of reasoning, scientific or otherwise—"the speaker, " the situation," and "the argument."

In an attempt at a full rhetorical understanding one can merge an internal and textual approach to reading sociological discourse with an external analysis of its social context. Even if one restricts comments to a particular essay, as with *Suicide,* one is still able to blend an internal analysis of the text with concerns for the social circumstances of its production. Thus, an internalist rhetorical consideration of Durkheim's morality tale on the decay of social integration would give place not only to the argument of the work but also to the moment in which it was produced, its rhetorical situation, to the authorial voice, the *persona,* in which he incarnates himself, and to the audience, the presumed public for such a textual intervention in human affairs. And all these are taken as conceptual moments within the text.

At the same time, it is important to recognize that such argumentation as is *Suicide* can be given an external context. It can have a context in which there is Emile Durkheim, and not his *persona*; his research and not his argument; his social circumstances and not his rhetorical situation; his sociological public and not his intended audience. Obviously, any claims—such as those above— are made *in* texts; but while some refer to texts alone, others allege a world which is extratextual. Of course, no such allegations *establish* an extratextual reality; rather, they give the limits of what a rhetorical discourse anticipates. Which is to claim that the "world" is not always *intended* as an element in texts, as some would maintain. There are textual assertions which discuss "the social relationships within which scientific discourse emerges"; and these can intend an extratextual reality.

Texts and relationships, analyzed and lived experiences, can be treated and indeed can be experienced as human realities of a different kind. Either realm might be taken as foundational for analytic purposes. We have little option but to formulate the world to be understood, and understood in some particular way: it would be inexcusable to claim that in so doing we have exhausted its possible meanings. Thus, I am not claiming that the rhetorical features of the text of *Suicide* account for the form and content of the work any more than I am suggesting that the social organization of French society in the late nineteenth century is the real explanation for its rhetorical character.

Hence, in this brief, sardonic note on the "committing" of *Suicide,* I am inclined to make use of an earlier paper (Overington, 1981), which tried to balance an external analysis of the social circumstances faced by Emile Durkheim, the bald guy in glasses, with the textual reality of translations of *Le Suicide,* in which the *persona* "Emile Durkheim" appears as the original, genre hero of multivariate, survey analysis.

First, however, let me situate *Suicide* in a milieu. It appeared originally in 1897, immediately after Durkheim had been elevated to the first chair in sociology at the University of Bordeaux. This was the first such professorial appointment in France: the second was to follow when he moved to the Sorbonne some six years later. This second appointment of his career was paralleled by *Suicide,* which was the second effort he made to account for the incidence and variation in the suicide rate (the first being 1888: 446-463). In conjunction with *Année Sociologique,* founded in 1896, *Suicide* became a key statement in which the message of Durkheimian sociology was sounded around France. To this milieu, Clark (1972) and Brown (1987) offer us a further, brief introduction.

From their analysis, two important factors can be identified. At the original appearance of *Suicide,* other people outside the universities were practicing a "sociology" that was quite different to Durkheim's. And, at the same time within the universities, philosophy, pedagogy and psychology were well entrenched and not inclined to be sympathetic publics for claims about a level of reality which was neither philosophical nor psychological. Second, senior bureaucrats in the Ministry of Education were supportive of efforts to reform pedagogical training in higher education. They hoped to bring this into contact with a secular, anticlerical, ethical scheme that could be presented as based on scientific principles. Clearly, much more than this was happening in *fin de siècle* France, but these social circumstances best constitute what I am calling a "rhetorical situation," the moment captured in the argument of *Suicide.*

I do think that what was "waiting to be done" by *Suicide* was to assist Durkheimian sociology become more acceptable among bureaucratic and academic elites in France. However, in constructing any rhetorical analysis, one must be very careful to discriminate among accounts which depend on matters outside the text—such things as authors' intentions and the responses of publics—*and* those which depend on the text itself. Here, I wish to exhibit an evenhanded disregard for the priorities of both the internal and the external, and any simple notion of dependence. This interpretation, then, depends on reading *Suicide* in the context of my sketchy characterization of its social circumstances, factors which are intended to be external to the text. I have allowed my claims about those "external" factors to place arbitrary limits on the interpretative freedom with which the text is encountered as an argument addressed to a rhetorical situation. Reciprocally, in order to display some of the analytic paradoxes that we sociologists had shelved under the old orthodoxy, I have chastened the constraints of these external factors by appeal to a concept of *persona.* This authorial "voice" is obviously internal to *Suicide* and is quite independent of any knowledge of the author or his intentions.

Therefore, in suggesting an answer to "Who committed *Suicide?*" it is my intention to explore some conditions for telling plausible stories about *Suicide,* without *depending* on either an external or an internal reality. In this moment of our intellectual history, there is profound ambivalence as to what is, or should be, plausible reasons for interpretation. We know that a plausible reading depends on a public's affirmative response: we don't know what will accomplish that. And obviously, the issue cannot be resolved within this or any other essay, save as a rhetorical device of this author's voice encouraging such a response.

Suicide is two books in one set of covers. It is an empirical study of suicide rates in nineteenth century Europe: it is also a sensitive and ethically concerned attempt to use changes in suicide rates as measures of the effects of rapid and important social *changes*. Nor is it necessary to choose between these two readings: both "books" can be read simultaneously, if we set the work up as the posing and answering of a pair of questions. These two questions would be "What causes major shifts in suicide rates?" and "What do these changes tell us about the moral health of society?" In answering them, *Suicide* claims for itself a sociological way of dealing with what was generally thought to be a specifically individual action; further, the text does this in order to show the moral consequences which flow from a breakdown in community integration. This volume, then, displays itself as the kind of sociology which can deal with a problem of individuals, typically within the field of psychology, and a scientific sociology with profound ethical implications, normally a philosophical concern.

In the preface to *Suicide,* "Durkheim" outlines his notions of sociology and the grounds which he assumes for this particular study. In that he chooses to distinguish his work from studies of "pure sociology." He does this by suggesting that his work, deals with a limited, well defined topic that has characteristics relevant to the present moment, and as such offers a place to locate "real laws...which demonstrate the possibility of sociology better than any dialectical argument" (1951:37). All this is compared invidiously to the other kinds of sociology, "pure sociology," which offer no more than "brilliant generalities" and rely upon "illustrations" for their proofs.

The preface continues with the suggestion that *Suicide* was a clear and distinct exemplar of the principles of sociological method which he had discussed earlier in the apodictic prose of *The Rules of Sociological Method* (1938). The oracular pronouncements of that earlier volume were widely treated by his school as canonic (Clark, 1972:168) and the following prefatorial advertisement connects *Suicide* with that earlier pronouncement:

"Sociological method as we practice it rests wholly on the basic principle that social facts must be studied as things, that is as realities external to the individual. There is no principle for which we have received more criticism; but none is more fundamental" (1951: 37-38).

And that was precisely the case; the vision of social facts *comme des choses* became *the* Durkheimians' battle cry.

At the very beginning of this volume, then, our *persona* offers a claim that his sociology is different from other kinds and this distinction is best available in its recognition of a new order of social realities which are above and beyond the individual level of explanation. As our textual voice says: "...there will emerge...from every page of this book, so to speak, the impression that the individual is dominated by a moral reality greater than himself: namely, collective reality" (1951: 38). In that claim, we can find Durkheimian sociology with a stake in an area of academic competence that need not be taken as an intrusion into those disciplines entrenched in the universities. And in the same vein, the *persona* is willing to allege that his sociology is competent to discuss matters that relate to ethics and the individual—the normal concerns of philosophy and psychology.

With such an appeal, Durkheim can hope to reach elite publics (both inside and outside academia) who would have shared in the contemporary individualism of psychology and philosophy. Moreover, he can hope to do that without falling foul of vested academic interests. Concretely, in this study, this meant that "Durkheim" had to establish suicide as a social, not an individual fact; at the same time he had to show that the social realities which produce suicide are still meaningful in individual terms. Quite a task! To accomplish this the *persona* works along a number of lines. In the first place, he defines suicide as a phenomenon interesting at the collective level. In the second, he carefully dismisses the major alternatives to this collective fact. Third and centrally, he exhibits the variations in suicide rates as they respond to collective factors. Lastly, he offers plausible images of collective types of suicide as they might appear in the mental states of individuals. First, how does "Durkheim" define suicide?

In his efforts to define "suicide" the *persona* has to set aside the act of *felo de se*, because it "...is an individual action affecting the individual only, ...thus belonging to psychology alone" (1951: 46). What, then, is left for him to study? Surely, it has to be something other than men and women, dead by their own hand. Indeed, that is the case. Individual suicide is not the issue; rather, it is suicide *rates*. These rates are not simply some aggregate of individual acts; rather, they are: "a factual order, unified and definite, as is shown by both its permanence and its variability" (1951: 51). For "Durkheim," then, rates of suicide are not the elemental sum of their individual parts; they represent a collective tendency in society. Using a metaphor from physics, the *persona* likens such tendencies to electric currents which flow through the walls of society turning on, not lights, stoves and vacuum cleaners, but setting off individual suicides, as these currents meet more or less resistance.

So, with *rates* of suicide clearly established as his sociological issue, "Durkheim" examines a variety of explanations for the stability and variation of these collective facts proposed by other writers. As a successful rhetor, speaker, writer, the *persona* contends with these other views as actual voices raised in opposition to his work (rather than voices formulated as oppositional); and he deals with them as would a newcomer to the field. He treats them at the beginning of his argument: each account—depending on race, climate, insanity, and the like—is given a careful presentation and equally carefully is rejected. No matter how well he states these alternative explanations for suicide rates—their variation and stability—he is able to show that they can be plausibly rejected as inadequate for statistical, conceptual or logical failings.

In Overington (1981), I explore at some length the issue of *climate* as a key explanation for seasonal variations in suicide. Could it be that excessive heat drives people to their death? Or, as Noel Coward much later had it: "Mad dogs and Englishmen go out in the midday sun"? Indeed, the *persona* offers us a vivid image of sailors afflicted by the incredible tortures of heat: "Those stricken by it are irresistibly impelled to throw themselves into water, whether overcome by dizziness in the midst of working at the mast-tops, or during sleep, from which they start up violently with frightful cries"(1951:110). But, he immediately notes, cold has similar effects as stories of Napoleon's retreat from Moscow suggest. Perhaps, then, it is neither heat nor cold but climatic extremes which cause changes in suicide rates? Rapidly, indeed on the same page, he gives us statistical data which exhibit an increase in suicide rates from January to June and thereafter a decline. There is nothing in those to suggest that there can be any easy relationship between extremes of heat and cold and variations in the suicide rate.

Thereafter, we are bombarded with average temperatures and suicide rates from around Europe which "Durkheim" uses to bolster his claim that nothing simple about climatic extremes can account for variations in suicide rates. So, what does? Well, he tells us, the obvious, smooth regularity of the increases and decreases in suicide rates can only be "caused" by some factor which varies with a similar regularity: like should cause like. There is, as he displays, an exact correspondence between the variation in length of daylight and variation in suicide rates: the more daylight the more suicides, the less daylight the fewer suicides. And this is not just a "SAD" tale turned on its head! It is not the seasonal variation in daylight which affects suicide rates; it is because "day...is the time of most active existence, when human relations cross and recross, when social life is most intense" (1951: 117). So, there is a relation between seasonal and climatic factors and suicide rates; but only when we understand them as face indicators of social factors, as keys to grasping the saturated intensity of social life from which suicide is the precipitate.

This pattern in his argumentation is repeated again and again. Some alternative explanation for suicide rates is presented; it is examined with both commonsense and statistics (insofar as they are different in any specific case!); the relationship between some "extrasocial" factor and suicide is annouced as concealing the actual social causes for fluctuations in the rates of suicide. Wading through pages of this easily arouses a reader's anticipation of "Durkheim's" social account which is to follow. The new explanation gains much rhetorical "presence" in this style of presentation. One eagerly waits its appearance in the argument: we know what doesn't account for rates of suicide. Tell us, please, what does? And Durkheim's *persona* does.

But "my" *persona* will not! The point of this essay is not once again to discuss the egoistic, anomic and altruistic types of suicide produced by variations in social integration and regulation. More to my point is to display Durkheim as the skillful creator of a sociological *persona* through which he established a receptive hearing from publics unsympathetic to "collective realities." We do need to recall that collectivist thought, represented by such figures as Bonald and De Maistre, had been a "reactionary" force opposed to republican individualism—the ideology espoused by the very elites that form key publics in Durkheim's rhetorical situation. In arguing for collective reality, social facts *comme des choses,* "Durkheim" could have been risking the complete alienation of his public.

I believe that Durkheim's rhetorical skill is particularly available in the strategies his *persona* uses to keep a public, sympathetic to individualist views, attracted to his collectivist explanations. There are, I believe, two main devices used in *Suicide* to "individualize" his *persona's* "social realities." In the first, we find society being treated as if it were an individual; in the second, we have striking anecdotes of mental states. Of course, this first strategy is frequently critized in commentaries on Durkheim's writing; plainly, in addressing some publics, I would be objecting to a mistake in levels of analysis. Here, however, I wish to suggest that this unstated characterization of society as an individual member of all societies—past, present or future—operates as a key, tacit premise in the argument of *Suicide.* Indeed, from the time of Aristotle, the enthymeme—incomplete arguments which rely upon the addressed public to supply missing premises—has been regarded as the essential rhetorical syllogism. In that sense, we are looking at a rhetorically crafted argument when we find such passages as:

> When society is strongly integrated, it holds individuals under its control, considers them at its service and thus forbids them to dispose wilfully of themselves. Accordingly, it opposes their evading their duties to it through death (1951: 209).

In this and dozens of similar instances, "society" is given a personality—with needs, desires, purposes and so on—tacitly appealing to the ethos of his elite public; allowing the unsettling, collective level of analysis to appear garbed in familiar, individualistic language.

The second device used in *Suicide* to give individual glamour to collective realities is less well noticed and rarely criticized as a theoretical or substantive "error." "Durkheim" provides evocative images of the *individual mental states* of the types of suicide; even though these types are only the names he attaches to polarities on cross-cutting continua and not individual things at all! Admittedly, he is somewhat apologetic about doing this, for it neither fits his advocated method of sociological research and analysis nor does he have statistical information from which to work. However, from my point of view, as "examples [that give] a more concrete character" (1951: 278) to the statistical material, they are helpful rhetorical methods for speaking to elite publics more used to individual level accounts of individual states.

Take one of the best known and most frequently quoted portions of *Suicide* which offers a vivid portrait of the "anomic" condition under the pressures of rapid growth in the economy:

> From top to bottom of the ladder, greed is aroused without knowing where to find the ultimate foothold. Nothing can calm it, since its goal is far beyond all

it can attain. Reality seems valueless by comparison with the dreams of fevered imaginations....A thirst arises for novelties, unfamiliar pleasures, nameless sensations, all of which lose their savor once known. Henceforth one has no strength to endure the least reverse...(1951: 256).

This is offered by "Durkheim" as an authoritative description of the anomic state at the individual level without either comment or further substantiation. It is fascinating that it is precisely such a "literary" description which is picked up by other writers in sociology to "show" what Durkheim's famous types of suicide "mean." But that is another topic which I take it up in Overington (1981: 457-459).

To engage the ethos of his elite publics, it is not sufficient merely to offer vivid illustrations of individual states. It is also important to use examples from sources which they are likely to find credible. What are they? Judging from the textual choices they are mainly literary sources. For example, from Lamartine's Raphael we are offered an "egoistic type" depicting his mental state as: "A human disease, but one the experience of which attracts rather than pains, where death resembles a voluptuous lapse into the infinite" (1951: 277). Nor does "Durkheim" miss the opportunity to rehabilitate documentary evidence collected by Brierre de Boismont (earlier rejected as "insufficiently objective" [1951: 146]) for illustrative purposes (1951: 281,283,286). Lively documents may not be grist for his methodological mill, but they can be vivid examples! What are dismissed in one place as not scientific enough for *his* sociology can be employed in another for rhetorical purposes, when they buttress the case he is making before his elite publics. One can have it both ways: in argumentation as in life, it is much more "both/and" than "either/or."

In reading this text as addressed to a set of social circumstances, I have suggested that it can be taken as two books in one set of covers, both embodying the same rhetorical situation. To this point, I have considered the first of those books—an empirical study of suicide rates. I have tried to show how we can understand the rhetorical skill of that effort by examining "Durkheim's" definitional skill, his "even-handed" elimination of alternative explanations, and his evocative individualization of collective realities. Nonetheless, there is a second book which is concerned with a different question; "What do these changes in suicide rates tell us about the moral health of society?" In speaking before the elite publics of his day, Durkheim would have taken due care to exhibit the ability of such a study, and the capacity of *his* sociology, to address the ethical consequences of major social change. In so doing, he would be able to offer an image of a scientific morality which could become the ethical core for training future teachers, and through them, their pupils.

It is "Durkheim" who suggests that changes in suicide rates are "really" indicative of major disturbances in the ethical integration of societies. The rhetorical sensitivity of this approach is plain. *Suicides* are not the issue; they are symptoms of something more profound. And what is that? At root, the actual problem is a growing isolation of individuals from involvement in meaningful group life: only by such involvement can people become responsive to the social morality which shapes life in ways that are acceptable to the collectivity. In a metaphor, part electric and part hydrologic, the *persona* speaks of suicidogenic "currents" which sweep through society carrying away those individuals not protected by their involvement in the group life of the social world. The great issue of the day was not a rise in suicide rates: it was the collapse of a morally regulating group life.

As the *persona* presents it, the social disruptions of the Revolution had taken the old world apart and on its ruins built a unified and centralized society. People were loyal to the nation, but that loyalty was insufficient to provide them with integrating ethical standards. In such a world, where people look to the center and a collective representation of the nation holds their loyalties; "...nothing about persons draws them out of themselves and imposes restraints upon them. Thus they inevitably lapse into egoism or anarchy" (1951: 389). Since the burden of his analysis of suicide rates turns around these issues of social integration and the moral regulation consequent on that, it is simple to take them up once again, only this time prescriptively. He can speak of moral collapse with a scientifically established method.

"Durkheim" concludes *Suicide* with a chapter that addresses "Practical Consequences." Through this he hopes to summon his elite public once again to understand just what *his* sociology can accomplish. It can display social problems with such clarity that one can address practical solutions with scientific rigor. In this case, he argues that some communal organization be developed that would stand midway between the individual and the state. This would restore stability to the social world by involving people in morally regulated activities that affected their everyday life. Consistent with his vision that it was through work that people are most significantly involved in the functions of society, he recommends that this new communal organization be occupational in character.

Few, and I am not one, consider this a workable proposal. Indeed, it was little more than an optimistic effort to revive the corporate societies of crafts which had ordered a much earlier world of work. Perhaps his elite publics, the intended audience, knew this. What would have mattered more to them was "Durkheim's" demonstrated willingness to tackle a "moral" issue with "scientific" techniques; to make recommendations towards solving a social problem that was identified by scientific inquiry. His conception of society as a moral collective which regulated individuals, or left them deregulated and subject to the terrors of self destruction when integration failed, gave scientific justification for a completely secular ethics.

As I concluded in an earlier paper when appreciating the rhetorical skill of this voice:

> In one sense, his notion of appropriate involvement and regulation was but a modern version of Aristotle's understanding of moral virtue as following a

moderate course between extremes. Durkheim, however, was able to argue that deviation from a middle course toward extremes of egoism and altruism, anomie and fatalism had *measurable* consequences in fluctuations of the suicide rate. Thus could moral virtue be scientifically established and, indeed, republican loyalty to the State justified (Overington, 1981: 456).

Richard Brown (1987) provides us with a brief commentary on my claim. Whether or not Durkheim captured the social "reality" of France at his time, Brown suggests that he did catch the attention of those publics influential in providing a place for his sociology within the French educational system, both in his time and in the decades immediately following. Considering those educational bureaucrats, crucial members of the elite publics addressed in "Durkheim's" rhetorical situation, it is plain that *Suicide* did no harm in advancing his sociology. And I do recognize the modesty of that claim. More usefully, let me quote Richard, if only to take advantage of his translations from the French:

> Said one supporter, 'The introduction of the teaching of sociology in our normal schools...marked a most important date on the sundial of republican spiritual power' (Thibaudet, 1927:222-223). Said one critic, 'The requirement that M. Durkheim's sociology be taught in the two hundred normal schools of France is among the gravest perils to which our country is subjected...[and further] such has been the influence of Durkheim in our University that he seems to have monopolized sociology....In our discussions, in our manuals, Durkheimian sociology and sociology *tout court* seem to be more and more synonymous' (Lacombe, 1926: 35; Brown, 1987: 94).

And so, what do we conclude? "Who committed *Suicide?*" and why does that question matter? By now, few readers will expect a definitive answer which opts either for Emile Durkheim or "Emile Durkheim." However, I do believe that we can find an answer which helps explain the survival of this classic text and in so doing suggests a reason for the ironic word play of the essay's title. Since Durkheim's death—"We die in earnest, that's no jest"—our encounters with him are solely textual. Only his voice lives on. Necessarily, then, living sociologists have encountered this profound scholar as the *persona* in one of his books or articles. For all that, it is usual for sociologists to read their classic texts in the context of biographical trivia and scholarly exegesis and to assume that these extratextual details give them better access to the great one. We are not generally trained to note that our textual meetings give us a unique and direct access to his mind.

It may well be this direct access which has given such longevity to *Suicide*. As sociologists we are impelled to worship at the shrine of social reality, to belong to the Church of the Social Relationship (or the synagogue, mosque, neighborhood bar, sacred community of your metaphorical choice). Reading *Suicide* is always, and one may read it several times in a career, an experience confirming one's belief in the reality of the collective and its difference to any individual level of understanding. We, sociologists, vary widely in what the "collective" means to us—there is no "sociology," there are diverse "sociologies"—nonetheless, we do recognize it as something different from the individual. Even methodological individualists recognize symbolic realities, like language, as a collective enterprise. More ironically, even arch positivists, whose discourse denies their membership in a social collective, have treated this work as classic.

The *persona* in *Suicide* provides us with an essential identification by means of his constant litany on the forms of collective reality. In this we are affirmed and our beliefs strengthened. From graduate school and earlier, we have been able to read this volume and find in the reasoning of its *persona* a continuing source of support. It supports our convictions about social realities which colleagues in other sciences doubt, which our students only write about under exam pressure, and which we share with intimates only outside the bedroom and the precarious social reality of our sexual scripts. We can identify with this rhetorical voice; we can find our beliefs supported in his claims; we can have a past which included his achievements, warts and all. "Emile Durkheim" never died: he certainly would not have committed *Suicide*.

REFERENCES

Bazerman, C. *Shaping Written Knowledge: The Genre and Activity of the Experimental Article in Science*. Madison: University of Wisconsin Press, 1988.

Bazerman, C., and Paradis, J. (eds.) *Textual Dynamics of the Professions: Historical and Contemporary Studies of Writing in Professional Communities*. Madison: University of Wisconsin Press, 1991.

Billig, M. *Arguing and Thinking: A Rhetorical Approach to Social Psychology*. Cambridge: Cambridge University Press, 1989.

Brown, R. H. *Society as Text: Essays on Rhetoric, Reason and Reality*. Chicago: University of Chicago Press, 1987.

Brown, R. H. *Social Science as Civic Discourse: Essays on the Invention, Legitimation and Uses of Social Theory*. Chicago: University of Chicago Press, 1989.

Bunge, M. A critical examination of the new sociology of science: Part 1. *Philosophy of the Social Sciences,* 1991, 21, 524-560.

Clark, T. N. Emile Durkheim and the French University. In A. Oberschall (ed.), *The Establishment of Empirical Sociology,* New York: Harper & Row, 1972.

Durkheim, E. Suicide et natalite: etude de statistique morale. *Revue Philosophique de la France et de L'Etranger,* 1888, 26, 446-463.

Durkheim, E. *The Rules of Sociological Method*. New York: The Free Press, 1938.

Durkheim, E. *Suicide: A Study in Sociology*. New York: The Free Press, 1951.

Feigl, H. Operationism and scientific method. *Psychological Review,* 1945, 52, 250-259.

Hunter, A. (ed.). *The Rhetoric of Social Research: Understood and Believed*. New Brunswick, NJ: Rutgers University Press, 1990.

Knorr-Cetina, K., and Mulkay, M. (eds.). *Science Observed: Perspectives on the Social Study of Science*. Beverly Hills, CA: Sage, 1983.

LaCapra, D. *Emile Durkheim: Sociologist and Philosopher*. Ithaca, NY: Cornell University Press. 1972.

Lukes, S. *Emile Durkheim: His Life and Work*. New York: Harper & Row, 1972.

Overington, M. A. The scientific community as audience: towards a rhetorical analysis of acience. *Philosophy and Rhetoric,* 1977, 10, 143-164.

Overington, M. A. A rhetorical appreciation of a sociological classic: Durkheim's *Suicide. Canadian Journal of Sociology,* 1981, 6, 447-461.

Pope, W. *Durkheim's Suicide: A Classic Analyzed.* Chicago: University of Chicago Press, 1976.

Simons, H. (ed.). *Rhetoric in the Human Sciences.* Newbury Park, CA: Sage, 1989.

Simons, H. *The Rhetorical Turn: Invention and Persuasion in the Conduct of Inquiry.* Chicago: University of Chicago Press, 1990.

Toulmin, S. From form to function: philosophy and history of science in the 1950s and now. *Daedulus,* 1977, Summer, 143-162.

Wallwork, E. *Durkheim: Morality and Milieu.* Cambridge, MA: Harvard University Press, 1972.

5

There are More Things in Heaven and Earth: Missing Features in Durkheim's Theory of Suicide

David P. Phillips, PhD, Todd E. Ruth and Sean MacNamara

Although it was completed nearly a century ago, Emile Durkheim's *Suicide* is still the most famous social-scientific treatise on self-destruction and one of the two or three best-known works in all of sociology. Written with magisterial force, and claiming to provide a complete and definitive explanation of suicide, it is still cited in contemporary research articles on suicide (as evidenced by the *Social Science Citation Index*). In addition, a generation of introductory texts has bestowed respectful attention on Durkheim's theory (e.g., Aron, 1970; Bierstedt, 1970; Biesanz and Biesanz, 1969; Bloch, 1952; Braude, 1974; Broom, Selznick, and Darroch, 1981; Caplow, 1971; Lazarsfeld, Sewell, and Wilensky, 1967; Lyon, 1983; Merton and Nisbet, 1971; Nisbet, 1970; Spencer, 1976; Wallace and Wolf, 1986; Wilson, 1971).

In this chapter, we will consider Durkheim's theory strictly on its merits as a theory of suicide, not as a part of Durkheim's more general theory of society. We will discuss some of the major dimensions of suicide which were left unexplored by Durkheim's theory; among other things, we will show that this theory provides an incomplete coverage of both independent and dependent variables related to suicide. We will begin with a brief summary of Durkheim's theory.

Durkheim defines suicide as "all cases of death resulting directly or indirectly from a positive or negative act of the victim himself, which he knows

This chapter was supported by an unrestricted grant to the senior author from a private foundation which wishes to remain anonymous. We thank J. Haydu, S. McGlocklin-Ruth, M. Phillips, E. Rapoport and G. Shafir for helpful comments and criticisms.

will produce this result." Perhaps the best compact summary of his theory has been provided by Lester:

> The basic concepts in Durkheim's analysis of suicidal behavior lead to four etiological types of suicidal behavior. These four types form two groups. The first group, which includes egoistic suicide and altruistic suicide, is based on the concept of *social integration*. A society is integrated insofar as its members possess shared beliefs and sentiments, interest in one another, and a common sense of devotion to common goals....Suicidal behavior is common in societies where there is a high degree of social integration (altruistic suicide) and in societies where there is a low degree of social integration (egoistic suicide)....The second social variable that Durkheim used was *social regulation*. A society is regulated insofar as the society has control over the emotions and motivations of the individual members. Suicidal behavior is common in societies with a high degree of social regulation (fatalistic suicide) and in societies with a low degree of social regulation (anomic suicide) (Lester, 1989, p. 21).

Durkheim maintains that social integration and social regulation are the only factors that determine the suicide rate (Durkheim, 1951; Lester, 1989; Coser, 1971; Pope, 1976). He divided *Suicide* into three sections and devoted all of the first section to arguing that nonsocial factors (e.g., psychological illness, alcoholism, genetics, and imitation) have no impact whatsoever on the suicide rate.

"Seek simplicity," said Einstein, "and distrust it." Durkheim seems to have given rather more emphasis to the first part of this maxim than to the second. Perhaps this was understandable because Durkheim was seeking to accomplish two separate goals in *Suicide,* and to some extent these imposed contradictory demands on his work. On the one hand, Durkheim wished to provide a complete, dispassionate explanation for the fluctuations of the suicide rate. To accomplish this goal Durkheim would have needed to acknowledge the contribution of a bewildering variety of variables, some of which were nonsocial, and some of which were social but had nothing to do with social integration and social regulation.

Durkheim was unable to accomplish this goal because it conflicted with a second one that was more important to him: he wished to establish and validate a new paradigm for the study of suicide and indeed for the study of social phenomena in general. To accomplish this second goal, Durkheim could not afford to overwhelm the reader with bewildering details about the relative impact of social and nonsocial variables; he needed instead to provide a powerful, clear, and necessarily oversimplified argument for the importance of social variables and of sociology.

In short, Durkheim the scientist was sometimes at odds with Durkheim the founder of a discipline, and the second Durkheim tended to predominate. Perhaps in the larger scheme of things, this emphasis was not altogether regrettable, because it enabled Durkheim to make a crucial contribution to the establishment of sociology. But, in the narrower scheme, Durkheim's overemphasis on simplicity has unfortunately limited our understanding of suicide.

The modern investigator of suicide is no longer concerned with the establishment and validation of sociology. Most investigators of suicide are not in fact sociologists, and sociological researchers take the existence of their field for granted (in part because of Durkheim's contributions). Thus, for the modern researcher, the most notable feature of Durkheim's theory may well be its insistence that the complex behavior of suicide is entirely determined by two factors alone. This is jarring to many current investigators, who have learned both from statistical precept and from bitter experience that human behavior is complex and determined by the interaction of many factors.

One of the ways to discover some of the missing dimensions in Durkheim's theory is to examine another famous discussion of suicide—in Shakespeare's *Hamlet*. Though Hamlet's soliloquy is only 34 lines long, it suggests aspects of suicide not covered at all in Durkheim's 405-page volume.

> To be, or not to be, that is the question:
> Whether 'tis nobler in the mind to suffer
> The slings and arrows of outrageous fortune,
> Or to take arms against a sea of troubles
> And by opposing end them....

Hamlet's soliloquy focuses our attention on two factors not sufficiently developed or not discussed at all in Durkheim's theory: the slings and arrows of outrageous fortune (or what would be called, in modern terms, *stressors*); and the varied *responses* to these stressors.

THE SLINGS AND ARROWS OF OUTRAGEOUS FORTUNE: STRESSORS

Durkheim's theory fails to consider the full range of stressors leading to suicide, restricting attention to those resulting from social factors. Thus, Durkheim considers people who commit suicide after divorce, but does not consider people who commit suicide after suffering chronic, excruciating physical pain (Fishbain et al., 1989, 1991; Foley, 1991). Nor does Durkheim acknowledge the possibility that stresses leading to suicide can arise from genetic rather than social factors. But studies of twins, reviewed by Roy (1992) strongly suggest a genetic component for suicide.

These findings on the importance of non-Durkheimian variables suggest the following "thought experiment." Imagine two groups that are equal with respect to social integration and social regulation. According to Durkheim's theory, these groups should display the same suicide rate. However, if one takes into account research linking suicide with biological stress factors, these two groups might nonetheless have different suicide rates because one group has an abnormally high rate of bone cancer or other illness that causes extreme physical pain. In order for Durkheim's theory to be correct and complete, one would need to assume that biological stress factors have no independent effect on suicide or that biological stresses are evenly distributed over the population. Neither of these assumptions is supported by the data, and indeed some evidence cited above suggests that these assumptions are incorrect.

WHETHER 'TIS NOBLER IN THE MIND: ALTERNATIVE RESPONSES TO STRESS

At one point or another, Hamlet hesitates between suicide, murder, and returning to his student life. Durkheim's theory of suicide fails to recognize that suicide is only one solution among many, and consequently the theory does not attempt to explain why a few anomic people choose suicide, while many more opt for alternative responses.

For example, fewer than 2 percent of all Americans commit suicide (U.S. National Center for Health Statistics, yearly volumes); the rest find other responses to life's problems. Why do some people develop negative, destructive responses, while others develop positive ones? Why do some alcoholics kill themselves, but many more join Alcoholics Anonymous? Why do a few unemployed people commit suicide, but a larger number collect welfare payments or find new jobs? Durkheim's theory fails to address any questions of this sort.

Let us consider a final example which is problematic for Durkheim's theory—individuals traumatized by divorce. They appear to have at least three general options: *stoical, constructive,* and *destructive.* Persons choosing the first of these options do not try to solve their problems, but avoid facing them or retreat from them. Some 'grin and bear it,' and live with their pain. Others ignore their own problems by developing an inordinate interest in the problems of others (e.g., through a passion for escapist literature, soap operas, talk shows, or sports). Still others retreat from their pain, either physically (through migration), or perhaps mentally (through excessive sleep or amnesia).

In contrast, persons choosing to respond *constructively* to their marital problems address these problems rather than avoid them. Mildly traumatized divorced persons may consult a clergyman or a divorce counselor, join a group with similar problems, read self-help manuals, or (very commonly) remarry. Those who are severely traumatized may consult social workers, psychologists, psychiatrists, or call suicide prevention centers.

Finally, persons choosing to respond *destructively* to their problems can direct their aggression either outward or inward. Some harass, batter, molest, rape, or even kill their ex-spouses. Others choose to hurt themselves, either nonfatally (through the abuse of alcohol or drugs) or fatally, through suicide. Thus, we see that suicide is only one of a very large number of alternative responses to divorce. Durkheim's theory is incomplete because it fails to explain why a few divorced persons opt for suicide, while many more find different solutions to their distress.

In sum, Durkheim aimed at producing a comprehensive theory of suicide, and believed he had done so. However, this theory is not in fact comprehensive, because it fails to consider

1. the full range of factors leading to suicide (including nonsocial factors and perhaps social factors having nothing to do with social integration or social regulation), and
2. factors prompting the individual to choose suicide over alternative responses.

In modern terms, Durkheim's theory fails to consider all the relevant *independent* variables.

His theory also provides inadequate coverage of *dependent* variables. Although Durkheim considers four types of suicide (egoistic, anomic, altruistic, and fatalistic), there are many types he does not consider, and these also need to be catalogued and explained in a comprehensive theory of suicide. Medical progress was accelerated when physicians stopped considering "fever" as a homogeneous phenomenon and began to distinguish subtypes with different etiologies (e.g., anthrax, malaria, yellow fever, diphtheria). Similarly, a comprehensive theory of self-destruction should seek to determine whether suicide is one unitary phenomenon or is in fact an inappropriately general term covering empirically separate phenomena with different etiologies. Durkheim's theory does not fully explore this topic, and consequently it fails to ask or answer a host of interesting and important questions, some of which will be mentioned below.

TYPES OF SUICIDE

Our survey of case studies and suicide statistics has uncovered examples of at least eight major types of suicide, which we have distributed along four continua. Each of these four will be considered in turn, together with some issues that they raise.

Overt versus Covert Suicide

The first type of suicide is illustrated by the extreme case of R. Budd Dwyer, the indicted Pennsylvania State Treasurer, who shot himself on camera, at the end of a televised news conference (Stevens, 1987). The second type of suicide is illustrated by the case of Willy Loman, Arthur Miller's unsuccessful salesman, who disguised his suicide as an automobile accident so as to provide insurance for his family (Miller, 1959). Durkheim tested his theory of suicide entirely with instances of overt suicide and omitted discussion of this second type.

Consideration of the overt-covert continuum leads us to ask some important questions which are not dealt with in Durkheim's theory of suicide. Why do some people commit suicide in an unmistakable, explicit fashion, while others disguise their cause of death, and still others choose to leave matters ambiguous? Is a theory of suicide designed to explain *overt* suicides also adequate for *ambiguous* and *covert* suicides? Even though covert suicides are intrinsically difficult to identify, any complete theory of self-destruction should seek to discuss and explain suicides of this sort.

Acute versus Chronic Suicide

Menninger first popularized this distinction, when he noted that "[i]n contrast to the sudden, acute manifestations of self-destruction represented by the act of suicide, those forms of self-destruction in which the individual commits slow suicide—suicide by inches as it were—could, I think, be called *chronic* suicide, or chronic self-destruction" (1938, p. 77). One of Menninger's many examples is that of the long-term alcoholic. Another example, not considered by Menninger, would be that of a man who persistently engages in unprotected sex with a lover he knows is infected with the AIDS virus.

The acute suicides (which Durkheim considers) and the chronic suicides (which he does not) fall on the same continuum. Recognition of this continuum raises questions which Durkheim fails to consider. Why do some people kill themselves slowly (as with alcohol or drugs) while others do so quickly? Can a theory designed to explain acute suicides explain chronic suicides as well? If not, how should one elaborate such a theory in order to make it more comprehensive?

Unassisted versus Assisted Suicide

In recent years, assisted suicide has become an increasingly important cause of death. This is due to three related social developments:

1. The Hemlock Society, under the direction of Derek Humphry, has grown and has begun to popularize and to some extent legitimize the idea of assisted suicide (Blendon, Szalay, and Knox, 1992). Humphry's 1991 book, *Final Exit,* was the subject of a *Newsweek* cover story (Ames, 1991) and was at the top of the *New York Times* Best Seller List in the hard-cover advice category (Altman, 1991).
2. Living Wills have become increasingly common; such wills specify the nature of the medical treatment to be applied to or withheld from the patient in circumstances where he cannot communicate with his physician. A typical example in this category is the instruction to refrain from heroic procedures in an effort to keep the patient alive.
3. Recently, Dutch physicians have begun to collaborate yet more

directly and actively in the patient's death; after meeting appropriate safeguards, physicians have annually "euthanized" an estimated 2000 patients who have requested death (Won, 1991).

All of these social movements are alike in that the patient is collaborating with others, to a greater or lesser degree, to precipitate his death. In these cases, the patient's actions constitute suicide by Durkheim's definition, because the patient's death results "directly or indirectly from a positive or negative act of the victim himself, which he knows will produce this result."

In developing his theory, Durkheim fails to examine assisted suicides; consequently, he fails to consider why some people choose this form of suicide over others. It is important to answer this question, because assisted suicides are becoming increasingly frequent and may at some point outnumber unassisted ones (Humphry, personal communication).

Murder-Suicide

Suicides seem to vary with respect to their desire to hurt others. Some suicide notes reveal a great desire to protect the survivors from pain, while other notes show a wish to elicit shame, guilt, or grief in those left behind (Leenaars, 1988). Some suicides are yet more extreme and strive to inflict not only psychological but physical pain on others. In the U.S. we have experienced highly publicized incidents of a gunman who shoots many in the workplace (Jennings, 1989) the marketplace (Jennings, 1991) or the schoolyard (Jennings, 1989) and then commits suicide. Despite these conspicuous examples, murder followed by suicide is quite rare in the U.S., constituting about 4 percent of all homicides, compared with an equivalent figure of 42 percent for Denmark, 33 percent for Britain, and 22 percent for Australia (West, 1967, Table 1). It seems reasonable to expect that a comprehensive theory of suicide should address and explain differences of this magnitude.

THEORETICAL WEAKNESSES IN SUMMARY

A complete theory of suicide should explain what prompts people to choose among the major types of suicide. In addition, such a theory should explain what prompts people to kill themselves at all, rather than choose a more common response to problematic situations. Because Durkheim failed to grapple with these two major questions, his theory is incomplete.

One could overlook the restricted scope of Durkheim's theory if it were a powerful predictive or explanatory instrument able to resolve fundamental theoretical puzzles. This is not always the case and derives partly from another fundamental weakness in Durkheim's theory: it fails to provide a method for measuring its two key explanatory variables—social integration and social regulation.

This failure has sometimes imparted a spurious validity to his theory, by enabling researchers with contradictory findings to claim that all of these findings support Durkheim's theory. For example, Powell (1958) found a U-shaped relationship between social status and suicide, while Maris (1969) found that suicides decreased with social status. Yet the authors of both studies maintained that their findings were consistent with Durkheim's theory of suicide.

In addition, Durkheim's failure to operationalize his key explanatory variables has resulted in an inability to predict or explain the variation of suicide with respect to the fundamental demographic factors of age and sex, as elaborated below.

Between 1950 and 1977 the suicide rate of youths nearly tripled; after 1977 this rate declined (U.S. National Center for Health Statistics, yearly volumes). Durkheim's theory neither predicted the increase before 1977 nor the decrease thereafter; nor does it provide a plausible explanation for these opposing trends.

In almost all societies and time periods examined, the male suicide rate is markedly higher than the rate for females (United Nations, yearly volumes). Supporters of Durkheim's theory often explain this fact by asserting (without documentation) that the social integration of males is weaker than that of females. However, the rate of suicide *attempts* (a topic not covered by Durkheim's theory) is much *lower* for males than for females (Maris, 1992; Stengel, 1964). It is difficult to reconcile these contradictory patterns by means of Durkheim's theory.

In sum, Durkheim's theory appears to be fundamentally flawed for at least five reasons:

1. The theory provides no measures for its two key explanatory variables (social integration and social regulation). This would appear to be a crippling problem in what Durkheim meant to be a scientific theory of suicide.

2. Durkheim's theory seems unable to provide plausible explanations for some major demographic variations in the suicide rate, e.g., the trebling of the youth suicide rate from 1950 to 1977 and the equally puzzling decline since that date.

3. The theory fails to explain why some distraught people choose suicide, while most choose nonsuicidal responses to their problems. For example, the theory fails to explain why some people choose destructive, fatal, inner-directed violence, while others choose constructive, nonfatal, outer-directed solutions.

4. Given that a small fraction of people do in fact choose suicide over a welter of competing alternatives, Durkheim's theory seems incapable of explaining why some people choose one major variant of suicide over another. It seems important for any theory of suicide to explain why some people choose to commit suicide alone, while others seek

to involve their physicians, family, or friends. It seems equally important to explain why some people choose a chronic suicide (through drugs or alcohol) while others opt for acute forms.

5. Finally, Durkheim's theory seems to suffer from a type of tunnel vision, claiming that the suicide rate is entirely determined by only two variables—social integration and social regulation.

In some ways, this tunnel vision had positive consequences for the validation and development of the sociological perspective, one which focused attention on the importance of social facts above all others. At the same time, this narrowed perspective has also had negative consequences, because it has prompted many sociological researchers to overlook the importance of biological and psychological factors in the etiology of suicide. Because of the importance of these additional variables, one can no longer view the suicide rate of a group in a strictly Durkheimian fashion, as a pure index of the degree to which a group is socially integrated or regulated.

Durkheim seems to have succumbed to a temptation common to many persons seeking to promulgate a new vision of life—he overemphasized the importance of the variables he personally had discovered. In this connection, it may not be unfair to compare Durkheim with a famous cellist who played the same note, over and over again, while practicing in his living room. His wife asked him why he didn't play up and down the scales, like other famous cellists. The cellist replied, "Madam, what they are searching for, I have found." Durkheim was less limited than this apocryphal cellist, because he played two notes, rather than one. But it seems reasonable to suppose that a comprehensive theory of suicide must involve all notes of the scale.

We are not faulting Durkheim for producing an incomplete theory of suicide. All theories are incomplete. We are faulting Durkheim for claiming that his theory was complete. Durkheim played two very sonorous notes, and the harmonies and themes built upon these notes have reverberated throughout his work and throughout much of twentieth-century sociology. But, in the long run, no matter how sonorous the notes or how great the virtuoso, the most satisfying music is produced when the full scale is employed.

REFERENCES

Altman, L. How-to book on suicide is atop best-seller list. *New York Times,* 1991, August 9, A10.

Ames, K. Last Rights. *Newsweek,* 1991, August 26, 40-41.

Aron, R. *Main Currents in Sociological Thought II.* New York, Anchor Books, 1970.

Bierstedt, R. *The Social Order.* New York: McGraw-Hill, 1970.

Biesanz, M., and Biesanz, J. *Introduction to Sociology.* Englewood Cliffs, NJ: Prentice-Hall, 1969.

Blendon, R. J., Szalay, U. S., and Knox, R. A. Should physicians aid their patients in dying? The public perspective. *Journal of the American Medical Association,* 1992, 267, 2658-2662.

Bloch, H. *Disorganization*. New York: Alfred A. Knopf, 1952.

Braude, L. *A Sense of Sociology*. London: Thomas Nelson and Sons, 1974.

Broom, L., Selznick, P., and Darroch, D. *Sociology*. New York, Harper & Row, 1981.

Caplow, T. *Elementary Sociology*. Englewood Cliffs, NJ: Prentice-Hall, 1971.

Coser, L. A. *Masters of Sociological Thought*. New York: Harcourt, Brace, Jovanovich, 1971.

Durkheim, E. *Suicide*. Glencoe, IL: Free Press, 1951.

Fishbain, D. A., Goldberg, M., Rosomoff, R. S., and Rosomoff, H. L. Homicide-suicide and chronic pain. *Clinical Journal of Pain*, 1989, 5, 275-277.

Fishbain, D. A., Goldberg, M., Rosomoff, R. S., and Rosomoff, H. L. Completed suicide in chronic pain. *Clinical Journal of Pain*, 1991, 7, 29-36.

Foley, K. M. The relationship of pain and symptom management to patient requests for physician-assisted suicide. *Journal of Pain and Symptom Management*, 1991, 6, 289-297.

Humphry, D. *Final Exit*. New York: Carol, 1991.

Jennings, P. Stockton, CA man wounds 30, kills 5 children and self in school. *ABC World News Tonight*. 1989, January 18.

Jennings, P. Louisville, KY man wounds 12, kills 7 and self in printing plant. *ABC World News Tonight*. 1989, September 14.

Jennings, P. Killeen, TX man kills 22 and self in cafeteria. *ABC World News Tonight*. 1991, October 16.

Lazarsfeld, P., Sewell, W., and Wilensky, H. *The Uses of Sociology*. New York: Basic Books, 1967.

Leenaars, A. A. *Suicide Notes*. New York: Human Science Press, 1988.

Lester, D. *Suicide from a Sociological Perspective*. Springfield, IL: Charles C Thomas, 1989.

Lyon, D. *Sociology and the Human Image*. Downers Grove, IL: Inter-Varsity Press, 1983.

Maris, R. W. *Social Forces in Urban Suicide*. Homewood, IL: Dorsey Press, 1969.

Maris, R. W. The relationship of nonfatal suicide attempts to completed suicides. In R. W. Maris, A. L. Berman, J. T. Maltsberger and R. I. Yufit (eds.), *Assessment and Prediction of Suicide*. New York: Guilford Press, 1992.

Menninger, K. A. *Man Against Himself*. New York: Harcourt, Brace & World, 1938.

Merton, R., and Nisbet, R. *Contemporary Social Problems*. New York: Harcourt, Brace, Jovanovich, 1971.

Miller, A. *Death of a Salesman*. New York: Viking Press, 1949.

Nisbet, R. *The Social Bond*. New York: Alfred A. Knopf, 1970.

Pope, W. *Durkheim's Suicide*. Chicago: University of Chicago Press, 1976.

Powell, E. Occupation, status, and suicide: Toward a redefinition of anomie. *American Sociological Review*, 1958, 23, 131-141.

Roy, A. Genetics, biology, and suicide in the family. In R. W. Maris, A. L. Berman, J. T. Maltsberger and R. I. Yufit (eds.), *Assessment and Prediction of Suicide*. New York: Guilford Press, 1992.

Shakespeare, W. *Hamlet* [The Arden Shakespeare]. New York: Methuen, 1982.

Spencer, M. *Foundations of Modern Sociology*. Englewood Cliffs, NJ: Prentice-Hall, 1976.

Stengel, E. *Suicide and Attempted Suicide*. Baltimore: Penguin Books, 1964.

Stevens, W. Official calls in press and kills himself. *New York Times*, 1987, January 23, A10.

United Nations. *Demographic Yearbook*. New York: United Nations, yearly volumes.

United States National Center for Health Statistics. *Vital Statistics of the United States*. Washington, DC: U.S. Government Printing Office, yearly volumes.

Wallace, R., and Wolf, A. *Contemporary Sociological Theory*. Englewood Cliffs, NJ: Prentice-Hall, 1986.

West, D. J. *Murder Followed by Suicide*. Cambridge, MA: Harvard University Press, 1967.

Wilson, E. *Sociology: Rules, Roles, and Relationships*. Homewood, IL: Dorsey Press, 1971.

Won, S. About 2000 Dutch patients choose euthanasia annually, forum told. *Canadian Medical Association Journal*, 1991, 145, 1341-1342.

6

The Whole, Its Parts and the Level of Analysis: Durkheim and the Macrosociological Study of Suicide

Ferenc Moksony, PhD

If there is a leitmotive in Durkheim's works, it is certainly the notion that society has an existence of its own, one that is quite distinct from and even superior to the behavior of individuals. This idea reflects, in part, Durkheim's desire for a firm social order that would constrain the growing freedom and self-interest accompanying the rise of modern industrial society (see Rex, 1973: 59-60). It also reflects his effort to establish sociology as an independent discipline, to secure for it a domain not shared with psychology.

This view of collective life as entirely different from individual attitudes and actions permeates Durkheim's methodological doctrine. It shows up in the distinction he makes between the isolated instances of a phenomenon and the total frequency with which it occurs in a group. The aggregate number of suicides—or what Durkheim uses synonymously, the suicide rate—is said to be more than merely the sum of the deaths taken separately; it is believed to constitute a reality *sui generis* (Durkheim, 1951: 46). Closely related to this idea of emergence is the famous principle of explaining social facts by other social facts, not by people's motives and behavior (Durkheim, 1978: 127). Indeed, if phenomena like suicide rates are not simply the result of hundreds or thousands of solitary decisions, but transcend those in some way, it may seem reasonable to seek their causes outside the minds of the actors, "in the nature of the societies themselves" (Durkheim, 1951: 299)

Durkheim's methodological program has greatly influenced the style of research on suicide and on deviance in general. Sociological inquiry has come to be seen as the effort to relate various kinds of rates[1] obtained for macro-level units such as countries or census tracts, to other characteristics of these units.

Typical studies in this field formulate what Inkeles (1965: 255) called an "S-R proposition, in which S is the state of society and R the resultant rate."

This chapter challenges the dominant mode of research by showing its irrelevance, even inappropriateness, for what is generally regarded as its ultimate justification—the explanation of emergent phenomena. Taking a closer look at the mechanisms that sometimes make social facts seem more than the simple aggregate of isolated actions, I shall argue that their operation does not warrant the purely macro-level form of analysis prevailing in the literature. I shall, moreover, suggest that this holistic approach hides rather than uncovers the causal processes that generally underlie paradoxical aggregate outcomes. In so doing I separate, in essence, from each other what Durkheim saw, and those following him still see, as strongly related: the distinctive nature of social phenomena and the need for a collectivistic type of inquiry.

EMERGENT PHENOMENA

In Part III of his book on suicide, Durkheim forcefully argues for a fundamental difference between social facts and subjective states of mind. He also distinguishes the "collective type of a society" from the "average type of its individual members" (Durkheim, 1951: 317). To support his position, he draws on an example that has to do with people's reaction to crime (316-317). At the sight of human violence such as murder, individuals, when acting alone, commonly feel indignation and ask for proper punishment. They do not, however, demand bloody revenge; nor do they usually make serious efforts to catch the offender. This is in sharp contrast with the way the crowd responds to the same type of delinquency. In that case, emotions are much more intense and people are very often satisfied only by the most severe form of retaliation. In that case, "anger is collective" (316).

What does this example tell us? It certainly shows that there are situations in which the behavior of a group as a whole cannot simply be deduced from what we know about each of its members taken separately. The fierce anger of the crowd much surpasses the average indignation each person, when alone, exhibits. But what does this unexpected excess of hostility at the group-level really demonstrate? Does it support the notion that social facts—that is, phenomena characterizing entire societies—are independent of the behavior of individuals and, consequently, need to be explained by reference to other macro-level properties? Or is it merely a sign of our having the wrong model of action, and of the way different actions combine to produce a social outcome?

There are two opposing forms the transition from individual action to macro-level results can take.[2] One is completely *atomistic* in nature; it consists of the summation of isolated instances of behavior. Max Weber's classic example can serve as an illustration. When it begins to rain, people on the street open their umbrellas. They all respond to a common, external stimulus—the weather—without regard to each other. They probably do not react at exactly the same time; individuals usually differ in the degree of wetness they tolerate. But the time lag only depends on their personal characteristics and the collective pattern is a simple function of the distribution of these characteristics. The phrase "aggregate psychology," a term coined by Coleman (1958), fully applies here.

The other way in which the micro-to-macro transition can proceed is much more complex; it involves manifold *relationships and mutual effects among actors*. Returning to Weber and the rain, the time sequence of responses may arise from people first looking, not at the sky, but at each other to see whether those around them have already opened their umbrella. In this case, behavior is governed both by individual traits and by the attributes of the others making up one's social environment. The aggregate outcome is still the result of individual action, but that action may be very different from the one produced in isolation. It may be different either because, as Durkheim seems to suggest, association transforms people themselves, or because, as I am inclined to believe (see also Granovetter, 1978), it changes the circumstances people respond to by their behavior.

Durkheim's example on crime clearly shows the importance of making the right choice between these contrasting modes of aggregation. The anger of the crowd seems unforeseen because our expectation is based on a wrong view of the micro-to-macro transition. By comparing the group-level outcome with the way each person, in isolation, reacts to murder, we *implicitly use an atomistic conception of the aggregation process*, we think of the crowd as made up of actors completely unrelated to each other. And this conception turns out, not surprisingly, to be false; members of crowds usually form a network of interaction and influence one another. It is this effect of being embedded in the web of social relations that changes people's behavior and makes the group's response more intense.

There is, then, nothing mysterious about so-called emergent phenomena. To understand them, there is no need to resort to the holistic approach often proposed in the literature. They can be explained fully in terms of individual behavior, albeit of one that is shaped *not only by the properties of the actor but also by the characteristics of the social context* in which the action takes place.

EFFECTS OF POPULATION STRUCTURE

Variables describing different aspects of population structure appear frequently in analyses of social phenomena. The age distribution and the sex ratio are but two of the many examples. Such characteristics of society can play their role in one of two distinct ways. The first is usually referred to as *composition effect*. Here macro-social demographic patterns possess no independent causal power; the impact they have derives entirely from the *corresponding individual-level relationship*. The aging of a society, for instance, can be expected to raise the suicide rate solely because old people have themselves a higher risk of taking their life. Similarly, the preponderance of men tends to push up the crime rate, since males are inherently more likely to become offenders than females. Cases like these are typically only of limited substantive interest to social scientists; indeed, they usually try to eliminate composition effects by employing standardized or adjusted measures. On the other hand, demographic explanations are based entirely on influences of this sort (see Stinchcombe, 1968: 60-79).

The second way is more complex, and it is also more interesting. In this case, the impact of population structure is genuine; it does not merely echo pre-existing relations at the level of individuals. For example, in a society experiencing what is often termed a "baby boom"—that is, an extreme rise in the number of births—young people encounter bottlenecks as they pass through the life-cycle. They attend schools that are more crowded, they face greater competition at the labor market, and they normally earn less than their fellows in smaller cohorts. These barriers may add up to a general sense of deprivation or anomie, which in turn may make people more vulnerable to suicide.[3] Note that here individuals take their life *not* because they are young; in fact, this should *lessen* their risk of self-destruction. Rather, they do so because they live in an environment in which their age-group constitutes an unusually large part of the population. They respond by their behavior to a characteristic of their social context; that is why influences of demographic structure like this are frequently called *contextual effects*.

The two kinds of impact can combine in more than on way. They can *reinforce* each other as in the case of age and crime: an increase in the proportion of the young can be expected to push up the crime rate both because people at lower ages are intrinsically more likely to violate law, and because members of large juvenile cohorts face greater obstacles to success or form deviant subcultures more easily. The effects can also *counteract* one another, as the previous example on age and suicide shows. Young people are generally less prone to self-destruction, thus a gain in the size of this age-bracket can be expected to *reduce* the total suicide rate. The same shift in demographic structure may, however, make, through the deleterious consequences of cohort size, these individuals more likely to take their life, thereby *raising* suicide level.[4]

The distinction between the two forms that the impact of population structure can take is closely related to the distinction made earlier between the two types of the micro-to-macro transition. Composition effect represents an aggregation process which is completely atomistic in nature. Here the behavioral regularities that translate demographic changes into changes in social phenomena are *independent of the shifts occurring in the distribution of the population* (see Stinchcombe, 1968: 61-62). Age-specific suicide risks, for instance, remain the same no matter how large the proportion of the elderly is; and to get the total impact, each unit increase or decline in that proportion *is weighted by these constant* behavioral propensities.[5] It is this very stability of responses against variations in circumstances that reflects the atomistic character of the process, the lack of interaction among individuals. The moving of an old person to a new area does not alter the exposure to self-destruction of those already living there; nor does the suicide risk of the newcomer depend on the kind of the people he or she joins.

Contextual effect, in contrast, represents the more complex of the two forms of the micro-to-macro transition, the one which involves manifold relationships among actors. In this case, the *behavioral regularities are no longer constant;* rather, they are a function of demographic patterns. Young persons, for example, are more likely to take their life, the greater the size of their cohort. Thus the contribution of population shifts to social phenomena cannot simply be determined by using a uniform weighting factor, such as a single set of age-specific suicide rates. The *changes in the weights induced by the changes in the demographic structure* also have to be taken into account; they have to be incorporated into our estimate of the total impact. And these changes in the weights occur because people do not live in isolation from each other, because they respond by their behavior to the actions or characteristics of those present in their social environment.

The implications for the problem of emergence of the two kinds of influence of population structure are parallel to the implications of the two forms of the aggregation process. Composition effects allow fairly easy inference from the micro-level to the macro-level.[6] What we know about each of its members can be extrapolated to the group as a whole. This is because the impact of demographic patterns is, in this case, merely a reflection of the corresponding individual-level relationships; it does not represent a separate causal force. It is when contextual effects are at work that difficulties arise. Here the distribution of the population plays a role of its own, one that may amplify, diminish or even reverse the original micro-level association. Unless we take these changes, brought about by the mutual dependence of actors on each other, into account, the aggregate outcome may indeed seem strange and difficult to grasp. It may seem to be *disproportionate to the composition* of the population; more or less than expected, depending on the way the two sorts of effects combine. The reason, again, is that our expectations are based on a wrong model of reality. Just as mistaking a complex aggregation process for a purely atomistic one makes collective phenomena unpredictable, mistaking a situation in which contextual mechanisms are also operating for one in which composition effects alone are at work makes suicide and other similar rates appear different from the simple sum of the individual events that comprise them.

DIVORCE AND SUICIDE

Marital status figures as a central variable in Durkheim's treatment of both egoistic and anomic suicide. He devotes considerable space to discussing the beneficial impact family life exerts on people by making them part of a highly integrated community. His focus is on marriage as a personal characteristic and on its relation to suicide at the level of individuals. This is true even though he often uses as evidence correlations across areas or time periods, and thus he runs the risk of committing what is called the ecological fallacy (Selvin, 1958).

Durkheim also pays much attention to divorce. And here his approach is completely different from the way he explains the impact of marriage. His aim is to understand why there is, across societies or regions, a fairly strong positive association between the suicide rate and the frequency with which couples break up their union. To do so, it would seem quite obvious to refer to the corresponding individual-level relationship: rates of self-destruction and of dissolution of marriage vary together because divorced people are *themselves* more likely to take their life. This would be an argument based on composition effect. Durkheim does not, however, proceed that way. He does not treat divorce as a characteristic of individuals; rather, he takes it to be a property of the social context. "The institution of divorce must itself cause suicide through its effect on marriage" (Durkheim, 1951: 270). And he also specifies the causal mechanisms involved:

> divorce implies a weakening of matrimonial regulation. Where it exists, and especially where law and custom permit its excessive prevalence, marriage is nothing but a weakened simulacrum of itself; it is an inferior form of marriage. It cannot produce its useful effects to the same degree. Its restraint upon desire is weakened; since it is more easily disturbed and superseded, it controls passion less and passion tends to rebel. It consents less readily to its assigned limit....One cannot be strongly restrained by a chain which may be broken on one side or the other at any moment. One cannot help looking beyond one's own position when the ground underfoot does not feel secure. Hence, in the countries where marriage is strongly tempered by divorce, the immunity of the married man is inevitably less....Consequently, the total number of suicides rises" (Durkheim, 1951: 271-272).

Durkheim thus identifies a contextual process as conveying the impact of divorce on self-destruction.[7] This process, moreover, involves complex interaction effects; that is, it varies with some characteristics of individuals. First, it depends on marital status. While Durkheim is silent on the issue of how the frequency of dissolution of marriage affects the suicide risk of divorced people themselves, it seems reasonable to assume that this influence, if any, is not the same as the one exerted on those still living together. For a high prevalence of divorce may lead to a change in the negative evaluation of marital disruptions, and it may also help those who broke up their marriage better organize themselves to defend their interests. These together may then mitigate the negative consequences of divorce, thereby reducing the danger of self-destruction. Second, the contextual mechanisms work differently for the two sexes: males lose their "moral calmness and tranquillity" (p. 271) and become more vulnerable to suicide as the spread of divorce increasingly undermines the institution of marriage, whereas females view the same process as liberation and their suicide risk declines accordingly.

These complex interactions make it difficult to trace the macro-level implications of the influence of divorce. Durkheim does not, in fact, address this issue explicitly. He stops at specifying what goes on at the level of individuals (including, of course, the role of the social environment) and only loosely refers to a possible rise in "the total number of suicides." While we cannot give a definitive answer without real data, we may at least think about the probable collective result of the combination of effects of various kinds. These effects partly reinforce each other: divorce as a personal characteristic and as a contextual variable for married men both elevate the suicide rate. Thus, if these two forces alone were operating, the macro-social outcome would be larger in magnitude than what the logic of composition effect would make us expect, but the direction of the impact—the more divorce, the more suicide—would be preserved. We would, then, be puzzled by the amount of the increase, but the very fact of the increase would come as no surprise.

Contextual processes other than those affecting married men are also at work. Females are less likely to take their life the more prevalent divorce is, and also may be divorced people themselves. This tends to counteract the growth arising from the heightened suicide risk for married males, although it does not probably reverse it completely, given the usual slight share of women (and also of divorced) in the total number of suicides.[8] Nevertheless, it is possible that the various kinds of influences produce, as a net result, an aggregate outcome which is not very far from what the erroneous assumption of composition effect only would lead us to expect. It is, in other words, possible that even a wrong model of reality yields correct implications, since the different contextual mechanisms destroy each other. This is mere coincidence, however, a result unique to the particular situation. Indeed, there are many examples (for instance, the one mentioned in note 2) that show the vast differences that may exist between predictions derived from an oversimplified view of society—one which disregards contextual processes—and the findings actually observed.

WOUNDED IDENTITIES AND MULTIPLIER EFFECTS

What Durkheim failed to do explicitly—the study of the macro-level consequences of various effects of population structure—has been accomplished by Farber (1968: 76-78), although only in a hypothetical example. The question he raises is how a high proportion of "individuals wounded in their sense of competence and therefore psychologically dependent" might be related to an increased frequency of self-destruction. An obvious answer would be that the association obtains because those individuals are *themselves,* due to their personality traits, more vulnerable to suicide. This would be an explanation based on composition effect, one which reduces the group-level correlation to its micro-level counterpart.

This explanation tells only part of the story, Farber says. The prevalence of mental health problems also has a contextual effect. People with such problems do not live in isolation; they constitute the social environment for each other. What is the impact of the psychologically injured being surrounded with individuals suffering from low self-evaluation? In such a society, there is extremely great demand for support, and that demand cannot be met because of the high probability of encountering people who are themselves in need of help. "We are thus confronted with the situation of the psychologically hungry demanding of those who cannot give" (Farber, 1968: 76).

Personality factors play, then, a *dual* role: they function both as characteristics of individuals and as characteristics of the social setting. A person's weak sense of competence precipitates *not only his own* death but also that of those for whom he is unable to provide support. These two sorts of influence tend to reinforce each other, producing what Farber calls "a kind of Keynesian multiplier effect, with a given increase in the number of vulnerable personalities in a society resulting in *disproportionately* large number of suicides" (Farber, 1968: 78, emphasis added). The word "disproportionately" in this sentence refers to what the term "emergent phenomena" also seeks to capture—the difference between the macro-level result actually observed and the one that would have obtained if composition effect alone had been operating.

PROBLEMS OF AGGREGATE DATA

Contextual effects are, we see, a major source of puzzling or "disproportional" collective outcomes. Such effects can fully be explained in terms of individual behavior as soon as we move beyond the narrow scope of "aggregate psychology." There is, then, no need to adopt the holistic approach proposed by Durkheim and many of his followers. But this approach is not only unnecessary; it is even inappropriate for a clear grasp of how environmental mechanisms work and how they give rise to emergent phenomena. This is because aggregate data, the raw materials of this perspective, very often make it impossible to identify contextual processes, to separate them from simple composition effects.[9]

To make this point clear, let us return to Durkheim's explanation of the effect of divorce on suicide. Let us, further, formalize his argument by using regression analysis, assuming, for the sake of simplicity, linear relationships among variables (we shall drop this restriction later). Our point of departure is the individual-level model connecting suicide, the dependent variable, and marital status. Without loss of generality, I take this latter variable to be a binary one, having only two categories: married (0) and divorced (1). I do this mainly because Durkheim is rather silent on how those in other categories might be affected by the prevalence of divorce. I also do this to keep the model as simple as possible.[10] Now the regression equation takes the following form:

$$y_{ij} = b_0 + b_1 x_{ij} + e_{ij}, \tag{1}$$

where y_{ij} indicates whether person i in area (country, region, etc.) j committed suicide or not,[11] x_{ij} is a dummy variable capturing the marital status of the same individual, b_0 and b_1 are regression coefficients, and e_{ij} is an error term. This model expresses the idea that the only determinant of one's likelihood of committing suicide is one's *own* marital status; that of *others* is believed not to affect that likelihood. It is this model that explanations based on composition effect aggregate to the macro-level in order to predict suicide rate for the society as a whole.

Let us accomplish this aggregation to see what happens to our original equation. To do so, we simply average y and x *within* areas and get

$$y_j = b_0 + b_1 x_j + e_j, \tag{2}$$

where y_j is the proportion[12] of suicides in area j, x_j is the proportion of divorced in the same area, and e_j is the error term for the macro-level observations. The result is, as we see, a linear relationship between the aggregate data.

Now let us modify the individual-level model we started with by incorporating into it possible contextual effects of the divorce rate. The simplest of such effects is an *additive* one; in this case, the prevalence of dissolutions of marriages has the same impact regardless of the individual characteristics, that is, regardless of whether a person himself is divorced or not. The regression equation reflecting this uniform influence of the frequency divorce looks like this:

$$y_{ij} = b_0 + b_1 x_{ij} + b_2 x_j + e_{ij}, \tag{3}$$

where b_2 is the coefficient indicating the strength of the contextual effect of divorce and all other terms are defined as before.

To see the implications of this model for the macro-level, we again average within areas and get

$$y_j = b_0 + b_1 x_j + b_2 x_j + e_j = b_0 + (b_1 + b_2) x_j + e_j. \tag{4}$$

The problem is obvious: equations (2) and (4) *cannot be distinguished from each other empirically*, although the individual-level behavioral processes underlying them [equations (1) and (3)] are completely different. Composition effect alone and its additive combination with contextual effect both lead to the *same* linear relationship among aggregate data. When regressing y_j on x_j, we get a *single* slope coefficient, and we cannot tell, without some information about individuals, whether it corresponds to b_1 or $(b_1 + b_2)$. Composition and contextual effects are, then, confounded in analyses using solely macro-level data. Given its exclusive reliance on data of this sort, the holistic approach proposed by Durkheim and adopted by the majority of sociologists studying suicide is of very limited help in explaining just what has given rise to it—emergent phenomena.

It could be argued, however, that equation (3) is an inaccurate representation of the behavioral processes contained in Durkheim's example. Specifically, the contextual effect of the prevalence of divorce is likely to be *interactive*, rather than additive. That is, its strength or direction depends on the characteristics of the individuals affected by it. For married people, the probability of suicide *increases* as the divorce rate rises. For divorced persons, in contrast, no change or even a *decrease* in suicide risk could be assumed, although Durkheim is, as already noted, silent on this issue. This differential impact of demographic structure could be captured by a regression equation with a cross-product term:

$$y_{ij} = b_0 + b_1 x_{ij} + b_3 x_{ij} x_j + e_{ij}, \tag{5}$$

where b_3 is the coefficient indicating the size of the interaction effect. (Given that x_{ij} is a binary or dummy variable, b_3 is simply the difference in the slopes for the two groups, married and divorced.[13])

What is the aggregate outcome this revised model leads to? Still again, we average within areas and get

$$y_j = b_0 + b_1 x_j + b_3 x_j x_j + e_j = b_0 + b_1 x_j + b_3 x_j^2 + e_j \tag{6}$$

As opposed to our earlier results, this time we have arrived at a *non*linear relationship among the macro-level variables. Moreover, from the estimable parameters of equation (6), all the coefficients of the underlying micro-level behavioral model represented by equation (5) can be determined and thus the two kinds of effects of population structure can be separated. Specifically, the regression weight attached to x_j in equation (6) reflects the size of composition effect, whereas the one attached to the quadratic term, x_j^2 indicates the strength of contextual effect. It seems, then, that even aggregate data allow us to distinguish empirically between the different forms of influences of demographic patterns and to isolate the forces that give rise to emergent phenomena.

The scope of this argument is rather limited, however. It is limited because it rests on two implicit assumptions. The first is that composition effect is *linear;* if it is not, then the departure of the aggregate relationship from linearity is no longer an unambiguous sign of the impact of the social environment. In fact, in such situations it can reflect either a (curvilinear) composition effect, or a contextual effect, or a mixture of the two. The second assumption is that the frequency of divorce exerts no *additive* or main effect on suicide; if it does, the two sorts of effects become again confounded. To see this, let us write a regression equation containing both additive and interactive terms:

$$y_{ij} = b_0 + b_1 x_{ij} + b_2 x_j + b_3 x_{ij} x_j + e_{ij} \tag{7}$$

The macro-level counterpart of this model is

$$y_j = b_0 + b_1 x_j + b_2 x_j + b_3 x_j x_j + e_j = b_0 + (b_1 + b_2) x_j + b_3 x_j^2 + e_j \tag{8}$$

If we now take, as we did in equation (6), the regression weights attached to x_j and x_j^2 to be the size of composition and contextual effects, respectively, we make a mistake to the degree that b^2, the additive component of the impact of the social environment, departs from zero. We overestimate or underestimate, depending on the sign of b^2, the role of individual marital status, and we get a biased picture of the overall importance of the social environment, since we attribute a part of it to micro-level characteristics. Even when interaction effects are at work, then, the exclusive reliance on aggregate data may well impede correct inference.

CONCLUSIONS

This chapter started from two major elements of Durkheim's methodological doctrine, both reflecting his fundamental aim to show the superiority of society over the individual. One was the idea of emergence: the notion that phenomena characterizing a group as a whole cannot be reduced to the attitudes or behavior of the members of the group taken separately. The other was the principle of explaining social facts by other social facts, not by people's motives and actions. Durkheim apparently saw this latter tenet to be a logical consequence of emergence: if social phenomena transcend individual behavior, then they cannot be accounted for by it either.

What conclusions can be drawn, on the basis of my analysis, as to the validity of these methodological rules? Durkheim was undoubtedly right in stressing the distinction between macro-social outcomes and simple aggregates of isolated actions. Suicide rates actually observed can indeed be very different from what an atomistic view of society would predict; that is, from the rate that would obtain if people were unrelated to each other.[14] Similarly, group response to crime can be considerably more severe than what we expect it to be if our expectation is based on the assumption of no interaction among individuals. In fact, much of our frustrations derive from our failure to realize how strongly our actions are tied to those of others and how deeply this connection affects the final result. We strive for better education in order to earn more, but we may well not attain our goal because *the similar efforts of others* may lead to an oversupply of well-trained individuals. While frustrating for those involved, paradoxical effects of this sort are the very phenomena that make sociology an exciting endeavor.

My agreement with Durkheim ends here, however. The distinctive nature of social facts—namely, that they are end products not only of people's intention but also of the characteristics of the situation—does *not* imply that we should abandon studying individual behavior and focus, instead, on relationships among properties of entire societies. For, even the most striking examples of so-called emergent phenomena can be explained, as we have seen, in terms of people's actions *if we take contextual effects into account.* Unexpected or puzzling aggregate outcomes are not a sign of the operation of macro-social forces *sui generis;* they are merely a sign of our using a wrong model of behavior and of the way behaviors combine. What we need to do, then, to accommodate the mode of our inquiry to the complexities of social life is not to adopt the collectivistic approach proposed by Durkheim. It is, rather, to trace contextual effects on individual behavior and the macro-level consequences such effects produce. This alternative strategy is not only sufficient; it is also more appropriate.

NOTES

1. The study of rates, as opposed to the examination of individual cases, is often seen as the hallmark of the sociological approach. As Merton (1957: 132) writes: "Our perspective is sociological. We look at variations in the rates of deviant behavior, not at its incidence" (emphasis in original; see also Gibbs [1968: 8-9]). Statements of this kind may make sense if they refer to the distinction between different levels of aggregation, although the holistic approach generally coupled with them is, as I shall argue, unacceptable. They are clearly wrong, however, if they imply the distinction between deterministic and probabilistic explanations. For, even psychological theories usually seek to explain average tendencies in attitudes or behavior, not single instances of them. There is thus, as Hanushek and Jackson (1977: 7) point out, an important difference between the analysis of the behavior of individuals—which involves looking at groups of persons with similar values on the explanatory variables—and the study of individualistic behavior.

2. This classification is one based on purely formal or logical criteria. For a typology grounded on more substantive considerations, see Coleman (1986: 1324-1327). For a useful discussion of the two kinds of aggregation process distinguished in the text, along with their implications for the discrepancy between individual and group behavior, see Barton (1968: 5-9).

3. For empirical evidence on the impact of large cohort size on suicide, see, e.g., Ahlburg and Schapiro (1984).

4. For a most famous instance of counteracting effects, see Stouffer et al. (1949: 250-253). A detailed treatment of this example is given in Moksony (1990a).

5. This can well be seen by examining the statistical techniques commonly used to isolate composition effects. In traditional demographic standardization, a single set of age-specific rates are employed to obtain the weighted average. In regression standardization, the difference between the population structures to be compared is multiplied by a single slope coefficient.

6. This applies, strictly speaking, to raw or metric regression coefficients only. Standardized measures such as correlations are affected even in the presence of composition effect. For a more detailed treatment of this issue, see, e.g., Hammond (1973).

7. Durkheim's treatment of divorce is indeed often cited as the first appearance of

the contextual approach in sociology. This is somewhat misleading, since what he did was merely to record an empirical fact, without conceptualizing it as a contextual effect. He did not reflect methodologically on his finding; he did not recognize his procedure as a particular instance of a broader analytical strategy. It was only half a century later—in papers that tried to generalize the results of Stouffer's famous study, *The American Soldier* (e.g., Kendall and Lazarsfeld, 1950)—that this more conscious attitude toward the study of impact of the social environment emerged. For the position that discoveries are really made only when observations have already been built into a theoretical or conceptual scheme, see Kuhn (1984).

8. While not treating macro-level implications explicitly, Durkheim does note, albeit only in a footnote, the unequal contributions that the contextual effects of divorce on males and females make to the aggregate correlation. As he writes (Durkheim, 1951: 273, note 20): "... as the wife's share in the total number of suicides is very slight, the decrease in female suicides is imperceptible in the whole and does not balance the increase of male suicides. Thus divorce is ultimately associated with a rise in the total number of suicides."

9. While the exclusive use of aggregate data is clearly the main obstacle to the empirical isolation of contextual mechanisms, even the combination of micro-level and macro-level information may raise difficulties in some situations. This is because of the functional dependency between the individual and the aggregate variables. For a more detailed treatment of this issue, see Moksony (1990b: 134) as well as the references given there.

10. To avoid unnecessary complexities, I do not consider possible sex differences either.

11. If we were really to estimate the parameters of this model, we would, of course, hardly use the binary variable suicide in its raw form. Instead, we would transform it to avoid the problems associated with the linear probability model, especially when, as in the case of rare events such as suicide, the distribution of the dependent variable is extremely skewed. One common transformation is to take the log odds of suicide (also called the logit) as the variable to be explained and employ what is known as logistic regression. My purpose here is, however, not the real estimation of the model; that is why I decided to present it in its simplest form.

12. Given the small number of suicides, we would, of course, usually multiply this figure by, say, 1,000,000 to get rid of the many zeros, thus transforming proportions into rates.

13. The lack of the additive term implies that the slope for divorced is zero.

14. Of course, even the most atomistic approach acknowledges social interaction when it uses concepts such as norms, values or socialization. The impact of factors of this sort is, however, different form contextual effects. It is not situation-bounded; that is, it becomes built into individuals and people carry it with them, so to speak, as they move from one setting to the next. Contextual effects, in contrast, are specific to the very place in which action occurs. The problem with the atomistic approach, then, is not that it disregards the social determination of behavioral dispositions; rather, it is that it disregards the social forces operating in the behavioral situation. For a useful discussion of the distinction made here, see Granovetter (1985).

REFERENCES

Ahlburg, D.A., and Schapiro, M.O. Socioeconomic ramifications of changing cohort size: an analysis of U.S. postwar suicide rates by age and sex. *Demography*, 1984, 21, 97-108.

Barton, A.H. Bringing society back in. Survey research and macro-methodology. *American Behavioral Scientist*, 1968, 12, 1-9. Coleman, J.S. Relational analysis: the study of social organizations with survey methods. *Human Organization*, 1958, 17, 28-36.

Coleman, J.S. Social theory, social research and a theory of action. *American Journal of Sociology*, 1986, 91, 1309-1335.

Durkheim, E. Suicide. *A Study in Sociology* (Translated by J.A. Spaulding and G. Simpson). New York: Free Press, 1951.

Durkheim, E. *A Társadalmi Tények Magyarázatához* (On the Explanation of Social Facts). Budapest: Közgazdasági és Jogi Könyvkiadó, 1978.

Farber, M.L. *Theory of Suicide*. New York. 1968.

Gibbs, J.P. Introduction. In J.P. Gibbs (ed.), *Suicide*. New York: Harper & Row, 1968.

Granovetter, M. Threshold models of collective behavior. *American Journal of Sociology*, 1978, 83, 1420-1443.

Granovetter, M. Economic action and social structure: the problem of embeddedness. *American Journal of Sociology*, 1985, 91, 481-510.

Hammond, J.L. Two sources of error in ecological correlations. *American Sociological Review*, 1973, 38, 764-777.

Hanushek, E.A., and Jackson, J.E. *Statistical Methods for Social Scientists*. New York: Academic Press, 1977.

Inkeles, A. Personality and social structure. In R.K. Merton, L. Broom, and L.S. Cottrell (eds.), *Sociology Today: Problems and Prospects*. New York: Harper & Row, 1965.

Kendall, P.L., and Lazarsfeld, P.F. Problems of survey analysis. In R.K. Merton and P.F. Lazarsfeld (eds.), *Continuities in Social Research*. Glencoe, IL: Free Press, 1950.

Kuhn, T.S. *A Tudományos Forradalmak Szerkezete* (The Structure of Scientific Revolutions). Budapest: Gondolat Kiadó, 1984.

Merton, R.K. *Social Theory and Social Structure*. Glencoe, IL: Free Press, 1957.

Moksony, F. Is the whole more than the sum of its parts? The contribution of contextual analysis to macrosociology. Paper presented at the conference "The Micro-Macro Link in Contemporary Sociology," Dubrovnik, Yugoslavia, 1990a.

Moksony, F. Ecological analysis of suicide: problems and prospects. In D. Lester (ed.), *Current Concepts of Suicide*. Philadelphia: Charles Press, 1990b.

Rex, J. The main types of sociological theory. In J. Rex (ed.), *Discovering Sociology*. London: Routledge & Kegan Paul, 1973.

Selvin, H.C. Durkheim's Suicide and problems of empirical research. *American Journal of Sociology*, 1958, 63, 607-619.

Stinchcombe, A.L. *Constructing Social Theories*. New York: Harcourt, Brace & World, 1968.

Stouffer, S.A., Suchman, E.A., DeVinney, L.C., Star, S.A., and Williams, R.M. *The American Soldier: Adjustment During Army Life, Vol.1*. Princeton, NJ: Princeton University Press, 1949.

7

"Suicide and the Birth Rate, A Study in Moral Statistics": A Translation and Commentary

Barclay D. Johnson, PhD

For too long, economists have taken a purely deductive approach to the population question.[1] Thanks to recent advances in the field of demography, we no longer have to be satisfied with mere theorizing about the abstract principle of the struggle for survival, or about the likelihood that production will sooner or later reach its extreme limit. This approach has not brought us one step closer to solving the problem because, however generally the law of competition may apply, it does not determine every social phenomenon all by itself. The attempt to use this single principle to solve the complex population question has yielded only partial solutions. Furthermore, nothing is more futile than to speculate about the future levels of population and of consumer goods. These will be determined by a thousand circumstances which the observer can neither know nor predict. Science studies first what is. Only then does it attempt to predict what will be, and it can only predict the future when it has a clear understanding of the present. Thus, the only way to decide whether an increase in population is good or bad for a country is to observe those societies where this growth is occurring and those in which it is not, and then to compare the two.

Nevertheless, we must be careful in choosing the social fact that we are going to examine. People often think that the happiness of individuals and societies increases proportionately as more goods are consumed. It has been suggested that a nation which consumes more will probably be happier, and

I am grateful to Fernand Fontaine, Judah Matras, W. Dain Oliver, and Whitney Pope for their comments on earlier versions of this translation.

some have inferred from this that to solve overpopulation one needs merely to determine whether changes in levels of consumption vary with changes in the birth rate.[2] But to say this would be to disregard the degree to which happiness is a relative matter. Improved circumstances do not make people happier if the needs that they feel increase equally or more so. If needs increase as soon as they are satisfied, they are not fulfilled; the gap between need and satisfaction remains the same. This is an elementary psychological fact which economists have not taken seriously enough.

The health of a society depends on many causes. The growth of resources, common and private, is only one of these. Often, it is not even one of the most important. In order for society to feel a sense of well-being, it is neither sufficient nor always necessary for it to burn a lot of coal or consume a lot of meat. What is necessary is that all of its functions develop in a way which is regular, harmonious, and proportionate.

The truth is that we do not have a criterion which permits us to measure the happiness of a society in a precise way. But it is possible to estimate the relative health or sickness of a society, because we can employ a rather well-known fact which expresses social ills numerically. That fact is the relative number of suicides. Without going into the psychology of this phenomenon here, it is certain that a consistent increase in suicide always points to a serious disturbance of the organic conditions of society. For these abnormal acts to increase, conditions of suffering must also have increased, and at the same time the power of the organism to resist must have decreased.

In this way, we can be sure that societies in which suicides are most frequent are less healthy than are those other societies in which suicide is less common. This observation provides us with a way of treating the controversial population problem. If it can be shown that an increase in the birth rate is accompanied by a rise in the number of suicides, we will be justified in inferring that too high a birth rate is an unhealthy phenomenon, detrimental to society. On the other hand, an opposite relationship would suggest the opposite conclusion.

Several facts which demographers have already pointed out seem to confirm the first of these propositions. Suicides are numerous in countries where the population is too concentrated. They decrease whenever emigration, acting as a safety valve, relieves the society of its excess population.[3] If we were to limit our attention to these observations alone, we would see Malthusianism proved by statistics. I have no intention of challenging these facts. But I would like to offer, in contrast to them, other facts which are no less numerous and no less important: If an excessive birth rate promotes suicide, an insufficient birth rate produces exactly the same result. Indeed, the purpose of the present study is precisely to call attention to the facts which prove the truth of this law, and then to interpret it.

SUICIDE AND THE BIRTH RATE IN
VARIOUS EUROPEAN COUNTRIES

If we put the European countries with high suicide rates into one category, and those with lower rates into another, and if we look at the average birth rates of the two types of societies, we obtain the results shown in Table 1.[4]

Table 1.

Country and time period	Suicides per million inhabitants	Births per thousand inhabitants
Countries where suicide is more frequent		
Denmark (1866-75)	267	30.9
France (1871-75)	150	25.7
Switzerland (1876)	196	30.4
Prussia (1871-75)	133	38.5
Austria (excluding Hungary) (1873-77)	122	38.7
Bavaria (1871-76)	90	39.2
Sweden (1871-75)	81	30.4
Norway (1866-73)	74	30.3
England and Wales (1871-76)	70	35.5
Average	131	33.3
Countries where suicide is less frequent		
Hungary (1864-65)	52	41.7
Belgium (1866-75)	67	32.1
Holland (1869-72)	35	35.6
Italy (1874-76)	31	37.1
Finland (1869-76)	31	34.5
Spain (1866-70)	17	35.7
Romania (dates not given)	25	30.2
Scotland (dates not given)	34	35.1
Average	36	35.7

Thus, in countries where suicide is more common there are 33.3 births for each 1000 inhabitants. But in countries with fewer suicides there are 35.7 births for each 1000 inhabitants. It is true that the difference between these two groups of countries is not very great. If we had no other proof to support our thesis, we would have to admit that the relationship between suicide and the birth rate is only remote and vague. But this first proof should not be slighted. We will give it greater importance when we realize that the growth of the suicide rate depends upon innumerable conditions, of which a low birth rate is only one. Since it does depend on so many factors, it is striking that the influence of the birth rate can be detected. To appreciate the significance of this fact, one must recognize that in some of the countries in the first group the abundance of suicides is certainly not due to a birth rate which is too low but rather to one which is too high. This is certainly the case in Germany. The presence of that prolific country in the first of our two groups is by itself enough to raise noticeably the average birth rate of the countries in that group. Indeed, if one omits Prussia and Bavaria from that group, here is what we find:

- In countries where suicide is more common, the average birth rate is 31.7 per 1000.
- In countries where suicide is less common, the average birth rate is 35.7.

The influence of a low birth rate on suicide can be seen even when the distorting case of Germany is included in the computation. This is so because this influence is so pervasive. Thus, Morselli, from whom we have taken the above table, cannot keep from recognizing this fact, even though he declines to explain it. He suggests that it should be submitted to a more detailed examination.[5] This is just what we will try to do.

This initial examination of evidence is doubly instructive. It provides us with a first proof of our hypothesis, though an imperfect one. It also indicates where we must seek the elements of a more complete proof. Clearly, we will find the facts we need neither in the countries where the birth rate is very high nor where it is only moderate. In the first countries, the birth rate would tend above all to produce suicide rather than to prevent it. In the others, we would not have a sufficiently varied set of observations. Thus, we must look at a nation in which the average birth rate is low. France satisfies that requirement only too well.

SUICIDE AND POPULATION GROWTH
IN THE DEPARTMENTS OF FRANCE

The birth rate is often measured by subtracting the number of stillborn babies from the annual number of births, and dividing the remainder (So) by the total population (N). In this way, one arrives at what is called the general birth rate.[6] But this measure is very imperfect, because the population as a whole includes a large number of children and old people, persons who either cannot reproduce yet or no longer can do so. Since these persons are unequally distributed geographically, it would be misleading to use this measure to compare the birth rates of the departments. Where children and old people are most numerous, the birth rate would appear to be lower, because they would increase the denominator N in the value So/N. For this reason, in calculating the birth rate, it would be better when possible to eliminate from N all those incapable of reproducing. In other words, it would be better to divide the annual number of births by the total number of fertile women, age 15 to 50.

But in this way one obtains the average rate of fertility,[7] and that is not what interests us right now. We want to study the social function of the birth rate, which is to maintain the life of the society. It is clear that we cannot appreciate the way in which that function is fulfilled by looking at the birth rate alone. Since deaths are the gaps which births will fill, we must take them into account also. The same reproductive activity can be a strengthening or a weakening factor, depending on whether the losses to be made up are more or less numerous. In other words, the only thing that matters to us is the socially useful effect of births, and this can only be expressed in relation to mortality. A prolific society in which mortality is also high is no better off than another in which there are fewer births and also fewer deaths. This is why we will compare the suicide rates in the different French departments not with the birth rate as such, whether general or special, but with the growth of population which results from an excess of births over deaths. This has been correctly called physiological growth. Population growth calculated in this way has the additional great advantage of not taking into account migration from one department to another, which clearly can only hinder our inquiry.

In the *Compte Général pour l'Administration de la Justice Criminelle en France* for the year 1880, M. Yvernès divided the departments into six classes, according to their annual rates of suicide from 1830 to 1880.[8] Let us look at the average physiological growth of each of these six classes, whether in that period or in something close to it. I will use M. Bertillon's figures for the first 69 years of this century (1801-69).[9]

In addition, since the first of these six groups includes only one department, the Seine, I include it in the second group in the figures shown in Table 2.

One sees from this table that average physiological growth rises, in a progressive and regular manner, as the suicide rate decreases. The two parallel movements continue from the first to the last group of departments, without interruption and without exception. Thus, we can conclude that these two social facts vary in inverse proportion to each other.

It is true that in this way we have compared only averages. But it has been necessary to proceed in this way because of the many accidental and local causes upon which the compared phenomena depend. If one examines a large enough number of departments, these causes must cancel each other out. Even so, if

Table 2.

Suicide Rate (1830-79) and Physiological Growth (1801-69) in the Departments of France

Department	Births per 1000 women, 15-50 minus crude death rate.[1]
1st Group (28-39 suicides yearly per 100,000 population)	
Seine	2.4
Seine-et-Oise	0.7
Seine-et-Marne	2.6
Marne	2.6
Oise	1.5
Average Increase	1.96[2]
2nd Group (17-21 suicides yearly per 100,000 population)	
Seine-Inférieure	3.6
Aisne	4.3
Aube	2.0
Eure-et-Loir	2.1
Var	0.3
Average Increase	2.46
3rd Group (12-16 suicides yearly per 100,000 population)	
Eure[3]	-0.6
Charente-Inférieure	1.7
Vaucluse	4.5
Basses-Alpes	2.9
Bouches-du-Rhône	2.0
Pas-de-Calais	5.6
Ardennes	6.0
Meuse	3.7
Côte-d'Or	2.8
Indre-et-Loire	2.5
Drôme	5.6
Somme	3.5
Rhône	5.8
Yonne	2.2
Loire-et-Cher	3.7
Loiret	3.4
Average Increase	3.46

Table 2. cond.

Department	Births per 1000 women, 15-50 minus crude death rate.[1]
4th Group (5-11 suicides yearly per 100,000 population)	
Doubs	5.1
Jura	2.7
Haute-Saône	4.7
Dordogne	3.4
Cher	7.8
Indre	6.2
Nièvre	5.9
Deux-Sèvres	4.8
Tarn-et-Garonne	0.6
Gironde	2.1
Isère	5.5
Maine-et-Loire	3.6
Saône-et-Loire	5.6
Mayenne	3.9
Haute-Marne	3.4
Calvados	-0.1
Hérault	4.0
Lot-et-Garonne	0.3
Orne	1.4
Sarthe	3.4
Manche	2.1
Charente	2.3
Nord	7.0
Corrèze	6.1
Haute-Vienne	4.7
Loire	8.3
Aude	5.1
Pyrénées-Orientales	6.6
Vosges	6.4
Ardèche	7.2
Landes	4.6
Basses-Pyrénées	4.9
Vendée	6.2
Vienne	5.6
Côtes-du-Nord	3.7
Finistère	5.0
Ille-et-Vilaine	2.8
Loire-Inférieure	5.7
Morbihan	4.4
Allier	5.7
Ain	2.3
Hautes-Alpes	3.5
Gard	5.5

Table 2. cond.

Department	Births per 1000 women, 15-5 minus crude death rate.[1]
5th Group (2-4 suicides yearly per 100,000 population)	
Corse	6.2
Creuse	6.3
Aveyron	5.6
Lozère	5.9
Hautes-Pyrénées	5.9
Cantal	3.8
Haute-Loire	5.5
Ariège	6.3
Tarn	5.4
Haute-Garonne	4.4
Gers	1.0
Lot	3.1
Puy-de-Dôme	3.6
Average Increase	4.85

[1] Durkheim calls this column "Yearly Surplus of Births over 1000 Deaths (1801-1869)."
[2] The average growth rates of the groups of departments, aside from the 4th group, appear to have been miscalculated. Correct figures have been substituted.
[3] M. Bertillion's table assigns a growth rate of +0.6 to Eure; we think that this figure involves a mistake in sign, and we have corrected it. We have also corrected his figure for the Calvados.

we are not satisfied with averages and choose to analyze the individual figures in the tables above, we will find nothing which disproves our conclusion.

In fact, for the whole of France, or rather for the 82 French departments which we have considered, the average growth in population is 4 (4.3 to be exact). Thus, if we look at how many departments are above and below the average in each of the five groups, we find that they are composed as shown in Table 3.

Thus, the groups of departments which have the most suicides are made up almost entirely of departments in which the population increase is below average. Then the relation reverses itself little by little, as the rate of suicides increases. The same result can be expressed in this way: Of the 26 departments which have the most suicides (the first, second and third groups), 20 show a population increase less than average, and of the 41 departments in which the increase is average or above, 25, or more than three quarters, belong to the fourth and fifth groups, those in which the number of suicides is lowest.[10]

Table 3.

Group and Frequency	Below the average increase in population	Above the average increase in population
1st Group (28-39 suicides)	100 % of the group	0 % of the group
2nd Group (17-21 suicides)	80 % of the group	20.% of the group
3rd Group (12-16 suicides)	68.8% of the group[1]	31.3% of the group
4th Group (5-11 suicides)	41.9% of the group	58.1% of the group
5th Group (2-4 suicides)	30.8% of the group	69.2% of the group

[1] Durkheim gives 68 and 32 percent for the third group, 40 and 60 percent for the fourth, and 13 and 77 percent for the fifth. These figures have been corrected.

THE EVIDENCE SEEN IN THE OPPOSITE WAY

Let us verify the above results by looking at the evidence the other way around. Let us group departments according to their physiological growth, and then look at the average rate of suicide of each department in each of the groups which has been defined in this way. The averages are based on the five years from 1872 to 1876. No doubt the period is short and does not correspond as closely as we would like to the period used to determine population growth. But these figures are the only ones at our disposal. M. Yvernès, in his *Compte Général,* provides us with only the upper and lower limits of each of his classes; he does not give the average number of suicides for each department. It is true that we could have calculated it ourselves, but we have drawn back from the considerable labor which would have been involved, a task which seems unnecessary in view of the agreement of all the proofs above and those which follow. Moreover, since suicide has evolved in a much more regular way than population growth since the beginning of this century, it is not as important to go further and establish its annual total over a very extended period.

We will divide the departments again, this time into four groups based upon their average growth (see Table 4).

This second examination confirms the previous one, and clearly shows the inverse relation between growth and suicide. The group of departments in which population growth is lowest is the one in which suicide is most frequent. From group to group, the second of these terms decreases as the first rises.

If, as before, we wish to go beyond mere averages, we obtain the following results: For the 82 departments studied, the yearly average of suicides per one million people is 138.9. Growth is greatest in the third and fourth groups, and these two groups include 36 departments. Of these 36 departments, only five have a higher than average number of suicides. Moreover, these five exceptions are all found in the third group. Not one of them is in the fourth.

But we can carry the analysis further.

Table 4.

Physiological Growth (1801-69) and the Suicide Rate (1872-76) in the Departments of France

Department	Suicides per year per million population[1]
1st Group (population growth of -0.6 to 2.5 - 20 departments)	
Eure	255.1
Calvados	147.5
Var	22.2
Lot-et-Garonne	84.5
Tarne-et-Garonne	74.0
Seine-et-Oise	388.8
Gers	61.8
Orne	96.9
Oise	407.2
Charente-Inferieure	160.2
Bouches-du-Rhône	202.9
Aube	284.8
Eure-et-Loir	273.5
Gironde	122.5
Manche	84.5
Yonne	219.3
Ain	128.2
Charente	164.3
Seine	400.3
Indre-et-Loire	213.2
Average	199.5
2nd Group (population growth of 2.6 to 4.5 - 26 departments)	
Marne	380.6
Seine-et-Marne	383.5
Jura	123.0
Haute-Marne	141.7[2]
Dordogne	115.3
Loiret	206.7
Ille-et-Vilaine	69.2
Côte-d'Or	187.4
Basses-Alpes	195.2
Lot	58.9
Sarthe	141.7
Hautes-Alpes	115.3
Somme	206.7
Seine-Inférieure	155.3
Maine-et-Loire	99.2
Puy-de-Dôme	219.3
Loire-et-Cher	186.0
Meuse	212.8

Table 4. cond.

Department	Suicides per year per million population[1]
2nd Group con't. population growth of 2.6 to 4.5 - 26 departments)	
Mayenne	82.7
Hérault	78.1
Haute-Garonne	65.9
Aisne	297.9
Morbihan	64.8
Vaucluse	208.7
Average	158.07[3]
3rd Group (population growth of 4.6 to 6.0 - 24 departments)	
Landes	83.1
Haute-Saône	118.1
Haute-Vienne	101.1
Basses-Pyrénées	64.2
Deux-Sèvres	111.0
Finistère	108.2
Doubs	113.9
Aude	74.8
Tarn	55.0
Haute-Loire	45.9
Isère	97.9
Gard	114.7
Aveyron	39.7
Drôme	162.2
Vienne	93.5
Pas-de-Calais	146.8
Saône-et-Loire	144.7
Allier	83.9
Loire-Inférieure	76.0
Rhône	166.8
Hautes-Pyrénées	39.9
Nièvre	94.1
Lozère	54.6
Ardennes	166.7
Average	98.2
4th Group (population growth from 6.1 to 8.3 - 12 departments)	
Corrèze	69.3
Corse	28.6
Indre	66.2
Ariège	103.6
Creuse	30.8
Vosges	69.2

Table 4. cond.

Department	Suicides per year per million population[1]
4th Group con't. (population growth of 6.1 to 8.3 - 12 departments)	
Pyrénées-Orientales	126.2
Nord	76.0
Ardèche	109.9
Vendée	84.6
Cher	104.9
Loire	70.8
Average	78.3

[1] Durkheim does not include the source of the suicide rates in Table 4. They are found in Morselli, *Suicide,* English editions, p. 43, and also on the folded map inside the back cover, "Intensity of Suicide in France in Each Department."

[2] In the chart below, the three departments on the left are listed consecutively, as they appear in Table 4. The three departments on the right are also listed consecutively, as they appear in the same table, but with the addition of the suicide rates that were originally assigned to them by Morselli.

Haute-Marne	141.7	Sarthe	141.7	(Morselli: 155.8)
Dordogne	115.3	Hautes-Alpes	115.3	(Morselli: 99.2)
Loiret	206.7	Somme	206.7	(Morselli: 219.3)

[3] The average growth rate of the third group of departments in Table 4 seems to be miscalculated. A correct figure has been substituted.

The highest suicide rate is 407.2 (the department of l'Oise) and the lowest is 28.6 (Corsica). Let us divide the interval which separates these extreme rates into four sets of departments, based on their rates of suicide. Then let us take note of the four groups of departments which have been defined on the basis of growth. Now we may ask about each of these four groups, In how many departments does the suicide rate exceed 300, in how many is it between 201 and 300, between 101 and 200, and between 28.6 and 100? The result of this procedure is expressed in Table 5.

It is enough to glance at the table to see confirmation of the relationship which has been stated.[11]

SUICIDE AND POPULATION GROWTH IN RELATION TO POPULATION DENSITY

This relationship also manifests itself in other ways. It is known that in France, as well as in all other European countries, suicides are much more common in cities than in rural areas. "[F]rom 1873 to 1878, 18,470 suicides were

Table 5.

Departments	In how many departments is the suicide rate between:				
	301 and 407	201 and 300	101 and 200	28.6 and 100	Total number of departments
1st Group[1] (growth between -0.6 and 2.5)	3	7	5	5	20
2nd Group (growth between 2.6 and 4.5 -the first two of the group[3])	2	6	9[2]	9	26
3rd Group (growth between 4.6 and 6.0)	0	0	11	13	24
4th Group (growth between 6.1 and 8.3)	0	0	4	8	12
Total	5	13	29	35	82

[1] The limits that define the four groups based on growth in Table 5 seem to include four typographical errors. These limits have been corrected to make them agree with the corresponding limits in Table 4.

[2] Durkheim gives the figures for the 2nd Group in the third and fourth columns as 8 and 10, respectively. These figures, and the two column totals, have been corrected.

[3] We learn from Tables 2 and 4 that these two departments (in the second row of this table) are Marne and Seine-et-Marne. Durkheim is pointing out that these two departments have the lowest rates of birth and the highest rates of suicide of the 26 departments. His implied point is that the two conform to his law and thus are an item of internal replication.

average, based on these numbers and the rural and urban populations as of 1876, we find that the suicide rate per million inhabitants in rural areas is 123.48, and that in cities it is 221.44."[12] Thus, if we were not mistaken in what we have said already, we would expect the population of cities to grow much less than does the population of rural areas. This is indeed what happens.

If one looks only at the chief town of each of the departments, he learns not only that the growth in these towns is very low, but that there are more deaths than births. In 1880 (and the same thing has been happening every year) 71 out of 86 of these towns had more deaths than births. The 15 which are exceptions to the rule are the following:

Nice, [283]. Privas, 102. Mézières, 5. Tulle, 231. Châteauroux, 43. [Mende, 1]. Saint-Étienne, 266. Chaumont, 62. Lille, 658. Tarbes, 39. Perpignan, 2. La Roche-sur-Yon, 2. Limoges, 57. Épinal, 4. Périgueux, 3.

The total increase of these 15 cities is 1758, whereas the deficit in the 71 others rises to the enormous figure of 13,641.[13]

For the urban and rural populations taken together, the statistics in France for 1884 are as follows:

- Urban population (all towns with more than 2000 inhabitants): 13,400,000 people.
- Rural population: 24,500,000 people.

The first figure is more than half as large as the second, and consequently we may say that the increase in the urban population should be more than half of the increase of the rural population. In reality it is only one ninth of it. In fact, in that same year of 1884 urban population growth was 8363, whereas rural population growth was 70,661.

In other words, if we represent the first figure by 100, we must represent the second not by 200 but by 875.

Finally, if we compare these two populations from the point of view not of population growth but of the birth rate alone, we get comparable results. Thus, we find[14] that for the year 1861 for the Seine [the French department which includes Paris], the birth rate is 21.1, for all other cities it is 34.5, and for rural areas it is 38.7.

This unequal population growth in cities and the country has long been recognized. M. Maurice Block[15] believed that it occurs because people marry sooner in rural areas than in cities. However, it is difficult to understand how the delay of a few years could produce such a large difference in the rates of growth of the two populations. More to the point, the connection which we have just drawn between population growth and the suicide rate proves that a declining population is a much more important phenomenon, and depends on deeper moral causes.

FAMILY SIZE AND SUICIDE ACCORDING TO OCCUPATION[16]

It is well known that occupations sometimes have a very marked effect on suicide. Thus, there is reason to study also their influence on population growth.

Although it is not known precisely how much each occupation influences the tendency to suicide, it has been proved that the occupation in which suicide is committed least is farming, and that the occupations in which suicide is committed most often are the liberal professions. In between are commerce and industry, though we cannot be certain which of the two has more suicides. However, those in commerce seem a little more prone than are those in industry. The influence of occupation on suicide has been studied the most in Italy. The table which Morselli has drawn up[17] is given here (see Table 7).

As can be seen, there are very few suicides among farmers, miners and

Table 7.

Occupational area	Number of suicides per million individuals in each occupation
Letters and science	618.3
Military	404.1
Public administration	324.3
Commerce	246.5
Law	217.8
Teachers	175.3
Medical professions	163.3
Transportation	154.7
Owners of personal and real property	133.5
Fine arts	94.0
Industrial production	56.7
Religion	45.3
Primary industry	25.0

trappers, few also among industrial workers, and more among workers in commerce. The liberal professions furnish an enormous number. We may suppose that these relationships are about the same in France. We find that population growth shows the opposite relation.[18]

According to the *Statistique de France*,[19] if we ignore domestic workers, we see that the average farm-owning family has 3.53 members, that in industry the average family size descends to 2.98, in commerce to 2.73, and among those in letters and science to 1.74. Thus, farm families are on the average almost one-sixth larger than are those of industrial workers, and more than one-fifth larger than those of men devoted to letters and science.[20] In short, the occupations in which people kill themselves most are also those in which there are the fewest births, and vice versa.

CONCLUSION

Now that the law has been established, it remains to interpret it.

The first conclusion which follows from the above is that the birth rate, when it is too low, is a pathological phenomenon. However one explains suicide, we have seen that it is always an index of sickness, and that it can only grow if this sickness itself grows. Since a low birth rate and an aggravation of the tendency to suicide are associated as regularly as we have just seen, we are justified in regarding them as two phenomena of the same species, and in attributing to the former the morbid character which everyone recognizes in the latter. As a result of their parallel development, the abnormal nature of one reveals the abnormal nature of the other.

Many sociologists have already claimed that too low a birth rate is harmful and a sickness for society. This study proves that it is also a misfortune and a sickness for individuals. A society which grows steadily is not only stronger and more capable of holding its own against rival societies, but the members who make it up have better chances of survival. They are physiologically more vigorous and have a greater power of resistance. Speaking of countries in which the birth rate is too low, M. Bertillon has said that such countries convert part of what would have been their descendants into savings, that is, into capital.[21] We have seen above how disastrous such an investment is both for society and for each individual.

But, as we said at the start, we do not mean to maintain that this relationship holds true for all levels of the birth rate.

Instead, it seems that when the birth rate reaches too high a level it becomes, again and for another reason, a cause of suicides. In a society in which the population multiplies too quickly, the struggle of life becomes too harsh, and individuals more easily relinquish an existence which has become too painful. These two propositions, although seemingly contradictory, are actually in agreement. It must not be forgotten that the birth rate is a social fact, and thus a living reality. There is no attribute of an organism which is good without any limit, and in an absolute sense. Every biological development is healthy only within limits. There is a normal zone for all living phenomena, below and above which they become pathological. This is true of the birth rate.

This is the meaning of the relationship we have established. But what is the cause of it? Once we have stated it, we must explain it. How is it that, within certain limits at least, the curve of the birth rate falls as that of suicide rises, and inversely?

Of course, these two facts, the rise in suicides and the decrease in births, must have one or several causes in common. But what are these causes?

As M. Bertillon has said somewhere, suicide is always a symptom of an organism in disequilibrium. But this lack of equilibrium can be due either to organic or to social causes. Sometimes it is the being himself who is tainted: it is his functions which are distorted and changed, even though his environment is healthy. Sometimes it is the environment itself which is not normal. Very probably there is no suicide in which these two causes do not operate together at the same time. A perfectly intact organism would resist its environment, and if the environment had no pathology in it, the morbid germs which the organism might contain could not develop. But if these two causes are always present, it is sometimes one and sometimes the other which has the greater influence, and which marks the suicide with its own character. Sometime suicides have been divided into two great types: those which are absurd, and those which are comprehensible and thought out. The first are those which result almost entirely from organic defects and in which social causes play only an occasional role. The others, on the contrary, derive logically from the nature of the environment and are for that reason intelligible.

The first of these causes is not common to the two phenomena being compared, and thus cannot account for the relationship between them.

It is a proven truth of demography that the birth rate is only very slightly dependent on race. A race is prolific or not according to the circumstances and environment in which it happens to be. The French race in France scarcely makes up for its yearly losses; in Canada, it multiplies with great rapidity. The Norman race is very fertile in England; it is very slightly so in Normandy. These facts, and others which could be mentioned, prove that the birth rate depends much less on organic predispositions than on the ruling customs and ideas in the society. Although the sterility of an individual can be due to a physiological condition, the sterility of a group results from other causes. Moreover, we know that when sterility prevails in a group it constitutes a desired practice, a sort of discipline, to which individuals submit themselves deliberately. It is not imposed on them by organic necessity. It is true that the departments in which there are the most suicides and the fewest births are also those in which there are the largest numbers of lunatics. But that only proves that madness, like suicide and births, is not only a result of individual and chance variations, but in large measure of social causes. Damaged nervous systems become more numerous in a group not only because of unfortunate cross-breeding and hereditary predispositions but also because of the bad social conditions in which individuals are placed. Organic causes are often only social causes transformed and fixed in the organism. Thus, only social causes are common to suicide and the birth rate, and can account for the relationship between them.

To determine more precisely the exact nature of these causes, let us consider the birth rate along with several other facts which equally confer immunity to suicide. We know that married couples are much less exposed to suicide than single people are, and that fathers are less exposed than are husbands without children. Where family bonds are strong, where domestic traditions are so strong that they resist struggles within the family which would otherwise dissolve a marriage—in short, where divorces and separations are rare, suicides are rare also, and where the former conditions are common the latter are also. All these facts prove that where the family exists it protects against suicide, and that the more alive and united it is, the more protection it confers. A high birth rate presupposes large families. But such families are only possible when men have a taste and habit for family solidarity, and prefer the pleasures of a common life over material comfort. Undoubtedly, these preferences usually become fixed, in an instinctive and unreflective way. But what if they do? Whether they are consciously worked out or not, they are not likely to change. It has often been said that families have become smaller because the parents are unwilling to compromise either their own well-being or that of their children. Perhaps so, but material prosperity would not have gained such importance in popular opinion if the joys of collective life had not also lost importance. Thus, any drop in the birth rate implies a weakening of family spirit. The latter, as we have just seen, also promotes suicide. It must, then, be the cause of both of them which we are trying to discover. If suicide grows when the birth rate declines, it is because these two phenomena are equally due, in part, to a decrease in family feeling.

But from where does this beneficial character of the family come? Surely not from the economic advantage which the family offers. When one thinks of the cares, the increased labor, the responsibilities, and the sorrows of all sorts which large families bring, who would dare to say that the balance of purely utilitarian advantages and inconveniences works out as a benefit or a deficit? Indeed, from this point of view, it is difficult to see why there are families at all, and one is forced, as M. Renan somewhere is, to regard paternal love as a device which has been contrived by nature in opposition to individuals, in order to compel them to serve its ends. Given what has been said above, only one answer to the question is possible. Family life is natural to the human organism as evolution has made him. As he is now constituted, man is made for union with some of his fellows in a more intimate community than is provided either by relationships in the world at large or by mere friendship. It is easy to explain why this need was born, and why it has become stronger since. Within his family, the individual belongs to a compact whole, with which he has solidarity, and which strengthens him. In this way, his power of resistance is increased. The less isolated he is, the better armed he is for the struggle. When, on the other hand, families are loosely knit and small in numbers, individuals, since they are less drawn together, allow spaces to exist between them. The cold wind of egoism blows through these spaces, and it chills the heart and weakens courage.

This short study is one more proof in support of this truth, that with regard to social questions the social approach is the most important. Usually the birth rate is studied mainly with regard to its economic consequences. Its effect on production or on the distribution of products, that is, on individual interests, is examined, and it is believed that changes in the birth rate can be explained by reference to these considerations alone. We have just seen that the birth rate is essentially a condition and index of the health of societies. Utilitarian calculations are too subtle to enter into the thinking of most people, and they do not change this state of health so much as social sentiments do. If these sentiments are present, they draw individuals into group life. If they are absent, people are diverted from it. It is the same with suicide. Often suicide has been attributed to the conflict of individual interests, and increases in suicide have been attributed to the growing intensity of competition, of the struggle for life (Morselli).[22] But it is also due to other, distinctly social, or, if one prefers, moral, causes. We have just pointed to one to these causes, and it is perhaps one of the most important ones.

COMMENTARY

Why should we study "Suicide et Natalité"? The brief answer is that Durkheim wrote it, it is about suicide, and it has not been available in English. In this unique document, Durkheim tries to account for variations in suicide rates when he is just beginning to study them, nine years before his book, *Suicide,* is to appear.

The indisputable value of the paper lies in what it reveals about Durkheim's intellectual development. "Suicide et Natalité" has been called a "highly illuminating source of information regarding the state of Durkheim's early thinking about explanations of suicide" (Huff, 1975). It can serve as a corrective to the common practice of approaching *Suicide* in something of a vacuum, without giving due attention to the man who wrote it, or to the setting in which he wrote.

Social and Intellectual Background

The decline in the French birth rate

Something may be said about the situation in which the essay was written— about the rates of birth and suicide in France and in Europe, and about some of the authors who influenced Durkheim.

For hundreds of years, France was the most powerful and populous country in Europe. But there came a time when her population grew more slowly than those of other countries. Before the year 1800, she was outstripped by Russia. Growing still more slowly in the nineteenth century, she was overtaken by Germany, Austria-Hungary, and Britain. Her relative decline in population occurred mostly because of a low birth rate among the married (Spengler, 1968).

The demographic transition is a model which describes how a premodern population, with high rates of birth and death, becomes a modern population, with low rates of birth and death. It is more or less accurate when applied to many countries. But although the population of France was actually the first to begin to modernize, it did not follow the model.

> The first [stage of the transition] began with the decline of mortality, the second with the decline of fertility, and the third with the decline, or at least the stabilization, of the population. In France, however, mortality and fertility fell at the same time. The drop in fertility was...at first [even] more pronounced than the decline in mortality, and perhaps preceded it. Hence the first stage in the demographic revolution did not occur in France, which moved straight into the second stage, only begun by other countries a hundred years later. Now it

I wish to thank Fernand Fontaine, Craig McKie, W. Dain Oliver, and Whitney Pope for their comments on earlier versions of this commentary.

is the first stage which is marked by a considerable increase in population, which is why, during the nineteenth century, the French population increased far less than the populations of surrounding countries: if France had maintained up to 1880 the fertility shown during the eighteenth century, it would have had by 1880 a population of 88 million, whereas it was in reality only 38 million (Bourgeois-Pichat, 1965, p. 490).[23]

In Durkheim's time, many French intellectuals were alarmed by what was happening. One of these was Louis Adolphe Bertillon, who was also a source of data for "Suicide et Natalité." M. Bertillon was one impassioned demographer. I translate his remarks rather freely:

...we have proved that it is only among us [the French] that the birth rate, already low, continues to decline, while those of most of our rivals remain at a high level, and even grow!

Will the downward trend come to an end? It must, unless the decrease is to be no longer merely relative [to the birth rates of other European countries] but absolute. We are in the presence of rival nations whose population growth is three or four times as great as ours. We must do more than merely stop our decline. Our birth rate must climb back up the slope which it has descended. It must be restored to what it once was!

If the present trend persists, where will it take us? We will become one of the least important countries in Europe. And on the earth as a whole, already teeming with throngs of Germans and Anglo-Saxons, we will be no more than a remnant. This result is as inevitable as the calculations which prove it.

Shall we allow this disgrace to happen without defending ourselves—without asking science to tell us the causes of our decline, and the means by which we can oppose it? [We must not let this happen. But if we are to defend ourselves, which of the sciences can help us?]

The science which we need is demography. It must offer to the legislator and the administrator what physics and chemistry now offer to industry. Yet our legislators, and even more our top administrators, do not know that it exists. They don't even know its name. There are, in France, fewer than half a dozen of us working in the field, and we are quite unknown. It is our duty to point out the disturbing demographic trends in France, to indicate their causes, and to determine their origins and their final outcomes.... We may or may not be understood. But we, having foreseen the danger, will have done our duty: To sound a cry of alarm to our imperiled native land! (Bertillon, 1864-1889, p. 491)

In the decades before World War I, those who shared M. Bertillon's anxiety thought that the low population growth of France might be having a number of dire effects. Most important, it was reducing her military power, especially in relation to Germany, whose population was growing rapidly (Spengler, 1968). Germany had won the Franco-Prussian War of 1870-71, and many attributed her victory to her advantageous demographic condition (Teitelbaum and Winter, 1985). That war was short, but it was a shock to the French (Adams, 1983; Swart, 1964). Germany annexed Alsace and southern Lorraine (Grenville, 1976), and the war made her into the preeminent power in Europe, so that the French felt that they could no longer stand up to her.

Some thought that the low French birth rate would be the occasion of further national woes. It was lessening the political prestige and influence of France in Europe. It would make the development of her colonies difficult or impossible. It was creating a labor shortage which was attracting foreign workers, and thus diluting the French racial stock. To Gustave LeBon, "[T]he worst disasters on the fields of battle will be infinitely less fearsome than such invasions." It was his fear that soon a third of those living in France would be German, and another third Italian (quoted in Swart, 1964, p. 173). LeBon's fears seem to be exaggerated. In 1851, immigrants were 1 percent of the French population; in 1872, they were 2 percent (Braudel, 1990). Immigration into the country during the nineteenth century was small potatoes in comparison to more recent French experience.

To some, the low birth rate was evidence of something more all-encompassing: a general loss of national vitality, a state of national decadence[24] (Swart, 1964). Here was a notion with a rather fuzzy empirical meaning and a large moral component. As one specialist in the field of decadence has written, "Until recently,…the best example of a decadent country in western Europe was France. This was not simply the view of France's critics; traumatized by [the war of] 1870 and the [Paris] Commune, the French themselves accepted for decades the stereotype that they were decadent" (Adams, 1983, p. 120).

Most of those who entertained such notions, and who inferred that the French should have more babies, were conservative and Roman Catholic. But others were liberals or socialists (Swart, 1964). Durkheim shared the same concerns, and wrote his paper partly because he was worried about the demographic, military, and moral weakness of France, especially in contrast to Germany. In the Conclusion of the essay, which is mostly about France, he argues explicitly that the French birth rate should be increased.

Despite the concern of some intellectuals, most Frenchmen remained apathetic about the low birth rate (Swart, 1964). The country was, after all, more prosperous than almost any other nation on the continent. There were also French economists and neo-Malthusians, believers in laissez-faire, who thought that population growth depends mainly on economic productivity. They argued that any effort by the state to increase the population would be an undesirable intervention in private affairs. These are the scholars whom Durkheim pooh-poohs in the very first words of his essay.

The rise in suicide

The preoccupation with the French birth rate was part of a larger trend of thought. Long before Durkheim, European governments began to compile statistics on births, deaths, marriages, murders, suicides, and other events thought to be good or bad. This evidence, together with progress in the natural sciences, awakened the belief that a new social science was possible, a science which might be used for social amelioration. The new science was moral statistics.

Durkheim tells us that the "true founder of moral statistics is Pastor Süssmilch," author of *The Divine Ordering of Change in the Human Sexes, as Demonstrated through Birth, Death, and Reproduction,* a three-volume study in theological demography which appeared in 1761[25] (Morselli, 1881, p. 276[26]). Most academic fields originally sprang from the undifferentiated study of divine science. Moral statistics came into being in this way, under the aegis of a man whom Durkheim calls a pastor and Morselli calls a theologian. The very name of the field, moral statistics, an oxymoron to us, aptly reflects the partially differentiated state of the enterprise. Morselli saw fit to argue polemically for metaphysical determinism, though this is not in itself a statistical issue. Durkheim, moving in the direction of further specialization, claimed that the field need take no stand on free will versus determinism. He also had a clearer idea than Morselli of the function of theory in science, as we will see. But even in Durkheim's day the process of differentiation was not complete. For example, he attempted to incorporate literary values into his work to a degree that is unusual in social science today.

If official statistics were to be believed, suicides had been multiplying all over Europe for decades. This trend excited the interest, and indeed the horror, of observers in various countries, and suicide rates were a major concern of the new science. "From statistics collected up to this time, is demonstrated this most painful fact, that suicide has increased from the beginning of the century, and goes on continually increasing in almost all the civilized countries of Europe and of the new world" (Morselli, 1881, p. 15, also pp. 18-22; Durkheim, 1951, pp. 46-51).

France did not have the highest rate of suicide in Europe. But her rate was higher than most, and Paris had the highest rate of any city in the world (Morselli, 1881). "It has been truly said," wrote Alfred Legoyt, an author whom Durkheim cites, "that France is one of the countries where men kill themselves most, and where the population grows the least" (Legoyt, 1881, p. 131). France, then, was unusual in both its low growth and its many suicides. Durkheim wrote his essay partly to learn why this was so, and whether the two unusual conditions might somehow be connected.[27]

Malthus, Darwin and social Darwinism

Some who wanted to interpret trends in births and suicides were attracted to the notion, expressed variously by Thomas Malthus, Herbert Spencer, and Charles Darwin, that the social process is, in Spencer's phrase, a "struggle for existence." The undertaking, called social Darwinism, put together ideas from all these authors, borrowing from Darwin in a rather loose way, and taught that the human struggle for existence is the source of social progress (Oldroyd, 1980).

In its commonest form, social Darwinism favored a policy of laissez-faire in the economy and in government, and taught that social reform was undesirable because it would only inhibit the natural selection which makes for progress (Himmelfarb, 1968). Durkheim was not this kind of social Darwinist, of course; he was highly critical of Spencer's individualism. But in 1888 the more general idea of the struggle for existence was in full flower. Authors with very diverse social ideals embraced it. Durkheim did so too in his early work, both in his article and five years later in the *Division of Labor.*

Morselli

Some social Darwinist ideas are to be found in *Il Suicidio* (1879), the work of the Italian psychiatrist and moral statistician, Enrico Morselli. I believe that Morselli had a greater impact than any other author on both Durkheim's "Suicide et Natalité" and his book, *Suicide.*

The best way to see the relationship between Morselli's work and "Suicide et Natalité" is to leave the essay to one side for a moment, and compare *Il Suicidio,* written nine years before Durkheim's essay, with Durkheim's *Suicide,* written nine years after. A comparison of the two books can help us to put the essay in perspective. They exhibit several similarities and one important difference. Selvin has called attention to one of the similarities: "...Durkheim did not invent the tabular procedures that he used in *Suicide;* he took them over from the 'moral statisticians' of the nineteenth century, especially Morselli, much of whose work on suicide reads like Durkheim's..." (Selvin, 1976, p. 41). Some of the pages of Morselli's book actually *look* like Durkheim's. A number of the tables presented by both authors are "arrays"— lists of cases (countries, religions, or whatever), together with the value of one or more variables for each case (Selvin, 1976; Wallis and Roberts, 1956). Neither book routinely presents tables which cross-classify cases, as do the two-variable tables familiar to us.

A second similarity between the two books is their overlapping content; some of the evidence in Morselli's study reappears in Durkheim's. Morselli's evidence is, if anything, more comprehensive than Durkheim's.

A third similarity is the interest of both authors in "facts" and "laws." For both authors[28], a "law" is a correlation between the suicide rate and some variable which is available from official sources, such as age, nationality, or religion. But in addition to these concrete relations between two variables, each author proposes one or more abstract variable as the actual cause of variation in suicide rates. The result of all of this is an ambiguity, once again in both authors, about what a "law" is. On the one hand, a law specifies a relation between, say, religion and suicide, and thus tells us that religion has *some property* which affects suicide. Looked at in this way, a law is a kind of explanation. On the other hand, the law itself does not say just *what* property of religion affects suicide. From this point of view, a law is little more than a statement that there is an association.

The one important difference between the two authors is their approach to explanation. Often Morselli explains a specific finding not by the application of some abstract principle but by an ad hoc suggestion.[29] For example, he asks why suicides are most common in the first ten days of the month:

> [F]rom whence this fact proceeds is not clear, unless it be that in the first days of each month debauchery, dissipation, orgies, especially in large cities, are more numerous (Morselli, 1881, p. 76). [This independent variable does not reappear in Morselli's account.]
>
> As to the strong tendency towards suicide of the Spanish women, it must be attributed to the force of their passions, which brings them nearer to the male sex, for certainly it is not the effect of the Southern climate, when we see that Italy, which is also insular, does not furnish so high a female proportion (Morselli, 1881, p. 192).

In spite of such atheoretical explanations, Morselli does have a general explanation of variation in suicide. He bases this explanation partly on the ideas of Malthus. When Malthus proposed "...a principle which constantly maintains the population on a level with the means of subsistence...," he was the "first person who recognized the importance of the battle of life for the happiness and moral conditions of men" (Morselli, 1881, pp. 367, 354). Morselli also pays respects to Darwin, whose *Descent of Man* (1871) appeared only eight years before his own book. "All the interesting phenomena of social life...have their origin in that constant struggle of man against nature, against other men, against himself..." (Morselli, 1881, p. 357). Morselli's general explanation of suicide incorporates these social Darwinist ideas:

> Suicide is an effect of the struggle for existence and of human selection, which works according to the laws of evolution among civilized peoples (Morselli, 1881, p. 354). Civilization intensifies the struggle for existence, which becomes more and more a mental one (Morselli, 1881, p. 360). When, in the struggle, the brain breaks down, in the exercise of the brain power some morbid aberration takes place which comes out in madness or that unsatisfied desire which terminates in voluntary death (Morselli, 1881, p. 362).
>
> [T]he principal element of civilization is the cultivation of the intellectual powers (Morselli, 1881, p. 130). Certain it is that in the upper classes of society the act of suicide spreads daily, owing to the direct ratio it has with the increased overuse of the brain power (Morselli, 1881, p. 249). The countries with the highest level of general culture, France and Germany, have the most suicide (Morselli, 1881, pp. 131, 132). The Protestant develops the inner, mental struggle for existence more than the Roman Catholic does, and is thus more prone to suicide (Morselli, 1881, pp. 125-126).

The merits of Morselli's explanation need not concern us right now. My point is that it plays a role in his study which is very different from the role that Durkheim's abstract explanation plays in *Suicide*. This contrast between the two studies is of decisive importance. Because of it alone, an examination of Morselli's book can strengthen our respect for Durkheim's.

Through the greater part of his book, Morselli shows little interest in the struggle for existence. He refers to it only occasionally, and he makes no serious attempt to measure its intensity. Instead, most of his pages are devoted to the search for laws, and his main goal seems to be to discover them. He accumulates his laws as if he were filling a bag with ping pong balls, which he then pours out on the floor before his reader. Then he picks up each one, identifies it, and tosses it back on the floor.

In his final chapter, when Morselli is finally about to announce his abstract explanation, he shows that he is quite aware of what he has been doing:

> …in investigating and summing up the laws of suicide from the aggregate of facts, *we have purposely passed over silently the opinion as to its nature which might be drawn from them.* But after analyzing all these laws, our opinion appears clear and certain (Morselli, 1881, p. 354, emphasis added).

"The opinion" is Morselli's idea about the struggle for existence which was quoted above. He intentionally ignores his general explanation of suicide through most of his book.

Durkheim's book offers just what Morselli's does not—a single theoretical explanation linked to a wide range of evidence. This is precisely what has made the book captivating to so many. It is true that Morselli has already proposed many of the laws which Durkheim presents. Both moral statisticians show that such variables as marital status, religion, and the business cycle affect the rate of suicide. But to Durkheim each of these variables embodies something more abstract. The sustained theme of his book is the pervasive effect of social integration and regulation on suicide.

Now, having drawn this contrast between the two authors, we can specify the relationship between Morselli's book and "Suicide et Natalité" which I have mentioned. Morselli offers his explanation of suicide almost as an afterthought. But Durkheim, with Morselli's work in mind, takes the decisive step beyond him. The scientific purpose of his essay is the development of an abstract explanation of suicide. Every item of evidence is chosen for its bearing on that explanation. *This is the most notable feature of "Suicide et Natalité."* I wish to emphasize that Durkheim takes this step *in his essay.* Nine years later, in his book, he approaches the explanation of suicide in the same way. But he is not doing so for the first time.[30]

Empirical Measures

The moral statisticians knew that the validity of suicide statistics is uncertain. Morselli points out that when a man kills himself the infamy of his act may cause his family and friends to conceal the details of his death (Morselli, 1881). But Durkheim's paper says nothing about the question of validity. It has been amply discussed in more recent times. There is no need to consider it further here.

Seven demographic measures

His indicators of fertility are another matter. He uses no fewer than seven of them. His short study actually contains as many measures of the birth rate as it does tables.

What is more, Durkheim makes no attempt to show that each measure is the most appropriate choice for the purpose at hand. He simply introduces each one in an ad hoc way, with the one exception of physiological growth, for which he does offer a rationale.

It is one of the most telling criticisms of Durkheim's paper that he simply cannot assume that the seven indicators are interchangeable. Whoever invented each of these indicators wanted to measure something which nothing else measured as well. For this reason alone, one would expect that the correlations among them would not be high.

With so many indicators to choose from, and with Durkheim offering no reason for choosing one rather than another, it is possible that he sometimes chooses an indicator because it shows the result which he wants to show.

But this unsatisfactory state of things is only partly his fault. We have already learned from M. Bertillon that the field of demography was then in a rudimentary state. With far less evidence to choose from than we have today, Durkheim is not as free as we would be to choose among birth rate indicators.

Physiological growth

Physiological growth appears in Durkheim's four tables representing the departments of France. This mixed measure is the only one of his seven which he discusses at length. He thinks that it is his best indicator of the birth rate.

The birth rate is a function of how many children the average married woman has. This number was low in France, and the French birth rate was low for this reason. This is, of course, the condition which concerns Durkheim. But the birth rate is also a function of how large a proportion of the population are physically capable of becoming pregnant. In a society other than France, a low birth rate might reflect an unusually small proportion of women in the child-bearing years. This proportion does not concern Durkheim, and he does not want it to affect his figures.[31]

In accordance with his concerns, he looks at the number of live births in a population, divided by the number of women within a range of ages meant to approximate the fertile years. (This range of ages must be set somewhat arbitrarily. In Durkheim's figures, it is 15-50. Now it is usually 15-44 or 15-49.) This statistic is now called the *general* fertility rate. The similar *marital* fertility rate represents *legitimate* births to women of the same ages. Durkheim uses the former statistic in Tables 2-5, probably because these figures were the only ones available. He uses the latter in Table 6. He never does say that the marital rate is the better of the two for his purpose. But I doubt that he would think that an increase in *illegitimate* births would betoken a healthier society.

To Durkheim it is not enough to look only at age-controlled birth rates. He wants "…to study the birth rate with regard to its social function, which is to maintain the life of the society." Thus, he resolves to examine not only births but also deaths, which "…are the gaps which births will fill."

To do this, he subtracts the *crude* death rate from the general birth rate. The crude death rate corresponds to the crude birth rate. It does not correct for the age structure of the population and is, therefore, a function both of the probability of death at each age and of the age structure (the proportion of people who are in each age group). The age structure can have a large effect on the crude death rate as can be shown by an example from our time. *Age-specific* death rates are higher in poor countries, such as Syria, than in prosperous ones, such as Israel. But since the population of Israel is older than that of Syria, the *crude* death rate is actually higher in Israel than it is in Syria.

Physiological growth represents an early attempt to devise a demographic measure more refined than either the crude birth rate or the crude rate of natural increase. Durkheim borrows the measure and the figures representing it from Bertillon.

Physiological growth has a decisive defect. Each of Durkheim's other measures refers to some understandable property of a set of people. But, even after trying with all my might, I cannot identify any set of people which a rate of physiological growth describes. To see the problem, let us consider another measure—the crude rate of natural increase. This is defined as births per 1000 population minus deaths per 1000 population. Births and deaths are measured in relation to the same denominator. But in calculating physiological growth, the two corresponding rates do not describe the same set of people. The denominator of the marital fertility rate is 1000 women within a certain age range, while the denominator of the crude death rate is 1000 members of the entire population. When the second rate is subtracted from the first, *the resulting number describes neither this set of women nor the population as a whole.*

Some of Durkheim's comments about the indicator unintentionally raise doubts about the other measures which he uses. For example, he says that the crude birth rate, in contrast to physiological growth, is "very imperfect." Yet he uses the crude birth rate in Table 1. Also, "the socially useful effect of births," which is what "matters to us…can only be expressed" by subtracting deaths from births. But most of his measures do not subtract deaths from births. It seems to follow that much of his own analysis is of doubtful value.

What is the "birth rate"?

One oddity about "Suicide et Natalité" is that, in spite of the multifarious indicators of the birth rate, our author does not make clear just what he is trying to measure. If he does in fact know what he wants to measure, we can be sure that it is not seven different things.

Durkheim is really not primarily interested in *births*. Instead, he is concerned with *population growth*—births minus deaths plus net migration.[32] We can see this if we look at specific evidence in his paper.

At three points in the essay we can see that Durkheim's "birth rate" includes deaths as well as births. First, physiological growth, his favorite measure, incorporates deaths. This is one reason why he values it as a measure of fertility. Second, there is his odd attitude toward Table 6 (see Note 11 at end of chapter). This table directly measures the demographic malady which distinguishes France from other countries. One would expect Durkheim to be keen about it. But he relegates it to a footnote. Maybe he does this because it does not incorporate death rates. Third, when he examines rural-urban differences in France, his figures would permit him to look at births by themselves. But he chooses not to. He examines births minus deaths instead.

Durkheim's "birth rate," as I reconstruct it, also incorporates migration between countries. The evidence for this is that on two occasions he uses measures of the birth rate which include migration.

First, he reports Legoyt's (1881) conclusion that a dense population can raise the suicide rate, as can be seen in the negative relation between emigration and suicide.[33] Durkheim would only mention this finding if thinks that migration alone can affect suicide, without regard to births or deaths.

Second, Durkheim's data on occupations uses mean family size as a measure of the birth rate. Family size is affected by migration and not only by births and deaths. In this way, it is like population density.[34]

If I have correctly identified what Durkheim means by the birth rate, it might be possible to reexamine and criticize his whole essay in the light of this conclusion. But he is not always consistent about what the birth rate really is, and I suspect that the exercise would not be very fruitful.

Suicide as a measure of abnormality

Evidence that human events are predictable led the moral statisticians to conclude that laws linking these events were waiting to be found. Durkheim's confidence that he can discover a law relating births to suicides shows him to be very much a moral statistician himself.[35]

The purpose of "Suicide et Natalité" is "to decide whether an increase in population is good or bad for a country." To determine this, our author wants an indicator of social ill-health (badness for society). He proposes the suicide rate, "a rather well-known fact which expresses social ills numerically."[36]

Durkheim is not plagued by doubts about the validity of his measure:

> ...it is certain that a consistent increase of suicides always points to a serious disturbance of the organic conditions of society. For these abnormal acts to

increase, conditions of suffering must also have increased, and the power of the organism to resist must have decreased at the same time.

He offers several arguments for this conclusion. First, "everyone recognizes" the "morbid character" of suicide. Second, Bertillon has said that "suicide is always a symptom of an organism in disequilibrium." Third, "...we have seen that [suicide] is always an index of sickness, and that it can only grow if this sickness itself grows." Durkheim thinks that he has proved his measure to be a good one. But I cannot find this proof in his essay. The case for his measure of abnormality is not as strong as one might wish.

In Durkheim's essay, social ill-health, individual unhappiness, and suicide are all strongly associated. But his view of these matters changed after 1888, and in *Suicide* things are not so simple.

His book continues to express the common sense view that men who kill themselves are unhappy. A "...state of disturbance, agitation and discontent...inevitably increases the possibilities of suicide" (*Suicide* p. 271; also see p. 213). But, he also insists, surprisingly, that suicide is associated with happiness.

Man prefers to abandon life when it is least difficult (p. 107). Facts...are far from confirming the current idea that suicide is due especially to life's burdens, since, on the contrary, it diminishes as these burdens increase (p. 201). Is life more readily renounced as it becomes more difficult? The explanation is seductively simple; and it agrees with the popular idea of suicide. But it is contradicted by facts (p. 242). The enormous [suicide] rate of those with independent means...sufficiently shows that the possessors of most comfort suffer most (p. 257).

It seems self-evident that unhappiness and suicide are positively associated. Durkheim's insistence in *Suicide* that they are *negatively* associated can fairly be described as eccentric, and evidence of this unexpected association might reasonably be expected. Yet he never does take a serious look, either in his essay or in his book, at whatever data might be used to test either proposition.

Another measure of abnormality

Durkheim criterion of the abnormality of nation is the suicide rate. Or is it? If we turn from what he says he does to what he actually does, several problems appear.

1. His *explicit* criterion of national health is the suicide rate. He offers the high French rate as evidence that his country is sick. The suicide rate is something internal to a society, calculated without reference to any other society. But what would he say if the German birth rate became *even higher,* while the birth rate and the suicide rate of France were unchanged? France, in such a case, might be even more vulner-

able than she was in 1870 to a German invasion. I think that in such a case Durkheim would say that France was sicker than she was before. I suggest this because his conclusion that France was unwell is based only partly on the internal state of France. It is also based on an implied *comparison* of France with the countries around her. In other words, he has a second, implicit criterion of national health. If both criteria were used to appraise a single set of countries, it is hard to see how the results could be the same.

2. Durkheim's twin criteria have implications which he does not explore. For example, how sick were Denmark and Switzerland? Each had a common frontier with Germany, and the two had the highest suicide rates in Table 1. Were they more or less sick than France? He does not say. In fact, he says nothing at all about these two countries.

3. He is distressed about the national "sickness" of France, just as some of his countrymen were troubled about national "decadence." Each of these two words is, of course, an organic metaphor. There might be nothing wrong with them. Perhaps societies actually have a measurable property which is in some ways like the health of organisms. But Durkheim should do more to define this dimension; the empirical meaning of the "sickness" of a society is hardly clearer than the empirical meaning of its level of "decadence." What Durkheim has in mind is even fuzzier because to him national sickness also means national *badness*. There are a number of social conditions which he regards as bad—a birth rate that is high or low, a suicide rate that is high or low, and some others. But what *empirical* property is common to these bad conditions?

4. His use of the organic analogy creates a problem of another kind. Durkheim applies his second criterion of national "health" by comparing a country with the countries around it. But when he does this, he draws an inappropriate organic analogy. He would say that an increase in the German birth rate can make France sicker. This comment does make sense in terms of the analogy, in that the health of an organism can be affected by changes in its physical environment. But he is also saying something more radical. An increase in the German birth rate will make France sicker *even if nothing changes within France*. To my knowledge, a comparable statement would not be made about an organism. It seems inappropriate to describe an event within Germany as a change in the health of France.[37]

Durkheim's Law

To learn more about Durkheim's law, I will now spell out the causal relations which he proposes. To common sense, there is no connection between the birth rate and the suicide rate. When Durkheim says that the first causes the second, he offers what is perhaps the most provocative assertion in his essay.

> ...if an excessive birth rate promotes suicide, an insufficient birth rate produces exactly the same result. Indeed, the purpose of the present study is precisely to call attention to the facts which prove the truth of this law, and then to interpret it.

Durkheim of course recognizes the need for data in support of his law. But that is not all that is needed. To make the connection plausible he should go beyond his statistical evidence and describe the link between births and suicides in greater detail. The need for such spelling out is especially acute because at first glance births and suicides seem to be unrelated to each other.

He does a lot of this kind of thing in *Suicide*. That is, apart from his statistical evidence, he offers extended commentaries on the associations he is proposing. Time after time, he delineates the ways in which the properties of social integration[38] and regulation act on men, either to predispose them to suicide or to protect them from it. He also tries to make the association meaningful when he defines psychological concomitants of egoism and of the other causes of suicide—conditions which he calls the "morphological types" of suicide (*Suicide*, Book Two, Chapter 6). He finds it worthwhile to do all of this, even though the connection which he is trying to establish is more meaningful in an intuitive way than is the one claimed in his essay.

In contrast, "Suicide et Natalité" offers little of this kind of commentary on the link between births and suicides. About all we are told is that there are two processes through which births affect suicides. These can be interpreted as intervening variables. Which of the two operates depends on whether the birth rate is high or low. When that rate is low, as in France, it makes the society weak, and this condition promotes suicide. When the rate is high, as in Germany, it intensifies the struggle for existence, which in turn encourages suicide. But Durkheim says very little about these conditions.

It may seem strange that he makes no effort to measure them, but this omission is really not surprising. The moral statisticians seem to have assumed that government statistics of various human events were the only data they could use. These pioneering sociologists did not take the further step of assuming an active role in generating their own data. This possibility would only be fully explored in the age of survey data, decades later. Yet Durkheim's discussion of his two intervening variables can be fairly described as perfunctory, even if we allow for the limitations of his times (Selvin, 1976).

Weakness of a society (France)

Durkheim has this to say about one of his two intervening variables.

> Many sociologists have already claimed that too low a birth rate is harmful and

a sickness for society. This study proves that it is also a misfortune and a sickness for individuals. A society which grows steadily is not only stronger and more capable of holding its own against rival societies, but the members who make it up also have better chances of survival. They are physiologically more vigorous and have a greater power of resistance.

He does not actually assign a name to this social condition, which we may call the "weakness" of a society. France suffered from this condition, and was less "capable of holding its own against rival societies" than other societies were. Durkheim may be thinking of France in the war of 1870-71, in future wars, in economic competition, in the scramble for colonies, or in other international struggles.

But what does it mean to say that the citizens of such a country show a lack of physiological vigor and resistance, and a lower chance of survival? Does it just mean that there are more suicides? Or that diseases are more prevalent, and the death rate is higher? Or is the lack of vigor and resistance somehow an immediate cause of a high suicide rate? It is not obvious why this national frailty, or any of the manifestations of it which he mentions, might lead to suicide.

Struggle for survival (Germany)

We know that the view of social life as a struggle for existence was very much in the air in Durkheim's time. It is interesting that his attitude to this idea is mixed.

At the start of his essay, he criticizes some unnamed authors for relying too much on the notion. "[T]he abstract principle of the struggle for survival" is of limited value for social science. "[T]he law of competition...does not determine every social phenomenon all by itself, [and] has yielded only partial solutions" to "the complex population question."

But he also accepts the principle, when he borrows from Morselli the idea that the struggle for existence can generate suicide, and suggests that this struggle is the link between a high birth rate and a high suicide rate.[39] "In a society in which the population multiplies too quickly, the struggle of life becomes too harsh, and individuals more easily relinquish an existence which has become too painful."

Durkheim does not say enough about the process through which a high birth rate intensifies the struggle for existence and how that struggle leads to suicide. Perhaps he says so little because he is less interested in Germany than in France. In any case, the link between births and suicides remains murky.

The range of operation of intervening variables

If we could accept Durkheim's claim that his two conditions link births to suicides, we still might wonder why each of them only operates across a limited range of birth rates. Why do variations in the weakness of society affect only societies with few births? Why does the varying intensity of the struggle for existence affect only societies with many births? Why, in fact, do the two conditions not operate in opposite directions along the whole range of birth rates, and thus nullify each other's effects? The result would be that every country has the same rate of suicide. The problem is that Durkheim says so little about the two conditions that one really cannot predict how each of them is related to suicide.

A cause of both births and suicide

Once Durkheim has presented his evidence, his Conclusion (which is mostly about France) moves off in an unexpected direction.

> This is the meaning of the relationship we have established. But what is the cause of it? Once we have stated it, we must explain it. How is it that, within certain limits at least, the curve of the birth rate falls as that of suicide rises, and inversely?
>   Of course, these two facts, the rise in suicides and the decrease in births, must have one or several causes in common. But what are these causes?

The only possible explanation, then, for the association between births and suicides, in France at least, is that both of them are caused by something else. This cause of both is family feeling, a factor not mentioned in Durkheim's essay up that point.

> Thus, only social causes are common to suicide and the birth rate, and can account for the relationship between them. To determine more precisely the exact nature of these causes, let us consider the birth rate along with several other facts which equally confer immunity to suicide.... A high birth rate presupposes large families.... Thus, any drop in the birth rate implies a weakening of family spirit. As we have just seen, it also promotes suicide. It must, then, be the cause of both of them which we are trying to discover. If suicide grows when the birth rate declines, it is because both of these phenomena are due, in part, to a decrease in family feeling.

Durkheim devotes the Conclusion of his paper to family feeling. But it is not so much a conclusion as a contradiction of what has gone before. When a third variable is introduced as a control and an apparently causal relation between two variables disappears, and when that third variable is prior to both, then what at first seemed to be a causal relation is said to be spurious. The relation between the two original variables only exists because each is affected by the prior variable. This is what Durkheim is suggesting about family feeling. Yet the *more* family feeling accounts for the association between births and suicides, the *less* that association is due to the effect of the birth rate on suicide. And, I may add, the less truth there is to the thesis of "Suicide et Natalité." In short, at this point Durkheim is unintentionally arguing against his own law.

Let us consider what relations might exist among Durkheim's two variables, or among any two variables for that matter. First, the causal relation between births and suicides might be real, as most of his essay claims. Second, some other factor might determine both births and suicide, so that the original relation is spurious, as his Conclusion seems to suggest. Third, the other factor might occur before births and after suicides, so that when the third variable is held constant, the original association disappears. In this case, the apparently causal relation between the two original variables is not spurious. The relation is actually causal, but it occurs through the operation of an intervening variable.

These are the possibilities which concern us, but they are not the only ones.[40] Durkheim seems to deny the first possibility, that births cause suicides, when he professes the second, that family feeling causes both births and suicides. But he does not consider the third, that births cause family feeling, and family feeling causes suicides.

The third possibility should not be disregarded. To choose between the second and the third we need to know the *time order* of the three variables. Suicide certainly comes last. But do births occur first and family feeling later, or is it the other way around? Either sequence seems possible. If family spirit is strong, couples might then decide to have more children. But the acquisition of another child might also strengthen family feeling. The two orders of events are not mutually exclusive. It may be that family feeling fosters and births, and that births also foster family feeling.

Perhaps Durkheim would actually agree that the time order goes in both ways. He says explicitly that family feeling causes births. Perhaps he also implies that births also increase family feeling. We might interpret his nebulous idea that the weakness of a society intervenes between a low birth rate and a high suicide rate as a statement about a very large number of highly associated symptoms of social illness and abnormality. Then we might infer that among these symptoms are low levels of solidarity in various social institutions, including the family. Hence, births lessen the weakness of a society and increase family spirit or feeling.

Durkheim's argument about family feeling can be summarized in the following way. In societies with low birth rates, family feeling affects the suicide rate, and it both affects and is affected by the birth rate. At the same time, the birth rate affects the suicide rate, though it does not totally determine it.

What can be said as a summary of the causal relations proposed in "Suicide et Natalité" as a whole? Durkheim accepts Morselli's idea that the struggle for existence can generate suicide, and adds that a high birth rate intensifies the struggle for existence. He suggests that a low birth rate weakens the society, which in turn promotes suicide. Then, in his Conclusion, he amends his interpretation of societies with low birth rates by adding the suggestion that the variable intervening between births and suicides is not weakness of the society (which he never really defines) but weakness of family feeling. We know that he is more interested in France than any other country. His brief mention of the weakness of society contrasts with his several pages of reflections on low family feeling in France. It seems that low family feeling is a subdimension of the weakness of society, but their relationship is not made explicit.

Antecedents of Durkheim's Law

Durkheim's claim that the birth rate causes the suicide rate may seem odd. But it was not unprecedented. A few earlier moral statisticians had already considered the relation of births and suicides. I will discuss several of them now.

No relation between births and suicides?

We have seen that Morselli had an important impact on Durkheim in several ways. Huff (1975) says that he also influenced Durkheim's thinking specifically about the relation between births and suicides.

According to Huff, Morselli claimed that no relation could be found between births and suicides. Durkheim probably interpreted this claim as a challenge and wrote his essay to meet it. Huff is the only author who has published a scholarly interpretation of Durkheim's paper. Thus, his suggestion deserves serious consideration.[41]

"[I]t seems likely," Huff writes, "that Morselli's work was one reason for Durkheim's 1888 study. For Morselli (1882, p. 34) claimed that the birthrate was one of the few social factors which could not be related to the suicide rate" (Huff, 1975, p. 247).

Huff is referring to a passage in Morselli's discussion of rates of various acts and events. Some of these, such as suicide and marriage, are voluntary. Morselli refers to the involuntary ones, such as birth and accidental death, as "unconscious phenomena of the social forces (demodinamica)" (Morselli, 1882, p. 33).

What Morselli is trying to do at this point is crucial for my argument. He is not trying to *account for* these events. Instead, he is asking the less usual question, *how much does each of them fluctuate* from year to year?

His procedure is to begin by looking at the rate of one such event in one country. For example, he examines the rate of illegitimate births in Cisleithan Austria for each of the years 1867 to 1876. He then subtracts the lowest from the highest of these rates, and adds 100. In this way, he arrives at a figure representing the "difference between the extremes, the smallest number being = 100." He does the same for rates of homicide, marriage, and other events in that country. Then he does the same thing for eight other countries of Europe. The result is a table which permits him to compare the amounts of fluctuation of all of the events which interest him. For example, it permits him to see whether there is greater fluctuation in rates of marriage than in rates of accidental death (Morselli, 1882, p. 34).

Morselli concludes that there is not much fluctuation of *any* of these classes of events. A secondary conclusion is that the voluntary acts, such as marriage and suicide, show even *less* variation than do the demodinamica, such as accidental death. Suicide rates, in turn, show less variation even than rates of other voluntary acts. The less rates vary, of course, the more they can be predicted. Morselli concludes that suicide rates are especially appropriate for scientific study[42] (see also Durkheim, 1951, pp. 46-51).

Morselli is looking at the variability, from year to year, of the rates of seven events. Of these seven, only the birth rate varies even less than the suicide rate. This finding prompts him to make the comment which Huff has in mind: "[T]he [only] demographical phenomenon [of those few listed here] which shows less variation [than the rate of suicide] is that of births, with which the rate of suicide cannot be compared" (Morselli, 1882, p. 34). Morselli is comparing the amount of fluctuation of birth rates with the amount of fluctuation of suicide rates. The birth rate varies a lot less than the suicide rate does, and in this sense the two rates "cannot be compared."[43]

It follows that Huff is mistaken. Morselli did not conclude in this passage is that "the birthrate was one of the few social factors which could not be related to the suicide rate." Morselli is *not* saying that no correlation can be found between rates of birth and suicide—that no law can be discovered relating the two rates. He is not discussing that question. Hence (and this is my point) Morselli's comment cannot have been the inspiration for Durkheim's essay.

A positive relation? (Masaryk)

Although I have not sought antecedents of Durkheim's law in a systematic way, I have come upon a partial statement of Durkheim's law in an interesting place, a study by Thomas G. Masaryk, a moral statistician who also found the time to serve as the first president of Czechoslovakia. He published his analysis of suicide in 1881, seven years before "Suicide et Natalité."

Masaryk considers several demographic factors in their relations to suicide, the age structure, population density, and over and underpopulation. (Each of these, by the way, is discussed at some point in this commentary.) Then he proposes what would later be part of Durkheim's law.

> The *speed of population growth* can favor the tendency to suicide insofar as this increase results in material and moral abuses. In Europe the rapid growth of population is most visible in England (including Wales), Saxony, and Prussia; it is least rapid in Portugal; in the former countries, suicide is frequent, in the latter, infrequent. Inversely, the population of France is increasing very slowly, is even decreasing here and there, but the tendency to suicide progressively increases. The parallelism here is therefore again not decisive (Masaryk, 1970, pp. 31-32).

For the moment, I will consider Masaryk's population growth and

Durkheim's "birth rate" to be identical. (They may indeed be identical. The problem, as we have seen, is that Durkheim is not all that clear about what the "birth rate" is.)

Masaryk suggests that between population growth and suicide there is a linear and positive relation—high growth is associated with high suicide.[44] But the relation is not perfect. The low growth and high suicide of France show that "the parallelism" is "not decisive."

Thus does Masaryk express part of Durkheim's law. He would move closer to it if he were to decide that France is not an exception to the general trend but evidence that the relation between growth and suicide is not linear. In other words, France shows that, when growth falls below a certain point, its relation to suicide is not positive but negative.

"Suicide et Natalité" does not mention Masaryk, and I have no evidence that his ideas influenced the article. But such a connection is possible. Masaryk's book appeared in 1881, in plenty of time for Durkheim to read it and draw some ideas from it.[45]

A negative relation? (Morselli)

Durkheim found the data which appear as his Table 1 in Morselli. But they were originally gathered, in 1876, by Luigi Bodio, a prominent Italian statistician whom Durkheim does not mention. Bodio collected rates of birth and suicide, along with rates of marriage and death, for at least 17 European countries. I have not been able to examine his book. But it is my guess that he merely listed the figures which he had gathered, and did not try to suggest what they might mean.[46]

Morselli reproduces Bodio's figures, representing four variables and seventeen countries. He concludes from this evidence that the relation of marriage rates to suicide is weak, that the relation of birth rates to suicide is negative and not so weak, and that the relation of death rates to suicide is also negative and somewhat stronger.

> But we are unable to give an adequate explanation of the...inverse relation of the birth rate [to suicide]. The influence of [the rates of birth, death, and marriage on suicide] is not shown clearly here. Since we lack the more profound and detailed investigation which would be needed to demonstrate that influence, this evidence cannot be found in this book. (Morselli, 1879, Tabella XIX, 198, 199).

Morselli sees that there is an inverse relation between the national rates of birth and suicide which will appear in "Suicide et Natalité." But he adds that this relation cannot be fully understood without more extensive study. It seems that his uncertainty leaves him less than pleased. After including the table and his comments in the Italian version of his book, he omits them from the later, English editions.

Durkheim comments directly on this passage from Morselli.

> The influence of a low birth rate on suicide can be seen even when the distorting case of Germany is included in the computation. This is so because this influence is so pervasive. Thus, Morselli, from whom we have taken the above table, cannot keep from recognizing this fact, even though he declines to explain it. He suggests that it should be submitted to a more detailed examination. This is just what we will try to do.[47]

Why did Durkheim write his essay? These scholarly minutiae about Bodio and Morselli provide part of the answer. He was predisposed to so by several currents of thought—social Darwinism, the belief that France was decadent, and others. But he also wanted to solve a specific empirical problem. Morselli posed that problem when he admitted that he could not make complete sense of his own data. Durkheim resolved to do better.

Evidence

Since this is a commentary on Durkheim's essay, the evidence which interests us is the evidence which Durkheim himself offers. I will introduce some further data, but only to augment some of his. I will not attempt a serious test of his law.

In looking at his evidence, I will try to keep two thoughts in mind. First, it would be unfair to criticize him when he does not use certain tools which were not available to him. But second, one should use the same standards in judging his inferences that one would use with a study which has just appeared.

Countries

Table 1

Durkheim's Table 1 contains his only data which compare countries, and his only data which bear on his law as a whole. Given his purpose, they are the most important evidence he has.

Morselli lists the 17 countries in order of their suicide rates, with a few out of place. This arrangement may have been all right for Morselli, but it makes things hard for us. Both Prussia and France have high suicide rates, and for this reason they appear close together in the table. But to Durkheim a high rate of suicide can result from either a high birth rate or a low one. Thus, the proximity of Germany and France in the table is misleading. They are where they are for opposite reasons.

Durkheim should have rearranged the countries in the order of their birth rates. Then the reader could learn whether suicide rates conform to Durkheim's law by scanning down the list of countries. They conform to it if they first decline, then remain low for an interval, and then rise.

In the accompanying scatter plot (Figure 1), I have added a line with three segments. It is not a curve which best fits the data, but one which represents Durkheim's law. To the degree that his law holds true, countries will be found on (or near) the curve. Since the range of birth rates is from 25.7 to 41.7, the horizontal scale has been truncated, and begins with 20. (Actual rates of birth and suicide for all countries are in the Summary Table for Europe in the Appendix.)

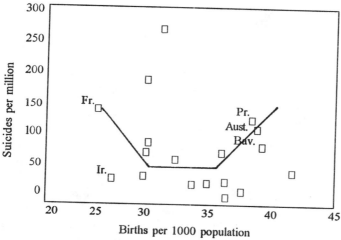

Figure 1

Crude birth rate (1865-76) and suicide in
18 European countries

Three German-speaking countries, Prussia, Bavaria, and Austria, are close to the righthand part of the curve. They support Durkheim, though Bavaria does so less strongly. After 1871, both Prussia and Bavaria were parts of the German Empire. Perhaps these three cases should be counted as two.

France, with the lowest rate of births and the third-highest of suicides, is the only country on or near the lefthand part of the curve, and the only case supporting Durkheim's claim that countries with few births have many suicides. (I have added Ireland to the scatter diagram. It is not in Table 1. I will discuss it below as a second European country with a low crude birth rate.)

No fewer than ten countries are near the horizontal part of the line. To Durkheim, their moderate birth rates are evidence that they are healthy. He seems to see these ten countries as having low suicide rates and *varying* birth rates. It follows (though he does not say so) that the differences in their suicide rates are due to variables *other then* the birth rate.[48]

Three countries are not close to any part of the curve, and therefore do not support him. Denmark and Switzerland have moderate birth rates. According to his law, they should have few suicides. Yet they have more than any other country shown. Hungary, with the highest birth rate, should have many suicides. Actually it has relatively few. Durkheim does not mention these three cases.

Let us ignore Durkheim's curve for the moment, and simply look at the way in which his 17 countries are distributed. The correlation coefficient of births and suicides is -.31. We have seen that Morselli recognizes this weak association. He does so without the use of Pearson's *r*, which had yet to be invented.[49]

Durkheim also acknowledges this relation, but only in passing. He comes to the evidence thinking of other things—the contrasting birth rates of Germany and France, the German victory in the war of 1870-71, the decadence of France, and the many suicides in both countries in contrast to most of Europe. He then inflicts these preoccupations on Morselli's data. No wielder of Occam's razor, he proposes a complicated association which has no clear basis in the distribution of cases before him. In all of this, he exhibits the "rather high-handed way with evidence" which Lukes finds elsewhere in his work (Lukes, 1972, p. 33).

When Durkheim takes leave of Table 1, he asks which countries he should look at for "a more complete proof." He decides on reasonable grounds not to look at those with moderate birth rates. But he adds that he will not look at those with high birth rates either, because "...the birth rate would tend above all to produce suicide rather than to prevent it." His reasoning is obscure. He badly needs confirmation of a positive association between births and suicide, and where might he find it except among those countries where he says that it exists? But perhaps he is satisfied with a specious argument if it frees him to look at France, which is what he wants to do. That is what the rest of his essay is about: The set of countries with few births and many suicides, of which his own country is his only example.

Evidence other than Durkheim's

Durkheim gives only brief attention to the countries which appear in Table 1. Yet we might want to learn more about them first, if we were seeking confirmation of his law. I will look at them now, using a set of data which are directly relevant to that law. I suspect that Durkheim does not use these figures because in 1888 they had not been published in a readily accessible form. They represent almost all of the countries which he studies, and most of them refer to 1865 to 1876, the same years as the rates in Table 1. They embody two indicators of the birth rate which he uses, marital fertility and natural increase, together with a measure of population growth. The third of these measures is what, as I have argued, Durkheim really means by the "birth rate," births minus deaths plus net migration. But it attains this result indirectly, being the difference in the size of a population over two successive years.

I will show the relation of each of the three measures to rates of suicide.

For each of the three, I will provide a scatter plot like the one for Table 1. Each chart will include a curve representing the law, attempting to make the segment on the left pass through France, the segment on the right pass through Germany (Prussia and Bavaria) and Austria, and the middle segment pass through whatever countries have moderate birth rates and few suicides. (As before, the actual figures which are the basis of what follows are in the Summary Table for Europe in the Appendix.)

I intentionally confine my attention to three unsophisticated indicators of the birth rate. I do not consider more sophisticated indicators which are used today. These more refined measures would be appropriate if my purpose were to determine how the birth rate was related to suicide in nineteenth-century Europe. But I am less concerned with this than with evaluating Durkheim's paper. As I have indicated, I am interested in the evidence which he presents and, secondarily, evidence which he might have used if he had sought it. He could not have used evidence employing measures which had yet to be invented.[50]

Marital Fertility Rate

The marital fertility rate, which appears in Durkheim's Table 6, is more refined than the crude birth rate of Table 1, and the most refined of the unrefined measures which I am using to compare countries. But no matter what age limits are set on the women included in its calculation, puberty and menopause take place at varying ages, and some infertile females will be included, or some fertile ones excluded, or both.

We know that many in Durkheim's time thought that low marital fertility was the specifically French demographic disease. These data show that France does have the lowest marital birth rate of the countries shown. But whether it also has the lowest "birth rate" depends on what measure of the birth rate one uses. If the "birth rate" is defined as natural increase, France does not have the lowest birth rate.

Germany[51] has the highest marital fertility of the countries listed. Table 1 contains a group of countries with a moderate birth rate and a low rate of suicide. The present chart (Figure 2) has eight countries of this kind.

This distribution of countries offers about as much support for Durkheim's law as does Table 1. The agreement between the two sets of data is not unexpected. On the y-axis, the figures are the same. On the x-axis, they represent two strongly correlated measures. It is known that the movements and changes of the *general* fertility rate are almost parallel to those of the crude birth rate.[52] The *marital* fertility rate, shown in the chart, is similar to the general fertility rate, except that the latter incorporates illegitimate births. Thus, if the general rate moves with the crude birth rate, we would expect the marital rate to behave similarly.

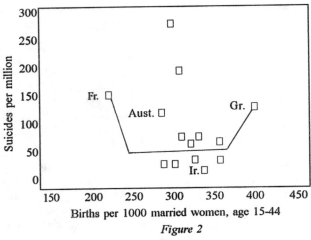

Figure 2

Marital fertility (1865-76) and suicide in
13 European countries

Crude Rate of Natural Increase

The crude rate of natural increase is simply the crude birth rate minus the crude death rate. If the "social function of births...to maintain the life of society, is only meaningful relative to deaths," this measure might be considered to be better for Durkheim's purpose than the crude birth rate.

Some demographers would say that this indicator is of little value, because it compounds the misleading effects of two rates which are themselves crude. Nevertheless, it is of interest because Durkheim uses it himself in his analysis of rural-urban differences (though he simply gives raw numbers of births and deaths). As before, the relation to suicide is shown in a scatter diagram (Figure 3).

France reappears as the one country with a low "birth rate" and a high rate of suicide. But there is no identifiable set of countries with moderate rates of natural increase and low rates of suicide, and the rest of Durkheim's curve can hardly be seen. He thinks that the rates of birth and suicide of Prussia, Bavaria, and Austria, as these are seen in Table 1, are "too high." But here we see that two of these three countries have rates of natural increase which are below the average of the 18 countries as a whole.

The two countries highest in suicide, Switzerland and Denmark, are also high in natural increase. Perhaps they support Durkheim better than they did in Table 1.

Yet consider the three countries in the lower right corner of the scatter plot. These countries are England (and Wales), Norway, and Scotland. They show even higher natural increase than Switzerland and Denmark. Yet they are fairly low in suicide. They are far from Durkheim's line, and do not support him.

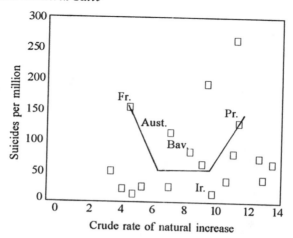

Figure 3
Natural increase (1865-76) and suicide in 18
European countries

I have noted that Durkheim is mistaken when he casually treats his fertility measures as interchangeable. *Findings based on one measure may not hold true if another is used.* The reader will see this point illustrated clearly if he compares the scatter plot representing Table A with the present one. The distributions of countries are rather different. It must be said that the natural increase figures do not give much support to Durkheim's law.

Population Growth

If what Durkheim really means by the "birth rate" somehow encompasses births, deaths and net migration, then a measure of population growth may bring us closest to that concept. His essay uses such an indicator only once and fleetingly, when he is examining rural-urban differences in France. Now we will compare European countries, using approximately the measure that he does. This indicator is simply the difference in the total population in two successive years, divided by the population in the earlier year, and multiplied by 1000 (Flora and Flora, 1987, p. 20; Barclay, 1958, p. 206).

Of all the measures we are using, only this one reflects migration, and for this reason the distribution of countries in the scatter diagram shown in Figure 4 is unique. Because of out-migration, the growth rate of Ireland is very low. It stretches the scale along the x-axis, so that the growth rates of the other countries seem to be more similar than they are.

The contrast between the birth rates of France and Germany is, of course, of special importance to Durkheim's argument. Ireland has a distorting effect in the present chart, which makes this contrast seem to be less than it is. But the contrast between France and Germany would be unimpressive even if Ireland were not in the chart.

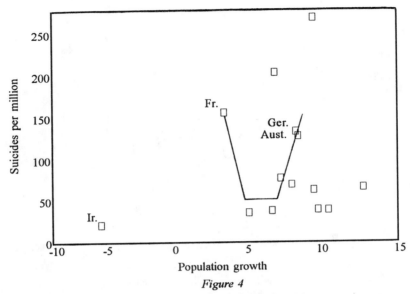

Figure 4

Population growth (1865-76) and suicide in 14 European countries

Ireland

Durkheim's essay does not mention Ireland.[53] But no other country in Europe cries out so piteously for recognition as a place of demographic infirmity. The social Darwinists did not always define the "struggle for existence" in the same way, and "Suicide et Natalité" does not define it at all. But, if the phrase is taken in its most naïve sense, that struggle in Ireland was brutal.

All of the nations in Table 1 were growing in the late nineteenth century. Even France was growing, though more slowly than her neighbors. All but two of the 82 French departments in Tables 2-5 were also growing, as Durkheim's evidence shows.

Even Ireland had grown at one time. Between the years 1767 and 1841, her population had grown spectacularly, from 2.5 to 8.2 million. One cause was the adoption of the potato as the main staple of the country. In the 1840s, it was so widely used that three million Irishmen ordinarily ate nothing else (Fry and Fry, 1988). But the country had become overpopulated. The potato crop was subject to repeated failures, and the Irish peasant, so heavily dependent on it, was vulnerable.

Then, in the fall of 1845, there came a visitation of the fungus, *Phyophthora infestans*, and half of the national potato crop failed. When several succeeding crops did also, the result was the Great Famine of 1845-48. During this "most cataclysmic event" in Irish history, one million died of starvation and disease.

Many others left. Between 1846 and 1849, nearly one million migrated to the U.S., Canada, and Britain (Fry and Fry, 1988, p. 237). A population of 8.2 million in 1841 shrank within a single decade to 6.5 million (Woodham-Smith, 1962, p. 411).

People kept leaving in large numbers, even after the famine ended, and partly for reasons apart from the potato. A long-term decline in the rural population is not unique to Ireland. It has taken place in many Western countries. But most of those who have left the farm in other countries have been able to find work in the city. In Ireland, because there was little mineral wealth, there was little industry, and because there was little industry, there were few jobs. The long decline in the Irish population seems to have ended only in quite recent years (Aalen, 1968, pp. 104, 106).

I will use the fertility indicators employed on the preceding pages to compare Ireland with other countries of Europe. I will approach each of the four charts in the same way, to see whether the predicted rate of suicide corresponds to its actual rate in Ireland. (The reader may wish to refer to the scatter plots in reading what follows.)

The *crude birth rate* of Ireland, roughly apparent in the scatter plot, was 27. Aside from France, it was the lowest of the 18 countries in the chart. Durkheim says that a low birth rate weakens a society and generates suicide, but offers only France in support of this assertion. If a low birth rate in France caused a high suicide rate, a low birth rate in Ireland should cause a high suicide rate there also. My estimate of the Irish suicide rate is 16.6 per million.[54] (This estimate is for 1865-1876, the years shown in Table 1.) This rate is lower than any in Durkheim's table. Thus, if we use the indicator of the birth rate which Durkheim himself uses, his prediction of the Irish suicide rate is not confirmed by the actual rate.

The *marital fertility rate* of Ireland was 333.1, placing it at the high end of the countries with moderate birth rates. Durkheim's law, if this measure were used, would predict a low suicide rate. In this case, his law is sustained. Ireland appears to have been a healthy country.

Or does it? Aside from this statistic, there are signs that Ireland may have been what Durkheim would consider a weak society, and that there was a low level of family feeling there: The average age of marriage was very late. There was "the lowest marriage rate in the world." A high proportion of people were in religious careers which committed them to celibacy (Aalen, 1968, p. 107).

The *crude rate of natural increase* (birth rate minus death rate) of Ireland was about 9.72, above the average of the countries represented. If I have correctly located the line representing Durkheim's law on the chart of natural increase, Ireland should have a higher rate of suicide than it does. If we use this indicator of the birth rate, Durkheim's law is not borne out.

The Irish *rate of population growth* was an exceedingly low -5.56. Using this indicator, the uniqueness of Ireland is dramatic. Furthermore, Ireland showed negative growth continuously over many years. The long-term decline in the Irish population has occurred because emigration has been so massive as to exceed natural increase. Using this indicator of the birth rate, Durkheim's analysis would suggest that Irish society was extremely weak, far weaker than France, and predict that the suicide rate would be very high. But its rate of suicide, once again, is the lowest of the 18 countries which we are studying.

Ireland is demographically peculiar, and one might not expect to learn much from one deviant case about the validity of Durkheim's law. But I think that two conclusions are justified:

1. Durkheim always uses only one fertility measure to describe a case, whether a country, a French department, or something else. But we have seen that the measures cannot be treated as interchangeable. As I have pointed out, the purpose of each indicator is to measure what it was uniquely designed to measure. Besides, as the Irish evidence suggests, different measures of the birth rate can lead us to expect different levels of suicide. The four predictions, for Ireland at least, are quite dissimilar.
2. Only France supports Durkheim's claim that a low rate of births causes a high rate of suicide. However atypical Ireland may be, it also qualifies as one case. And, when we use three of the four available measures of the birth rate, that case contradicts Durkheim.

French departments

Tables 1-5

Durkheim thinks that Tables 2-5 contain his best evidence. They present average growth rates of the French departments over many decades. The suicide rates in Tables 2 and 3 are also averages over many decades, although those in Tables 4 and 5 refer to a much shorter interval. None of these periods corresponds to 1865 to 1876, the 12 years which are depicted in Table 1. But in spite of the several noncoinciding intervals of time, one might say that the French data do offer internal replication of *part* of the nonlinear relation in Table 1.

Poor Durkheim! He wants to present his evidence in a way which is easy to understand, but he does not know how. As a result, his Tables 2 and 4 are fiendishly hard to read. They are arrays—lists of all 82 French departments, together with the rates of birth and suicide of each department. He knows that it is hard to make sense of all of the numbers, and he adds Tables 3 and 5 as more readable summaries.[55]

In Tables 2 and 3, he groups departments according to their suicide rates, and gives the growth rates of individual departments. This would be the way to set up these tables if he were looking at the effect of suicide on growth, which of course he is not. He presents Tables 4 and 5 in the appropriate way:

He creates groups of departments on the basis of their growth rates, and he lists the suicide rates of specific departments.[56]

Table 5 looks more like something that might be published today than does anything else in the article. To bring it fully up to date, one would only have to percentage it in the direction of physiological growth, the independent variable.

Even though Durkheim considers the figures in Tables 2 and 4 to be his best evidence, they have three limitations:

1. Physiological growth as a measure has the defects which I have mentioned before.

2. As replication, Tables 2 and 4 are of limited value. Durkheim undoubtedly thinks that they offer internal replication of part of the curvilinear relation which he claims to have shown in Table 1. But their contribution is limited for no fewer than four reasons. (a) The French data replicate only one third of his law, the association between few births and many suicides. (b) The one country in Table 1 supporting this association is France. The case of Ireland contradicts it. What is needed most is not further evidence from France but supporting evidence from other countries. (c) The crude birth rates of Table 1 and the growth rates of Tables 2-5 measure somewhat different things. The findings from Europe and France are, strictly speaking, not comparable. (d) The birth rates of Table 1 represent the years 1865 to 1876, whereas the growth rates of Tables 2-5 are averages reckoned over many decades. For this reason also, the two sets of findings are not comparable.

3. *Why* are the average growth rates in Tables 2-5 reckoned over many decades, while the average suicide rates in Tables 4 and 5 represent only a few years? Durkheim would have all of the figures in the four tables represent the longer interval. But he thinks that the data he wants are not available, and he offers rates for the shorter period as a less desirable substitute.

He is mistaken. The figures which he wants are available, but he has overlooked them. The Appendix includes an explanation of this situation and also provides the figures which he would prefer to use.

What, after all of these qualifications, can we conclude from Tables 2-5?

In a sense, these four tables are only one. For each department, the growth rate appears only once, in Table 2, and the suicide rate only once, in Table 4. Between these two sets of rates, the correlation coefficient is -0.49. There is a moderate negative relation between growth and suicides in the departments of France. This association is stronger than the linear correlation which we found in the European data. But of course Durkheim's law does not predict a linear relation in Table 1.

We know on other grounds that marital fertility and the crude death rate were declining at the same time. But the former was declining more rapidly. The *difference* between these two declining rates is expressed, albeit obscurely, as a decline in physiological growth—the general fertility rate minus the crude death rate.

Aside from the negative relation between births and suicides, one conspicuous pattern can be seen in the scatter diagram. Every department which is high in growth is low in suicide. Not one of them is high in both growth and suicide.

But not every department which is low in growth is high in suicide. The five departments which are conspicuous at the top of the scatter plot include and surround Paris. All of them are low in growth, and Paris has the highest suicide rate of any city in the world (Morselli, 1881, p. 181; Durkheim, 1951, pp. 134-135) But there is also a set of three departments which are similar in growth to those in the Paris region yet have few suicides. The three are adjacent departments in the southwest of France (Gers, Lot-et-Garonne, Tarn-et-Garonne).

Apparently, high growth, or something associated with it, is a *barrier* to suicide. As the rate of growth decreases, higher suicide rates become more likely. But they are not inevitable. *The lower the growth rates, the wider the range of suicide rates.* (Actual rates of growth and suicide of the departments are listed in the Appendix.)

Evidence other than Durkheim's

I will say more about the departments, as they are distributed in the scatter plot. I will limit my comments to a few groups of outliers in the chart.

Durkheim's growth rates pertain to the years 1801 to 1869, and I would like to describe the departments during those years. But it is hard to find information on specific departments during exactly these years, and I can offer only rough impressions.

What I can say is also limited because we are concerned here with physiological growth, and it is a troublesome indicator indeed. A rate of physiological growth is determined by a birth rate and a death rate, yet the growth rates itself reveals neither of these. Two departments with very different birth rates might have the same physiological growth rate, while two other departments with the same rate of physiological growth might have very different birth rates. The meaning of a physiological growth rate is even more obscure because, as I have pointed out, the birth and death rates which constitute it have different denominators. For such reasons, I will tread lightly in what follows on the meaning of the growth rates of specific departments.

Aveyron, Corse, Creuse, and *Hautes-Pyrénées* are widely scattered geographically. They had high growth rates, and they had the lowest suicide rates in

France. They were low in several dimensions of modernity. None had a large city, all were thinly populated (Camp, 1961; Angeville, 1969), and three were very low in industrialization (Price, 1987). Literacy was about average for France as a whole. When authorities of the Catholic Church judged the levels of "religious vitality" of the 82 departments, they rated three of this group as "good," which was the highest of the four ratings which were assigned. But they also rated one of them, Creuse, as only "mediocre," and this was the lowest rank. (Note that these evaluations were carried out in 1880.)

Ardèche, Cher, Loire, and *Nord* are widely dispersed geographically, as are the first group. This set of four cases had few suicides. They also had the highest growth rates in the country, and for this reason can be readily identified in the chart. One would expect them to be low in various dimensions of modernity, but they turn out to have been quite diverse. In population density, they varied from low (Cher) to very high (Nord, on the Belgian border). One of them (the Nord, again) was more urban than only six departments in France. In literacy, three were average and one moderately below average. In 1831, two of the four departments were among the twelve most rural departments in France. If we may take the number of steam engines in 1841 as a measure of industrialization, two of these departments had between 5 and 15 (more than most departments), another (Loire) had between 101 and 300, and the Nord had more than 400, the most in France (Price, 1987, p.40). The Nord was, in fact, the fourth-wealthiest department in the country. Yet in spite of these indications of its modernity, in the Nord the church detected a "good" level of religious vitality. This was the highest level among the four departments, and the highest rank assigned to any department by the ecclesiastical evaluators.

Clearly, the Nord was the one really odd case in this group. It was highly modern in several ways. Yet its religious vitality was high, and its rate of growth was actually the fourth highest in France. Why did this wealthy department have a suicide rate of 109.9, while the nearby Oise had a rate of 407.2? In *Suicide*, Durkheim recognizes that the Nord was not typical.

> Within the northern region, two departments stand out because of their moderate aptitude for suicide, the Nord and Pas-de-Calais. In this respect, the Nord is especially surprising, because it is highly industrial, and high industrialization favors suicide.... In these two departments, the average family is large, although in the adjoining departments it is very small (Durkheim, 1897, pp. 211-212).

Somehow, the Nord succeeded in retaining *large families* while being highly modern. And, of course, in "Suicide et Natalité" family size is a measure of the birth rate which is negatively associated with suicide in France. In the book *Suicide*, family size appears as the main indicator of a low level of egoism in the family, which is negatively associated with suicide.

Perhaps the average family in the Nord was large because so many foreigners lived there. In 1872, only 2 percent of French residents were immigrants. But of that small percentage, fully 40 percent were Belgians living in the Nord (Braudel, 1990). I suspect that the distinctiveness of the Nord reflected some qualities of Belgian society which distinguished it from France.

Seine, Marne, Oise, Seine-et-Marne, and *Seine-et-Oise* are all in the Ile de France, and make up Paris and its environs. They were low in physiological growth. They were also dramatically higher in suicide than any other depart- ment and, for this reason, are easy to see in the scatter diagram. All were industrialized, had high rates of crime, and had little agriculture (although Seine-et-Marne differed slightly from this pattern). The Seine was by far the most populous of the four.

I have mentioned Morselli's comment that suicide was commoner in Paris than anywhere else in the world (Morselli, 1881, p. 181). But some comments by Durkheim in *Suicide* suggest that Morselli's statement requires amplifica- tion. It is not obvious why the departments which are only *near* Paris should have rates comparable to the Seine itself, which embraces Paris, or why the rate of Paris proper was actually lower than those of several districts near her (Durkheim, 1951, pp. 134-137).

The obvious step would be to attribute the high suicide rates around Paris to urbanization, or to something associated with it. To see whether this explanation has any basis, we may look at departments which contained large cities but were not near Paris. If urbanization is the explanation we are looking for, these departments would have more suicides than the rest of France. But they would also have fewer suicides than the Parisian departments, because Paris was much larger than any other French city. (In 1851, Paris was about five times the size of the next largest city, which was Marseilles.) Along with Marseille (in *Bouche-du-Rhône*), the cities which interest us are Lyon (in *Rhône*), Nantes (in *Loire Inférieure*), Bordeaux (in *Gironde*), and Toulouse (in *Haute-Garonne*).[57]

The suicide rates of these five departments were between 65.9 and 202.9. The rates of the four Parisian departments were dramatically higher, between 380.6 and 407.2. The five departments had rates of suicide and of growth which placed them much closer to the regression line in the scatter plot than were the four departments around Paris. Therefore, the very high frequency of suicide around Paris does not seem to be due to urbanization alone. These high rates also seem to reflect the operation of other factors. This is true whatever may be the explanation of the differing rates of suicide among the French departments as a whole.

Gers, Lot-et-Garonne, and *Tarn-et-Garonne* are adjacent departments in the southwest, though not on the Spanish border. They appear as a diagonal row in the lower lefthand corner of the scatter plot. In France, low growth is associated with modernity, and low suicide with an absence of modernity. These three agricultural departments were atypical—low (modern) in growth and low (not modern) in suicide. The three ranged from somewhat above to somewhat below average in urbanization. They were low in industrialization through the relevant period, intermediate in religious vitality, and a bit below average in percent literate. I have tried to learn more about these unusual departments, but I remain unable to account for the discrepancy between their rates of growth and suicide.

Eure and *Calvados* are in Normandy, on the English Channel. Because they were the only departments with *negative* growth rates, they can be readily seen on the chart. They were also among the wealthiest, along with the Nord and the departments around Paris. They were industrialized (especially Eure), and densely populated, with high crime rates. All of these conditions were associated with low growth. They were above average in literacy (as we would expect) and in religious vitality (as we would not).

The growth rates of these contiguous departments may have been negative because of certain cultural patterns which were specific to Normandy. There were few marriages in that region in the nineteenth century, and the marriages which did take place produced few children. With low growth *and* low marital fertility, Eure and Calvados were low in two of Durkheim's measures of the birth rate. They might be expected to have many suicides. In fact, the suicide rate of Eure was rather high.

To the moral statisticians, the long-term rise of suicide in Europe was somehow a result of "civilization." We would speak instead of "modernization." The decline in physiological growth is one aspect of modernization, and it tends, at least in France, to be accompanied by a rise in suicide. One main generalization, which is not unexpected, can be drawn from the characterizations just given: Both low growth and high suicide are associated with various other dimensions of modernization. But this is only a tendency, and there are striking exceptions.

Table 6

Durkheim believes that Tables 2-5 have shown that there is a negative relation between births and suicides in France. Table 6 is meant only to confirm this association, and he commits it to a footnote. Yet this table, as he apparently is not aware, contains the most remarkable findings in his essay (see Note 11 at end of chapter).

According to this evidence, the effect of the birth rate on suicide is compressed into a *very narrow range* of birth rates. Within that range, the effect is *extremely strong*. A small increase in the birth rate brings about a dramatic decrease in suicide. When the birth rate is 140 per year, the suicide rate is 280 per million. When the birth rate rises to only 185, the suicide rate shrinks to 20 to 40 per million. In other words, an increase in the birth rate of 25 percent produces a decrease in suicide of between 86 and 93 percent.

This effect is spectacular. The figures suggest that the births which fall within that narrow band possess some singular property which distinguishes them from other births. It is not apparent what that property might be. I doubt that an increase in births from 140 to a mere 185 could bring about the enormous effect shown in the table.

The obvious course would be to examine the source of Durkheim's evidence. But he does not say what it is, and I have not been able to uncover it.

Table 6 justifies an aside about the strength of an effect.

The strength of an *effect* and the strength of an *association* are two different things. One might find a very large effect which is somewhat unpredictable—a large effect and a *low* association. Or, one might discover a small effect which is highly predictable—a small effect and a *high* association.

Although Table 6 shows that the *effect* of marital fertility on suicide is very strong, it does not follow that the *association* of the two is strong also. Let us imagine a different version of the table, in which an increase in births of 25 percent caused a decline in suicide of only 25 percent. In this case, the effect of births would be a lot less than the one in Table 6. But the association between the two variables might be the same.

The table shows a strong effect over a narrow range. Something comparable can be seen in another field. The effect of electromagnetic radiation on bacteria is extremely variable. Most of the spectrum has little effect, but certain parts of it are deadly (Pelczar, Reid and Chan, 1970, pp. 434-435).

Population density

Durkheim's purpose is to demonstrate the truth of his law. He is only interested in rural-urban differences (and, in the section of his essay which follows, occupations) as they bear on that law. Now that he has left his European evidence, he is concerned solely with France, and with that part of his law which posits an *inverse* relation between births and suicides.

His argument concerning population density can be expressed thus: (1) suicide is *more* common in cities than in rural areas, (2) births are *less* common in cities than in rural areas, and (3) therefore, rates of birth and suicide are inversely related.

He gives evidence in support of the first two statements, and from this he *infers* that the third statement is true. This indirect form of proof is not the most secure basis for inference. But it may be of some value if the relations among the variables involved are strong enough.

We may note in passing that, although the three statements are about three variables, Durkheim is trying to show only that there is a *two*-variable relation between births and suicides. He is not using population density as a test factor. If he were to succeed in demonstrating this two-variable relation, he might then introduce further variables as controls (though in fact he does not do this).

He gives little attention to rural and urban suicide rates, except to report that the rate for the cities of France is 221, while in the rural areas it is 123.

The birth rate is another matter. In his brief discussion of rural-urban contrasts, he employs three indicators of the birth rate, two of which he has not used before.

The first is births minus deaths, a measure of natural increase which does not take the size of the populations into account. Durkheim shows that the chief towns of the departments had a great predominance of deaths over births. He implies that natural increase is higher in the rest of France, but he gives no figures.

Next, population growth makes a fleeting appearance. This is the indicator which comes closest to measuring the "birth rate" as Durkheim conceives it.[58] He defines the urban population as all those living in towns of 2000 or over, and the rural as the rest, and finds that in France the urban population, in proportion to its size, grew far less than the rural. (The growth in question apparently took place during the year 1884.)

Finally, he gives three crude birth rates, which he obtains from Legoyt. For this one moment, one might use a single indicator of the birth rate to compare his data from Europe with some of his data from France.

Durkheim's brief discussion of population density embodies some of his recurring problems. He is trying to show that there is *some* association in his evidence. But he does not consider *how strong* this association is. This question is even more important than usual, because his indirect method of inference makes the validity of his conclusions depend very much on the strength of the association.

If all three indicators of the birth rate measured the same thing, he would only need to use one of them. But he can hardly be unaware that the three cannot be equated. One includes only births, the second births and deaths, while the third reflects births, deaths, and migration. He does not discuss these differences. Why then does he use all three measures?

Perhaps he thinks that if he can show an association between births and suicides with one birth rate measure, he will show a *stronger* association if he uses three measures. It might have been wiser to decide which of the three indicators best measures what interests him and use that indicator only.

Occupations

Durkheim's treatment of occupations also encounters problems.[59] Table 7 gives occupational suicide rates from Italy. He supposes that the relations of occupation and suicide are about the same in France.

This table, like Table 1, is taken from Morselli. But this time Durkheim does some rearranging, and presents the occupations in the order of their suicide rates. Perhaps he does this merely to show that occupations have widely varying rates of suicide. The figures do make this dramatically clear, at least for Italy.[60]

But should the table be set up this way? The question is one of time order. No one chooses an occupation because he has killed himself. The dependent variable in Table 7 can only be suicide. In order to show the degree to which occupation affects suicide, the rates should be listed in the order of occupation, the independent variable.

But how can anyone arrange suicide rates "in order of occupation"? Occupations do not lie along a single dimension. They are not inherently ordered in terms of more or less. In this respect, they are like countries.[61]

It seems that Durkheim wants to apply to occupations the same indirect method which he has used with population density. But Table 7 permits him to conclude only that suicide varies by occupation, and this statement is *not comparable* to either of the statements about rural-urban differences which were presented above. Let us grant that suicide rates vary by occupation. Let us grant also what his few figures suggest, that birth rates also vary by occupation. From these two statements, no conclusion about an association between births and suicides can be derived. Yet his purpose is to show that there is such an association: "...the occupations in which people kill themselves most are also those in which there are the fewest births, and vice versa."

Perhaps realizing this, he drops his indirect method and takes up the direct approach which is more familiar to us, that is, having given the suicide rates of 13 occupations, he now gives the birth rates of four of the same occupations: letters and science, commerce, industry, and farming. At this point, the other nine suicide rates in Table 7 become irrelevant to his argument.

Let us make three assumptions. First, the four occupations show the same relation between births and suicides as we would see if we had evidence on all occupations. Second, occupational suicide rates bear about the same relation to one another in Italy and France, though their absolute levels may be different in the two countries. Third, both physiological growth and average family size are valid measures of the birth rate. On these assumptions, these few figures are consistent with Durkheim's conclusion from Tables 2-5 that the birth rate and the suicide rate are inversely related in France.[62]

Data and Theory: Four Issues

There remain four general issues to consider. Each has to do with the relation between Durkheim's theory and his evidence: (1) an assumption he makes about the *strength* of relations between two variables, (2) his use of ecological data, (3) the period of time which separates a set of births from the suicides which they cause, and (4) a way which Durkheim does not mention in which the birth rate *does* cause the suicide rate.

The strength of an association

Durkheim's thinking about the strength of a relation between two variables will seem strange today. His views on the matter can be summarized in four statements.

(1) *Any relation between two variables is perfect.* There are no *degrees* of association. He never makes this odd assumption explicit, nor does he consistently maintain it. But Selvin (1961) finds it in *Suicide*,[63] and I find it in "Suicide et Natalité." I have mentioned several points in the article where Durkheim's reasoning is perplexing. Now I will argue that the source of our puzzlement is his odd assumption.

One instance is his discussion of the suicide rate as an indicator of the abnormal state of a society. He assumes at that point that several states of ill-health—the suffering of individuals, the rate of suicide, and the ill-health of society itself—*exist to a corresponding degree.* Some might ask for evidence of these strong associations. But Durkheim's assumption seems to make him think that such evidence is unnecessary.

The same assumption can be found in his discussion of the weakness of a society, the variable which intervenes between a low birth rate and a high suicide rate. In this case, his assumption leads to several ideas. In France, all manifestations of decadence will occur together. The rates of all human diseases are highly correlated with each another. The decadence of a society is highly correlated with the rates of all diseases. And suicide is highly correlated with all of them. Thus, if a low birth rate causes national decadence, this social condition is closely associated with all forms of individual weakness, including suicide, and the link between a low birth rate and a high suicide rate has been clarified. But if we do not assume with Durkheim that any relation between two variables is perfect, his line of argument is not persuasive.

Yet another instance is his argument that low physiological growth is abnormal. His evidence shows that in France there is a negative relation between growth and suicide, and he thinks that he has proved that a high rate of suicide is abnormal. On these grounds, he infers that a low rate of growth is also abnormal.

Once again, his faulty assumption leads to an unwarranted inference. Let us concede that there is a *moderate* negative relation between growth and suicide. Let us suppose also that the word "abnormality" has an clear empirical referent.[64] Let us also for the moment agree with him that abnormality is associated with a high rate of suicide. Even given all of this, it follows only that abnormality *may* also, *in some measure,* be associated with a low rate of growth. Durkheim's confident inference that the abnormality of a high suicide rate proves the abnormality of a low growth rate assumes that the relation between a low birth rate and suicide is perfect.

We come upon a final example in his analysis of rural-urban differences. He shows that suicide is *more* common in cities than in rural areas, and that births are *less* common, and infers that the rates of births and suicides are inversely related. But he does not ask how strong the associations must be to justify his inference. Once again, he seems to assume that the first two associations are perfect. If this is not so, and if the first two statements describe only weak associations, the third statement may not be true of this particular set of data.

(2) If there are a number of items of evidence that an association exists, Durkheim concludes that the association is a strong one.

> Since a low birth rate and an aggravation of the tendency to suicide are associated as regularly as we have just seen, we are justified in regarding them as two phenomena of the same species, and in attributing to the former the morbid character which everyone recognizes in the latter.

In other words, since the birth rate and suicide are in *some* measure associated in several sets of data, the association between them is strong. But a moderate association is only moderate, however many sets of data may show it. A strong association is no less strong, even if it is shown only once.

(3) Durkheim is not aware that an association can be expressed as a single number. He presents Tables 2-5 in order to accomplish two things. To offer the data ("the facts") and to show that there is an association between births and suicides ("the law"). Table 2 does contain a lot of facts, but the surfeit of numbers obscures the relation which Durkheim wants to show. To demonstrate it more clearly, he summarizes the data in Table 3, and also summarizes both tables in words. Then, with the thought that Tables 2 and 3 are still not enough, he presents the "expérience inverse" in Tables 4 and 5.

He says that he adds Tables 4 and 5 because Table 2, in spite of its vastness, does not list the average suicide rates of each department. But he may also do so because he is not conversant with the correlation coefficient. This statistic might teach him that an association can be effectively presented as a single number. It might also teach him another truth, upon which the first depends, that an association between two variables *objectively exists*. For want of such a statistic, and the understanding which comes with it, his custom is to treat an association as something to be come at from various angles, and to be approximated with words.

In such things Durkheim was adhering to the norms of his time. The moral statistician was a solo practitioner, fighting against whatever schools of thought opposed his own. He worked with limited evidence, no textbooks to guide his labors, and no experience as a student in methodology courses. Even in *Suicide*, Durkheim "…had not formalized his analytical procedures" (Selvin, 1961, p. 136).

(4) Sometimes he recognizes that moderate associations exist. He indicates on several occasions that some condition is *due to many causes*. Future levels of population and consumer goods will be determined by a thousand circumstances, the health of a society depends on many causes, the suicide rate depends on "innumerable conditions," and increases in physiological growth and the suicide rate depend on "many accidental and local causes." He makes some of these comments in order to play down the weakness of a relation which, if it were stronger, would help his argument. But each of the comments

is also an acknowledgment that sometimes an association is less than perfect. It must be, if there is more than one cause. By implication, an association is only perfect when something is totally determined by something else. But if there is one thing that social research has established since Durkheim's time, it is that most correlations in the social world are not very high. Almost all explanations must appeal to multiple causation.[65]

Ecological hypotheses, data, and inferences

The most effective tables in *Suicide* show the level of integration or regulation of the social environment of each person represented in the table, and also whether he has killed himself or not. In other words, these tables show that there is a relation between births and suicides *on the individual level*. This is multivariate evidence.

"Suicide et Natalité" is different. Durkheim claims that one rate causes another rate. A birth rate brings about another social condition, some level of the struggle for existence or of the weakness of a society, and this condition, in turn, affects the rate of suicide. This is an ecological hypothesis. Multivariate evidence, that is, evidence of a relation between births and suicides on the individual level, would not be needed to test it. Since Durkheim's hypotheses are ecological, it is appropriate that his evidence is also ecological. It characterizes not individuals but either countries or departments of France.

His evidence is ecological, and so, appropriately, are his inferences. For example, here are two of his ecological findings:

1. The group of departments in which population growth is lowest is the one in which suicide is most frequent.
2. The occupations in which people kill themselves most are also those in which there are the fewest births, and vice versa.

From the second of these findings we cannot infer that the same relation obtains *among individuals*. We cannot infer, for example, that female lawyers who have babies are less likely to kill themselves than are female lawyers without babies. Such an inference would display the "ecological fallacy." Some of Durkheim's inferences in *Suicide* show this defect, as Pope (1976, pp. 63, 89) has shown. But his essay is innocent of it.

But whatever basis we use to subdivide a social category, there will always be variation *within* each subcategory. *Internal variation* is an inherent limitation of ecological data.

For example, the suicide rates in Table 4 represent averages for the years 1872 to 1876. If we take these years as a single period, the average suicide rate for France as a whole is a single figure. But for the same period there are as many departmental rates as there are departments, and these show that there is great internal variation in France. The department with the highest suicide rate is the Oise, near Paris, whose rate of 407.2 is substantially higher than the highest suicide rate in Table 1. The department with the lowest rate is Corsica, whose rate of 28.6 is lower than all but two of the rates in Table 1.

The data in *Suicide* suggest similar conclusions. Durkheim introduces many test factors in his book. Each time he does this, he displays the resulting subgroups in a table. *Every one* of these tables shows internal variation. Not once does every subgroup exhibit the same rate of suicide.

By definition, any social group or category will have a single rate of suicides (or of births). But any hope of introducing enough controls to uncover internally homogeneous units would prove forlorn. The rate of the group as a whole will almost always be different from the rate of most or all of the subunits which appears when a control variable is introduced.

Because of variation of this kind, some inferences from ecological data are uncertain. Durkheim says that in France low birth rates are associated with high suicide rates. But it is possible that suicides in departments with low birth rates occur mainly in the minority of subgroups within those departments which have relatively *high* birth rates. In such a case, there would be a kind of *positive* relation between births and suicides which would be concealed by ecological evidence. Although such a possibility may be remote, it remains true that his ecological data do not rule it out.

Durkheim's experience in preparing his article may have made him more aware of the pervasiveness of internal variation, and of the resulting limits of ecological data. In *Suicide* he works with hypotheses which call for multivariate data, and therefore do not suffer from this limitation.

The lag between births and suicides

The third issue has radical implications. It is possible that much of the evidence in "Suicide et Natalité" is irrelevant. It is also possible that there is no way to test Durkheim's law, no matter what evidence we have.

To approach this issue, we may think about the rates of suicide in the book, *Suicide*. Every rate represents deaths which have taken place over a certain interval of time. Some of these intervals are a single year. Others are two or more years, represented by an average of the suicide rates over those years. A few represent as many as ten years, or even a few more.[66] These time intervals vary in this way, without any apparent rationale, from table to table, and sometimes even within a single table.

Why the variation? Durkheim does not seem to choose these intervals because of theoretical considerations. He rarely claims that he has chosen a given interval because it is the best possible choice, given the specific question he is addressing. Instead, he adopts it because it is the one which was used by whoever assembled the evidence which he is using.

He seems to think that one interval is about as good as another. Data based on a single year are neither better nor worse than data based on ten years. His procedure only makes sense if he is making a further assumption, that the effect of a given level of integration or regulation on suicide can be seen after a *short* period of time. This period seems to be a matter of days or weeks. Sometimes readers of *Suicide* have accepted this assumption without reflection. But the truth of it is not obvious.

Things are different in "Suicide et Natalité." It is not immediately clear what assumption the essay makes about these time intervals. But I will argue that the implicit assumption is that there is a lag of *decades* between a set of births and the suicides which result from them.

Several considerations lead to this conclusion. First, it is suggested by the periods represented in Tables 2-5. Someone who is familiar with *Suicide* may be taken aback to find average rates of growth and suicide reckoned over decades. But Durkheim does not include these figures for want of something better. He thinks that these data are the best in his paper.

They are the best partly because they employ physiological growth, which he considers to be his best measure of the birth rate. But they are the best for another reason as well. If births only cause suicides which occur many years later, rates which are calculated over decades are not only desirable but essential. Only rates of this kind can ensure that a set of births will appear in the same table as the suicides which result from them. If the time intervals shown in a particular table are too short, one will be looking at births without the suicides which result from them, and suicides without the births which caused them. Obviously, such a table can tell us nothing about the relation between births and suicides.

A second reason to think that there is a long lag is that most of the effects of babies on society are not immediate.

Durkheim says that a low birth rate makes a society weak, and that this weakness in turn causes suicide. But to know how long the lag is we need to know more. We need to know just which effects of births make the society stronger. Once we know this, we can estimate how long after a birth these effects will take place. This information, in turn, may help us to determine the length of the lag between births and suicides.

Since Durkheim does not tell us any of these things directly, we will first consider the matter without reference to him. How, in general, does a birth affect a society? Obviously, a birth has certain effects right away, and other, delayed effects continue through the lifespan of whoever has been born. A baby does not participate in society, but he does require money and the withdrawal of a women from the labor force. A boy, 20 years later, becomes available to fight in a war. A young adult is ready to produce children. As a man grows older, his economic contribution changes. And so on.

Although Durkheim does not say which of the repercussions of births matter to him, we know that most of these repercussions do not occur until years or decades later. For this reason alone, it seems likely that the effects which interest Durkheim do also. If this is so, the lag which we seek to identify is prolonged.

A third reason is that the one effect of a birth which Durkheim almost certainly has in mind only takes place after a long lag.

He wrote his essay only 17 years after the defeat of France in 1871. He seems to have this defeat in mind. So strong is his preoccupation with France and Germany that it leads him to ignore evidence, both when he interprets Table 1 and when he formulates his law. Many believed that the low birth rate caused the defeat. If more Frenchmen had been born, the country could have had a larger army. But the birth rate which had this dire effect was not that of 1871 but of roughly 20 years earlier. If only there had been more of these earlier births, they might have prevented the defeat. I suggest, on these somewhat conjectural grounds, that the lag is on the order of 20 years.

Durkheim never says that the birth of more boys would make France a stronger society when they become soldiers 20 years later. He never even mentions the war of 1870-71. But he does not have to. He was not writing for us. He was writing for Frenchmen who, not long before, had suffered defeat in a war. And he does at least hint at such things: "A society which grows steadily is...stronger and more capable of holding its own against rival societies...." These considerations only suggest that there is a long lag between births and suicides. They do not prove it. And there are some reasons which suggest that there is no lag.

Sometimes Durkheim seems to assume that the effect of births on suicides is almost immediate. "If it can be shown that an increase in the birth rate is *accompanied by* a rise in the number of suicides, we will be justified in inferring that too high a birth rate is an unhealthy phenomenon, detrimental to society" (emphasis added). The same seems to be suggested by some of his comments about his data on countries, rural-urban differences, and occupations.

These considerations, taken together, have some force. What is more, his Conclusion also seems to imply that there is no lag. He claims there that family feeling affects both births and suicides. If this is so, how long would it take family feeing to have these effects? With regard to its effect on births, if family spirit is strong, a couple will not wait 20 years before they decide to have a child. With regard to its effect on suicide, strong family feeling will not deter a family member from killing himself 20 years after it exists. The intervals of time which these processes require seem comparable to the brief intervals of *Suicide*. Considered in this way, Durkheim's Conclusion makes the lag disappear.

But we must reject this solution. An acceptable interpretation of Durkheim's article must be consistent with the law which it is his aim to establish. Since his Conclusion contradicts his law, we can only accept his ideas about family feeling if are prepared to say that in Durkheim's view the birth rate does not cause the suicide rate. Thus, his Conclusion cannot be taken as proof that the lag is not prolonged. I conclude that, although the evidence is not conclusive, there probably is a long lag between births and suicides, and it probably lasts about 20 years.[67]

The long lag may be an unexpected idea, and it has an implication which may also be unexpected. If there is a lag, Durkheim is actually concerned with *two* associations. The first is shown directly in his data. It is the association between births and suicides during whatever period of time a particular table represents. To see this association, one looks at birth rates and suicide rates over the *same* period of years.[68]

The second association is only implied. It is the association between a set of births and those *later* suicides which they cause. In other words, it is the association between the birth rate over some limited period and the suicide rate of a *later* period, which is separated from the first by the lag. Durkheim never mentions this second association. But it is what really matters. The only evidence which can support him directly is evidence of this association.

He may not be fully aware that the second association is implied by his analysis. In any case, he only looks for his first association. Consider his comments on Tables 4 and 5, which contain long-term average growth rates and short-term average suicide rates:

> ...since suicide has evolved in a much more regular way than population growth since the beginning of this century, it is not as important to go further and establish its annual total over a very extended period.

Durkheim wants to factor out fluctuations in births and suicides. Because the growth rates have been so variable, he thinks it best to smooth them out by using long-term averages. But because suicide rates have not varied so much, averages representing a few years are sufficient.

Here is a truly awkward situation. It is essential that Durkheim identify the second association. To do this, he should locate a swell in births, move ahead in time the distance of the lag, and then look for a corresponding decline in suicides in that later period. There is simply no other way to find evidence of the second association. Instead, he sets out, perversely, to flatten out these variations. *He tries to obscure precisely the fluctuations which he should be examining.* As a result, his tables prevent his reader from distinguishing suicides caused by a given set of births from suicides caused by earlier or by later births. Yet the second association could not be more important—evidence of it would be central to any adequate test of his law.[69]

At the start of this section, I mentioned two implications of the lag. Now these may be restated. First, it is possible that much of Durkheim's evidence is irrelevant. There probably is a lag between births and suicides, and my best guess is that it is 20 years long. But his evidence, aside from Tables 2-5, represents shorter periods of time. It seems that the births which appear in his tables cause suicides which do not appear, because they will occur years later. And the suicides which appear are the results of births which are not shown, because they occurred years before. It is true that his evidence shows in various ways that there is a relation between births and suicides. But *it is a relation between births and the wrong suicides.* This relation has only a remote bearing on his thesis that births *now* will affect suicide at a *later* time. Thus, much of Durkheim's evidence is irrelevant to his law.

It is also possible (and this is the second implication of the lag) that no evidence could be relevant because there is no way to test his law. His argument probably implies that there is a lag, but we cannot be sure about this. If there is one, it may last 20 years, but maybe it does not. Since this period is not defined, it is not clear what evidence would be relevant. And if we do not know what evidence would be relevant, how could we test his law?

How births cause suicides

Durkheim encounters no dearth of problems when he tries to show that births affect suicides. There is an irony in this, because births *do* cause suicides, and they do so in a rather straightforward way. In saying this, I am using the word "cause" in the weak sense which Durkheim himself sometimes employs: a "cause" of suicide is anything which has *some effect* on it.

Any population shows a distribution of people according to age. The familiar population pyramid expresses this distribution as the percentage of the total population of each sex, in each age group: 0-4 years, 5-9 years, and so on. Therefore, those populations with high birth rates are likely to have many young people (Lauro, 1982, p. 99).

Births do not determine the age structure all by themselves. Deaths are of course also a determinant (Spengler, 1974, p. 65). The birth rate may be high, but if it is counteracted by a high death rate among the young, the population as a whole may not be very young. Migration also affects the age structure. Those leaving a country in a given year are not likely to be representative of the age structure as a whole; nor are those entering it. We can accommodate these complications by simply defining the "birth rate" as births minus deaths plus net migration. Such a definition should not be disconcerting. I have suggested that Durkheim himself, according to the best reading of him, defines the birth rate in this extended sense. If we do the same, we can still say that the "birth rate," through its effect on the age structure, is one cause of the suicide rate.[70]

Many variables affect the suicide rate. But one of those with the greatest effect is age. The evidence in *Suicide* reveals, as Pope has shown, that age, sex, and region all have "far more explanatory power" than do variables to which Durkheim gives greater attention, such as religion and family size (Pope, 1976, p. 142).

Suicide is rare among children. It grows more frequent with increasing age, and "...is often ten times as great at the close of life as at its beginning" (Durkheim, 1951, pp. 100, 324; Dublin, 1963, pp. 22-26). These comments describe men more clearly than women. But men commit most suicides, and the statement also describes the suicides of the two sexes taken together.

In short, since the birth rate determines the age structure, and since age has a powerful effect on the frequency of suicide, the birth rate causes the suicide rate.[71]

Now we have two explanations, Durkheim's and the present one, for whatever association is found between births and suicides. Since both use the word, cause, in a weak sense, the two are not mutually exclusive. On the other hand, some of the relations between births and suicides which Durkheim presents may be due to the age structure, rather than to the processes which he proposes.

This is true of France and Germany. Durkheim says that the low French birth rate weakens the society and causes more suicides. I have suggested that a low birth rate also causes more suicide by producing an older population. In France, then, the age structure and the weakness of the society influence the suicide rate in the same direction. Most of Durkheim's evidence—all that appears after Table 1—is meant to show that births and suicides are inversely related in France. But how much of this association is a result of the age structure, rather than of the weakness of French society?

In Germany, a high birth rate intensifies the struggle for existence, and tends to generate a high rate of suicide. But the same high birth rate will also produce a *young* population, and this tends to cause a low rate of suicide. Thus, in Germany the two tendencies act against one another. In this regard, France and Germany are contrasting cases.

Durkheim's only evidence that there is a positive relation between births and suicides in Germany is in Table 1. If we think that this limited evidence has some force, the struggle for existence in Germany acquires a certain plausibility. It seems to be powerful enough to show its effects even though the age structure is operating in the opposite direction.

What of the age structure in relation to a pattern of another kind, the dramatic growth of suicide in the nineteenth century (Durkheim, 1951, pp. 50-51, 367)? "Suicide et Natalité" does not explicitly attempt to account for this increase. But Durkheim does think that the declining birth rate in France during the nineteenth century made the society grow weaker, with the rise in suicide a result. Is it possible that the birth rate caused suicide to increase, not by weakening the society but by acting through the age structure?

A decline in fertility is one of the processes which define the demographic transition. As the birth rate drops, there are fewer children and more old people, and the average age tends to rise. This process was taking place during the nineteenth century in the European countries which Durkheim studies. The average age was rising, and so was the suicide rate.

It seems certain that the first change partly brought about the second. As the average age rose, the strong effect of age on suicide must have contributed to the increasing suicide rate. This is so even if Durkheim is right, and the birth rate was *also* affecting the suicide rate through its effects on the weakness of society, the struggle for existence, or both.

The Essay and the Book

Much of what is most interesting about "Suicide et Natalité" is its similarities to and differences from *Suicide*. I already considered Durkheim's changing (or unchanging) approaches to a number of specific problems: the diagnosis of French society, how to present evidence, and others. But what is the relationship between the central propositions in the two documents? Does "Suicide et Natalité" anticipate the explanatory concepts which are developed in *Suicide*? And, looking at things the other way around, is the law proposed in the essay reaffirmed in the book?

Suicide in the essay: Huff's thesis

I have mentioned Toby Huff, the one author who has published an analysis of "Suicide et Natalité." Huff (1975) initially proposes a specific view of what a scientific explanation is. His thesis is that Durkheim presents such an explanation in *Suicide*. "Suicide et Natalité" plays an important role in Huff's argument because it reveals just how far Durkheim had progressed in 1888 toward the explanation which he would advance in 1897.

Huff concedes that much of what we find in *Suicide* is not original. The moral statisticians had published hundreds of studies of suicide before Durkheim entered the field (Douglas, 1967, p. 16). Morselli brought their main findings together in 1879, 18 years before Durkheim's book appeared, and expressed most of the laws which Durkheim would later subsume under such concepts as egoism and anomie. It may be that Morselli's compilation is even more inclusive than Durkheim's (Huff, 1975, p. 247).

Durkheim's contribution was an act of "abduction," which is the essential term in Huff's analysis. The expression is not a new one. Aristotle used it to refer to a syllogism whose major premise is certain, but whose minor premise is only probable. The philosopher Charles Sanders Peirce wrote of abduction in a related sense, as the process by which explanatory constructs in science are created. To Huff, who follows Peirce, abduction is "...the only logical operation which introduces any new idea...." It is not deduction; there is no set of premises from which propositions inescapably follow. Nor is it induction; it is not a process of recording new sensory reports (Huff, 1975, pp. 241-242). A scientist engages in abduction when, in the process of reorganizing available evidence, he proposes a certain set of hypothetical entities, arguing that these entities can be presumed to exist because they can make sense of that evidence. Abduction is a form of conjecture. By itself, it proves nothing (Huff, 1975, pp. 249-250).

Durkheim's contribution was an act of abduction in just this sense. He took data provided by his predecessors and reorganized it using new principles of his own invention. Such hypothetical social conditions as egoism cannot be observed and measured. But they are of value to the scientist because they enable him to explain the known by the unknown. The "only justification for introducing them in the first place [is] the hoped-for demonstration that the known facts of rates of suicide could be arranged in a fashion consistent with a belief in them" (Huff, 1975, pp. 249-253).

What then of "Suicide et Natalité"? In 1888, Durkheim gave "a demographic explanation [of suicide] which is far removed from the theory of social integration." It is "radically different" from the one he was to offer in 1897. The theoretical categories which appear in *Suicide* are not to be found in "Suicide et Natalité." Their very *absence* (and this is Huff's point) shows that the process of abduction was yet to occur (Huff, 1975, pp. 247-248).

We can treat Huff's claim as an exegetical hypothesis that certain ideas from *Suicide* are not in the essay. What happens if we look in the essay for the concepts which Huff says are not there?

There is no hint of fatalism in the article. With regard to altruism, Durkheim makes no reference to nonliterate or non-Western societies, and, though he lists a suicide rate for the military in Italy, he says nothing about it. Thus, we need only look for signs of egoism and anomie.

We seem closer to the book *Suicide* when we encounter the discussion of family feeling in the Conclusion of "Suicide et Natalité." This social condition confers immunity against suicide, and is clearly akin to what *Suicide* calls social integration, a low level of which is egoism. The question is, Does the *absence* of family feeling and family spirit have the properties of egoism, as Durkheim was to define it in 1897?

We can only answer this question if we have a clear idea of the properties of egoism. It has been argued that "egoism," in *Suicide,* has three such properties, and that these are indicated by certain recurring terms. This only means that it is clear what these defining terms are. The question of how egoism is to be identified empirically is another matter. The defining terms are: a low rate of social interaction, few common beliefs, and weak social regulation (Johnson, 1965, p. 883).

Here, drawn from the Conclusion to "Suicide et Natalité," are the phrases and sentences which are the most relevant to egoism:

> Where family bonds [and] domestic traditions are…strong, they resist struggles within the family which would otherwise dissolve a marriage… [L]arge families…are only possible when men have a taste and habit for family solidarity, and prefer the pleasures of a common life…. Within his family, the individual belongs to a compact whole, with which he is solidary….[But when] families are loosely knit and small in numbers…spaces…exist between [the members]….The cold wind of egoism blows through these spaces, and it chills the heart and weakens courage…. If [social] sentiments are present, they draw individuals into group life.

The theme of these comments is social integration in the family. Yet this is only true in some vague sense. A nebulous idea of social integration is one thing; Durkheim's later concept of integration is another. The defining terms and phrases from *Suicide* which I listed above are striking by their absence from these excerpts. It is true that the comments actually include the *word* egoism, this being its one appearance in the article. But in this case the word does not seem to refer to the condition of low social integration as this is defined in *Suicide*.

Huff quotes Durkheim's conclusion in *Suicide* that *"Suicide varies inversely with the degree of integration of domestic society"* (Durkheim, 1951, p. 208) and comments that Durkheim "made no such claim in 1888" (Huff, 1975, p. 247). Actually, this is not quite true. Even in 1888, Durkheim was claiming that the stronger family bonds are, the less suicide there is. It is his later *concept* of integration that was lacking—an abstract property common to domestic, religious, and political society, which affects the suicide rate of *any* group.

What then of anomie? At an early point in his article, Durkheim argues that happiness depends not on the absolute level of satisfaction but on the gap between *felt* need and satisfaction. "If needs increase as soon as they are satisfied, they are not fulfilled; the gap between need and satisfaction remains the same." This is a familiar idea. It recurs in the discussion of anomie in *Suicide*. But in 1888 he does not associate this gap with a social condition of the kind which he will later call anomie. In fact, the word anomie does not appear in his essay.

In *Suicide*, again visiting the same gap, he adds several ideas. If human nature is unregulated, its needs are unlimited. But society can provide the regulation which will weaken the intensity of needs, thereby lessening the gap between these needs and their satisfaction. Since some acts of suicide grow out of unlimited needs, social regulation can lower the suicide rate (Durkheim, 1951, pp. 246-254). These assertions are of course part of Durkheim's characterization of anomie. But in his essay there is only a hint of such things to come.

We may say, then, that there is a notion of solidarity in the family in "Suicide et Natalité," but that it lacks the defining properties of egoism. There is also one idea which will later be associated with his concept of anomie, but this is only a foreshadowing. In short, the fully developed concepts of egoism, anomie, altruism, and fatalism cannot be found in the essay.

Durkheim's *Division of Labor* appeared five years after "Suicide et Natalité." Huff concludes that this book makes "no significant advance" over the analysis of suicide in the article. It devotes only five pages to the topic, and this brief discussion draws no connection between egoism or any of the other categories of 1897 and suicide (Durkheim, 1933, pp. 246-251; Huff, 1975, pp. 248-249).

Huff's reading of *Division* calls for a few comments. In that book, following Morselli and others, Durkheim observes that France and Germany exhibit the highest levels of civilization in Europe, and that they are also high in suicide.

But he does *not* say, as he did in 1888, that there are too few births in France and too many in Germany, and that these levels of fertility cause high rates of suicide in both countries. Nor does his discussion of suicide mention either the birth rate or "Suicide et Natalité." If he still believed that the birth rate causes the suicide rate, he would certainly say so. In this way, *Division* moves away from his essay.

But it does not move toward *Suicide*. We are not told, as we are in *Suicide*, that France and Germany have high levels of egoism and anomie. When *Division* discusses suicide, it does not mention egoism, altruism, anomie, fatalism, integration, or regulation. It does speak of "anomie" in another context (Durkheim, 1933, pp. 353-373), but it draws no connection between this social condition and suicide. In short, the abduction of which Huff writes had yet to occur in 1893.

Most of my comments so far are consistent with Huff's thesis. But three further things may be said.

First, Huff takes the view that Durkheim's "real originality" lies in the abduction which he performed, and not, as others have claimed, in his contribution to multivariate analysis (Huff, 1975, pp. 242, 252, 253). But I think that Huff poses a false antithesis. Developing explanatory concepts and doing multivariate analysis are not mutually exclusive activities. Durkheim's idea that all relations are perfect is partly a mistake about what happens when one carries out multivariate analysis. But it also creates problems for him when he tries to formulate abstract propositions.

Second, it is Huff's view that the data in *Suicide* are consistent with the ideas which Durkheim abducted. But this conclusion can only be justified by a close examination of Durkheim's evidence. No one had published such an examination until soon after Huff's article appeared, when Pope provided the one thorough examination of the relation of Durkheim's evidence to his theory which has appeared. This meticulous analysis shows that Durkheim's evidence supports his theory less well than many have supposed (Pope, 1976). However estimable is Huff's analysis of theoretical discovery, Pope's study leads one to ask to what extent Durkheim arrived at his categories by abduction, and to what extent he just dreamed them up somehow and then inflicted them on his data.

Third, if Durkheim abducted something, what did he abduct? What, in other words, is his theory in *Suicide*? I have maintained elsewhere (Johnson, 1964, 1965) that two possible constructions of his theory are possible. According to the first of these, egoism and altruism form the opposite ends of a dimension of social integration. Anomie and fatalism form the opposite ends of a second dimension, of social regulation. Suicides are high when any one of the four causes is high, and highest when two of them are. The two dimensions cut across one another. Each society, group, or social condition lies at a position along each of the two. The point at which these two positions intersect corresponds to a rate of suicide. This will be the rate of the group in question, according to the theory. If this interpretation of Durkheim's theory is the best reading of *Suicide,* then Huff's argument may be sustained.

But I have argued that a second construction of the theory is *more consistent with Durkheim's own statements* and is therefore to be preferred. According to this second reading, altruism and fatalism are not part of his theory, and egoism and anomie are identical. There is one cause of variation in suicide rates, and there is a linear relation between egoism/anomie and suicide. This means, of course, that Durkheim himself was not fully aware of the most consistent interpretation of his own theory.[72] If this second reading of *Suicide* is accepted, then the theory which Huff claims that Durkheim abducted was not in fact Durkheim's theory.[73]

The essay in *Suicide*: the law is left behind

What then of the opposite relation between Durkheim's two studies? What is the role of the birth rate and of the law of 1888 in *Suicide*? The book does mention the birth rate (Durkheim, 1951, pp. 200, 201). But it never says that it has an effect on suicide. Variations in suicide are caused by social conditions such as egoism, not by the birth rate.

We have seen that Durkheim, in both his article and his book, sometimes sees any relation between two variables as perfect. He is thinking in this way whenever he says that something "causes" something else and means that it *totally determines* it. If we assume that he is thinking in this way, then if egoism and the others determine suicide, it follows the birth rate does *not* "cause" the suicide rate. He has abandoned his law of 1888.

But sometimes he recognizes that some relations are less than perfect. If he is thinking in this way in *Suicide,* he might suggest that both the birth rate and such conditions as egoism in some measure *affect* the suicide rate. But he never does suggest this. His book never says that births have any effect on suicide at all.

The book does refer to "Suicide et Natalité," however, (Durkheim, 1951, pp. 172, ftn. 3, 198) and one passage explicitly comments on it. This passage is found in a discussion of egoism in the family. It reveals that Durkheim, without actually saying so, no longer believes in his law of 1888.

He says that he has "already stated and proved," by the evidence on physiological growth in his essay, that immunity from suicide increases with family size.[74] But he adds that he now has a better measure of family size, the average membership of family households. He employs this better indicator in two tables (Durkheim, 1951, pp. 198-200; see also the two maps in Appendix IV).

Thus, Durkheim claims that in 1888 (a) he used his growth figures in order to measure family size, and (b) he maintained that those figures prove that immunity from suicide increases with family size. Each of these claims is false, as the following considerations will prove.

First, the only independent variable in his article is the birth rate. There is nothing else for physiological growth to measure. Thus, it is certain that he did not intend his growth figures to measure family size. It is true that there is a discussion of family size in his essay. But it is found in the section of the paper on occupations, and is quite unrelated to Durkheim's discussion of physiological growth.[75]

Second, if he wanted to use growth to measure family size, his article would discuss the two together. But it does not. His long discussion of physiological growth mentions its relations to various things: births, the birth rate, births minus deaths, and population growth. But it does not mention the relation of growth to family size.

Third, although the birth rate and family size are probably in some degree *associated,* the strength of their association has no bearing on the question at hand. The point is that conceptually they are two different things.

Fourth, although growth might serve as a suitable measure of family size in another context, the issue is whether Durkheim intended to use it in this way in 1888. And he did not.[76]

Apparently, by the time Durkheim wrote the *Division of Labor,* he had turned his back on his law. But even four years later, in *Suicide,* he is disinclined to say so. Durkheim rarely concedes that he has changed his mind,[77] and maybe he misrepresents his original purpose in using his growth measure because he wants to obscure his own change of opinion. I am sure that he puts aside his law of 1888 because of some of the weaknesses in his essay which have been documented here. But he never says so.

Conclusion

I have identified three kinds of shortcomings in "Suicide et Natalité": those resulting from our author's *lack of knowledge* of ways of dealing with evidence, those relating to his *scholarship,* and those relating to his *law itself.* The shortcomings of the third kind are the most important.

The deficiencies of the first kind are not Durkheim's fault. No one in his time knew about such things as correlation coefficients, scatter diagrams, and today's refined demographic indicators. But we have seen that these gaps in his knowledge sometimes prevent him from seeing what his own figures show and from conveying their meaning to his reader.

The problems of the second kind arise because sometimes he is, by our standards, insufficiently objective and painstaking as a scholar. This charge is most believable when one confronts several items of evidence that "Suicide et Natalité" was prepared in haste.

1. His tables contain some wrong headings, and various figures in them are miscalculated.

2. He tells us that M. Bertillon and M. Renan each said a certain thing "somewhere."

3. At one point, he needs certain figures which are provided in the source which he is using. But he does not notice them, and his own inattention compels him to substitute inferior data. (This situation is explained in the Appendix.)

4. Every citation in his paper is imprecise. Because of this vagueness, I was unable to identify and locate one of his sources at all. Even worse, he offers several items of evidence with no indication of where he found them.

It is difficult not to speak sharply about Durkheim's repeated carelessness. But we may choose to judge certain other deficiencies in his scholarship less harshly.

All that we know of Durkheim suggests that he was far from indifferent to society's dictates. His approach to life was highly conventional. His personal style was "tres comme il faut." He was a diligent worker. He followed the academic standards of his time so well that he was rewarded with an appointment at the Sorbonne. The appointment was in two fields, and one of them, sociology, was new and untried. In short, he was obedient to the norms of his own time.

But these norms were somewhat different from ours. Sociology was just beginning to separate itself from other kinds of activity. It was a less specialized pursuit then, and some of the oddities in his paper are there for that reason. Above all, an essay in sociology was expected also to be a literary creation. It seems that this is why Durkheim analyzes a table as if he were a critic reviewing a play. There is no one best way to do it, and literary merit is one criterion of a good interpretation.

He presents some figures from Morselli without rearranging them. The result is Table 1, and it is hard to read. But Durkheim, again thinking as might a literary man, may have thought that in this case a passage from another man's book should be reproduced exactly as its author originally presented it.

The polemical tone of the essay is another literary feature. His conclusions about Table 1 are influenced not only by the data but also by his patriotic concerns about France in relation to Germany. When he uses an indicator of the birth rate which pleases him, in Tables 2-5, he argues for its excellence. But when the measure is less appropriate, as in some of his other data, he passes silently over it. If Durkheim thinks that the proper task of a sociologist is not merely analysis but argumentation, he may consider such deviations from objectivity to be appropriate.[78]

In short, it is true Durkheim's scholarship is not always objective and painstaking. But it would be arbitrary to ignore differences of time and place, and to condemn all of what may seem to be failings of this kind.

The third, and most important, group of shortcomings has to do with Durkheim's law itself. I have mentioned these at various points. I will now use the main assertions of his essay as an outline within which to summarize the shortcomings of this third kind.

Durkheim wants to "...decide whether an increase in population is good or bad for a country...." He chooses suicide rates as his indicator of how bad the condition of a country is.

Durkheim's law suggests that the relation of births and suicides is not a linear one—a high or a low birth rate will cause a high rate of suicide. Germany had a high birth rate and many suicides. France had a low birth rate and many suicides. A moderate birth rate, as in ten other European countries, caused a low suicide rate.

Durkheim's data on European countries do not support his law very well. I have introduced further evidence, measuring the same countries with indicators which he does not use. It provides even less support for his law.

His seven measures of the birth rate present another problem. Each of them measures something unique, but Durkheim treats them as if they all measured the same thing. They are not interchangeable, and for this reason alone his findings are of uncertain meaning.

Durkheim is satisfied that he has proved his law. But he also wants to "interpret" it—to show *why* births and suicides are related in the way in which they are. Actually, he only does this for that part which says that a low birth rate is positively related to suicide. He suggests that the level of family feeling in a society affects rates of both birth and suicide. Varying levels of family feeling, then, partly account for the observed association between births and suicides.

This "interpretation" of the law seems to contradict it. To the extent that family feeling causes both births and suicides, there cannot be a causal relation between births and suicides. But we do not know the extent of this contradiction, since he does not specify the relative impact of the birth rate and of family feeling on suicide.

The effect of births on suicides is not immediate. Certain conditions (the weakness of a society, the struggle for existence) intervene between births and suicides. But these conditions are only vaguely defined. Partly for this reason, we do not know how long after a given set of births the suicides which they cause will take place. It is probably a matter of decades, and this delay has an awkward implication. Since most of Durkheim's evidence covers much briefer periods, one of his tables may include births but not the suicides which they cause, and suicides but not the births which caused them. To the extent that this is so, any apparent association between the births and suicides in the table is of doubtful meaning. The lag is probably long. But, since it is of uncertain length, we cannot know whether his data, or perhaps any data, have any bearing on his law.

Durkheim says enough to show that his findings may be irrelevant to his law. But he does not say enough to tell us what evidence would be relevant. To make a test of his law possible, we would need at least the following: (1)

an explicit definition of the "birth rate," so that an appropriate indicator of it might be chosen, (2) more information about the variables which intervene between births and suicides, (3) a less ambiguous idea of the length of the lag between births and suicides, and (4) specification of the degree to which suicides are determined by births, and by family feeling.

Durkheim's essay is imperfect and unfinished. But he managed to overcome some of its defects as he went on to prepare *Suicide,* as I have pointed out from time to time. The essay, then, did have value to him as a working paper. It provided him with something which he might improve upon, and to this extent it can be counted a success.

Apart from this, "Suicide et Natalité" has one outstanding virtue. Everything in it pivots on Durkheim's theory. Each item of evidence is introduced because of its bearing on his law of suicide. We have seen an instructive contrast in Morselli. He leads his reader on a prolonged stroll through a zoo of correlates of suicide. For want of direction by an abstract explanatory principle, he wanders aimlessly. It is clear that Durkheim understood something about the explanation of suicide which Morselli did not. But Durkheim did not show this understanding for the first time in his famous book. He showed this nine years before, in an essay which has remained almost completely unknown since his time.

APPENDIX

Notes to the Summary Table for Europe

Sources of data in the table

The rates of birth, natural increase (calculated) and suicide are from Morselli (1879, p. 198). (The first and third columns also appear in "Suicide et Natalité," Table 1.) Rates of marital fertility and population growth are from Flora, passim.

Calculation of rates of marital fertility and population growth

These rates represent averages for the years 1865 to 1876. When the figures for these years are not available, I approximate them by using the most appropriate years that are available.

The marital fertility rates of six countries are estimates of this kind. For each of the following countries, the average rate which I have used is based on the years indicated: Cisleithan Austria (1880-1882), Finland (1880-1884), Germany (1872-1875), Italy (1871-1876), the Netherlands (1874-1876), and Switzerland (1871-1876).

The estimated growth rates of five countries are arrived at in the same way: Belgium (based on two average rates, for 1857-1866 and 1867-1880), Frank (based on rates for the wanted years, except for 1871), Italy (based on rates for the wanted years except 1867 and 1872), the Netherlands (1871-1876), and Switzerland (1872-1876).

A suicide rate for Germany

Morselli gives suicide rates for Prussia and Bavaria which represent part of 1865 to 1876, the period he is interested in, but he does not give figures for Germany as a whole. I have found rates of marital fertility and growth for Germany as a whole, but not for Prussia or Bavaria. I need a suicide rate for Germany, for the years 1865 to 1876. But even a credible estimate of this rate is hard to arrive at.

The source of the problem is the unification of Germany in 1871. This political change took place within the period which we are studying, and it caused a hiatus in record-keeping.

The earliest available suicide figure for the whole of Germany is 211, for the years 1881 to 1884 (Halbwachs, 1978, pp. 5, 72). These years are later than what we need, and the figure seems too high to serve as an estimate for 1865 to 1876. Morselli's suicide rates for Prussia and Bavaria are quite a bit lower, and 72 percent of all Germans lived in these two states.

To arrive at another estimate, I have used Morselli's suicide rates for Prussia and Bavaria, weighted by population. The defect of this estimate is that it does not reflect suicides among the 28 percent of Germans who were neither Prussians nor Bavarians. The figure, 126, is used in the marital fertility and growth charts.

A suicide rate for Ireland

My estimate of the Irish suicide rate (16.6) is based on extrapolation from census figures for 1861, 1871, and 1881 (Hickley and Doherty, 1980, p. 485) and on raw number of suicides (Masaryk, 1970, pp. 131-132). Legoyt (1881, p. 134) also provides rates for each year from 1865 to 1875. Using his figures, the average suicide rate over these 11 years is 17.3. (Also see Masaryk, 1970, p. 46; Morselli, 1879, pp. 128-129, Table XVII; and Durkheim, 1951, p. 351.)

A second French distribution using Yvernès' suicide rates

The discussion of the French departments above is based on a scatter plot containing suicide rates taken from Morselli. Now I wish to suggest a second possible distribution of these departments, using the same growth rates but suicide rates taken from Yvernès. The actual rates of growth, and of suicide according to both sources, are listed in a table at the end of this Appendix.

All of this requires an explanation. The figures in Durkheim's Tables 2-5

Summary Table for Europe

COUNTRIES	Births per 1000 population: 1865-76[1]	Births per 1000 married women 15-44: 1865-76[2]	Natural increase per 1000 population 1865-76[3]	Population growth 1865-76[2]	Suicides per million	Years of suicide rates
Averages	34.04	316.23	8.65	6.96	85.14	
Austria (excluding Hungary)	38.7	286.10	7.10	7.98	122.0	(1873-77)
Bavaria	39.20	?	8.10	?	90.0	(1871-76)
Belgium	32.10	360.30	8.60	9.07	67.0	(1866-75)
Denmark	30.90	297.90	11.10	9.53	267.0	(1866-75)
England & Wales	35.50	318.30	13.30	12.78	70.0	(1871-76)
Finland	34.50	301.30	5.10	5.02	31.0	(1869-76)
France	25.70	217.40	4.50	2.96	150.0	(1871-75)
Germany	38.40[4]	396.30[2]	10.60[2]	7.82	126.0	(1871-76)
Holland	35.60	355.40	10.40	10.53	35.0	(1869-72)
Hungary	41.70	?	3.30	?	52.0	(1864-65)
Ireland	26.80[2]	333.10	9.72[2]	-5.56	16.6	(1865-76)
Italy	37.10	289.70	7.00	6.33	31.0	(1874-76)

Summary Table for Europe

	Births per 1000 population: 1865-76[1]	Births per 1000 married women 15-44: 1865-76[2]	Natural increase per 1000 population 1865-76[3]	Population growth: 1865-76[4]	Suicides per million	Years of suicide rates
Norway	30.30	327.60	12.80	7.63	74.00	(1866-73)
Prussia	38.50	?	11.10	?	133.00	(1874-76)
Rumania	30.2	?	4.00	?	25.00	(not given in Morselli)
Scotland	35.1	321.70	12.90	9.80	34.00	(not given in Morselli)
Spain	35.7	?	4.50	?	17.00	(1866-70)
Sweden	30.4	315.00	11.00	7.09	81.00	(1871-85)
Switzerland	30.4	307.10	9.30	6.48	196.00	(1876)

[1] From Chapter 7, Table 1
[2] From Flora
[3] Calculated from Morselli

actually represent *three* periods of time. All four tables use a single set of growth rates, representing averages for the years 1801 to 1869. But the two sets of suicide rates correspond in time neither to the growth rates nor to each other.

The suicide rates in Tables 2 and 3, from Yvernès, are for the years 1830 to 1879. These years substantially overlap with the years of the growth rates. Durkheim apparently thinks that the two periods are similar enough for his purpose, and he does not mention the difference between them. But Morselli's suicide rates in Tables 4 and 5 are averages for 1872 to 1876, an interval which is both later and much shorter. Why is this second set of figures introduced?

Durkheim is aware that the Yvernès suicide rates correspond better than Morselli's rates to the years of the growth rates. He would prefer to use Yvernès' suicide rates in all four of his tables. But Durkheim says that Yvernès provides average suicide rates for *groups* of departments only, and in order to construct Tables 4 and 5, Durkheim needs the mean rate of suicides of *each department*. The Morselli rates are based on a less appropriate time interval, but they do represent individual departments.

Durkheim is right that Yvernès' *map* of the suicide rates of groups of departments does not provide the evidence that he wants. But he overlooks a *chart* in the same book which provides just what he needs—the average suicide rates of each department, for the years 1830 to 1879. Yvernès' distribution is based on the evidence which Durkheim himself would have liked to use, and it seems appropriate to acknowledge it.

Since I have discussed the Morselli scatter plot at length, my comments on Yvernès'findings will be brief.

For both periods, there is a moderate negative relation between growth and suicide in the departments of France. The correlation between growth and the Yvernès suicide rates is -0.43; the same statistic, using Morselli's suicide rates, is -0.49.

Since suicide increased a lot in France in the nineteenth century, it is not surprising that Yvernès' suicide rates are generally lower than Morselli's. My discussion of age and suicide above would suggest that the difference must be partly due to the changing age structure of France. In the earlier years, there were more children, few of whom kill themselves, and fewer old people, who have very high rates of suicide. In spite of these and other social changes, each of the outlier groups which we found in the Morselli data also appears in the Yvernès data.

Especially striking in the earlier data is the conspicuous position of the one department with low growth and the highest suicide rate. This is the Seine, the department which includes Paris itself. It is odd that the suicide rate in the Seine did not increase during the interval we are looking at. It is also odd that over the same interval the rates of the other four departments were identical (280), and that all of these rates increased by roughly the same amount.

Summary Table for France

Department	Physiological growth rates: 1801-69 (from Bertillion)	Suicide rates: 1872-76 (from Morselli)	Suicide rates: 1830-79 (from Yvernés)
Averages	4.0	136.66	99.15
Ain	2.3	128.2	90
Aisne	4.3	64.8	210
Allier	5.7	83.9	50
Ardèche	7.2	109.9	50
Ardennes	6.0	166.7	130
Ariège	6.3	103.6	20
Aube	2.0	284.8	190
Aude	5.1	74.8	50
Aveyron	5.6	39.7	20
Basses-Alpes	2.9	195.2	140
Basses-Pyrénées	4.9	64.2	50
Bouches-du-Rhóne	2.0	202.9	150
Calvados	-0.1	147.5	90
Cantal	3.8	61.2	30
Charente	2.3	164.3	110
Charente-Inférieure	1.7	160.2	120
Cher	7.8	70.8	70
Corrèze	6.1	69.3	50
Corse	6.2	28.6	20
Côte-d'Or	2.8	187.4	120
Côtes-du-Nord	3.7	52.7	50
Creuse	6.3	30.8	40
Deux-Sèvres	4.8	111.0	90
Dordogne	3.4	115.3	80
Doubs	5.1	113.9	80
Drôme	5.6	162.2	120
Eure	-0.6	255.1	160
Eure-et-Loir	2.1	273.5	170
Finistère	5.0	108.2	80
Gard	5.5	114.7	90
Gers	1.0	61.8	40
Gironde	2.1	122.5	90
Haute-Garonne	4.4	141.7	40
Haute-Loire	5.5	45.9	30
Haute-Marne	3.4	141.7	100
Haute-Saône	4.7	118.1	60
Haute-Vienne	4.7	101.1	80
Haute-Alpes	3.5	115.3	80
Hautes-Pyrénées	5.3	39.9	30
Hérault	4.0	78.1	60

Summary Table for France cond.

Department	Physiological growth rates: 1801-69 (from Bertillion)	Suicide rates:1872-76 (from Morselli)	Suicide rates: 1830-79 (from Yvernés)
Ille-et-Vilaine	2.8	69.2	50
Indre	6.2	66.2	70
Indre-et-Loire	2.5	213.2	150
Isère	5.5	97.9	80
Jura	2.7	123	80
Landes	4.6	83.1	60
Loire	8.3	70.8	50
Loir-et-Cher	2.7	186	120
Loire-Inférieure	5.7	76	60
Loiret	3.4	206.7	160
Lot	2.1	58.9	40
Lot-et-Garonne	0.3	84.5	60
Lozère	5.9	54.6	40
Maine-et-Loire	3.6	99.2	100
Manche	2.1	84.5	50
Marne	2.6	380.6	280
Mayenne	3.9	82.7	60
Meuse	3.7	212.8	140
Morbihan	4.4	64.8	60
Nièvre	5.9	94.1	70
Nord	7.0	76.0	100
Oise	1.5	407.2	280
Orne	1.4	96.9	60
Pas-de-Calais	5.6	146.8	120
Puy-de-Dôme	3.6	219.3	40
Pyrénées-Orientales	6.6	126.2	60
Rhône	5.8	166.8	120
Saône-et-Loire	5.6	144.7	90
Sarthe	3.4	141.7	100
Seine	2.4	400.3	390
Seine-et-Marne	2.6	383.5	280
Seine-et-Oise	0.7	388.8	280
Seine-Inférieure	2.6	155.3	180
Somme	3.5	206.7	150
Tarn	5.4	55	40
Tarn-et-Garonne	0.6	74	60
Var	1.5	221.2	170
Vaucluse	4.5	208.7	140
Vendée	6.2	84.6	50
Vienne	5.6	93.5	70
Vosges	6.4	69.3	90

Notes to the Summary Table for France

Durkheim's figures for the French departments come from several sources, and the departments listed vary somewhat from one source to another. Bertillon gives the growth rates of 89 departments (for the years 1801-1869), Morselli lists the suicide rates of 85 departments (for 1830-1879), and Yvernés lists suicide rates of 86 departments (for 1872-1876), and Yvernés lists suicide rates of 85 departments (for 1830-79). Since Durkheim wants his tables to show relations among these rates, his tables include only the 82 departments which appear in all three lists. (Nadaillac, in 1881, mentions 86 chief towns of the departments. Morselli, writing at about the same time, also lists 86 departments, and I think the two lists are the same.)

In 1860, France acquired Nice and Savoy from the Kingdom of Sardinia, and in 1871 she ceded parts of Alsace-Lorraine to Germany. These political developments caused the elimination of old departments and the creation of new ones. The shifting number of departments in "Suicide et Natalité" is the result.

NOTES

1. Nadaillac, one of Durkheim's sources, discusses a number of these authors (Nadaillac, pp. 114-18; full citation below). Durkheim later cites one of them, M. Block, "one of our most eminent economists," who argues that too rapid population growth can lead to poverty and national weakness.
2. See Nadaillac, (le Marquis de), *Affaiblissement [Progressif] de la Natalité en France, [ses Causes et ses Consequences]*, Paris, [Vendôme: impr. de Lemercier,] 1881, pp. 121ff. Durkheim uses the first edition and I have had to use the second (Paris, G. Masson, Librairie de L'Academie de Médecine, 1886), but the pagination and the passages he cites appear to be identical in the two editions.
3. [Alfred] Legoyt, *[Le] Suicide Ancien et Moderne [Étude Historique, Philosophique, Morale et Statistique*, Paris, A. Drouin, 1881], p. 257.
4. Durkheim's table is taken from Enrico Agostino Morselli, *Il Suicidio; Saggio di Statistica Morale Comparata*. Milano: Dumolard, 1879, p. 199. Translated as Henry Morselli, *Suicide: An Essay on Comparative Moral Statistics*. New York, D. Appleton & Co., 1882; reprinted in several identical editions. (International Scientific Series, number 36.) This table is omitted from all of the English editions.
5. Morselli, *Il Suicidio*, p. 199. This passage is omitted from the English editions of Morselli's book.
6. What Durkheim calls the general birth rate is now called the crude birth rate. His discussion of the general and special birth rates is based on Louis Adolphe Bertillon, "Natalité (Démographie)," in A. Dechambre, Directeur, *Dictionnaire Encyclopédique des Sciences Medicales*, Paris, G. Masson/P. Asselin, 1864-1889 (in 100 volumes), whole number 63 (Series II, Vol. II), pp. 444-491. In another essay, Bertillon proposes a set of "signs and symbols" for demography, and Durkheim obtains the symbols N and So from this source. (Bertillon, "Demographie, Démologie" in *Dictionnaire Encyclopédique*, whole number 27, Series I, Vol. 26, pp. 655-657.
7. This statistic is now called the "general fertility rate," except that the usual denominator now is women 15-44 or 15-49.

8. Emile Yvernès (no author listed on title page), *Compte Général de l'Administration de la Justice Criminelle en France pendant l'année 1880 et Rapport Relatif aux Années 1826 á 1880,* Paris, Imprimerie Nationale, 1882, see Plate II.
9. See the articles, "France, Démographie," in the *Dictionnaire Encyclopédique des Sciences Médicales.* I include only 82 departments in my calculations: I have had to omit Alpes-Maritimes, Savoie, and Haute Savoie, for which demographic information is only available for recent years, and also the departments which were annexed, and are no longer included in the map of suicides presented by M. Yvernès.

   The three departments which Durkheim names belonged to the Kingdom of Sardinia but became French in 1860. The "departments which were annexed" are those of Alsace and part of Lorraine, secured by Prussia at the end of the Franco-Prussian War in 1871. Durkheim has several sets of data on the French departments. During the periods which these data represent, political events caused the number of French departments to change more than once. Therefore, Bertillon presents the physiological growth rates of 89 departments, Morselli gives the suicide rates of 86, and Yvernès gives the suicide rates of 85. Durkheim himself lists only those 82 departments whose rates of growth and suicide he can compare— that is, the departments which are listed by all three of his authorities, Bertillon, Yvernès and Morselli. In a passage below, Durkheim cites Nadaillac, who gives figures which represent the chief towns of the departments. He lists 86 of these towns; the corresponding list of departments must be the same as Morselli's.

   Durkheim provides no page numbers in the citation above. His reference to "the articles, 'France, Démographie'" is misleading. The *Dictionnaire Encyclopédique* contains no article called "France." It does contain a book-length *collection* of articles with this title, and this collection includes the one essay which Durkheim has in mind, Louis Adolphe Bertillon, "France: Démographie" (*Dictionnaire Encyclopédique,* whole number 41, (Series IV, Vol. 5), pp. 405-559). The physiological growth figures are found in Bertillon's Tableau III, which is appended to his essay (pp. 560-561). Bertillon briefly discusses physiological growth on pp. 418, 420-422, and 458-459. But I have not found the *formula* for physiological growth in Bertillon, and have had to rely on Durkheim for it.
10. With three figures corrected, the second part of this sentence reads thus: "...of the 40 departments in which the increase is average or above, 34, or 85 percent, belong to the fourth and fifth groups, those in which the number of suicides is lowest." Also, Durkheim describes the 40 departments both as "Above the Average Increase in Population" and as "average or above" in population increase.
11. In what has been said so far we have concerned ourselves only with growth. We think it is interesting to make the same comparison for the special birth rate, or fecundity (the number of children born each year to 1000 married women between the ages 15 and 50). These are the results we get:

   Except for the irregularity which appears suddenly in the sixth group, this result agrees with the preceding ones.

   Durkheim does not mention the source of these fertility rates, and I have not been able to find it. The measure now called the "marital fertility rate" is the one that he uses, except that it is usually calculated for married women, 15-44 or 15-49. The "special birth rate" and "fecundity" now have different meanings.

   The groups of departments in Table 6 are based on suicide rates, not on fertility rates. They are almost the same as the groups in Tables 2 and 3. M. Yvernès is the source of these groups, and of the suicide rates in Table 6, though he gives the suicide rate of the first group as 39. (See Yvernès' map, and a *chart* in the same book, titled "22. Renseignements divers," on pp. clxii-clxiii.)

Table 6.

Departments	Suicides per year per 100,000 population, 1830-79	Special birth rate: births per year among 1000 married women, 15-50 [1]
1st group	38	133
2nd group	28	139.25
3rd group	17-21	150.2
4th group	12-16	161
5th group	5-11	190
6th group	2-4	185

[1] Years are not indicated.

12. Legoyt, *Suicide Ancien and Moderne,* p. 195.
13. Durkheim does not indicate the source of these figures. It is Nadaillac, *Affaiblissement,* p. 74, ftn. 1 and p. 141 (Appendix C).
    Durkheim's figures show a discrepancy. He lists only fourteen cities, not fifteen, and the total number of deaths minus births for the fourteen is 1657, not 1758. A comparison with Nadaillac shows that Durkheim reports the deaths minus births of Nice as 183 rather than Nadaillac's 283, and that Durkheim omits "Mende 1," which appears in Nadaillac's list. These corrections resolve the discrepancy. I include them, in brackets, in the translation.
    I have not found the source of the numbers representing urban and rural population growth.
14. Legoyt, [Alfred,] *La France et L'Étranger, [Études de Statistique Comparée]* [Paris, Veuve Berger-Levrault et Fils, 1864-1870. 2 vols., vol.] II, 38.
15. [Maurice Block,] *Statistique de [la] France, Comparée avec les Divers Pays de l'Europe,* I [tome premier, Paris, Guillaumin et Cie. 1875, p.] 63.
16. Durkheim's heading for this section refers to *"physiological* growth," but the section is actually about family size.
17. The immunity of Italian industry is quite exceptional. It probably exists because Italian industry is not sufficiently developed.
18. Durkheim means that in larger the average family in an occupation, the lower its suicides rate is likely to be. At this point, family size is his measure of the birth rate.
19. 2d series, XVII, XLVII. Durkheim's citation has proved to be too vague to permit me to identify and examine this source.
20. Durkheim says that "farm families are...more than one-fifth larger than those of men devoted to letters and science." But his figures show them to be about twice as large I cannot say more, for want of access to his source.
21. Bertillon, article "Natalité" in the *Dict. Encyclopédique des Sciences Médicales,* 2d series, II, 490.
22. Morselli, *Suicide,* English editions, "Second Part. Synthesis" (pp. 353-374), esp. p. 354.
23. Durkheim does not ask *why* marital fertility declined in France when it did, a question which seems to be somewhat unsettled even today (Goldscheider, 1991; Braudel, 1990).
24. In *Suicide,* Durkheim calls some who thought this way "theorists of sadness":

their gloomy ideas reflect the egoism of the society around them (Durkheim, 1951, p. 214, footnote 48).

25. Durkheim writes that it appeared in 1742; Baechler, that it appeared in 1761 (Durkheim, 1951; Baechler, 1979).

26. Since all English versions of Morselli's book seem to be identical, any reference to particular pages in his book should refer to all versions.

27. One attraction of the suicide rate as an object of scientific study is that it has few effects on society. For this reason, its relationship in time to another variable is almost always clear; it can be confidently interpreted as a dependent variable. We may note in passing, however, that suicide does have a few social effects. One of these is its repercussions for the families of victims. Another is the effect of its continuous growth through the nineteenth century on the thinking of the moral statisticians.

28. Morselli (1881, p. 354); Durkheim "Suicide et Natalité," first paragraph; Durkheim (1951, pp. 178-79).

29. Durkheim also offers ad hoc explanations of suicide, though less often then Morselli does. The relation between sex and suicide is one of the strongest that Durkheim discusses, yet his explanation of it is partly biological, and thus contradicts the thesis of his book. The relation between age and suicide is also dramatic, yet he discusses it only briefly, with the suggestion that suicidogenic currents build up in a person only gradually, over many years. Apparently, a man's susceptibility to suicide is determined by the residua of social environments experienced over a lifetime, a notion which wreaks havoc on much of the rest of his book, since his tables show associations between suicide and *present* social conditions. But perhaps no one explanation could be found which would account for all variation in suicide.

30. One difference between the two studies should be mentioned. In his essay, Durkheim acknowledges that variation in suicide is due to "many causes." It cannot be entirely attributed to differences in the birth rate. But in *Suicide* he is disinclined to admit that explanations to supplement his own are needed.

31. The birth rate is also affected by marital patterns (Mauldin, 1982).

32. Durkheim's concern is with "vital events," births and deaths. This means that most of the time he thinks of population growth as a process of *replacement* over a given year. The crude rate of natural increase attempts to identify this process of replacement by counting the vital events of birth and death. But it is also possible, without counting these events, to determine the change in the total number of persons from one year to the next by simply comparing the size of a given population for those two years. This method reflects changes from all sources, so that if net migration is added to natural increase, the two measures show the same result, even though they are calculated differently (Barclay, 1958).

33. Here is the relevant passage from Legoyt: "Among economic influences [on suicide], let us also mention emigration. It seems probable that acts of discouragement [suicide] are less frequent in those countries where the poor go abroad to find the means of subsistence than in those countries where they remain at home and persist in the struggle against misery, in hope of a better future there." To show that emigration and suicide are inversely related, Legoyt then lists the numbers of emigrants and the rates of suicide, over several years, for Denmark, Sweden, and Germany. Then he asks: "Can not the constantly and rapidly growing number of suicides in France also be explained by the insignificant number of our emigrants...?" (Legoyt, 1881, pp. 257-259, my translation).

Something funny has happened here. When he cites Legoyt, Durkheim accepts emigration as an inverse measure of population density. Both (low) emigration and density are the "birth rate." But when Legoyt applies his ideas to France a problem arises. If emigration from France were to rise, the population would be less concentrated—that is, the birth rate would be lower. If the birth rate were lower, the suicide rate would be lower also. Thus, Legoyt's analysis implies that it is the *high* birth rate of France which causes the high suicide rate there. Yet Durkheim is at pains to prove the opposite, that a *low* birth rate in France causes the high suicide rate.

It is true that Durkheim mentions Legoyt only briefly, and does not refer to his thoughts about France. But we may say these things: The purpose of "Suicide et Natalité" is to prove Durkheim's law. He introduces the passage from Legoyt in support of that law. But when he does so he does not recognize that part of the passage contradicts the law.

34. There remain two loose ends in all of this. First, what of migration *into* a country? When the birth rate is high, out-migration makes a society healthier. Does it follow that when the birth rate is *low, in*migration makes a country healthier? Durkheim does not say so, but his argument might seem to imply it. Other Frenchmen, not making his assumptions, see in-migration as unhealthy—even catastrophic. LeBon takes this view, as I have remarked.

Second, the comments above refer only to migration *between* countries. To Durkheim, migration *within* a country is not relevant to his problem: Physiological growth "has the...great advantage of not taking into account migration from one department to another, which clearly can only hinder our inquiry." Similarly: "If one looks only at the chief town of each of the departments, he learns not only that the growth in these towns is very low, but that there are more *deaths than births*" (emphasis added). That is all that matters to Durkheim—deaths and births. Because of migration from the country, these towns probably grew during this period, but Durkheim intentionally ignores this migration within France and looks only at births and deaths. Thus, both explicitly and implicitly, he treats migration within France as something which does not concern him. He does not say why he looks at the two kinds of migration differently. Perhaps he thinks that since internal migration does not affect the size of the French population as a whole, it has no effect on the health of the country.

35. He assumes in *Suicide* that there must be an association between two variables even when none is apparent. The coefficient of preservation of widowed persons with reference to the unmarried "...changes with age, but following an irregular evolution the law of which cannot be determined" (p. 180).

36. Nadaillac suggests levels of consumption as an indicator of individual and social happiness. But Durkheim rejects this alternative to the suicide rate. It is an "elementary psychological fact" that satisfaction of needs alone does not make people happier if "the gap between need and satisfaction remains the same." This thought anticipates both his discussion of anomie in *Suicide* and his use of the argument by elimination in the early chapters of that book.

37. In its frequent biological terminology, "Suicide et Natalité" resembles Durkheim's *Division of Labor* (1893) more than it does *Suicide* (1897). But, in spite of such terms, there is at least one problem of which the article is innocent. Sometimes social thinkers, especially those in the vague category of social Darwinists, have been faulted for directly inferring the properties of groups from those of organisms. I think that "Suicide et Natalité" does not do this. On the other hand, it does use organic analogies in what might prove to be a fruitful way when it suggests the possibility that societies are, in some specific respect, like organisms. For example, Durkheim says that the birth rates of certain "healthy" countries of Europe lie within "a normal zone...below and above which they become pathological," and that, in France, "too low a birth rate is harmful and a sickness for

society." (Lukes, 1972, pp. 34-36) But it remains true that his paper does not *demonstrate* this particular parallelism between organisms and societies.

38. There are three: common ideas, a high frequency of social interaction, and social regulation (Johnson, 1965).

39. Morselli and Durkheim disagree about various things. Morselli, as we know, offers the struggle for existence as a general explanation of variations in suicide rates. To Durkheim, this struggle is only an intervening variable between births and suicides, and it plays this role only in some societies. Morselli attributes the high suicide rates in Germany and France to their *similar* social condition: A high level of civilization, with which an intense struggle for existence is associated. Durkheim attributes the same high rates to the *contrasting* birth rates in the two countries. We will see below that Morselli, looking at the same European figures as Durkheim, sees an *inverse* relation between births and suicides. Durkheim acknowledges this inverse relation in passing, but immediately postulates the nonlinear relation which is expressed in his law.

40. From this discussion, it is clear that Durkheim had some awareness of the scheme which was much later codified as the elaboration formula (Lazarsfeld and Rosenberg, 1955, Section II). In addition to possibility (1), mentioned above, conventional names for the others are: (2) "explanation" and (3) "interpretation." There are other possible outcomes. (4) In "replication," the original association reappears within the subgroups which appear when a control variable is introduced. After Durkheim's first table, his evidence takes the form of several approximations to replication. The most complex outcome is (5) "specification," in which the original association does not disappear, but varies in strength, depending on the value of the test factor. His paper does not discuss this possibility.

41. Lukes' summary of the paper is the only other discussion of it which I have found (Lukes, 1972, pp. 194-195).

42. Morselli believes that metaphysical determinism must be a presupposition of sociology as a science. He suggests that the predictability of suicide supports determinism. (Morselli, 1882, pp. 16, 70, 187-189, 268-276.) Durkheim, however, takes the view that sociology does not need to take a stand on this question (Durkheim, 1938, p. 141; 1951, p. 39, ftn. 2, p. 325, ftn. 20) My guess is that Durkheim's comments do not reflect a serious metaphysical position so much as a concern that others will find both him and his (new) field to be seemly and acceptable; he may think of an insistent determinism as unnecessarily abrasive.

43. The Italian phrase is: "...con cui suicidio non può stare a confronto..." (Morselli, 1879, p. 101). The English translation gives "stare a confronto" as "stand for comparison," which I have changed to "be compared."

44. Masaryk proposes a positive relation between population growth and the suicide rate. Legoyt (1881) proposes the same positive relation, though between other dimensions of the "birth rate" and the suicide rate, as I explained in a footnote to the section, "What is the 'birth rate'?"

45. Nine years later, in *Suicide*, Durkheim does cite Masaryk's book, as one of a set on "studies of suicide in general" (Durkheim, 1951, pp. 52-53 ftn. 8).

46. Bodio's book is the 1876 edition of a yearly publication of the Italian government (Bodio, 1876). Morselli gives no indication that Bodio tried to assign any meaning to the figures he had collected. He probably merely listed them. The same conclusion is suggested by two collections of statistics of the Italian government which I have been able to examine. These two anonymous reports are similar to the 1876 volume, were published soon after it, and may also be the work of Bodio: Each of them says little about the possible meaning of the figures presented. (Italy, 1878, 1880) The import of all of this is that Morselli was probably the first to attempt an interpretation of the figures in Durkheim's Table 1.

47. In this passage, Durkheim agrees with Morselli that the relation between births and suicides is *negative,* and he describes Germany as a "distorting case." But Durkheim takes a different view in the rest of his essay. Although the relation is negative among societies with low birth rates, it is positive among societies with high birth rates. Moreover, Germany is not a "distorting case," but Durkheim's main evidence of this positive relation.

48. As of passing interest, among the ten countries the correlation coefficient (Pearson's r) between rates of birth and suicide is -.51.

49. This statistic was being developed at about the time *Suicide* appeared in 1897. Durkheim did not know about it even then, for reasons which Selvin has explored (Selvin, 1976).

50. Such measures have been used more recently to analyze data from Durkheim's time (Camp, 1961, p. 99).

51. "Germany" is the German Empire, made up of Prussia, Bavaria and the other German states which united in 1871. Further information on figures for Germany is in the Appendix, in the Notes to the Summary Table for Europe.

52. The general fertility rate is a larger number, because it represents the same births over a smaller denominator, but the curves typically have about the same shape (Matras, 1971, p. 202).

53. Durkheim has this to say in *Suicide*: "There is very little suicide in Ireland, where the peasantry leads so wretched a life" (Durkheim, 1951, p. 245; see also pp. 107, 108, 114-115, 351).

54. Information on figures for Ireland is in the Appendix, in the Notes to the Summary Table for Europe.

55. In *Suicide,* our author seems to have realized that the most important thing to show in a table is the association and that not all of the facts have to be given in order to do this. His book never lists all of the departments of France, a procedure which can only obscure things, and there are no megatables of the form of Tables 2 and 4. He presents the departments, when he does, in groups rather than individually. There are large tables (e.g., Durkheim, 1951, pp. 196, 260), but their purpose is not to list a large number of cases, but to exhibit some multivariate relation, that is, to show how the association between some variable and suicide changes when other variables are introduced as controls.

56. Durkheim does not say what criteria were used to establish the boundaries between the groups of departments in both Tables 2 and 4. The problem is that the way the groups are defined, whether those based on growth or on suicide, might affect the strength of the association shown. That is, one might produce doctored results by defining the groups in such a way that the apparent relation between the two variables would be stronger than it would otherwise be.

57. Durkheim's growth figures refer to 1801-1869, and omit Nice and Strasbourg, two of the largest cities in present-day France. Nice is now in the department of Alpes-Maritimes, and Strasbourg in Bas-Rhin. Another large city, Nantes, was in the department of Loire-Inférieure. This department appears in Durkheim's data, but it was renamed Loire-Atlantique in 1957.

58. Since he is looking at the population growth of parts of France rather than of the country as a whole, the measure also incorporates *internal* migration. I argued earlier that his implicit definition of the "birth rate" excludes this.

59. I suggested above that, when Durkheim sees family feeling affecting both suicides and the birth rate, he seems to contradict his own law. Now we find him saying that since occupations affect suicide, "...there is reason to study also their influence on population growth." This is another error of the same kind.

60. Durkheim omits several of the suicide rates in Morselli's table: vagrant professions (259.3), domestic servants (68.1), industrial supernumeraries (30.9), and "de-

pendents, and without fixed profession" (8.0). (See Morselli, 1881, p. 244, for the original table.)

61. Occupations actually vary along a number of dimensions—income, level of education, and others. If Durkheim wished, he could settle on one of these dimensions as the property of occupations which matters to him, and then arrange occupations along that dimension. But he does not do this.

62. It may not be obvious what occupations are included in "letters and science," the group with the highest suicide rate. The category *does* not include law, teaching, the "medical professions," fine arts, and religion, since each of these is separately listed in Table 7. According to Morselli, the category *does* include "...the literary, scientific, journalists, engineers, geometricians, all those in short who make the greatest use of their brain power" (Morselli, 1881, p. 248).

63. Durkheim regarded anything much less than perfect rank correlation as "independent" (Selvin, 1961, p. 136, ftn. 21): "...the presence of a few cases that depart from a perfect relation is enough to convince Durkheim that there is no relation at all. As Boudon has remarked, Durkheim's methodology was still that of John Stuart Mill's *System of Logic* (Boudon, 1973). In Mill's "canon of concomitant variation" there is room only for perfect positive and perfect negative relations—nothing in between (Selvin, 1976, p. 41).

64. Durkheim (1938) says that it does. In "Suicide et Natalité," he describes a number of social conditions as "abnormal." But, as I have said earlier, I wonder whether they have any common property, except that he thinks that they are undesirable.

65. From this point of view, he did not take a step forward when he declared in the *Rules* that "A given effect always has a single corresponding cause" (Durkheim, 1938, p. 128).

66. Here are some pages of *Suicide* on which various intervals are found: one year (258, 268), two years (167), three (178, 196), four (154), five (177, 258), six (191, 258), more than six (153, 245, 258). Often there is a mixture of intervals in a given table (101, 154, 258, 262).

67. I will mention two complications which I otherwise ignore. First, the "lag" which has been discussed is the interval of time between births and the weakness of a society. This weakness, in turn, has an impact on suicides, which amounts to a second part of the lag. But this second part need not trouble us. It represents the effect on the suicide rate of a condition of the social environment which is similar to low social integration or regulation. This part of the process, like the operation of the independent variables in *Suicide,* should take a relatively short time. The second part of the lag does not make the lag between births and suicides appreciably longer.

   Second, how we are to apply all of this to a country with a high birth rate, such as Germany? In such a country, the variable which intervenes between births and suicides is not the weakness of a society but the struggle for existence. Thus, to determine how long the lag between births and suicides would be in such countries, we would have to start over. What identifiable events constitute the struggle for existence? In what ways do births intensify that struggle? How long after a given acceleration of births does the struggle for existence become more intense? How long after that intensification does the rate of suicide increase? Durkheim tells us so little about countries with high birth rates that it would be fruitless to pursue these questions here.

68. Durkheim's birth rates usually do not describe exactly the same periods as his suicide rates. But these usually small discrepancies need not concern us.

69. There is another problem with the second association. The two intervening processes must involve many small and contingent social events which take place over a long time. However clearly these processes were defined, they could hardly

have uniform effects over a fixed number of years. In practical terms, their outcome would be somewhat unpredictable. Thus, no one could say that births which occurred, say, in 1837 caused *all* of the suicides which took place in a single, identifiable year later on, and that they caused no others. More likely, those births caused *some* of the suicides in each of a *series* of years. To make Durkheim's ideas testable, we would have to know how those suicides are distributed over those years, and have some idea of what proportion of them occurs during each year. These questions may appear to be unanswerable. But we would need answers to them in order to subject his law to meaningful empirical test.

70. The rates of fertility, mortality, and migration which determine the age structure are all *age-specific* (Matras, 1971, pp. 174-178, 202-203, 374). I pass over this further complication.

71. Halbwachs offers some similar observations, which are paraphrased here:
    The age composition of the population varies from one country to another. For example, in 1910 the population of France was older than that of Germany, with a higher proportion of persons over 60. Thus, even if the suicide rates of the two countries were the same, one could say that "more men and women in a given age category kill themselves in Germany than in France." The suicide rate of a particular population can rise simply because its members are growing older, without reflecting any moral and social disequilibrium (Halbwachs, 1978, pp. 60-62)

72. Although some have challenged this last statement about Durkheim's theory, it is actually an implication of a familiar idea. If culture consists of systems of concepts, and these concepts are partly independent of any one person's awareness of them, a thinker's (subjective) ideas about his theory may not entirely coincide with that (objective) theory in itself. The theory may contain self-contradictions and other implications of which its originator is unaware. When someone else not only recognizes these implications but persuades the theorist to accept them, their objective reality is shown. If this line of thought is accepted, there is nothing strange in the suggestion that Durkheim is unaware of the most consistent interpretation of his own theory.
    This way of thinking about culture has many further implications, of course. For example, Durkheim hit upon parts of the elaboration formula which Lazarsfeld and his colleagues later more fully *discovered*. Neither Durkheim nor the Columbia scholars *invented* it.
    Sorokin and the early Parsons distinguish between culture and thought processes (Parsons' "action"). Popper proposes a similar distinction between mental processes ("world 2") and objective knowledge ("world 3"), the latter being knowledge which is real even if no one knows it (Sorokin, 1937-41, vol. I, pp. 59, 61; vol. IV, p. 11; 1943, pp. 16ff, 24; Parsons, 1937, pp. 762-765; Popper, 1972; Johnson, 1976, chaps. II-IV).

73. Because the first reading of *Suicide* is the more conventional, I assume the truth of it when I refer in this commentary to "Durkheim's theory." The second, more radical, reading is demonstrably preferable, but to show this here would lead us too far afield.

74. We find that even in 1897 he has a good word for physiological growth which he describes as a "not unreasonable" measure of family size.

75. There is a complication here. In "Suicide et Natalité," physiological growth is a *measure*. In *Suicide*, egoism is *the thing measured*. But family size seems to be both. It is a measure of egoism in the two tables in *Suicide*. It is (or so Durkheim claims in *Suicide*) what physiological growth is meant to measure in "Suicide et Natalité." There is no reason why family size cannot play both roles. The problem is that his description of what he was trying to do in his essay is not accurate.

76. The table on p. 199 of *Suicide* (Durkheim, 1951) also raises a problem of another kind. It shows that the number of members of a family household has an exceedingly strong effect on the rate of suicide. This can be most readily seen if we ignore most of the table and simply compare two of Durkheim's groups of French departments, those in which the average household size is the smallest and those in which it is the largest. This comparison shows that an increase in household size from 347 to 434 results in a decrease in suicide from about 405 to about 50. In other words, a 25 percent increase in household size causes an 82 to 93 percent decrease in suicide. This represents an enormous effect over a narrow range. It is similar to what we found in Table 6, and is as hard to believe as that table was. It seems that we have come upon one kind of mistake or inaccuracy in Durkheim which he did not overcome between 1888 and 1897.

77. He does do this in the *Rules* (Durkheim, 1938, p. 115, ftn. 22).

78. I have quoted the impassioned words of the demographer Bertillon, another polemical sociologist of the time. We might expect polemic in the popular press, but Bertillon's comments were published in a medical encyclopedia.

REFERENCES

Aalen, F. H. A. The Irish people: demography. In V. Meally (ed.), *Encyclopedia of Ireland*. Dublin: Allan Figgis, 1968.

Adams, R. M. *Decadent Societies*. San Francisco: North Point Press, 1983.

d'Angeville, Comte A. *Essai sur la Statistique de la Population Française considérée sous quelques-uns de ces Rapports Physiques et Moraux*. Bourg. impr. de F. Dufour, 1836 (1837 in fact), reprinted 1969, Paris: Editions Mouton, Seconde Partie, Études Statistiques qui Concernent Chaque Département.

Baechler, J. *Suicides*. New York: Basic Books, 1979.

Barclay, G. W. *Techniques of Population Analysis*. New York: Wiley, 1958.

Bertillion, L. A. Natalité (Démographie). In A. Dechambre (ed.), *Dictionnaire Encyclopédique des Sciences Médicales*. Paris: G. Masson/P. Asselin, 1864-1889, number 63, series II, volume II.

Bodio, L. *Introduzione al Movimento dello Stato Civile 1862-1877*. Rome: [publisher unknown], 1876.

Bourgeois-Pichat, J. The general development of the population of France since the Eighteenth Century. In D. V. Glass and D. E. C. Eversley (eds.), *Population in History*. Chicago: Aldine, 1965.

Braudel, F. *The Identity of France, Volume II: People and Production*. London: Collins, 1990.

Camp, W. D. *Marriage and the Family in France Since the Revolution*. New York: Bookman, 1961.

Darwin, C. *The Descent of Man*. New York: Appleton, 1871.

Direzione Generale della Statistica. *Populazione. Movimento della Stato Civile, Anni 1862-1878*. Rome: Tipografia Cenninani, 1878.

Direzione Generale della Statistica. *Populazione. Movimento della Stato Civile, Anni 1862-1878*. Rome: Tipografia Cenninani, 1880.

Douglas, J. D. *The Social Meanings of Suicide*. Princeton, NJ: Princeton University Press, 1967.

Dublin, L. I. *Suicide*. New York: Ronald Press, 1963.

Durkheim, E. *The Division of Labor in Society* (translated by George Simpson). Glencoe, IL: Free Press, 1933.

Durkheim, E. *The Rules of the Sociological Method* (translated by S. A. Solovay and J. H. Mueller). New York: Free Press, 1938.

Durkheim, E. *Le Suicide: Étude de Sociologie* [1897]. Paris: Presses Universitaires de France, 1960.

Durkheim, E. *Suicide, A Study in Sociology* (translated by J. A. Spaulding and G. Simpson). Glencoe, IL: Free Press, 1951.

Flora, P., Kraus, F., and Pfennzing, W. *State, Economy, and Society in Western Europe, 1815-1975. A Data Handbook in Two Volumes.* Chicago: St. James Press, 1987.

Fry, P., and Somerset Fry, F. *A History of Ireland.* London: Routledge, 1988.

Goldscheider, C. *Population, Modernization, and Social Structure.* Boston: Little, Brown, 1971.

Grenville, J. A. S. *Europe Reshaped, 1848-1878.* Hove, UK: Harvester/Fontana, 1976.

Halbwachs, M. *The Causes of Suicide* (translated by H. Goldblatt). London: Routledge & Kegan Paul, 1978.

Hickey, D. J., and Doherty, J. E. (eds.), Population. In *A Dictionary of Irish History Since 1800.* Totowa, NJ: Gill and Macmillan/Barnes & Noble, 1980.

Himmelfarb, G. *Darwin and the Darwinian Revolution.* New York: Norton, 1968.

Huff, T. Discovery and Explanation in Sociology: Durkheim on Suicide. *Philosophy of the Social Sciences,* 1975, 5, 241-257.

Johnson, B. D. *Emile Durkheim and the Theory of Social Integration.* Unpublished master's thesis, University of California, Berkeley, 1964.

Johnson, B. D. Durkheim's One Cause of Suicide. *American Sociological Review,* 1965, 30, 875-886.

Johnson, B. D. *Some Philosophical Problems in Parsons' Early Thought.* Unpublished doctoral thesis, University of California, Berkeley, 1976.

Lauro, D. Composition. In J. A. Ross (ed.), *International Encyclopedia of Population.* New York: Free Press, 1982.

Lazarsfeld, P. F., and Rosenberg, M. (eds.), *The Language of Social Research.* Glencoe, IL: Free Press, 1955.

Legoyt, A. *Le Suicide Ancien et Moderne.* Paris: A Drouin, 1881.

Lukes, S. *Emile Durkheim: His Life and Work.* New York, Harper & Row, 1972.

Masaryk, T. G. *Suicide and the Meaning of Civilization* (translated by W. B. Weist and R. G. Batson). Chicago: University of Chicago Press, 1970.

Matras, J. *Populations and Societies.* Englewood Cliffs, NJ: Prentice-Hall, 1973.

Mauldin, W. P. Fertility and Population Growth. In J. A. Ross (ed.), *International Encyclopedia of Population.* New York: Free Press, 1982.

Morselli, E. *Il Suicidio: Saggio di Statistica Comparata.* Milan: Dumolard, 1879.

Oldroyd, D. R. *Darwinian Impacts: An Introduction to the Darwinian Revolution.* Bristol, PA: Open University Press, 1980.

Parsons, T. *The Structure of Social Action.* New York: McGraw-Hill, 1937; Glencoe, IL: Free Press, 1949.

Pelczar, M. J., Reid, R. D., and Chan, E. S. C. *Microbiology.* New York: McGraw-Hill, 1972.

Petersen, W., and Petersen, R. *Dictionary of Demography, Biographies A-L.* Westport, CT: Greenwood, 1985.

Pope, W. *Durkheim's Suicide: A Classic Analyzed.* Chicago: University of Chicago Press, 1976.

Popper, K. R. *Objective Knowledge, an Evolutionary Approach.* London: Oxford University Press, 1972.

Price, R. *A Social History of Nineteenth-Century France.* New York: Holmes & Meier, 1987.

Selvin, H. Durkheim's *Suicide* and Problems of Empirical Research. In S. M. Lipset and N. J. Smelser (eds.), *Sociology: The Progress of a Decade.* Englewood Cliffs, NJ: Prentice-Hall, 1961.

Selvin, H. Durkheim, Booth, and Yule: the nondiffusion of an intellectual innovation. *Archives Européens de Sociologie*, 1976, 17(1), 38-52.

Smelser, N. J., and Warner, R. S. *Sociological Theory: Historical and Formal*. Morristown, NJ: General Learning Press, 1976.

Sorokin, P. *Social and Cultural Dynamics*. New York: American Book Co., 1937-41.

Sorokin, P. *Sociocultural Causality, Space, Time*. Durham, NC: Duke University Press, 1943.

Spengler, J. J. *France Faces Depopulation*. New York: Greenwood Press, 1968. (Originally published by Duke University Press, 1938.)

Spengler, J. J. *Population Change, Modernization, and Welfare*. Englewood Cliffs, NJ: Prentice-Hall, 1974.

Süssmilch, J. P. *Die Göttliche Ordnung in den Veränderungen des menschlichen Geschlechts, aus der Geburt, dem Tode und der Fortpflanzung desselben Erwiesen* (3 vols.). Berlin: Verlag der Buchladens der Realschule, 1761-1762.

Swart, K. W. *The Sense of Decadence in Nineteenth Century France*. The Hague: Martinus Nijhoff, 1964.

Teitelbaum, M. S., and Winter, J. M. *The Fear of Population Decline*. Orlando, FL: Academic Press, 1985.

Wallis, W. A., and Roberts, H. V. *Statistics: A New Approach*. New York: Free Press, 1956.

Woodham-Smith, C. *The Great Hunger*. New York: Harper & Row, 1962.

8

Durkheim and the Immunity of Women to Suicide

Howard I. Kushner, PhD

Whatever other iconoclastic views he may have held, Emile Durkheim assumed, as his predecessors had, that modernity was a primary contributor to increases in the suicide rate. Thus, he endorsed the view that traditional (especially, rural) family life provided the best protection against self-destructive behavior. A logical corollary to these assumptions was that women, since most were subsumed in the family, were much more immune to suicide than were men. As a result, Durkheim never questioned the alleged resistance of women to suicide. In 1897 he enshrined these beliefs in his classic *Suicide: A Study in Sociology* (Durkheim, 1951, p. 166). And, due in no small part to the continued influence of Durkheim's typology, these assumptions have remained largely undisputed ever since.[1] Yet, as I will argue below, Durkheim's assertion of the immunity of women to suicide rests more on the assumptions that he brought to his investigation than to any compelling statistical or logical evidence.

THE CONTEXT

Durkheim's assertion in *Suicide* that women were relatively immune to suicide was informed by almost a century of expert opinion that had associated suicide, with vice, urbanization, and modernity. Ancient fears that the growth of cities

Much of the material in this chapter (although revised and in different form) is taken from my article, "Suicide, Gender and the Fear of Modernity in Nineteenth-Century Medical and Social Thought," *Journal of Social History*, 26 (Spring, 1993), 461-490 and appears here with the permission of the editors of the *Journal of Social History*. I thank Elizabeth Colwill, Lisa Lieberman, Carol R. Kushner, and David L. Ransel for their critical comments. All translations from French are mine, unless otherwise noted.

would lead to an increase in a variety of social and mental illnesses had intensified in early nineteenth-century Europe and North America. The assertion in 1820 by Etienne Esquirol (1838, pp. 400-401), the leader of the French asylum movement, that "madness is the disease of civilization" was emblematic of these views. By mid-century this view had become common-place. For instance, the influential American alienist Edward Jarvis attributed insanity to "the price we pay for civilization. The causes of the one increase with the developments and results of the other" (Jarvis, 1852, pp. 333-364).

Devotion to domestic virtues was depicted as the best defense against the forces of social disintegration. These assertions were bolstered by statistical compilations of rates of disease, insanity, and violence, all of which reinforced dogmas about the evils of the city (see Porter, 1986; Bourguet, 1989). Because self-destructive behavior became a *prima facie* example of the corrupting effects of urbanization, the incidence of suicide developed into a barometer for social health in Western Europe and the United States. "Suicide," writes Barbara Gates, "took on the status of trope quite readily." It "became an indicator of social illness, a measure of what was wrong with late Victorian" society (Gates, 1990, pp. 64-72; see also Hacking, 1990).

From the first, hypotheses about the causes of suicide were tied to senti-mental visions of the family and to an ambivalence toward social change. Thus, warnings of suicide epidemics were coupled with nostalgic portraits of rural life, which concluded that the best safeguards against suicide lay in the restoration of traditional values, especially the patriarchal family.[2] Given the logic of these assumptions, experts insisted that women, because they were most fully subsumed in traditional familial hierarchies, would prove more immune to suicide than men.

These views had gained intensity in the beginning of the nineteenth century as the generalized anxieties of earlier eras were translated into social "facts" by the swelling urban populations and by the growth of urban classes less attached to traditional authoritarian structures. Informing and exacerbating all of this was a fear of gender chaos: women it seemed were becoming more like men, and men more like women. These concerns surfaced in revolutionary France, and they intensified throughout the nineteenth century (Colwill, 1991). Thus, as experts defined suicide as a male activity, they simultaneously labeled women who killed themselves as entering the male sphere. Within the rules that defined who was at risk for self-destruction lay the warning that, if women persisted in acting like men, they endangered not only themselves, but also the family. Often these gender issues were submerged in a formulaic and generalized set of caveats about the dangers of urban life which portrayed those most subsumed in it (men) at greatest risk of suicide. In this construction, women (because suicide was gendered as male) rarely appear. This absence, however, both obscures and reveals concrete fears that increasing numbers of working urban women were themselves among the forces of modernity that posed a "threat" to the moral fabric (DeGroat, 1991; Stansell, 1986). So, while anxiety about the changing role of women was no mere abstraction, any more than the fear of class conflict was, it remained subterranean in the highly structured and ritualized jeremiads about the connections between suicide and urban life.

To the extent that modern urban life was identified as the cause of suicide, traditional familial values were presented as the "natural environment" which guarded against self-destruction. Looking at the assumptions of nineteenth-century French statistical investigations of work, historian Joan W. Scott found that "the collection of population according to households...reveals and constructs a certain vision of social organization based on a particular idea of the family that is 'naturalized' in the course of presenting data." That is, the family was portrayed as "the natural environment that fostered those qualities of individual discipline and orderliness necessary for the health and prosperity of society" (Scott, 1988a, pp. 115, 129).

Indeed, the replication of an ideal "family" was often the aim of the "moral treatment" in British, French, and American asylums, even among those who, like Philippe Pinel, advocated removing patients from particular familial situations which they saw as contributing to a disorder.[3] Alexandre Brierre de Boismont, editor of the *Annales médico-psychologiques,* argued in 1856 that the "treatment which renders the greatest service" to the suicidal is "family life," which itself can remove "the moral suffering in the vast majority" of cases (Brierre de Boismont, 1856, p. 633).[4]

It became axiomatic that, if traditional family life protected its members from suicide, those most subsumed in traditional roles—women—ought to demonstrate the greatest resistance to suicide. Not surprisingly, this was exactly what the earliest statistics showed—that approximately three out of every four completed suicides in both Europe and North America were men (Falret, 1822; Quételet, 1835, 1848; Winslow, 1840; Etoc-Demazy, 1844; Hunt, 1845; Cook, 1849). "Although women were more exposed to mental illness than men," wrote Esquirol in 1821 (1838, vol. 1, p. 584), "suicide is less frequent among them. Observers from all nations are in agreement on that issue."[5] Esquirol attributed this to women's "overexcitement of their sensibilities, their flights of imagination, their exaggerated tenderness, their religious attachments," all of which "produce in them illnesses opposed to suicide, in addition to which their mild character and natural timidity distances them" from suicidal thoughts (Esquirol, 1838, vol. 1, pp. 584-585).

Esquirol's explanations for women's resistance to suicide reflected widely held assumptions which were repeated almost reflexively throughout the century. While "civilization" was attached to male behavior, "mother," "wife," and "woman" served as a representation of a set of socially constructed behaviors attached to females that translated vaguely into an assortment of attributes that included passivity, frailty, modesty, patience, loyalty, acceptance, and self-renunciation. (In French, of course, "femme" is used interchangeably for "woman" and "wife.") In this scheme "civilization" and "women" were opponents if not opposites. Social constructions (gender), as opposed to biological distinctions (sex), became the operative metaphors used to explain the alleged immunity of women to suicide. This circumstance, of course, did not preclude the conflation of gender and sex; rather, it ensured it.[6]

Thus, throughout the century, physicians and other experts offered almost the same sentences in different languages, to explain the relative resistance of women to suicide (Falret, 1822; Winslow, 1840; Brierre de Boismont, 1856; Bertrand, 1857; Anon., 1861). Indeed, the same reasoning continued to be presented throughout the century with such regularity, that hardly anyone doubted the assertion in a widely republished 1881 British article entitled "Suicidal Mania," that "religious restraints" and the possession of "a larger measure of that hope which springs eternal in the human breast," accounted for the fact that women "were less prone to commit suicide...than men" (Knighton, 1881, p. 376; see also Mulhall, 1883, p. 907).

Even when Darwinian metaphors replaced earlier nostalgic portrayals of family life, conclusions were familiar. "The difficulties of existence, those at least which proceed from the struggle for life," wrote Henry Morselli (1882), professor of psychological medicine at the Royal University of Turin, "bear more heavily on man. Woman," he insisted, "only shares in these through the affections, and although she has a more impressionable nervous temperament, yet possesses the faculty of resigning herself more easily to circumstances" (pp. 195, 197). "The comparative immunity of the female sex from self-destruction," according to British psychiatrist and barrister S. A. K. Strahan (1893, p. 178), "depends in part upon the relatively less harassing part she takes in the struggle for existence; in part upon the less indulgent and vicious life she leads; and in part upon her lack of courage and natural repugnance to personal violence and disfigurement."

No matter what the statistics showed, the fact remained that *some* women committed suicide.[7] Commentators explained this in two ways. First, they insisted that the motives for male and female suicides were very different. Suicide among women was portrayed as an individual emotional act and, thus, inconsequential, while male suicide was seen as a barometer of national economic and social well-being. Second, building on the first assumption, because male suicide was a consequence of the stresses inherent in men's roles and responsibilities (i.e., the price of "civilization"), female suicide occurred when women *deviated* from their less conflicted (traditional) roles.[8]

Again, Esquirol's explanations were emblematic. "Women kill themselves more rarely than men," he wrote in 1821, and when they do, "more often it is [amorous] passion which impels them to this aberration" (Esquirol, 1838, vol. 1, p. 585). In the United States, an anonymous "Southern Physician" wrote in *The American Whig Review* in 1847 that "in men, real or fancied impotence is very apt to induce self-destruction—and among women, we cannot help always suspecting the dread of the consequences of secret loss of honor" (Anon., 1847, p. 42).[9] Morselli found that men's suicides were caused by "financial embarrassments," "weariness of life," and other "egoistical motives, whilst among women, after mental diseases, there predominate passions, domestic troubles, shame and remorse." In contrast to men, explained Morselli, "among the causes which urge them to leave this life women always exhibit that spirit of self-denial, that delicacy of feeling and of love, which inspire all her acts" (Morselli, 1882, p. 305).

If a women's suicide could not be attributed to passion or shame, it invariably was tied to women's adopting roles that nature and society had assigned to men. When women left the security of their families, explained Brierre de Boismont, they substantially increased their risk of suicide (Brierre de Boismont, 1856). The higher suicide rates of women who "take an active part in the business of life," according to an 1883 English essay entitled "Insanity, Suicide, and Civilization," "serve as a caution to prevent them from taking part in politics, or matters best suited for men" (Mulhall, 1883, p. 908). "It has been observed," wrote the American Richard N. Reeves in 1897, "that as woman approaches man in her mode of life she also becomes more familiar with those abnormal conditions which have previously been peculiar to man." This leads to an increase in suicide among women because "the comparative immunity of women from self-destruction in the past has depended greatly upon the relatively less harassing part she has taken in the struggle for life" (Reeves, 1897, pp. 189-190).

By the end of the century, joining the chorus of his French and American cousins, Reginald Skelton summed up the view which had become commonplace:

> Though every woman has to traverse certain critical periods in her lifetime, which are dangerous both to her bodily and mental condition, yet she is exempt from many of the factors most favorable to suicide. Her affection for home and children is greater, and the religious sentiment has diminished less in woman than in man; her intellectual faculties are usually less developed, and hence also her sensibility to mental pain; inured to continual petty troubles, her patience is fortified to resist greater ones. It is without surprise, therefore, that we learn that there are four times as many men as women suicides. In the large towns, however, these factors tending to the exemption of women from suicide largely disappear (Skelton, 1900, p. 417).

DURKHEIM AND THE IMMUNITY OF WOMEN

These nineteenth-century assumptions about women and suicide were codified in Durkheim's *Suicide: A Study in Sociology* (1897). Along with his predecessors, Durkheim assumed that "mental illnesses go hand in hand with civilization" and that insanity was more common "in towns than the countryside, and in large rather than small towns." And Durkheim too connected suicide with modernity. What appeared to be suicide among primitive people, he characterized as not "an act of despair but of abnegation...On the contrary, true suicide, the suicide of sadness, is an endemic state among civilized persons." Its incidence is a function of "the level of civilization," with the greatest numbers of suicides among the most developed societies. "Everywhere," wrote Durkheim, "suicide is more prevalent in towns than in the countryside. Civilization is concentrated in large towns, as is suicide" (Durkheim, 1984, pp. 191-192, 215).[10]

Given these views, it was not surprising that Durkheim reached the same conclusions that his predecessors had about the protective influence of the traditional family against suicide. In an 1888 essay entitled "Suicide et natalité: Etude de statistique morale," Durkheim linked low birthrates in France to increases in the rate of suicide: "If suicide progresses when the birthrate declines," wrote Durkheim, "it is that these two phenomena are equally due in part to a decline of domestic sentiments." "All facts," he insisted, "demonstrate that where the family exists, it protects against suicide and that it has even more of this protective force when it is...dense enough." From this perspective, a low birthrate led to the weakening of the family. And, Durkheim found, those areas with the least population growth experienced the highest rates of suicide. A "good birthrate" was "only possible where...domestic solidarity" was chosen over a life of "material ease." Thus, the more children a family produced, the safer its members were from self-destruction. "In these conditions in fact," concluded Durkheim, "the individual becomes part of the solid mass with which he is unified and which multiples his strengths: his power of resistance is thus increased. The less isolated he is, the much stronger he is for the struggle." But, Durkheim warned, "where on the contrary families are sparse, poor, or meager, individuals, less closely joined to one another, allow spaces between them where the cold wind of egoism blows freezing their hearts and weakening their courage" (Durkheim, 1888, p. 463).[11] Because the health of society depended upon the density of families, women were expected to be mothers of many children. And by extension, women were healthiest and least prone to suicide themselves to the extent that they were subsumed in traditional roles. "Woman is less concerned than man in the civilizing process," Durkheim asserted in 1893, "she participates less in it and draws less benefit from it. She more recalls certain characteristics to be found in primitive natures" (Durkheim, 1984, p. 192). These presumptions alone go far in explaining why Durkheim assumed that women were "naturally" immune to suicide.

Durkheim's assertion in *Le Suicide* that "in all the countries of the world, women commit suicide less than men," was based then, not only on the statistical data of his predecessors, but also on their gender assumptions (Durkheim, 1951, pp. 99, 166).[12] Thus, Durkheim attributed what he called the relative immunity of women to suicide to the fact that women were "fundamentally traditionalist by nature, they govern their conduct," Durkheim asserted, "by fixed beliefs and have no great intellectual needs" (Durkheim, 1951, p. 166).

Durkheim insisted that his explanation for the incidence of suicide rested on purely social factors. And, in his text, Durkheim sometimes attributes women's lower rates to their socialization. "The two sexes do not share equally in social life. Man is actively involved in it, while woman does little more than look on from a distance. Consequently, man is much more highly socialized than woman" (Durkheim, 1951, p. 385). Nevertheless, throughout his study he mainly ascribed the low incidence of women's suicide to organic influences.[13] For instance, in explaining the immunity of women to suicide, Durkheim concluded that "being a more instinctive creature than man, woman has only to follow her instincts to find calmness and peace" (Durkheim, 1951, p. 272).

Indeed, whenever it came to issues of gender, Durkheim's sociology was displaced by biologisms. Although Durkheim insisted that he was concerned with the social rather than the biological causes of suicide, he was, nevertheless, influenced by the popular, if sometimes vague, "degeneration" theory, especially its neo-Lamarckian variety.[14] In *The Division of Labor in Society* (1893), drawing upon Lamarck's "law of use and disuse" and Gustave Le Bon's neo-Lamarckian writings, Durkheim argued that as the division of labor increasingly separated men from women in modern societies it had the effect of enlarging men's brains (and intelligence) while diminishing women's:

> labor became increasingly divided up...between the sexes. At first limited to the sexual functions alone, it gradually extended to many other functions. The woman had long withdrawn from warfare and public affairs, and had centered her existence entirely round the family. Since then her role has become even more specialized. Nowadays, among civilized peoples the woman leads an existence entirely different from the man's. It might be said that the two great functions of psychological life had become as if dissociated from each other, one sex having overcome the affective, the other the intellectual function (Durkheim, 1984, pp. 20-21).

These sexual divisions in labor, Durkheim asserted, were "made perceptible physically by the morphological differences they have brought about." As a result, "not only are the size, weight and general shape very dissimilar as between a man and a woman, but, as Dr. LeBon has shown, ...with the advance of civilization the brain of the two sexes has increasingly developed differently." Thus, explained Durkheim, "the progressive gap" between men and women "may be due both to the considerable development of the male skull and to a cessation, even a regression in the growth of the female skull" (Durkheim, 1984, pp. 20-21).

Durkheim's assumptions about women's biological (thus intellectual) inferiority rested on a deeper set of unexamined racist views. For Durkheim's proof of women's intellectual inferiority rested upon a comparison with others whom Durkheim and his contemporaries unquestionably believed to be inferior to white French males. Quoting and endorsing Le Bon, Durkheim explained that "Whilst the average size of the skulls of male Parisians places them among the largest known skulls, the average size of those of female Parisians places them among the very smallest skulls observed, very much below those of Chinese women and scarcely above those of the women of New Caledonia" (Durkheim, 1984, pp. 20-21). Although Durkheim drew on Le Bon for his discussion of women's inferior brain size, this was a widely held view in mid-nineteenth-century French, Italian, British, German and American medical communities. Its leading exponent was the influential and respected French neurologist, Paul Broca.[15]

All the preceding suggests that, at least when it came to issues of gender, Durkheim's view of suicide was less a novel contribution than a restatement of a widely accepted convention. Durkheim's conventional views on women's intelligence and social roles may seem somewhat perplexing to those familiar with his sometimes otherwise unconventional views. For instance, in *The Division of Labor in Society* (1893), Durkheim suggested that traditional moral values could no longer effectively regulate modern, industrial society. Unlike many of his more nostalgic contemporaries, Durkheim sought adoption of a moral system more attuned to the social realities of modern life (Durkheim, 1984, pp. 329-341). To a great extent, a similar project underlay and informed much of Durkheim's *Suicide*. Nevertheless, a number of scholars (e.g., La-Capra, 1972) have found Durkheim's assumptions to be more conservative than his rhetoric. Nowhere does that conservatism display itself more clearly than in Durkheim's discussion of women. This resulted, in part, from Durkheim's failure to extend the logic of his social critique of morality to the issue of women's suicide. But (as I will argue) this was no mere oversight, for Durkheim's entire project rested on assumptions about the (natural) immunity of women to suicide. If Durkheim had challenged this notion, the foundation of the rest of his enterprise would have been considerably undermined.

What was new, then, in Durkheim's *Suicide* was not his presentation of the etiological role of social disintegration or the immunity of women to suicide, but a definition and a classificatory system (typology) which allowed him to use the incidence of suicide as a yardstick for social pathology.[16]

Durkheim's definition of suicide as *"death resulting directly or indirectly from a positive or negative act of the victim himself, which he knows will produce this result"* was, on the one hand, irrelevant to the statistics he used, while, on the other, it ensured that suicidal behavior by women could not be considered as suicide (Durkheim, 1951, p. 44). It was irrelevant because all of Durkheim's conclusions about the incidence of suicide were drawn from official statistics which defined suicide in ways that were incompatible with Durkheim's definition. For instance, those who sacrificed their lives for others ("un acte positif") were never listed as suicides in official statistics. And, those whose deaths resulted only "indirectly" from their acts generally did not appear in the statistics either.[17] Indeed, Durkheim must have known that those officials charged with the determination of whether an act was a suicide almost always labeled antisocial (socially disintegrative) acts as suicide, while they almost never called a socially sanctioned (integrative) behavior (heroism) suicide. The unquestioned assumption that suicide was an antisocial act was, after all, why Durkheim had chosen it as an indicator of social pathology in the first place. Apparently Durkheim never considered the possibility that the belief—shared by official statistics collectors and interpreters of suicide—that suicide was antisocial behavior had, *a priori*, distorted suicide statistics.

In addition, Durkheim's definition guaranteed that attempted suicide, the most commonly acknowledged women's suicidal behavior, would be excluded from consideration.[18] For, although Durkheim admitted that attempted suicide fit his definition of suicide *as a behavior*, he excluded it from his typology because attempted suicide fell "short of actual death."[19] By confining his categories to completed suicides, Durkheim excluded most suicidal behavior by women from subsequent investigations of suicide. If he had included attempted suicides, women rather than men would have emerged as the group at greatest risk of self-destructive behavior.[20]

Moreover, data just as good (or just as bad) as that on completed suicides were available had Durkheim's preconceptions not prevented him from considering them. For instance, beginning in 1826 (until 1961) the French Administration de la justice criminelle (under the direction of le Ministère de la santé) published suicide statistics that made no distinction between attempted and successful suicides ("suicides tentés ou effectués"). In the nineteenth century these were published in the *Annales d'hygiène,* which recorded the incidence of suicide (including, but not separating out attempted suicides) by age and by sex. Although these statistics suffered from the same weaknesses as data on completed suicides, there was no "objective" reason why they could not have been considered (Baudelot and Establet, 1986).

The decision to exclude attempted suicide from consideration was odd because the entire enterprise of the sociological study of suicide was aimed at describing social behavior. Certainly, attempting to kill oneself must be considered suicidal behavior. Yet, suicidologists since Durkheim have relied on statistics which, by defining only completed suicide as suicide, have effectively eliminated the majority of suicidal behavior from their analysis of suicidal behavior.

The data on attempted suicide could have been used to demonstrate that women were less content with their social roles than men were. Curiously, no suicide study has ever come to that conclusion. Thus, while suicidologists continue to refine their statistical methods, they rarely have questioned the assumption that only completed or successful suicides should constitute the data base for suicidal behavior.[21]

If Durkheim's definition of suicide ensured that women's suicidal behavior would be trivialized, his typology guaranteed that even those women who completed suicide would be excluded from the suicide equation. That is, in creating a "scientific" sociology Durkheim enshrined the unquestioned assumptions about both the effects of modernity and the immunity of women to suicide.[22] Thus, Durkheim's classificatory system contributed to and sustained the underreporting of women's completed suicides.

Although Durkheim described four types of suicide—altruistic, egoistic, anomic, and fatalistic—he elaborated only the first three and assigned the fourth, fatalistic, to a footnote. Because Durkheim wanted to demonstrate that the rate of suicide provided a way to measure social pathology, his typology was created to uncover the "regular and specific factor[s] in suicide in our modern societies." As Durkheim defined them, both anomie and egoism resulted from the collapse of traditional restraints and, thus, their incidence could be used as an index for social pathology. The rate of anomic suicide measured alienation, while the rate of egoistic measured the decline of self-restraint. Altruistic suicide, on the other hand, reflected socially sanctioned self-sacrifice and, as such, provided the base rate of suicide against which Durkheim could contrast the increase of suicide brought on by the breakdown of social integration, which he attributed to anomic and egoistic behavior (Durkheim, 1951, pp. 241-258). Of course, given the reality of social statistics, the reported number of anomic and egoistic suicides would always be significantly greater than altruistic suicides. But, as we shall see, there could be almost no fatalistic suicide.

As Durkheim explained in his footnote, fatalism "derives from excessive regulation, that of persons with futures pitilessly blocked and passions violently choked by oppressive discipline." Durkheim declined to look in detail at fatalistic suicide because he claimed that "it has so little contemporary importance and examples are so hard to find...that it seems useless to dwell upon it" (Durkheim, 1951, p. 311).[23]

Durkheim's definition of fatalism described the psychological and social condition of many nineteenth-century women. Like those before him, Durkheim assumed that, as an antisocial act, suicide was exacerbated by social disintegration. Accepting the belief that traditional family life offered the best safeguard against suicidal behavior, Durkheim never questioned the supposition that those most subsumed in the family (women and children) would be most immune to suicide (Durkheim, 1888, p. 450).[24] Given this paradigm, suicide and integrative (women's) behavior—what Durkheim labeled "fatalism"—were opposites. Because social integration was alleged to be the cure for suicidal ideation, there was no way for Durkheim to suppose that suicide could be a female behavior. Thus, classifying women's suicide as fatalistic guaranteed that women would be defined *a priori* as immune to suicide.

But, on its own terms, did Durkheim's data demonstrate that those who were most subsumed in particular social institutions were more immune to suicide than those who were less "socially integrated"? The answer is much more ambiguous than Durkheim and his predecessors were willing to admit. For, even accepting the equivocal data that women completed suicide less frequently than men, the high rate of attempted suicide by women suggested that suicidal behavior was a common way for women to express their profound unhappiness. Given the social role of most nineteenth-century women, it is fair to assume that submersion in the family provided no special protection for women from suicidal behavior (see Kushner, 1989, pp. 109-111). And, although his evidence was no more "value free" than Durkheim's, the Dutch anthropologist Steinmetz (1894) found that women living in the most socially integrated (primitive) societies had a greater incidence of suicide than men.[25]

The greatest challenge to the belief that social integration provided protection from suicide, however, came from Durkheim's own data. Official statistics consistently reported that the highest rates of suicide were in the military. "It is a general fact in all European countries," wrote Durkheim, "that the suicidal aptitude of soldiers is much higher than that of the civilian population of the same age" (Durkheim, 1951, p. 228; see also Morselli, 1882, Skelton, 1900). Durkheim's definition of fatalistic suicide as resulting "from excessive regulation," whose "passions [were] violently choked by oppressive discipline," seemed to describe nineteenth-century military life perfectly. Durkheim's understanding of official statistics and his own typological definitions could have led him to classify military suicide as fatalistic. Given the reported incidence of military suicide, Durkheim could have concluded that fatalism was the most important type of suicide.[26]

Durkheim, however, overcame the obvious inconsistency that military suicide exposed for his typology by arbitrarily classifying military suicide as "altruistic," even though the greatest number of reported military suicides could hardly be attributed to self-sacrifice (Durkheim, 1951, pp. 228-239).[27] Given his familiarity with suicide statistics, Durkheim must have known that those who sacrificed their lives for their military comrades in battle were never categorized as a suicide in any official statistics. Indeed, to be reported as a suicide, a military death would have to have occurred *outside* a combat situation.

Durkheim was not the only commentator who was forced to perform logical and classificatory gymnastics to account for the extraordinary rate of military suicide. Skelton, whose explanations for the immunity of women to suicide mirrored Durkheim's, tied what he found to be the "truly appalling" rates of military suicides to "training" which "is essentially destructive of individualism." Laying out a pattern of socialization that could have as easily described women as it did soldiers, Skelton attributed military suicide to the fact that a soldier "learns to consider himself a mere unit in a huge aggregate of individuals....The soldier's very trade consists in placing at the disposal of others that of all possessions most valued by man—his life. Is it, then, surprising that he should have less hesitation than other men in removing it?" (Skelton, 1900, pp. 473, 475).[28]

Given their assumptions about the "nature of women" and the prophylactic impact of family life, neither Skelton nor Durkheim could acknowledge the parallels that they had drawn between soldiers' and women's social situations. The point, of course, is *not* that women's and soldiers' socialization was the same, for it was not. Rather, Durkheim's description and discussions of military suicide fit into his category of fatalism more clearly than it fit into altruism. The reason that Durkheim could not see this was that he was tied to a set of rules that assumed that high rates of suicide were attached to the anomie and egoism brought on by modern urban life. If military suicide were categorized as fatalistic, Durkheim would have had to question his basic assumptions. This he could not do because it seemed self-evident to him that low rates of suicide were associated with social integration. Since fatalism was attached to social integration, women's low rates of suicide could be categorized as fatalistic—so infrequent a cause as hardly worthy of notice. Because the reported high rate of military suicide could not be attributed to modernity, it was placed in a special category, altruism, which effectively eliminated it from consideration.[29] Altruism became the baseline of suicide that all societies could condone—sacrifice for others.

This is not to suggest that Durkheim (or for that matter, Morselli, Masaryk, or Skelton) consciously set out to distort evidence. Rather, Durkheim was bound to a set of assumptions that framed his conclusions before he began his research. Given these assumptions, it would have been surprising if Durkheim had reached different conclusions. Thus, Durkheim's typology sanctioned the antimodernity and nostalgia that had "discovered" the suicide "problem" in the first place. His sociology provided (and continues to provide) "scientific" justification for traditional assumptions about women's behavior.[30] Had it been otherwise, Durkheim's *Suicide* might never have achieved the overwhelming influence that it has.

CONCLUSION

No conspiracy existed to exclude women's suicides from consideration. Rather, we must return to the rules that shaped Western considerations of suicide in the first place, that is, the fear of modernity was based upon a set of nostalgic beliefs that identified the growth of urban society as a challenge to traditional (patriarchal) authority. In this context, the motivation for the collection and analysis of suicide rates was to illustrate that modernity caused self-destructive behavior. Given these preconceptions, it was assumed that women were insulated from suicide to the extent that they were subsumed within the bounds of traditional family life. In other words, given the set of rules for defining and classifying suicide, there was no way in which suicide could have been seen as a female behavior. By refusing to reexamine these assumptions about women's roles and behavior, Durkheimian sociology was doomed to endorse the underlying values that Durkheim had hoped to challenge. As a result, neither Durkheim nor his followers could construct a classificatory system or adopt a methodology that would expose traditional life to the same scrutiny that they had insisted upon when it came to modernity.

NOTES

1. Unlike many classic texts, Durkheim's *Suicide* remains, according to French sociologists Baudelot and Establet (1986, p. 9), "un livre vivant. Et rares, en sciences sociales, les ouvrages qui survivent à leurs auteurs ou circonstances historiques qui ont motivé leur publication. *Le suicide* est une exception." In particular, Baudelot and Establet conclude that one social fact that has not changed is that "les hommes se suicident plus souvent que les femmes, les vieux plus souvent que les jeunes" (Baudelot and Establet 1984, pp. 59-70). See also Baudelot and Establet (1986, pp. 101-104).
2. For a discussion of the persistence of this view see Kushner (1989, pp. 100-101). For an example of this persistence in experts' thinking about suicide see Baudelot and Establet (1986, pp. 99-104) who conclude that "la protection dont bénéficie un individu à l'égard du suicide est fonction du nombre et de la profondeur des relations qu'il noue avec son milieu familial" (p. 101).
3. For a discussion of the origins and development of the moral treatment in France see Goldstein (1987, pp. 65-66, 80-119); for Britain see Scull (1979, 1981 pp. 107-118); for the U.S. see McGovern (1985, pp. 62-85); for Pinel see Castel (1988, pp. 201-205).
4. For similar views see Rhodes (1876) and Mulhall (1883).
5. That women should have been viewed as less suicidal than men is particularly puzzling given the long-held connection between suicide and insanity (Showalter, 1981; 1985).
6. Gender, as opposed to sex, is used here as the grammatical way of describing the properties associated with the distinctions of sex. My use of gender in this essay parallels that of historian Joan W. Scott (1986, 1988).
7. As I have demonstrated elsewhere (Kushner, 1985, 1989), even within the set of rules used by statistics gatherers, both nineteenth- and twentieth-century official suicide statistics can be characterized as having underreported the number of completed suicides by women. In fact, given the way suicide statistics have been and continue to be collected, the assertion that women complete suicide less frequently than men is questionable. Although official statistics continue to report that men are three to four times more likely to commit suicide than women, as Douglas (1967) demonstrated, these statistics are fatally flawed. As the British sociologist Taylor (1982, p. 62) has written, "Despite the general critical acclaim that [Douglas's] *The Social Meanings of Suicide* quite rightly received, it has had very little influence on the ways in which sociologists actually study suicide. In the first place many subsequent studies of suicide rates make no reference to Douglas and second, those who do mention him tend to side-step, rather than confront his arguments." Unlike their Anglo-American colleagues, a number of French sociologists have directly confronted Douglas. For instance, French sociologists Baudelot and Establet (1986) concede Douglas's main point that "a difference always exists between theoretical definitions expressed by sociologists and those given in existing statistics." Although they admit that the inaccuracies of suicide statistics "prohibit making refined international comparisons and measuring the evolution of suicide over long periods," they, nevertheless, insist that these data present an accurate picture of "the variations of suicide according to sex, age, marital state, region, and, although in moderation, social category." Besnard (1976) examines both Douglas's critique of Durkheim and Baechler's (1975) assertions of a constant rate of suicide. Besnard rejects Baechler's assertion that suicide statistics are invalid because they ignore attempted suicides (p. 334). Besnard concludes that official statistics, if carefully used, can avoid the errors that both Baechler and Douglas uncover: "il ne serait pas impossible, par une recherche

appropriée, d'estimer la marge d'erreur maximale qui peut affecter les statistiques officielles du suicide. Une telle étude permettrait sans doute aussi de voir si les erreurs se répartissent de manière aléatoire ou systématique" (p. 339). Reviewing the arguments of Baudelot and Establet as well as Besnard, Merllié (1986), on the one hand, defends Durkheim against charges that he used suicide statistics as objective reflection of reality, while, on the other hand he accepts Douglas's and Taylor's critiques of official statistics. Suicide statistics, Merllié concludes are, nevertheless, useful for social analysis "comme object et non seulement comme instrument, pour l'analyse sociologique" (p. 324).

8. This remains the dominant view. For instance, at the 22nd Annual Meeting of the American Association for Suicidology, in her keynote address entitled "Gender Socialization and Suicide," Sanborn (1989) tied the alleged maleness of suicide to men's socialization, which made it subsequently difficult for them to express a "softer side." If men would act like women, Sanborn suggested, suicide would be reduced substantially. See also Harnisch (1989) and Huchcroft (1989).

9. This essay was widely circulated and reprinted in several journals, including the *Democratic Review* (1854, 34, 405-417) and *Harper's New Monthly Magazine* (1859, 18, 516-520). Rhodes, an American author who lived in Paris and whose articles on "social issues" appeared regularly in American, French, and British periodicals, explained in 1876 that women committed suicide for very different motives from those of men: "Women appear to be more subject to moral influences, such as disappointed love, betrayal, desertion, jealousy, domestic trouble, and sentimental exaltation of every description." Men, on the other hand, "are rather affected by trials of a material order, such as misery, business embarrassments, losses, ungratified ambition" (Rhodes, 1876, pp. 192, 194).

10. For more on Durkheim's connection of suicide with the "intensity" of modern urban civilization see Nye (1982).

11. Durkheim also believed that populations that were too dense also caused suicide. His interest was in locating what he believed to be a healthy norm in order to contrast it with the pathological. Also see Nye (1982, pp. 114-115).

12. In a recent essay Berrios and Mohanna (1990) argue that Durkheim drew very selectively from the writings of nineteenth-century psychiatrists, exaggerating alienists' linking of suicide with psychopathology in his chapter, "Suicide et les états psychopathiques." Although I have no quarrel with Berrios and Mohanna, my argument rests on the congruence of Durkheim and nineteenth-century psychiatrists on the characterization of the etiology of women's suicide.

13. For a discussion of this contradiction in Durkheim's *Suicide* see Besnard (1973).

14. Durkheim was interested in the social effects of degeneration rather than its contribution to individual suicides. Thus, in his *Suicide,* Durkheim insisted that "a society does not depend for its number of suicides on having more or fewer neuropaths or alcoholics. Although the different forms of degeneration are an eminently suitable psychological field of action of the causes which may lead a man to suicide, degeneration itself is not one of these causes. Admittedly, under similar circumstances, the degenerate is more apt to commit suicide than the well man; but he does not necessarily do so because of his condition. This potentiality of his becomes effective only through the action of other factors which we must discover" (Durkheim, 1951, p. 81). For a discussion of Durkheim's debt to the degeneration model see Nye (1982, 1984). For an analysis of the roots of generation theory in French psychiatry see Dowbiggin (1985). For a comprehensive discussion of degeneration see Pick (1989).

15. For more on gender and brain size see Gould (1981) and Harrington (1987).

16. "Suicide was of primary interest to Durkheim," LaCapra reminds us, "not as an

isolated tragedy in the lives of discrete individuals, but as an index of a more widespread pathology in society as a whole" (LaCapra, 1972, p. 144).

17. For a discussion of the failure of official statistics to report those (particularly women) who die indirectly from their suicidal acts, see Kushner (1989, pp. 103-104).

18. While statistics on attempted suicides suffer from the same limitations as all suicide statistics, Durkheim never questioned their reliability. Also see Brierre de Boismont (1856, pp. 65-66).

19. "An attempt is an act thus defined but falling short of actual death" (Durkheim, 1951, p. 44).

20. Estimates since the early nineteenth century have indicated that for every completed suicide there have been six to eight attempts. These same statistics have concluded that women attempt suicide at a rate approximately two to three times greater than men (Shneidman and Farberow, 1961; Maris, 1981; Dublin, 1963; Hendin, 1982). Hendin sees the ratio as 10:1.

21. Although suicidologists have offered various ex post facto explanations justifying the exclusion of attempted suicides from measures of suicidal behavior, none of these can be sustained on close examination. This decision has no logical basis other than one of convenience—that is, completed suicides are readily available to researchers as part of national vital statistics on death rates. But, epidemiologists have persuaded their governments to collect data on many nonlethal diseases and modern statistical methodology has made it possible to develop many measures of other forms of behavior and belief. In retrospect it seems bizarre that suicide attempts should have been excluded from all considerations of the incidence of suicide just at the moment when sophisticated statistical methodologies were developed that could have been used to include attempted suicide, that is, unless, of course, the reason for excluding attempted suicide from the equation rested ultimately upon a set of beliefs that only could conceive of suicide as a male behavior (see Kushner, 1989, pp. 102-103).

22. As the French sociologist Philippe Besnard pointed out, Durkheim was interested in female suicide only to the extent that he could use it for elaboration of his wider concerns about social pathology. In no case, Besnard finds, did Durkheim view women's suicide itself as a category for systematic analysis. "Durkheim face au suicide des femmes n'a pas qu'un intérêt anecdotique. Elle est peut-être l'origine, et en tout cas au moins un symptôme, d'une carence plus fondamentale dans l'élaboration de sa théorie du suicide" (Besnard, 1973 p. 33).

23. Most subsequent studies, even those which claim to reevaluate Durkheim's *Suicide,* have ignored fatalistic suicide. For instance, in their attempt "lire *Le suicide,* pour en extraire une méthode d'analyse aujourd'hui encore applicable au suicide et à d'autres faits sociaux" Baudelot and Establet review only the "trois grands types de suicides...le suicide égoïste...le suicide altruiste," et "le suicide anomique." In fact, their study never mentions fatalistic suicide. It is, therefore, not surprising that they have concluded that Durkheim's assertion that men were more suicidal than women has stood the test of time (Baudelot and Establet, 1986, pp. 10-11, 99-103). Also see Baudelot and Establet (1984, pp. 59-70). Although he briefly mentions fatalistic suicide, Pope (1976) ignores it in his evaluation of Durkheim's *Suicide,* while devoting a chapter each to egoistic, altruistic, and anomic suicide.

24. One of the very few claims that women who are most submerged in the family display the greatest female suicidal behavior is found in Johnson (1981).

25. More recently, the historian Lane (1979) challenged Durkheim's logic that increased suicide rates supplied an index for social disintegration. Using the same type of data as Durkheim, Lane found that, as nineteenth-century Philadelphia

urbanized, its suicide rate grew proportionally greater than its homicide rate. Murderers, Lane reasoned, defy civil order, while suicides, he argued, by turning violent urges inward, internalize social regulation. Lane concluded that the increasing incidence of suicide in late-nineteenth-century cities served as a barometer of social integration because suicide, unlike homicide, indicated internalization of social anger.

26. As early as 1821 Esquirol had attributed the high incidence of military suicide to factors which seem consistent with Durkheim's fatalistic category. "L'esprit militaire, qui inspire l'indifférence pour la vie, qui n'attache pas une grande importance à un bien qu'on est prêt à sacrifier à l'ambition du maître; l'esprit militaire, dis-je, doit être favorable au suicide" (Esquirol, 1838, vol. 1, p. 590).

27. As Besnard points out "Après tout, le seul exemple «moderne» qui soit donné [by Durkheim] du suicide altruiste est le suicide militaire qui pourrait d'ailleurs tout aussi bien être interprété en termes de régulation excessive (Durkheim évoque la discipline rigide, «compressive de l'individu») qu'en invoquant la trop forte intégration en l'en-groupe" (Besnard, 1973, p. 42).

28. Masaryk's explanation for the high suicide rate in the military was especially convoluted given his algebra of the more "civilized" a society, the greater its suicide rate. "The philosophy of life, which at present is manifested by the military services," wrote Masaryk in 1881, "is wanting throughout in either true moral or religious content, and suicide therefore appears more frequently among soldiers than among civilians" (Masaryk, 1970, p. 171). For Morselli's discussion of military suicide see Morselli (1982, pp. 256-257).

29. If Durkheim contradicted his own logic by portraying military suicide as altruistic, he ignored entirely the fact that official statistics regularly reported extremely high rates of suicide among prisoners. "Prison life," according to Masaryk, "disposes very strongly to suicide, as the relatively high frequency of among prison inmates indicates" (Masaryk, 1970, p. 39). Given his typology, Durkheim would have had to categorize the majority of prisoner suicides as fatalistic. Recent studies continue to report high rates of prisoner suicides: "In most countries," according to Kerkhof and Bernasco (1990), suicide "in correctional institutions is higher than in the population at large." See also Bernheim (1987, pp. 315-317)

30. For examples of the persistence of Durkheim's conclusions about women's suicide by Anglo-American experts see Kushner (1989, pp. 100-102). An example of the persistence of similar thinking in France is provided in the work of French sociologists Chenais and Vallin (1981) who attribute the increase of suicide among women in industrial countries since the Second World War to the breakdown of traditional institutions like the family. Thus, the increase of suicide among women is directly related to this increased exposure to those economic fluctuations that previously had their greatest impact on men: "L'influence de la situation économique sur le suicide dépend beaucoup de la manière dont les individus en difficulté se trouvent insérés dans la société. L'existence et l'efficacité de réseaux de solidarité (qu'il s'agisse de la famille ou d'autres institutions) peuvent écarter le recours à un geste de désespoir" (pp. 2-3). Also see Chenais (1973) and Baudelot and Establet (1984).

REFERENCES

Anonymous. Suicide. *The American Whig Review,* 1847, 6 (August), 137-142.
Anonymous. Suicides in New York City in 1860. *New York Times,* 1861, January 17, section 2, page 1.
Baechler, J. *Les Suicides.* Paris: Calmann-Levy, 1975.

Baudelot, C., and Establet, R. Suicide: l'évolution séculaire d'un fait social. *Economie et Statistique*, 1984, 168, 59-70.

Baudelot, C., and Establet, R. *Durkheim et le Suicide*. Paris: Presses Universitaires de France, 1986.

Bernheim, J. C. *Les Suicides en Prison*. Montréal: Edition du Méridien, 1987.

Berrios, G. E., and Mohanna, M. Durkheim and French psychiatric views on suicide during the 19th century. *British Journal of Psychiatry*, 1990, 156, 1-9.

Bertrand, L. *Traité du Suicide*. Paris: J. B. Baillière, 1857.

Besnard, P. Durkheim et les femmes ou le *Suicide* inachevé. *Revue Française de Sociologie*, 1973, 14(1), 27-61.

Besnard, P. Anti- ou anté-Durkheimisme? *Revue Française de Sociologie*, 1976, 17, 313-341.

Bourguet, M. N. *Déchiffrer la France*. Paris: Editions des Archives Contemporaines, 1989.

Brierre de Boismont, A. *Du Suicide et de la Folie Suicide*. Paris: J. B. Baillière, 1856.

Castel, R. *The Regulation of Madness*. Berkeley: University of California, 1988.

Chenais, C. L'évolution de la mortalité par suicide dans divers pays industrialisés. *Population*, 1973, 28(2), 419-22.

Chenais, J. C., and Vallin, J. Le suicide at la crise économique. *Population et Sociétés*, 1981, 147(May), 6-9.

Colwill, E. Transforming 'women's empire.' Ph.D. dissertation, State University of New York, Binghamton, 1991.

Cook, G. P. Statistics of suicide, which have occurred in the state of New York from Dec. 1, 1847 to Dec. 1, 1848. *American Journal of Insanity*, 1849, 5, 308-309.

DeGroat, J. The work and lives of women in Parisian manufacturing trades, 1830-1848. Ph.D. dissertation, University of Rochester, 1991.

Douglas, J. D. *The Social Meanings of Suicide*. Princeton: Princeton University, 1967.

Dowbiggin, I. Degeneration and hereditarianism in French mental science, 1840-90. In W. F. Bynum, R. Porter and M. Shepherd (eds.), *The Anatomy of Madness*, Vol. 1. London: Tavistock, 1985.

Dublin, L. I. *Suicide*. New York: Ronald Press, 1963.

Durkheim, E. Suicide et natalité. *Revue Philosophique de la France et de l'Etranger*, 1888, 26, 446-463.

Durkheim, E. *Suicide: A Study in Sociology* (Translated by J. A. Spaulding and G. Simpson). Glencoe, IL: Free Press, 1951.

Durkheim, E. *The Division of Labor in Society* (Translated by W. D. Halls). London: Macmillan, 1984.

Esquirol, J. E. De la hypémanie ou mélancholie. In J. E. Esquirol, *Des Maladies Mentales*, Vol. 1. Paris: J. B. Baillière, 1838.

Etoc-Demazy, G. F. *Recherches Statistiques sur le Suicide*. Paris: Germer-Baillière, 1844.

Falret, J. P. *De l'Hypochondrie et du Suicide*. Paris: Croullebois, 1822.

Gates, B. T. *Victorian Suicide*. Princeton, NJ: Princeton University Press, 1988.

Goldstein, J. *Console and Classify*. New York: Cambridge University Press, 1987.

Gould, S. J. *The Mismeasure of Man*. New York: Norton, 1981.

Guerry, A. M. *Essai sur la Statistique Morale de la France*. Paris, 1833.

Hacking, I. *The Taming of Chance*. Cambridge: Cambridge University Press, 1990.

Harnisch, P. Suicide and gender. *AAS NewsLink*, 1989, 14(Summer), 1, 3.

Harrington, A. *Medicine, Mind and the Double Brain*. Princeton, NJ: Princeton University Press, 1987.

Hendin, H. *Suicide in America*. New York: Norton, 1982.

Huchcroft, S. What can we learn from female suicides? *AAS NewsLink*, 1989, 15(Fall), 12-13.

Hunt, E. K. Statistics of suicide in the U.S. *American Journal of Insanity*, 1845, 1, 225-234.

Jarvis, E. On the supposed increase of insanity. *American Journal of Insanity*, 1852, 8, 333-364.

Johnson, K. Durkheim revisited. *Suicide and Life-Threatening Behavior*, 1981, 11, 145-153.

Kerkhof, A. J. F. M., and Bernasco, W. Suicidal behavior in jails and prisons in the Netherlands. *Suicide and Life-Threatening Behavior*, 1990, 20, 123-137.

Knighton, W. Suicidal mania. *Littel's Living Age*, 1881, 148, 376-381.

Kushner, H. I. Women and suicide in historical perspective. *Signs*, 1985, 10, 537-552.

Kushner, H. I. *Self-Destruction in the Promised Land*. New Brunswick, NJ: Rutgers University Press, 1989.

LaCapra, D. *Emile Durkheim*. Ithaca, NY: Cornell University Press, 1972.

Lane, R. *Violent Death in the City*. Cambridge, MA: Harvard University Press, 1979.

Le Bon, G. *L'homme et les Societé*, Vol. 2. Paris: J. Rothschild, 1881.

Maris, R. *Pathways to Suicide*. Baltimore: Johns Hopkins University Press, 1981.

Masaryk, X. *Civilization and the Meaning of Civilization*. Chicago: University of Chicago Press, 1970.

McGovern, C. M. *Masters of Madness*. Hanover, NH: University Press of New England, 1985.

Merllié, D. Le suicide et ses statistiques. *Revue Philosophique de la France et l'Etranger*, 1987, 1086, 303-325.

Morselli, H. *Suicide*. New York: D. Appleton and Co, 1882.

Mulhall, M. G. Insanity, suicide and civilization. *The Contemporary Review*, 1883, 63, 901-908.

Nye, R. A. Heredity, pathology and psychoneurosis in Durkheim's early work. *Knowledge and Society*, 1982, 4, 102-142.

Nye, R. *Crime, Madness, and Politics in Modern France*. Princeton, NJ: Princeton University Press, 1984.

Pick, D. *Faces of Degeneration*. Cambridge: Cambridge University Press, 1989.

Pope, W. *Durkheim's Suicide*. Chicago: University of Chicago Press, 1976.

Porter, T. M. *The Rise of Statistical Thinking, 1820-1900*. Princeton, NJ: Princeton University Press, 1986.

Quételet, A. *Sur l'Homme et le Développement de ses Facultés*. Paris: Bachelier, 1835.

Quételet, A. *Du Système Social et des Lois qui le Régissent*. Paris: Guillaumin et Cie, 1848.

Reeves, R. N. Suicide and the environment. *Popular Science Monthly*, 1897, 51(June), 186-199.

Rhodes, A. Suicide. *The Galaxy*, 1876, 21, 192-195.

Sanborn, C. Gender socialization and suicide. *Suicide and Life-Threatening Behavior*, 1990, 22, 148-155.

Scott, J. W. Gender: a useful category of historical analysis. *American Historical Review*, 1986, 91, 1053-1075.

Scott, J. W. A statistical representation of work. In J. W. Scott (ed.), *Gender and the Politics of History*. New York: Columbia University Press, 1988a.

Scott, J. W. *Gender and the Politics of History*. New York: Columbia University Press, 1988b.

Scull, A. *Museums of Madness*. New York: St. Martin's Press, 1979.

Scull, A. Moral treatment reconsidered. In A. Scull (ed.), *Madhouses, Mad-Doctors, and Madmen*. Philadelphia: University of Pennsylvania Press, 1981.

Shneidman, E. S., and Farberow, N. L. Statistical comparisons between attempted and committed suicides. In N. L. Farberow and E. S. Shneidman (eds.), *The Cry for Help*. New York: McGraw-Hill, 1961.

Showalter, E. Victorian women and insanity. In A. Scull (ed.), *Madhouse, Mad-Doctors, and Madmen*. Philadelphia: University of Pennsylvania Press, 1981.

Showalter, R. *The Female Malady*. New York: Random House, 1985.

Skelton, R. A. Statistics of suicide. *The Nineteenth Century*, 1900, 48(September), 465-495.

Stansell, C. *City of Women*. New York: Knopf, 1986.

Steinmetz, S. R. Suicide among primitive peoples. *American Anthropologist*, 1894, 7, 55-60.

Strahan, S. A. K. *Suicide and Insanity*. London: Swan Sonnenschein and Co., 1893.

Taylor, S. *Durkheim and the Study of Suicide*. New York: St. Martin's Press, 1982.

Winslow, F. *The Anatomy of Suicide*. London: H. Renshaw, 1840.

9

Applying Durkheim's Typology to Individual Suicides

David Lester, PhD

Durkheim designed his theory and typology of suicide to be applied to *societies* as a whole, but both he and others utilized it also with the *subgroups* that exist within society and to *generalized figures*. For example, Durkheim mentioned fatalistic suicide in a footnote attributing this type to young husbands with no children and to slaves. In this chapter I plan to explore whether Durkheim's typology can be usefully extended to *individual* cases of suicide.

Sociologists can be rather traditional. For example, I have been scolded by various reviewers for applying Durkheim's theory of suicide to primitive societies (Durkheim himself did not do so). Clearly, applying Durkheim's typology to individual suicides may also arouse the ire of some sociologists. However, if we cannot modify the theory and research paradigms of scholars in the past, then we cannot expect social science to advance.

Sociologists typically justify every study of suicide by first citing Durkheim's writing on the topic. Indeed, it is a good starting point. According to Lukes (1972), Durkheim was profoundly affected by the suicide of one of his student peers, Victor Hommay. Hommay had found his adolescent life empty and isolated, but his years at the Ecole Normale Supérieure in Paris were enjoyable. He missed the company of his friends during his vacations and also, after graduation, when he taught in a provincial lycée. He worked hard on his thesis, which relieved to some extent the tedium of his days. In 1886, Hommay died, perhaps killing himself, by falling from a window as he was about to leave to teach one day. Lukes notes that the description that Durkheim later gave of *egoistic* suicide closely fitted Hommay's situation. Thus, Durkheim provides some justification for the task I have set myself in this chapter.

CLASSIFYING SOCIETIES

Sociological studies of suicide have not typically classified societies into Durkheim's four types of suicide. Rather, particular social variables, objectively measured, are assumed to reflect the underlying social dimensions. For example, societies with higher divorce rates typically have higher suicide rates (Lester, 1988). Divorce is thought to directly reduce the strength of social integration in the society (by splitting up families) and perhaps also to reflect a lack of social regulation (since only the socially unregulated would consider divorce).

In a study of the impact of social integration and social regulation on suicide which permits a classification of societies (Lester, 1989), I subjected measures of seven social variables in 53 nations of the world to a factor analysis and extracted two factors. One, with high loadings from political rights, civil rights, political freedom, and religious liberty, seemed to tap social regulation. The second, with a high loading from the marriage rate, perhaps tapped social integration. Each of the 53 nations was classified as high, moderate or low on each of the factor scores.

High scores on both factors were obtained by Bulgaria, Czechoslovakia, Egypt, Hungary, Poland, Singapore, South Korea and Yugoslavia. Suicides in these nations might be fatalistic/altruistic. Low scores on both factors were obtained by Sweden and Switzerland, and suicides in these nations might be anomic/egoistic.

Honduras, Jordan, Mexico, Panama, and the Philippines were high in social regulation and low in social integration; while Australia, Canada, New Zealand and the United Kingdom were low in social regulation and high in social integration.

This study was meant to be provocative rather than definitive, but a revised set of social variables might provide two factors which adequately measure Durkheim's constructs, thereby permitting a classification of nations on these contructs.

CLASSIFYING SUBGROUPS

Several discussions have appeared of whether one of Durkheim's four types of suicide is characteristic of a particular of a society. Let us look at just a few of these.

Suttee

Sharma (1978) has discussed whether suttee, the suicide of a Hindu widow on her husband's funeral pyre, is altruistic suicide. In altruistic suicide, the individual is well integrated into the society, perhaps to the extent that the ego is not the individual's own property. The person belongs to the state. Since suttee is performed as a duty, it may be termed *obligatory altruistic suicide*. Sharma noted that, though some Hindu widows may commit suttee because there is strong public pressure to do so (obligatory altruistic suicide), other widows presumably do so because they dread life alone without their husband (optional altruistic suicide).

Sharma noted that the term altruistic for Durkheim meant that the act was performed as a duty. Suttee was not regarded as a religious duty until the tenth or eleventh century and for many years was only found in the warrior class. Hindu society allowed for the separation of husband and wife, and often relatives tried to dissuade widows from suttee. Furthermore, Sharma argued that the widow kills herself for the future good of both herself and her husband. Suttee ensures that wife and husband will dwell in heaven. The wife's suttee affects her husband's destiny. As such, Sharma views it as sacrifice rather than suicide, or perhaps a combination of the two.

Primitive Societies

Two basic forms of suicide have been described in contemporary Austronesian-speaking Oceania. Some individuals in these societies commit suicide in order to avoid the consequences of public exposure of their immoral or illicit behavior. The suicide spares victims and their family from shame and humiliation. Other individuals, usually young men, kill themselves after being slighted or offended, typically by a family member. The suicide expresses the victim's anger at being mistreated. Since most Oceanic societies discourage the direct expression of anger, especially toward the family, the anger is turned inward onto the self.

MacPherson and MacPherson (1985, 1987) viewed the first type of suicide described above as altruistic suicide since the act affects the honor and prestige of the group as a whole. The victim commits suicide to make amends to the community.

The MacPhersons viewed the second type of suicide as anomic since such suicides occur more frequently during times of social disequilibrium and change when the consensus on social norms and customs is breaking down. The desires of people, especially the young, may rise beyond realistic chances of fulfillment, and they commit suicide when reality indicates that those desires will never be satisfied.

Other Examples

Ofstein and Acuff (1979) suggested that suicide in the elderly could be seen as egoistic. They noted that disengagement theory (Cummings, 1963) suggests that the elderly and the society to which they belong experience a mutual withdrawal with advancing age, leaving the elderly individual in a state of social isolation.

Hitchcock (1967) explored the consequences of the shortage of marriageable women among the Nauthars in Nepal. This shortage led to complex arranged marriages being agreed upon involving young children and extreme conflict when the arrangements became difficult to implement. The suicides in young women in the group were viewed by Hitchcock as fatalistic in nature.

APPLYING SOCIAL INTEGRATION AND SOCIAL REGULATION TO INDIVIDUALS

Breed's Suicide Syndrome

It is clear that the basic elements involved in Durkheim's concepts of social integration and social regulation can be applied to individuals. For example, Breed (1972) proposed five basic components for the suicidal syndrome in individuals: commitment, rigidity, failure, shame, and isolation.

By *commitment,* Breed meant having an internalized set of culturally defined roles and goals, a notion which resembles social regulation. *Failure* for women included separation/divorce and childlessness, components of social integration. *Shame* included low self-esteem, feelings of shame from failure, and loss of hope, an anomic state. *Isolation* included living alone, few social contacts and frustration of dependency needs, aspects again of social integration.

Breed (1970) applied his concepts to suicide in blacks. In his study of suicide among young, lower-class, single black males in New Orleans, Breed was struck by the oppression of black society by the white society. He found that blacks remain largely segregated, powerless and less well-protected than whites from arbitrary authorities. For example, he identified a high incidence of difficulties with the police and other authorities in the black suicides. Interviews with blacks in the community revealed a widespread fear of the police, and several respondents said that they would commit suicide rather than go to jail. Breed saw fatalistic suicide as a result of the absence of freedom from unjust and arbitrary authorities, and he felt, therefore, that black suicide was fatalistic in nature.

Altruistic and Fatalistic Suicide in Chinese Women of the Ch'ing Dynasty

Young (1972) examined suicide among Chinese women during the Ch'ing Dynasty in China (1644-1912). Traditional Chinese society was guided by an emphasis on familism rather than individualism and, as subordinate members of the family, women were expected to perform their roles according to the Confucian principles of filial piety and chastity. Among some groups, the notion developed that people should sacrifice their lives in order to preserve these values, and female suicide in the name of chastity began to appear from the twelfth century on.

At the *community level,* suicide as an act to preserve chastity inspired admiration, and the victim was glorified. Some *clans,* however, disapproved of suicide for any cause, while other clans tacitly encouraged suicide to preserve chastity because of the honor it would bestow on the clan. *Families* almost uniformly disapproved of suicide for any cause.

Young noted that, during the Ch'ing Dynasty, some women committed suicide after their husband or fiancé had died, while others committed suicide because they felt that their hitherto unblemished reputation as chaste women had been damaged (perhaps by an attempted rape). Young saw both of these types of suicide as altruistic. Women also committed suicide rather than undergo a forced remarriage or after capture by armed rebel bandits. Young saw these suicides as fatalistic.

In a study of 626 cases of female suicide from selected local gazetteers, Young classified 59 percent of the suicides as altruistic and 41 percent as fatalistic. He noted that the methods used by the two types of suicide differed, with the altruistic suicides using hanging much more often than the fatalistic suicides (who used drowning and other methods more often).

Fatalistic Suicide in American Youth

Peck (1983) identified Durkheim's concept of fatalism with Rotter's (1966) concept of an external locus of control. If people have an external locus of control, they think that their lives are determined by external forces beyond their control rather than being affected by how they themselves behave. Peck saw this attitude as similar to fatalism.

Peck examined suicide notes written by suicides under the age of 35 from a midwestern city and found evidence of an external locus of control (fatalistic thinking) in 33 percent of the notes, for example,

> I have attempted suicide because I could no longer take my father's sadistic nature. My mother was a "machine"—lacking in human emotions. This was the only way to get away from my parents (Peck, 1983, p. 321).

Anomic Suicide in Japanese Youth

Iga and Ohara (1967) proposed that suicide in Japanese youth after the Second World War was anomic in nature. They argued that the components of anomie (egocentrism, goal-means discrepancy, emotional dependency, and insecurity) were prominent in Japanese youth and reinforced by the culture. For example, Japanese place great value on "rising in the world," and parents are highly competitive in striving to enhance their children's chances for geting ahead. On the other hand, channels for social mobility are limited. Firms often look at family background and influential connections before hiring staff, and the government for a long time gave preference (almost exclusively) to graduates of Tokyo University. Thus, it is not easy for Japanese youth to realize the aspirations set up for them.

Iga and Ohara moved from this general level of discourse to studies of the individual by giving personality inventories to suicidal and nonsuicidal Japanese youth and noting that the suicide attempters obtained high scores on such scales as lack of cooperativeness, inferiority feelings and worries over possible misfortune. They interpreted these differences as indicating anomie in the suicidal Japanese youth.

Altruistic Suicide in Greek Tragedy

Faber (1970) used the suicides in the plays of Euripides to illustrate the nature of altruistic suicide as defined by Durkheim. For example, in *Alcestis*, Apollo is fond of Alcestis' husband, Admetus, and, when he finds out that Admetus is going to die at a young age, tries to persuade the Fates to spare him. The Fates agree to do so, but only if a substitute willing to die in his place can be found. Admetus cannot find anyone willing to die in his place, and so eventually his wife, Alcestis, volunteers to do so. Thus, Faber saw Alcestis' suicide as altruistic.

Incidentally, Faber notes that the motivations in the play are more complex than this simple analysis indicates. For example, Alcestis is shocked that her husband is willing to let her make this sacrifice and comes to feel great resentment toward him. She then tries to induce guilt through her death, and her self-sacrifice becomes tinged with unconscious aggression, which in turn suggests that her initial offer to die in Admetus' place was not serious—that she hoped he would reject her offer.

Kaplan (1987) took all of the suicides discussed in Faber's book, from the plays of both Sophocles and Euripides, and classified them into Durkheim's typology. For Sophocles, Kaplan classified the suicides as follows:

Ajax	egoistic
Oedipus	egoistic
Jocasta	egoistic
Haemon	egoistic
Eurydice	egoistic
Deineira	egoistic
Heracles	anomic/egoistic
Antigone	anomic/egoistic

while, for the suicides in Euripides, Kaplan suggested the following classification:

Hermione	anomic/egoistic
Phaedra	anomic/egoistic

Evadne	altruistic
Iphigenia	altruistic
Menoeceus	altruistic
Macaria	altruistic
Polyxena	altruistic
Alcestis	altruistic

Kaplan also examined the six suicides mentioned in the Hebrew Bible, and found that only four possibly fitted into Durkheim's types. The suicides of Abimelech (Judges 9:54) and Saul's armor bearer (I Samuel 31:5) were possibly altruistic, and the suicides of Ahitophel (II Samuel 17:23) and Zimri (I Kings 16:18) possibly egoistic. However, Kaplan felt that the suicides of Samson (Judges 16:30) and Saul (I Samuel 31:4, II Samuel 1:6, and I Chronicles 10:4) were the result of a differentiated *and* integrated relationship with their God, and Kaplan called such suicides *covenantal*. (The suicides of Saul's armor bearer and Zimri were also thought to be possibly covenantal.)

Famous Suicides

Shulman (1987) classified three famous suicides into Durkheim's types. Ernest Hemingway stressed courage and machismo. His heroes were boxers, soldiers and bullfighters. His orientation was American individualism and his suicide egoistic.

Virginia Woolf was sexually abused as a child and frigid throughout her marriage. She had several episodes of psychiatric disturbance and was generally pessimistic in her outlook on life. Shulman saw her suicide as anomic.

Nikolai Gogol was politically conservative but often criticized by Russian nobility. After the death of a woman who had served as a mother figure for him, he fell under the influence of a priest who convinced Gogol that his writings were sinful. Gogol fasted and prayed for forgiveness for his sins for three weeks and died of starvation in 1852. Shulman saw this as an altruistic suicide.

Van Hoesel's Empirical Study

Van Hoesel (1983) obtained cases of suicides from two medical examiners and made summaries of the cases. An independent judge decided whether the cases might fit more than one typology of suicide, and 404 such cases formed the basis for the study. Undergraduate and graduate student judges then sorted the set of cases into one or more of ten typologies, including Durkheim's. The concordance rate (percent agreement between judges) for Durkheim's typology was 79 percent, and 71 percent of the cases could be classified. None of the suicides were seen as altruistic, 5.7 percent as egoistic, 8.7 percent as fatalistic and 56.7 percent as anomic.

CRITERIA FOR CLASSIFYING INDIVIDUAL SUICIDES

Shulman's analysis of three famous suicides discussed above highlights two important problems which must be addressed before applying Durkheim's typology to individual cases of suicide. First, it is necessary to specify formal criteria for classifying a suicide into each of the four Durkheimian types. When I read Shulman's decisions on Hemingway, Woolf and Gogol, I found myself disagreeing with his placement, and the disagreement is because Shulman and I use different criteria.

A second decision is whether we are going to rely on objective, externally observable, criteria or subjective criteria. For example, a reliance on observable and external criteria might lead to social integration being operationalized in terms of such variables as married/divorced, attends church/does not attend, and lived in same community for 10 years/moved in last 10 years. In contrast, a reliance on subjective personal criteria would necessitate knowing how the individual felt about his or her social integration and social regulation. It is obvious that a person may appear to be socially integrated, with a family, friends and colleagues, yet feel alienated and alone.

One source of ideas for a Durkheimian classification comes from Van Hoesel (1983) who prepared the following set of guidelines for classifying suicides into Durkheim's types:

1. **Egoistic suicide**. This suicide stems from a lack of integration of the individual into society. People most likely to commit egoistic suicide are not dependent enough on their group and are left too much to their private interests.

    Example: A 78-year-old black male was found in his apartment in a decomposed state. Neighbors reported they had not seen the man for three weeks, but said this was normal since he usually "kept to himself." There was no known family or friends to contact for funeral arrangements. Autopsy results showed the man died of a self-inflicted gunshot wound and had a considerable amount of alcohol in his blood at the time of death.

    Comment: This man was an older person living alone and clearly alienated from society. He had no friends or family and very limited contact with his neighbors. The fact that he lacked any meaningful social interaction would place him as an egoistic suicide.

2. **Altruistic suicide**. This suicide is characterized by very high social cohesion. Unlike the individual who commits egoistic suicide, the individual described in the altruistic category is overly integrated into a group and feels that no sacrifice, even that of one's own life, is too much if it would benefit the group as a whole.

    Example: A 23-year-old white male poured gasoline over himself and set himself on fire. Prior to this act he had given an antiwar speech and had said he would kill himself to show that "the peace movement was serious."

Comment: This would be an example of altruistic suicide because this man gave up his life for a cause he believed in.

3. **Anomic suicide**. This occurs in a crisis situation. The person is not capable of dealing with the crisis in a rational manner and chooses suicide as a solution to the problem.

Example: A 35-year-old white female was found hanging in the basement of her house. She had been very depressed after her husband left her two days prior to her death. About an hour before her death he had visited her and talked about a divorce. She then called her mother and said she couldn't deal with the situation anymore and would kill herself.

Comment: This is an example of someone experiencing the loss of a loved one which clearly constituted a major crisis in her life. Other examples of an anomic suicide would be the person who experiences a sudden increase or decrease in wealth or the death of a loved one.

4. **Fatalistic suicide**. This can be an extreme response to excessive regulation. Victims feel that they have no freedom and no future.

Example: A 27-year-old black male was found hanging from the top of his cell door in a state penitentiary. A week before his death he had received a 40-year sentence for his involvement in several armed robberies.

Comment: This man was in a situation where he had very little free choice. He was "choked by oppressive discipline" and had no freedom (Van Hoesel, 1983, 64-66).

If one focuses solely on the definitions of social integration and social regulation given by Durkheim, definitions which, however, have been greatly criticized (see Lester [1972] for a review of the criticisms), then one is forced to look solely at the degree to which a suicide is integrated into and regulated by society. However, Durkheim chose particular labels for his four types. *Altruistic* goes beyond the concept of social integration and suggests that such suicides must intend to help others by their suicide. Altruistic suicide is, therefore, a sacrifice by a socially integrated person. *Fatalistic* indicates that people are overwhelmed by their fate and suggests, therefore, either that a socially determined fate requires their suicide or that suicide is an escape from too strong a regulation. The first type might be illustrated by the mass suicides of Americans in Guyana who were followers of Jim Jones (Kilduff and Javers, 1979) while the second type might be illustrated by the Jews in Austria who killed themselves rather than be sent away by the Nazis to concentration camps (Kwiet, 1984).

Thus, we must also look at the psychological state of the individual and the motives behind the suicide. From Iga and Ohara the sources of motivation

Table 1.

The Classification of Thirty Suicides

	Social Integration	Social Regulation	Comment	Type
Craig Badialis	high	average	committed suicide to bring peace	altruistic
Povl Bang-Jensen	high	average	fired from UN; felt persecuted	fatalistic
John Berryman	low	low	feelings of failure; alcoholism	anomic
Bruce Clark	low	average	felt he was a failure	anomic
Hart Crane	low	low	felt he was a failure; violent alcoholic	anomic
James Forrestal	high	?	schizophrenic, forced resignation	anomic
Sigmund Freud	high	?	fled Nazis; dying of cancer	fatalistic
Judy Garland	average	low	addict; feelings of failure	anomic
Kenneth Halliwell	low	low	losing lover; failure	egoistic/ anomic
Tom Heggen	low	average	alone; needed mentor	egoistic
Ernest Hemingway	high	high	feared being institutionalized	fatalistic
Christopher Jens	low	low	schizophrenic	egoistic/ anomic
Paul Kammerer	mixed*	average	losing wife & lover; accused of fraud; schizophrenic	anomic/ egoistic
Vachel Lindsay	low	low	schizophrenic	anomic
Ross Lockridge	high	average	obsessed with novel; anticipating failure	anomic
Jack London	average	average	threatened and real loss; illness	anomic/

The Classification of Thirty Suicides, cond.

	Social Integration	Social Regulation	Comment	Type
Yukio Mishima	high	low	tried to overthrow government	anomic
Marilyn Monroe	low	average	alone; rejected	egoistic
O.H. Mowrer	average	high	widower; depressed	egoistic
Cesare Pavese	low	average	alone	egoistic
Sylvia Plath	mixed*	average	husband left her	egoistic/ anomic
Freddie Prinze	average	low	drug addict; impulsive	anomic
Mark Rothko	mixed	low	distrustful; separated from wife	egoistic/ anomic
Gabrielle Russier	mixed	low	lost lover; threatened with imprisonment	fatalistic/ egoistic
Victor Tausk	mixed	low	rejected fiancé; forced into marriage	fatalistic
Sara Teasdale	low	average	alone; fear of illness	egoistic
Vincent van Gogh	low	low	disturbed	egoistic/ anomic
Jody White	mixed	low	lost girlfriend	egoistic/ anomic
Virginia Woolf	high	low	feared insanity	fatalistic
Stephan Zweig	mixed	average	feared Nazis; fear of old age	fatalistic/ egoistic

* "Mixed" indicates that these individuals had social ties, but they are not the ones they most desired.

and psychological condition are relevant and from Van Hoesel the descriptions given for anomic and fatalistic suicide are also relevant.

AN APPLICATION OF THESE
PRINCIPLES TO THIRTY SUICIDES

A recent study was made of the lives of 30 suicides whose lives and deaths were sufficiently interesting to warrant a biography (Lester, 1991). Table 1 applies the concepts discussed above to their lives and deaths. The ratings of social integration and social regulation are based more or less on objective information about the social network and degree of regulation of each individual. The final classification uses the criteria both of Van Hoesel and of Iga and Ohara.

Nine of the suicides were classified as anomic, eight as anomic/egoistic, five as egoistic, five as fatalistic, two as fatalistic/egoistic and one as altruistic. All of the 30 suicides could be classified. The problem was not whether they fitted into the typology, but rather which type did they fit best.

As expected, given the problems that sociologists have had in distinguishing between social integration and social regulation (Johnson, 1965), the mixed label of anomic/egoistic was common. However, interestingly, two suicides had elements of both fatalistic and egoistic suicide. This possibility suggests the usefulness of the Johnson suggestion that social integration and social regulation should be viewed as two independent dimensions giving nine (three-by-three) cells in the cross-tabulated array if each dimension is scored as high, moderate or low.

As Johnson and others have suggested, altruistic and fatalistic suicide may not be common in modern society. However, almost all of the suicides considered in this analysis took place in countries where political and religious oppression are relatively absent. If we had been able to obtain suicides from nations where oppression is strong, then fatalistic and altruistic suicides might have been more common.

CONCLUSIONS

The task attempted in this chapter, namely to explore whether individual suicides can be fitted into Durkheim's typology, has been successful. We have observed that several other scholars have played with this idea. The present analysis has shown that it may well be possible to apply Durkheim's typology to individuals, and we have explored some of the difficulties encountered in doing this. In particular, it has been found that the derivation of a set of criteria for the classification of individuals is the major hurdle to be overcome.

REFERENCES

Breed, W. The Negro and fatalistic suicide. *Pacific Sociological Review,* 1970, 13, 156-162.

Breed, W. Five components of a basic suicide syndrome. *Life-Threatening Behavior,* 1972, 2, 3-18.

Cummings, E. Further thoughts on the theory of disengagement. *International Social Science Journal,* 1963, 15, 377-393.

Durkheim, E. *Suicide.* Glencoe, IL: Free Press, 1930.

Faber, M. D. *Suicide and Greek Tragedy.* New York: Sphinx Press, 1970.

Hitchcock, J. T. Fatalistic suicide resulting from adaptation to an asymmetrical sex ratio. *Eastern Anthropologist,* 1967, 20, 133-142.

Iga, M., and Ohara, K. Suicide attempts of Japanese youth and Durkheim's concept of anomie. *Human Organization,* 1967, 26, 59-68.

Johnson, B. D. Durkheim's one cause of suicide. *American Sociological Review,* 1965, 30, 875-886.

Kaplan, K. J. Jonah and Narcissus. *Studies in Formative Spirituality,* 1987, 8(1), 33-54.

Kilduff, M., and Javers, R. *The Suicide Cult.* New York: Bantam, 1979.

Kwiet, K. The ultimate refuge. *Leo Baeck Institute Yearbook,* 1984, 29, 135-168.

Lester, D. A regional analysis of suicide and homicide rates in the U.S.A. *Social Psychiatry and Psychiatric Epidemiology,* 1988, 23, 202-205.

Lester, D. *Suicide from a Sociological Perspective.* Springfield, IL: Charles C Thomas, 1989.

Lester, D. The study of suicidal lives. *Suicide and Life-Threatening Behavior,* 1991, 21, 164-173.

Lukes, S. *Emile Durkheim.* New York: Harper & Row, 1972.

MacPherson, C., and MacPherson, L. Suicide in Western Samoa. In F. X. Hezel, D. H. Rubinstein, and G. M. White (eds.), *Culture, Youth and Suicide in the Pacific.* Honolulu: East-West Center, 1985.

MacPherson, C., and MacPherson, L. Toward an explanation of recent trends in suicide in Western Samoa. *Man,* 1987, 22, 305-330.

Ofstein, D. H., and Acuff, F. G. Durkheim and disengagement. *Free Inquiry in Creative Sociology,* 1979, 7(2), 108-111.

Peck, D. L. The last moments of life. *Deviant Behavior,* 1983, 4, 313-332.

Rotter, J. B. Generalized expectancies for internal versus external control of reinforcement. *Psychological Monographs,* 1966, 80(609).

Sharma, A. Emile Durkheim on suttee as suicide. *International Journal of Contemporary Sociology,* 1978, 15, 283-291.

Shulman, E. A Durkheimian analysis of three famous writers. In R. Yufit (ed.), *Proceedings of the 20th Annual Conference.* Denver: American Association of Suicidology, 1987.

Van Hoesel, F. M. T. An empirical typology of suicide. Master's thesis, American University, 1983.

Young, L. C. Altruistic suicide. *Sociological Bulletin,* 1972, 21(2), 103-121.

10

Reformulating Durkheim
One Hundred Years Later

Steven Stack, PhD

Aspects of Durkheim's theory of suicide have dominated the sociological work on suicide for nearly 100 years (Stack, 1982; Lester, 1989:22). The present chapter will first briefly outline the essential features of Durkheim's perspective. This consists of two parts: his neglected long-term or historical theory of suicide, and his much celebrated short-term theory on suicide. Second, I draw special attention to empirical work which questions either level of Durkheim's perspective and offers ideas on how we might reformulate his theory in light of this negative evidence. Third, I critically assess Durkheim's treatment of selected "extrasocial factors," such as imitation and alcoholism, and contend that they need to be incorporated into a full model of suicidal behavior. Finally, the discussion offers some suggestions for future research.

DURKHEIM'S THEORY OF SUICIDE

Analyses of Durkheim's theory have tended to focus on its ahistorical aspects. These parts of his theory are more amenable to empirical tests. For example, divorce rates, measured in the short term, have often been linked to suicide through Durkheim's twin concepts of anomie and egoism (e.g., Wasserman, 1990; Stack, 1980; Breault and Barkey, 1982; Trovato and Voss, 1990; Kowalski et al., 1987). Data on divorce and suicide rates at one point in time, for example, are abundant and encourage such analyses. Further, divorce represents the state of high egoism and anomie, two key aspects in Durkheim's conceptual scheme.

But divorce was used in Durkheim as an illustration of anomie and egoism, psychological states which characterized the greater fabric of social life in Durkheim's times. The historical changes taking place such as urbanization and industrialization were viewed as the principal sources of egoism and anomie. Hence, modern research, by focusing on short-term and even cross-sectional analysis of phenomena like divorce, has often missed the heart of the Durkheimian theory. The driving forces of modernization which cause egoism and anomie throughout society's institutional apparatus, have been neglected.

The Historical Theory

The modernization process and the greed of industrial capitalism were linked to suicide (Durkheim, 1966). The former bred egoism, while the latter increased anomie. Egoism increases suicide risk by decreasing the subordination of the individual to group life. Anomie increases suicide potential by unleashing limitless appetites and by bringing abrupt changes to the lives of individuals.

Urbanization, industrialization, and secularization are three concepts fundamental to Durkheim's historical theory of egoism and suicide. Basically, as Travis (1990:225) points out, Durkheim often equated social change with the erosion of social control. Durkheim (1966:391) described his times as constituting "collective sadness," given the deterioration of the old order based on rural feudalism, the Catholic Church and a general subordination of the individual to collective life. The processes of secularization in religion and education increased egoism and suicide potential. The rise of Protestantism in the religious institution opened the door to "religious individualism." The number of shared beliefs and practices fell, making life presumably less meaningful for the individual and increasing suicide risk (Durkheim, 1966:152-170).

Secularization of education from moral to scientific was taking place throughout Europe. The quest after knowledge broke down automatic obedience to cultural traditions and fostered "free inquiry" or "scientific culture" (Durkheim, 1966:162-170). Individualism in education was linked to individualism in Protestantism. Protestant nations had higher student enrollment ratios than Catholic nations, for example (Durkheim, 1966:163).

Individualism associated with the revolutions in religion and science was further buttressed by social change in the family. The process of urbanization broke down ancestral homes based on the extended family. Bonds to relatives were weakened as part of this transformation. Decreased responsibilities and contact with kin translated into greater egoism and suicide risk (Durkheim, 1966:171-216). Further, industrialization and urbanization tend to lower the birth rate. This reduces family size and, as such, the amount of responsibilities and interaction with children. As this "family density" decreases, suicide risk follows (Durkheim, 1966:200-201).

Through promoting Protestantism, science, the breakdown of family ties and a lower birth rate, the process of modernization increased suicide risk through promoting individualism.

The second major thrust of Durkheim's historical theory was based on the economy or "industry." This is the theory of economic anomie (Durkheim, 1966:254-258; 1964). The rise of laissez faire capitalism was equated with the relative lack of regulation of the economy. As Durkheim (1966:255) put it, "Government, instead of regulating economic life, has become its tool and servant." The thirst of the capitalist class for profit was associated with the rise of a world economic system. Profit could not only be derived from local markets, as in the past, but also from the world as a whole. Potential profit-making was, indeed, unlimited. In this context, economic goals of industrial production were seen as destructive, as encouraging anomie among the captains of industry (Durkheim, 1966:255). Once the drive after unlimited profits fails, which will be the case in most instances, the heavy disappointment and downward social mobility increase the risk of suicide.

Economic anomie also spreads to the class of consumers wherein "a thirst arises for novelties, unfamiliar pleasures, nameless sensations, all of which lose their savor once known" (Durkheim, 1966:256). Durkheim's argument is an antecedent of the "one-dimensional man" thesis of Herbert Marcuse (1966) more than a half century later.

Durkheim (1966:47,49,50,106,367) presented relatively little longitudinal data on suicide to support his historical theory. He reports (1966:369) that in the last 50 years suicide rates have at least tripled in nations where data were available. The data for this contention are not given but he lists the percent change in the sheer numbers of suicides for eight nations (Durkheim, 1966:367). These changes in suicide are reproduced in Table 1.

An important issue of how much of the increase was due to economic anomie vs. social egoism is not dealt with. Further, for the 35-year period from 1841 to 1875, the amount of change reported varies from a low of 35 percent

Table 1.

Durkheim's Data on Modernization and Suicide: Trends in the Number of Suicides in Eight European Nations

Nation	Years	Change in Suicide
Prussia	1826-1890	411%
France	1826-1888	385%
German Austria	1841/45-1877	318%
Saxony	1841-1875	238%
Belgium	1841-1889	212%
Italy	n.a. (20 years)	109%
Sweden	1841-1871/75	72%
Denmark	1841-1871/75	35%

Adapted from E. Durkheim, *Suicide* (New York: Free Press, 1966), p. 367.

in Denmark to a high of 318 percent in German Austria. There is no explanation for the variation in suicide rates in response to the modernization process. Possibly the variation in the level and rate of change in the modernization process could explain the differences in suicide trends. Given these largely unexplored issues in Durkheim's own book, it is not surprising that empirical researchers have neglected them.

The Cross-Sectional Theory

Much of Durkheim's book and most of the research that followed his paradigm is based on his treatment of egoism and anomie in the family and religious institutions in society (Durkheim, 1966:152-276).[1] Subordination of the individual to group life constitutes the main social safety net against suicide. In the family such subordination amounts to serving the needs of a spouse or children. In religion it is primarily to the sheer number of religious beliefs and practices (Stack, 1982).

Durkheim's data on marital status and religious affiliation largely support his views. For example, single men have a higher suicide rate (975 per million) than married men without children (644 per million). In turn, married men without children have a higher suicide rate than married men who do have children (336 per million) (Durkheim, 1966:187). Further, Protestants, who in Durkheim's time had fewer shared beliefs and religious practices to subordinate themselves to than did Catholics, had a higher suicide rate than Catholics in various European nations (Durkheim, 1966:152-155).

Turning to economic factors, Durkheim dealt with socioeconomic status, arguing the poor should have a relatively low suicide rate. Poverty was seen as a school of social restraint, where anomie was relatively low (Durkheim, 1966:245, 254, 257, 298).

Short-term changes in the business cycle were also connected to suicide. Durkheim (1966:241-246) contended that both economic recession and economic prosperity should increase the suicide rate through their promotion of economic anomie. For example, sudden downward mobility thwarts the meeting of appetites for masses of people who experience economic hardship in a recession.

The business cycle, however, represents another source of secondary, short-term variation in suicide. Other sources of secondary variation include an upswing in divorce or a decline in Catholicism. The main driving force behind the long-term suicide problem, however, is modernization.

RESEARCH EVIDENCE AND REFORMULATIONS

The Historical, Long-Term Model

The most understudied aspect of Durkheim's theory is his historical thesis. Suicide will continue to increase in the times of "collective sadness" brought about by the collapse of major social institutions and the increased greed in the economy. Only the "occupational group" could save society from the suicide risk inherent in industrial capitalism (Durkheim, 1964). The occupational group would be an organization based on work and composed of both employers and employees in a given industry. A joint council of the employers and employees would govern each industry, such jointedness being necessary to curb appetites for both unlimited profits and unlimited wages. Since such groups have not developed, it would be anticipated that suicide should have kept rising in the twentieth century.

The only systematic paper on these matters finds that in the twentieth century, industrial nations have followed remarkably different suicide patterns (Pope, Danigelis, and Stack, 1984). In response to increases in modernization, in one third of the nations the suicide rate increased, in one third it decreased, and in one third it remained relatively unaffected by modernization. A recent investigation of Finland covering the period 1750 to 1980 found an overall positive association between urbanization and suicide (Stack, 1992b). However, the strength of the association weakened in the twentieth century. Presumably the sources of this change included the notion that as the initial shocks of urbanization subsided, second- and third-generation city dwellers became more typical.[2]

Explaining these divergent patterns is certainly worthy of considerable theoretical work. Explanations might be anticipated from a Durkheimian perspective. First, the theory of economic anomie needs to be reformulated given the emergence of state regulation of the economy. Durkheim wrote well before the Great Depression, a period which brought substantial reform to industrial capitalism. The rise of labor parties with strong ties to large labor unions, the establishment of social security, the welfare state, progressive income taxation, corporate profits taxes, and numerous other institutions which placed a restraint on profits and regulated the economy came largely after Durkheim died. The variation in such regulation may explain some of the variation in suicide trends in this century. To the extent that a nation regulates its economic system through direct government involvement in the economy, economic anomie will be decreased. Given decreased economic anomie, if all else is equal, suicide should decline.

In industrial nations the process of urbanization has been largely completed for some time. The initial shock of rural-to-urban migration certainly increases suicide risk (as in Durkheim's day). However, once urban populations stabilize, and once second and third generations are born and raised within a given city, ties to the city develop and suicide risk is apt to abate. Durkheim may have underestimated the ability of urban dwellers to adapt, maintain kinship ties, develop social networks based on neighborhoods, and create a gemeinschaft or village reality within an urban world (Gans, 1962).

Durkheim was largely wrong that suicide is lowest among the poor (Stack, 1982). Therefore, differences among nations in the degree of income transfers to the poor might explain some of the variance in suicide trends. If such transfers are growing, suicide rates should be decreasing if all else is equal. This is precisely what Marshall (1978) found in the U.S. in the case of elderly suicide.

Further, Durkheim failed to foresee the tremendous increase in female labor force participation. Instead, he viewed women as having a higher morality than men. Women were protected from suicide given their home-centered, subordinate roles. This has changed substantially in the twentieth century. Much unlike Durkheim's time, today most women in industrial countries are in the labor force. Female labor force participation is often viewed as decreasing family integration and increasing suicide risk (e.g., Stack, 1978). The effect is, however, more pronounced in males than females (e.g., Stack, 1987b). In fact, in times of cultural support for female labor force participation, the relationship between it and female suicide vanishes. It is contended that with such cultural support, women are more able to take advantage of the benefits of work. For example, additional income and adult companionship with coworkers will be more of a benefit when there is less guilt associated with working. Cultural support reduces the amount of guilt (Stack, 1987b). The level of female labor force participation is assumed to be inversely related to guilt and role conflict between home and work responsibilities for working women. The variation in the modernization-suicide linkage may depend upon the level of female labor force participation.

Finally, a proposition from the opportunity theory of suicide needs to be woven into Durkheim's theory (Clarke and Lester, 1989). Durkheim failed to consider inequalities in access to the means of self-destruction. Nevertheless, factors such as the availability of firearms and the detoxification of natural gas have been found to influence suicide rates. For example, the detoxification of natural gas is associated with downswings in the suicide rate both in the United Kingdom (Kreitman, 1976) and Switzerland (Lester, 1990).

In a study of 77 metropolitan areas, Gundlach (1990) found that the relationship between divorce and suicide was much stronger in cities with high gun availability. Similarly, master trends in suicide may be sensitive to interaction effects between social suicidogenic conditions and opportunities for suicide.

The Short-Term Model

Most of the work on Durkheim's theory of suicide has tested his famous propositions on religion, and the family (e.g., Pope and Danigelis, 1981; Breault and Barkey, 1982; Stack, 1980a; 1982; 1992c). Religious affiliation, church membership, and religiosity indicators have dominated the work on religion. Divorce rates have constituted the main operationalization of work on the family and suicide.

Research on the institutions of marriage and religion have been mixed.

Short-term analysis of Durkheim's theory of divorce and suicide has nearly always yielded positive results (e.g., Breault and Barkey, 1982; Stack, 1982; Wasserman, 1990). His cross-sectional view of religion's impact on suicide has, however, been the subject of much debate.

Cross-national analyses of a large number of nations have found that the percent Catholic-suicide relationship is spurious once a control is introduced for modernization (Pope and Danigelis, 1981) or when a control for divorce is incorporated (Stack, 1981:215). For the 50 American states, a control for divorce, in like manner, rendered the Catholic-suicide relationship insignificant (Stack, 1980b). Turning to American counties, the percent Catholic is unrelated to suicide (Kowalski et al., 1987). However, if we employ higher levels of aggregation (county groups) and restrict the analysis to an n of 404 such groups (Pescosolido and Georgiana, 1989), percent Catholic is negatively related to suicide. Breault (1988) also reports a negative relationship between the percent Catholic and suicide for American counties. However, the percent Protestant is more closely related to suicide than the percent Catholic. Further, the percent Lutheran, percent Methodist, and percent Southern Baptist are all associated with reductions in suicide (Breault, 1988).

This work tends to suggest that Catholicism is largely no longer a protection against suicide. Theoretical interpretations often point to the convergence of different faiths in various measures of religiosity (Stack, 1980b; 1983).

Durkheim's theory of religion and suicide has been reformulated along the lines of religious commitment theory (Stark et al., 1983; Stack, 1983). Therein commitment to a few core religious beliefs is all that is needed to lower suicide risk. Belief in an afterlife, for example, can assuage all manner of worldly suffering through offering eternal salvation in return for perseverance through divorce, unemployment, illness, and other life crises. Hence, the sheer number of beliefs and practices, stressed in Durkheim's concept of religious integration, may be irrelevant to suicide potential.

Research using a cross-sectional methodology has tended to find a negative relationship between suicide and indicators of religious commitment (e.g., Stack, 1983; Breault and Barkey, 1982; Stack, 1992a). Time series analysis of post-World War II European data series has tended to find no effect (Stack, 1989, 1990a); but see Stack (1991a) for an exception. For the case of the U.S., religious trends are negatively associated with suicide, but they are collinear with family trends. Possibly in the case of the U.S. this pair of institutions reflects larger societal trends in the level of individualism (Stack, 1985).

While the research evidence is mixed for religious commitment theory, most evidence suggests a linkage between religious commitment and suicide. This generalization also holds for data at the individual level. A recent study found that while Catholicism was unrelated to suicide ideation, religious commitment was significantly related to suicide ideation (Stack and Lester, 1991).

A second reformulation of Durkheim's theory on religion and suicide, religious networks theory, has been advanced by Pescosolido and Georgiana

(1989). Herein, religious social networks offer a shield against suicide. Social support offered by coreligionists is the essence of religion's protection against suicide. This is fostered through organizational features of religion that encourage primary ties. Such organizational features include theological conservatism and nonecumenicalism.

Pescosolido (1990) further develops network theory arguing that the influence of religion on networking is greatest in that religion's "historical hub." If a religion has been in place for a long while, it has had the chance to develop an infrastructure (e.g., religious schools, hospitals, and social clubs) that promotes networking and social support for coreligionists. Support is found for most of the premises of network theory in two studies of U.S. county groups (Pescosolido, 1990; Pescosolido and Georgiana, 1989).

In both reformulations of Durkheim's religious integration theory, however, there is a departure from the basic premise that it is the sheer number of beliefs and practices that lowers suicide potential. In the case of religious commitment theory, commitment to just a few key beliefs is all that is needed to reduce suicide risk. In network theory, it is not the beliefs that matter but the social support one receives from people. The networking process and the social support derived therein might be viewed, however, as an extension of subordination through such "practices." Social support is contingent on at least some subordination of one's individualism to the interests of the collectivity.

Research on economic class and suicide in Detroit, Chicago, and elsewhere has refuted Durkheim's thesis of an inverse relationship (Stack, 1982). Durkheim's theory of class and suicide was fundamentally flawed. He did not have the kind of detailed data which are needed to test the class-suicide link. Lower-income people simply have a higher suicide rate than is found in the upper socioeconomic classes (Stack, 1982).

Research on Durkheim's historical theory of suicide is very thin. Much more needs to be done in assessing the considerable variation in suicide trends both in Durkheim's time and today. His cross-sectional theory has received very mixed support. The theory of family integration has been supported in nearly all of the research done in the last 100 years. In contrast, the theory of religious integration has been the subject of much debate. The theory of religious integration might be reformulated through Stack's (1983) theory of religious commitment and Pescosolido's (1990) theory of religious networks. Finally, Durkheim's theory of economic anomie has been supported in terms of the link between economic recession and suicide. It has not been supported in terms of the theory of socioeconomic class and suicide.

EXTRASOCIAL FACTORS

Durkheim dismissed a series of "extrasocial factors" as irrelevant to suicide. As Pope (1976) contends, this was done without any rigorous marshalling of evidence against many of them. This chapter contends that at least two of these extrasocial factors are clearly related to suicide and need to be incorporated into a reformulation of Durkheim.

Perhaps the weakest proposition in Durkheim's work was that the process of imitation or contagion could not affect the national rate of suicide (1966:123-142). In actual fact, that the media affects the national suicide rate has been firmly established in the literature of the 1970s and 1980s (see review in Stack, 1990b).

Durkheim did not adopt modern methodologies testing this assertion (e.g., Stack, 1987a). There was no testing, for example, of the impact of a publicized news story concerning suicide on the national suicide rate. Perhaps this was so since Durkheim was writing in a period marked by high illiteracy. For example, less than a third of the adult population of Northern Italy (6 to 12 percent in the South) was literate (Durkheim, 1966:164). With such high illiteracy rates it would be unreasonable to expect much of a copycat effect based on the newspapers. Further, the media channels of television and radio did not exist. These buttress modern-day copycat suicide through both echoing the messages of the press and reaching the remaining illiterate population.

Durkheim's theory of social integration and suicide has been synthesized with an age-specific theory of media impacts on suicide. Elsewhere (Stack, 1991c) it was found that media news stories on suicide were related to the suicide rates of the young and the elderly. The middle-aged were immune from copycat effects. Both the young and the old are viewed as low in social integration. The young have less of a stake in social institutions. The elderly are also relatively isolated from institutional life. In contrast, the middle-aged are generally at the peaks of their careers and are more integrated into community social institutions.

There has been a relative dearth of research in sociology on alcoholism and suicide. Durkheim's strong stand against such a connection may have discouraged such work. This is unfortunate. Durkheim's own data even suggest a powerful relationship. Pope (1976:164) calculated a correlation coefficient using Durkheim's own data and found a substantial ($r = 0.94$) correlation between alcohol consumption and suicide. Wasserman (1989) has demonstrated a close link between alcohol consumption and suicide in the U.S. for the period 1910 to 1933. DeLint (1981) notes a strong association between alcohol consumption and suicide for the period 1950 to 1975 in the Netherlands. Theoretical interpretation of this link includes the notion that alcohol fosters both mental and physical problems including depression, cancer, and cirrhosis of the liver. These problems contribute to suicide risk (Wasserman, 1989).

A reformulation of Durkheim's theory needs to take into account the extrasocial factors of media influences and alcohol consumption. These variables may have some bearing on the explanation of long-term swings in the suicide rate in various nations.

DISCUSSION

Durkheim wrote in a time of great macrosociological change. Modernization was transforming social institutions and suicide was increasing substantially in most nations. These changes, however, tended to slow down in the twentieth century. National suicide patterns in the present century include long swing declines and in some nations suicide has long since leveled off. These changes warrant a rethinking of many of Durkheim's basic axioms.

This chapter calls for more research tailored to the explanation of divergent suicide trends among nations. This is critical to the active reformulation of Durkheim's theory which would predict a universal upswing in suicide. It is clear that the magnitude of the modernization-suicide relationship varies considerably, and even reverses in sign for some nations in the twentieth century. I suggest investigation of the degree of state regulation of the economy. This includes the extensiveness of transfer payments to the elderly and poor. More generally, such state regulation involves subordination of interests and placing a cap on limitless appetites for profits.

A number of other factors may help to explain divergent trends in suicide. Trends and levels of female labor force participation, a factor unaddressed in Durkheim, should be explored as a mediating condition. Work by Pope, Danigelis, and Stack (1984) on these differences among 18 nations suggests that the religious base of society (whether Catholic, Protestant, or mixed) conditions the nature of the modernization-suicide relationship. Opportunity factors such as the wide variation among nations in gun availability might condition the relationship. Finally, extrasocial factors such as alcohol consumption levels might also explain some of the variation among nations.

New explanations need to be developed for findings contrary to Durkheim's short-term theory of suicide. Cross-sectional theories linking marital/parental status to suicide and associating religious affiliation with suicide have met with mixed results. While there is nearly universal support for Durkheim's theory of marital/parental integration and suicide, his theory of religion and suicide has been extensively debated. Research indicates that religion affects suicide through commitment to a few core beliefs and/or through social networking with coreligionists. These processes are somewhat removed from Durkheim's classic arguments that the sheer number of beliefs and practices formed the core of religion's protection against suicide. While his theory of domestic integration has held up, his theory of religious integration may need substantial reformulation, perhaps including the lines of argument of religious commitment theory and religious networks theory.

Durkheim's propositions on the economy and suicide were largely wrong. These theses have been viewed as a polemic against Marxism (e.g., Zeitlin, 1968). Prosperity as well as high socioeconomic standing simply do not increase suicide. On the contrary they decrease it (Stack, 1982). Durkheim greatly underestimated the pressures of life in the underclass, the many social problems that can chip away at the will to live. Instead, a more sociological question might be why don't more of the impoverished commit suicide?

Extrasocial factors need to be incorporated into theoretical and empirical studies. In particular, much more empirical work is needed on the badly neglected factor of alcohol consumption. Further, media impacts need further theoretical work. For example, media influences may follow interaction effects in addition to the age-based interaction. Future work might explore interactions with suicidogenic conditions. Herein the concepts of integration and regulation can be applied. That is, the mood of the audience needs to be taken into account. In times of high unemployment, divorce, and other suicidogenic conditions, a widely publicized suicide story might provoke more audience identification. If so, such times should multiply any copycat effect.

Finally, Durkheim's theory might be improved through a combination with psychoanalytic theory (Simpson, 1966:13-32). That is, a life history perspective which stresses the early childhood experiences in the genesis of a "suicidal career" or life style could be merged with the sociological interpretations of Durkheim. For example, why do some divorcees commit suicide while others do not? Both groups experience anomie and egoism. Perhaps those with negativistic early childhood experiences are the ones who carry the highest suicide risk. This line of thought was developed extensively by Maris (1984), but an explication of this point of departure for reformulation of Durkheim is beyond the scope of the present analysis.

NOTES

1. Durkheim's theory also considered other variables such as wars and political crises. A discussion of these other less researched areas of his theory is outside the parameters of this chapter.
2. Cross-sectional work investigating large numbers of nations at one point in time has generally found a positive association between level of economic development and suicide (e.g., Stack, 1978; Quinney, 1965). Quinney (1965:405), for example, contends that industrialization institutionalizes individualism. As such, people in industrial societies are at higher risk than people in preindustrial nations since suicide is more of a personal choice for those who fail to achieve their aspirations in social life.

REFERENCES

Breault, K. Beyond the quick and dirty. *American Journal of Sociology,* 1988, 93, 1479-1486.

Breault, K., and Barkey, K. Comparative analysis of Durkheim's theory of egoistic suicide. *Sociological Quarterly,* 1982, 23, 321-331.

Clarke, R. V., and Lester, D. *Suicide: Closing the Exits.* New York: Springer-Verlag, 1989.

DeLint, J. The influence of much increased alcohol consumption on mortality rates. *British Journal of Addiction,* 1981, 76, 77-83.

Durkheim, E. *The Division of Labor.* New York: Free Press, 1964.

Durkheim, E. *Suicide.* New York: Free Press, 1966.

Gans, H. *The Urban Villagers.* New York: Free Press, 1962.

Gundlach, J. H. Absence of family support, opportunity, and suicide. *Family Perspective,* 1990, 24, 7-14.

Kowalski, G. S., Faupel, C., and Starr, P. D. Urbanism and suicide. *Social Forces,* 1987, 66, 85-101.

Kreitman, N. The coal gas story. *British Journal of Preventive and Social Medicine,* 1976, 30, 86-93.

Lester, D. *Suicide from a Sociological Perspective.* Springfield, IL: Charles C Thomas, 1989.

Lester, D. The effect of detoxification of domestic gas in Switzerland on the suicide rate. *Acta Psychiatrica Scandinavica,* 1990, 82, 383-384.

Marcuse, H. *One-Dimensional Man.* New York: Beacon, 1966.

Maris, R. *Pathways to Suicide.* Baltimore: Johns Hopkins University Press, 1981.

Marshall, J. Changes in aged white male suicide. *Journal of Gerontology,* 1978, 33, 763-768.

Pescosolido, B. The social context of religious integration and suicide. *Sociological Quarterly,* 1990, 31, 337-357.

Pescosolido, B., and Georgiana, S. Durkheim, suicide, and religion. *American Sociological Review,* 1989, 54, 33-48.

Pope, W. *Durkheim's Suicide.* Chicago: University of Chicago, 1976.

Pope, W., and Danigelis, N. Sociology's one law. *Social Forces,* 1981, 60, 495-516.

Pope, W., Danigelis, N., and Stack, S. The effect of modernization on suicide. Paper presented to the American Sociological Association, San Antonio, 1984.

Quinney, R. Suicide, homicide, and economic development. *Social Forces,* 1965, 43, 401.

Simpson, G. Editor's Introduction. In E. Durkheim, *Suicide.* New York: Free Press, 1966, 13-32.

Stack, S. Suicide. *Social Forces,* 1978, 57, 644-653.

Stack, S. The effect of marital integration on suicide. *Journal of Marriage and the Family,* 1980a, 42, 83-92.

Stack, S. Religion and suicide. *Social Psychiatry,* 1980b, 15, 65-70.

Stack, S. Suicide and religion. *Sociological Analysis,* 1981, 14, 207-220.

Stack, S. Suicide. *Deviant Behavior,* 1982, 4, 44-66.

Stack, S. The effect of religious commitment on suicide. *Journal of Health and Social Behavior,* 1983, 24, 362-374.

Stack, S. The effect of domestic/religious individualism on suicide, 1954-1978. *Journal of Marriage and the Family,* 1985, 47, 431-447.

Stack, S. Celebrities and suicide. *American Sociological Review,* 1987a, 52, 401-413.

Stack, S. The effect of female labor force participation on suicide. *Sociological Forum,* 1987b, 2, 257-277.

Stack, S. The impact of divorce on suicide in Norway. *Journal of Marriage and the Family,* 1989, 51, 229-238.

Stack, S. The effect of divorce on suicide in Denmark. *Sociological Quarterly,* 1990a, 31, 359-370.

Stack, S. Media Impacts on Suicide. In D. Lester (ed.), *Current Concepts of Suicide.* Philadelphia: Charles Press, 1990b.

Stack, S. The effect of religion on suicide in Sweden. *Journal for the Scientific Study of Religion,* 1991a, 30.

Stack, S. Social Correlates of Suicide by Age. In A. A. Leenaars (ed.), *Suicide Across the Life Span.* New York: Plenum, 1991b.

Stack, S. Religiosity, Depression, and Suicide. In J. Schumaker (ed.), *Religion and Mental Health.* New York: Oxford University Press, 1992a.

Stack, S. The effect of modernization on suicide in Finland, 1750-1980. Paper presented to the American Association of Suicidology, Chicago, 1992b.

Stack, S. Marriage, Family, Religion, and Suicide. In R. Maris (ed.), *Assessment and Prediction of Suicide*. New York: Guilford, 1992b.

Stack, S., and Lester, D. The effect of religion on suicide ideation. *Social Psychiatry and Psychiatric Epidemiology*, 1991, 26, 168-170.

Stark, R., Doyle, D. P., and Rushing, L. Beyond Durkheim. *Journal for the Scientific Study of Religion*, 1983, 22, 120-131.

Travis, R. Halbwachs and Durkheim. *British Journal of Sociology*, 1990, 41, 241-243.

Trovato, F., and Vos, R. Domestic/religious individualism and youth suicide in Canada. *Family Perspective*, 1990, 24, 69-82.

Wasserman, I. The effects of war and alcohol consumption on patterns of suicide. *Social Forces*, 1989, 68, 513-530.

Wasserman, I. The impact of divorce on suicide in the United States, 1970-1983. *Family Perspective*, 1990, 24, 61-68.

Zeitlin, M. *Ideology and the Development of Sociological Theory*. Englewood Cliffs, NJ: Prentice-Hall, 1968.

11

Self-Harm During the Nineteenth Century: A Conceptual History

G. E. Berrios, MD

Non fortitudinis laudandae, sed pusillanimitatis vituperandae testimonia.

St. Augustine

Sometime during 1853, Antoine Wierz[1] completed one of his strangest paintings, "The Suicidal." It depicted a man with naked torso, head wrapped in clouds, blowing a sort of wind instrument; his left arm was raised high, his hand clawed; his figure was floating forward and flanked by a praying angel and, somewhat lost in the penumbra, by a winged devil. This dreamlike vision allegorizes well nineteenth-century views on suicide as a personal event reflecting polarity, despair, insanity and loss of individuality.

These nineteenth-century views on self-harm were but a continuation of concepts debated in previous centuries.[2] For example, the debate during the Enlightenment reflected a clash between religious views and the new liberalism. A good illustration is the work of one individual, Madame de Staël, who after writing an apology of suicide in 1796, published a rejoinder in 1812, a much-neglected work entitled *Réflexions sur le suicide:* "In my work on the 'Influence of Passions' I defended the act of suicide, but I repent now of having penned those thoughtless words. I was then a proud and vivacious young woman: but what is the use of living but having the hope of improving oneself?"[3] Another representative of the liberal view was Cesare Beccaria[4] who in his *Dei delitti e delle pene* wrote: "Suicide is a crime that cannot be punished for when punishment is meted out it either falls upon the innocent or upon a corpse. In the latter case it will have no effect upon the living, in the former it is tyrannical and unfair as political rights dictate that punishment must be personal."[5]

After the 1820s, this moral debate became medicalized, and shaped by changes in the notion of mental disease and in psychological theory. As

Lanteri-Laura and del Pistoia have observed: "at the end of the eighteenth century [suicide] ceased to be condemned on the basis of religiously inspired tradition: the secularization of the law no longer made it permissible to punish it as a revolt against God. Nevertheless, it remained a shocking act; so psychiatry was invited to take charge of it, since society still regard it as a threat to established order."[6]

The rise of the anatomo-clinical model of disease transformed the concept of mental illness and this, in turn, led to a disintegration of "total insanity." The "partial" insanities (e.g., monomania and lypemania) offered a new medical way of explaining suicide. Changes in psychological theory were equally important: the rise of faculty psychology made possible the clinical existence of nonintellectual insanities (i.e., insanities whose primary disorder was to be found in the emotions or volition).[7] This concept, once again, offered the medical establishment a second model of self-harm behavior as such persons might now be called "insane" or "alienated" without, in fact, showing delusions or hallucinations. One way or the other, alienists became able to protect families of suicidal persons from religious and legal persecution. In fact, by the end of the eighteenth century, laws against completed suicide had ceased to be regularly enforced as they caused as much trouble to the enforcers as they did to the families of the deceased.[8]

There is no full agreement among scholars[9] as to the balance of arguments, during the first half of the nineteenth century, in regard to the view that all suicidal acts were "pathological." To explore this, a definitional baseline of representative eighteenth-century views is needed, and these are nowhere better expressed than in the French Encyclopedia. Diderot stated that the imputation of suicide should depend upon the ascertaining of mental state *(situation d'esprit)*; subjects being unimputable when found to be suffering from a brain disorder *(cerveau derange)*, depression *(tombe dans une noire melancolie)*, or delirium *(phrénesie)*.[10] The French doctrine, up to the 1760s, seems to have been that at least some among the mental ill could not be declared *felo de se*; and although only three categories of mental disorder are mentioned, it is clear that the first—*cerveau derange*—was meant to include cases without obvious clinical features. The idea that some mental disorders could lead to suicide was not, of course, new: as J.C. Schmitt has shown, since the medieval period states such as *accidia, tristitia, desperatio, taedium vitae,* and *frenesia* had been regularly mentioned; the problem for the historian is to identify these states from a clinical point of view. Indeed, some may have not had even recognizable clinical boundaries.[11]

Toward the end of the eighteenth century, the abuse of the "psychiatric" view of suicide encouraged some to put forward narrower views: for example, the French Protestant Jean Dumas, in his book of 1773, attacks the defense of suicide contained in both Montesquieu's LXXVIth *Lettres Persane* and Holbach's *Système de la Nature*.[12] In England, E. Burton, a former Fellow of Trinity College, Cambridge, also worried about the medical excuse and stated:

"where ten destroy themselves through insanity, hundreds destroy themselves coolly and deliberately…"; unfortunately, "a state of lunacy becomes a matter of purchase…thus it generally happens that the result of all these public inquiries into the cause of voluntary death is a state of lunacy; which implies that no one can in the full possession of his senses, resolutely and deliberately destroy himself."[13] Bayet has made a similar commentary in regard to the French situation.[14] C. Moore, also from Trinity College, in his magnificent two-volume book, wrote: "that suicide implies no necessity of an absolute and permanent madness is agreed on all hands,"[15] and "suicide, then, whether deliberate or precipitate, no more 'necessarily' implies madness or lunacy that every other great crime can be said to do,"[16] and even in the case of known madness, Moore claimed, there might be imputability. He was only echoing Blackstone who earlier on had commented: "if a lunatic can be proved to have committed suicide during a lucid interval he is adjudged in the eye of the law a *felo de se*."[17]

So the view that only a proportion of persons who committed suicide were actually mentally ill, or that mental illness may not be an explanation even when present, was already present during the eighteenth century.[18] Indeed, the same claim was to continue into the following century, except that, as has been mentioned above, new concepts made the debate drift into other directions. It is, therefore, surprising that at the very end of the nineteenth century, and with the benefit of hindsight, Durkheim still felt able to say that the "psychiatric" conception of suicide was an absolute belief among nineteenth-century alienists. Since we have elsewhere shown that this was an inaccurate interpretation by Durkheim, the topic will not be touched upon again.[19]

The nineteenth-century debate, however, is interesting in its own right because it generated new questions—some of these still current—such as the relationship between suicide and heredity and brain localization, and the value of national statistics.[20] This issue became particularly important toward the end of the century when, under the influence of degeneration theory, suicide began to be considered as a stigma of degeneration.[21] By the 1880s, much agreement existed between French, German, British, Italian and Spanish alienists on the definition and classification of suicide, and also on the role played by heredity, mental illness, and social factors. This consensus was reached through the publication of some major works, all translated into the main European languages[22] in which was formulated what will here be called the "standard view." This view was reached by steps, and these will be here briefly described.

ESQUIROL: CREATOR OF THE "STANDARD" VIEW

Accounts of nineteenth-century psychiatric views on suicide tend to start with Etienne Esquirol: "suicide shows all the features of mental alienation of which is but a symptom. There is no need to search for a special brain site for suicide as it can be found associated with all kinds of clinical situations being, as it is, secondary to both acute delirium and to the chronic delusional states; post-mortem studies have not thrown much light on the subject."[23] This quotation comes from his 1838 book, a final summary of his work. The original version of the chapter on suicide, however, was published in 1821, and is different in various ways. This is, perhaps, the reason why Esquirol is quoted both by those who see him as the champion of the "psychiatric" thesis, for example Durkheim,[24] Halbwachs,[25] Achille-Delmas,[26] and Giddens[27] and also by those who see him as the representative of the "standard" view,[28] namely, that some suicides are caused by mental illness and some are not.[29]

In 1821,[30] Esquirol defined suicide in a very wide fashion: "this phenomenon is observed in the most varied circumstances ... and shaped by the same uncertainties that affect mental illness; doubtless, suicide is idiopathic, but it can frequently be secondary." He listed[31] dying "for the highest motives," "for social delusions" *(idées fausses, mais accréditées)*, impulsive emotion, organic delirium, mania (in the old-fashioned sense of this term),[32] hypochondria, lypemania (Esquirol's transitional term for depression), and parasuicide (which Esquirol called suicide simulé). He then concluded: "from what has been said it can be concluded that suicide is a phenomenon that follows a large number of, and has diverse presentations; this phenomenon cannot, therefore, be considered as a disease. The general conclusions drawn from having considered suicide as a *sui generis* disease have been proven wrong by experience."[33] Some of these views are tightened in the 1838 version, his definition of suicide became narrower, and hence the "psychiatric" explanation acquired relatively more importance. But even then his later views were not as absolute as Durkheim presented them. For example, when discussing treatment Esquirol stated: "suicide is an act secondary to severe emotional upheaval *(délire de passion)* or insanity *(folie)*...treatment should rest on the understanding of causes and determinant motives of suicide."[34] It is unlikely, therefore, that for Esquirol suicide was always a form of monomania; indeed, it is unlikely that it was always a form of insanity. A recent interpretation of Esquirol's view has also given him the benefit of the doubt,[35] making the point that although Esquirol might have claimed that most suicides entailed some sort of abnormal or upset state of mind, the French alienist was very aware of the role of social factors. Blondel also accused Esquirol's successors of having hardened his views, particularly neglected his acceptance of social factors, in order to bolster their own views.[36] Giddens has also considered Esquirol's views as more flexible than Durkheim's version of them.[37]

Interpretation of what Esquirol really said is bedeviled by the ambiguous meaning of a number of French clinical concepts: *aliénation mentale, folie, délire de passion,* and *symptomatique.* A detailed analysis of these issues is beyond the scope of this chapter. Briefly, however, the word *"folie"* was a generic term used to refer to various states of madness and hence to long lasting diseases.[38] Things are more complicated in relation to *"délire,"* which has no direct English rendition; from the beginning of the nineteenth century, untold confusion has been caused by translators rendering *délire* into the English term "delirium." In fact, it very rarely means this (in the sense of organic brain syndrome); almost always it simply means delusion (i.e., a *temporary* dislocation of psychological function affecting intellect, motility or affect).[39] Hence, its presence does not necessarily indicate a diagnosis of *folie* or madness. Spaulding and Simpson (the English translators of Durkheim) rendered "délire" as "delirium" throughout, thereby causing much confusion. In the case of "délire de passion," meaning is clearer: Esquirol believed that "*délire*" could follow any major emotional upheaval: "passions (i.e.,emotions) can so affect our sensations, ideas, judgments and decisions that is not surprising that violent excitement may cause 'délire': in this case it is sudden in onset and short lived; it can also be the lingering product of lasting emotions (*passion chronique*)."[40] This means that both Esquirol and many of his followers would use "délire de passion" to refer to an upset of mind, to a temporary emotional upheaval following a social or personal crisis; this description did not entail at all the presence of a disease (i.e., *folie*).[41]

It can be concluded, therefore, that Esquirol was saying that, during the suicidal act the individual *was always in an altered mental state* but that this might only be a *short-lived emotional upheaval,* and not insanity. This interpretation is shared by Blondel: "it is a fact that madmen kill themselves and that such suicides are pathological. It is a different fact that men said to be normal also kill themselves. But they are not normal in the moment of the act. They only do it under the effect of a strong emotion...." He then goes on to say: "this disorder of the emotions that Esquirol makes the basis of his second category of suicide can be precipitated by life events and the tendencies of individuals."[42] This interpretation is reinforced by the view, expressed by Esquirol himself, that the treatment of suicide must focus on the subject's "motivations and reasons."

OTHER FRENCH HOLDERS OF THE "STANDARD" VIEW

In a popular book, Brierre de Boismont[43] also presented a balanced view of the association between insanity and suicide. For unclear reasons, Durkheim totally ignores Brierre de Boismont's repeated claims that "suicide is not always evidence of mental illness"[44] and that "the disease of spleen, when accompanied by tendency to suicide, cannot be considered as a variety of mental illness unless it is accompanied by a disorder of emotions or thinking. To make such state yet another form of insanity is to justify the reproach, ofttimes addressed at alienists, that they see their fad every where...Spleen has more social than personal origins."[45]

Another important representative of the "standard" view was G.F. Etoc-Demazy[46] whose views were expressed in a book that appeared in 1844,[47] and in a paper published in 1846 as a rejoinder to Bourdin's book.[48] Etoc-Demazy confessed that he had never been able to convince himself that all suicides were the result of mental illness. He criticized the a priori (and clinically weak) approach taken by Bourdin, and offered instead his notion of *aberration morbid passagère*,[49] a continuation of Esquirol's notion (discussed above) of *délire de passion*. He rejected the view that made all suicides into mental diseases, and concluded: "the insistence with which some authors want to consider suicide as a form of mental alienation, stems from an exaggerated human fondness for life."[50]

E. Lisle also defended the "standard" view. His book, which appeared the same year as Brierre's, was awarded the coveted Imperial Academy Prize of Medicine.[51] Lisle, perhaps unfairly, attacked Esquirol whom he interpreted (wrongly) as defending the psychiatric thesis; he explained Esquirol's shift from moderate to absolutist as resulting from the fact that he had always worked in mental hospitals and thus lost perspective. Lisle then proceeded to reduce *ad absurdum* the view that all suicide is madness by saying that a similar argument should apply to homicide; he also attacked Falret for inventing the notion of *melancolie suicide*[52] and made fun of him by claiming that perhaps all the classical suicidal heroes were at the time suffering from melancholia! He also dismissed Bourdin's book as insignificant, and as trying to propagate the doctrine of monomania.[53] More importantly, he criticized his method of reasoning by induction, i.e., trying to demonstrate a point of view from theoretical premises without resorting to empirical evidence. He denied the existence of a "suicidal monomania" in cases when suicidal behavior is the only evidence for the existence of the disease, and concluded that if the clinical facts were observed, the view that all suicides are "pathological" would soon be dispelled.

But not all defenders of the "standard" view had a medical perspective; Bertrand, for example, wrote from a deeply religious viewpoint, and his award-winning book received the imprimatur of Gousset, then Archbishop of Reims.[54] Predictably, Bertrand started by saying that suicide is an act against God, family and fatherland. He believed that moral freedom must be preserved at all costs, and this led him to accuse Bourdin of believing that man was like a clock, and paradoxically, to deny the view that all suicides must be the result of madness. He concluded that "to put forward the view that all suicides are the result of mental alienation, and hence not imputable, is a dangerous and serious mistake which can give rise to undesirable moral consequences."[55] Interestingly, he again differentiated between acute and chronic suicide (the terminology was Esquirol's)[56] and included among the latter alcoholism (this about 100 years before Menninger's identical claim in the book *Man Against Himself*).

NON-FRENCH HOLDERS OF THE "STANDARD" VIEW

The standard view was held by most renowned alienists of the period. For example, Prichard wrote: "the prevalent opinion is that insanity is not always the cause of suicide, though the verdict of lunacy is generally brought by juries, owing to the extreme barbarity of the law on this subject. M. Fodéré[57] has expressed long ago the opinion that suicide is always the result of madness. Though every one would wish to be of the same sentiment, it seems difficult to maintain it when we consider the frequent and almost ordinary occurrence of suicide in some countries...like the impulse to homicide, this propensity to suicide is simply a moral perversion,[58] and therefore neither of these affections fall within the restricted definition of insanity."[59] Griesinger was equally balanced in his views: "the pathological and aetiological history of suicide does not belong entirely to psychiatry; in fact, whatever some writers have said, we cannot conclude that suicide is always a symptom or a result of insanity."[60] Bucknill and Tuke wrote: "We have had occasion, previously, to remark that the act of self-destruction may originate in different, and even opposite conditions of mind. Hence, it is quite clear that the suicide act cannot always be properly referred to disorder of the same group of feelings...and here it may be observed, in regard to suicide in general, that the question so often asked *Is suicide the result of cerebromental disease* [italics in original] must be answered both affirmatively and negatively. That the act may be committed in a perfectly healthy state of mind cannot, for a moment, be disputed."[61]

DEFENDERS OF THE "PSYCHIATRIC" THESIS

During the first half of the nineteenth century there were, however, some whose views approached the caricature drawn by Durkheim; one was Cazauvieilh on "rural" suicide.[62] Cazauvieilh put forward an extreme view: there were three types of suicide and all were psychiatric disorders. In the purest Faculty Psychology tradition he listed suicides resulting from disorders of thought, affection and volition *(délire de intelligence, affections,* and *actions)*. "Real" suicides he defined as acts accompanied by willingness and clear consciousness. He considered as "accidental" all deaths in the insane when there was no formed intent to die. Loyal to Esquirol, he defended a concept of monomania that, at the time, had already been called into question.[63] He dealt with both suicide and homicide as related acts and reported 16 postmortem studies searching for the *siège de l'organe dont les souffrances portent au meurtre de soi-meme.*[64]

THE AFTERMATH

By the 1880s, the psychiatric debate on whether suicide was *always* due to mental illness (the "psychiatric" thesis) had been decided in favor of the view that it was not (the "standard" view). Most alienists entertained a broad definition of suicide, and consequently all manner of "social" events were accepted as potential causes.[65] Of this view many nonmedical men—except perhaps, Durkheim—were aware: for example, Westcott[66] listed among the supporters of the standard view Blandford, Leuret, Gray, Bucknill and Tuke,

Des Etangs,[67] and Littré.[68] Morselli, whom no one could accuse of softness,[69] expressed a similar sentiment: "just as madness may go on without any attempt at suicide, so the suicidal determination is formed in the healthiest of minds, which then carry it out with the coolness inspired by the most perfect logic."[70] Brouc discussed suicide as a "social event,"[71] and Legoyt went as far as discussing the very social variables that played such an important role in Durkheim's argument.[72] The "standard" view was carried without difficulty into the twentieth century. In his assessment of the controversy, Viallon restated that Etoc-Demazy, Cerise, Belhomme, Chereau, Palmer and Gray "had reacted with force against the 'psychiatric' thesis";[73] Pilcz agreed with Kraepelin that only 30 percent of suicides seem to be related to diagnosable mental illness;[74] and Serin concluded, after a detailed survey, that "a third [of suicides] were conceived and executed in the absence of psychopathology."[75]

Things should have been allowed to rest there. With hindsight, it seems clear that much of the nineteenth century debate (including Durkheim's contribution toward the tail end of it) was conceptual rather than empirical, i.e., resulted from confusion in regard to the definition of suicide; but after Durkheim's book, disagreement also resulted from the way in which "social" was defined. It is beyond dispute that most nineteenth century alienists managed to include "social facts" as causes of suicide. However, by the time of Durkheim, and probably as a result of his contribution, "social fact" had acquired a wider and more abstract meaning.[76] Analysis of this shift, which has to do with the gradual development of sociology during the nineteenth century, is beyond both the scope of this chapter and the ken of its author. However, it seems as if "the social" had, by the very end of the century, become accepted as a higher, irreducible, and omnipresent level of explanation.[77] This was good for sociology and for the professionalization of her practitioners, but created explanatory splits in a number of regions of reality, one of which was mental illness and suicide. Durkheim was, in a way, unfair to accuse early nineteenth-century psychiatrists of not fully accepting the social explanation of suicide for, during this period, such concepts were not yet part of the intellectual fare of alienists. For example, for Esquirol "social" meant environmental in relation to specific individuals; he had little thought for social laws; for Durkheim, on the other hand, it meant general, the result of objective laws equally applicable to all people. Whilst for Esquirol the "dependent" variable for social explanations was the behavior (e.g., suicide) of a given individual, for Durkheim it became the social facts, as expressed in large group statistics.

And these differences became more obvious by the time the controversy flared up again in France in the 1930s. It started in 1926, with the publication by Maurice de Fleury[78] of an update of the "psychiatric" thesis whose only new feature was the incorporation of the "neuroses." It must be remembered that up to the 1880s, "mental disorder" basically referred to the "insanities" (organic states, melancholia, etc.). Between this time and the 1930s, however, and thanks to the work of Janet, Freud and others, the neuroses[79] and the personality disorders were included under the rubric "mental disorder." When Fleury and Achille-Delmas[80] claimed that all suicides resulted from mental disorder, they meant both the old insanities and the new neurotic conditions, particularly the anxiety states. This is why, few years later, Deshaies felt able to claim that about one-third of the psychiatric causes of suicide fell into this latter category.[81]

Maurice Halbwachs replied in 1930 in a classical book that went further than Durkheim's in its reaffirmation of the "social" thesis of suicide.[82] By Halbwachs's time, the "social" explanation had become fully consolidated, and he had no difficulty in making the claim that all suicides were socially originated, including those in which alienists might show clear mental illness for, after all, mental illness was also social in origin. This claim, legitimate from the conceptual point of view, did upset alienists then as much as it might upset some now; the reason for this being that psychiatrists always deal with individual cases, and grand social causes seems to be beyond their perception and remedial manipulation. Consequently, they deny their existence, or try to redefine them in simpler and tangible ways. This was the problem with Achille-Delmas, when he retorted in 1932.[83] His book, which on occasions sounds naive and conceptually uncouth, conveys the perplexity of a generation of alienists *vis-à-vis* the sociological explanation of suicide.

But the obvious thing to do, when faced with multiple levels of explanation, might be to blend them. This is precisely what Blondel, a man who since the 1910s had shown great sensitivity for the "sociological,"[84] did in his book of 1933.[85] He chastised Achille-Demas for "inventing a phrenology without organology"[86] but also stated that Halbwachs had resuscitated a conflict, and hence both were wrong *(En cette querelle les partis extrêmes semblend tous deux dans leur tort)* [87]: "in regards to suicide, it would be dangerous to reject the sociological explanation; but it would be equally dangerous not to acknowledge the role of the pathological which although may have social causes and lead to social effects, *may not be social* at all."[88] Whether or not Blondel was successful in his quest remains to be seen. To many current clinicians, old issues such as the definition of suicide, the informational value of suicide statistics, and the ways in which these should be collected and interpreted[89] have not yet been solved; as has not the crucial question of whether they are susceptible to empirical solution.

NOTES

1. Joseph Antoine Wiertz (1806-1865) was a Belgian painter whose style changed twice: earlier in his career he followed Michael Angelo and Rubens, and later, after establishing himself in Brussels, he developed an increasingly phantasmagoric, visionary, and on occasions morbid style, similar to Goya's a century before. During this period he painted "Child in Flames," "Buried Alive," "Famine," "Insanity and Crime," "Thoughts and Visions of an Executed Man's Head," and "The Suicide." Most of these works are at the Wierz Museum in Brussels.
2. See the excellent chapter on suicide by professor John McManners in *Death and*

the Enlightenment, Oxford, Oxford University Press, 1985; also Rosen, G., History in the study of suicide, *Psychological Medicine*, 1971, 4:267-285; Crocker, L.G.,The discussion of suicide in the 18th century, *Journal of the History of Ideas*, 1952, 13:47-52; Doughty, O., The English Malady of the 18th century, *Review of English Studies*, 1926, 2:257-269; Bartel, R., Suicide in 18th-century England, *Huntington Library Quarterly*, 1960, 23:145-158; pp. 204-246 in Fedden, H.R., *Suicide*. London: Peter Davies, 1938.

3. Mme. la Baronne de Staël. De l'Influence des passions sur le bonheur des individues et des nations. New Edition. Paris: Treuttel et Würtz, 1820, p. 296. This volume also includes her "Réflexions sur le suicide." In 1821, Esquirol also commented about her change of mind: "In the enthusiasm of youth, Madame de Staël seemed to have approved of suicide, later she recanted." Esquirol, E., Suicide. In Adelon, Alard, Alibert et al. (eds.), *Dictionnaire des Sciences Médicales par une Société de Médecins et de Chirurgiens*. Paris: Panckoucke, 1821, pp. 213-283.

4. Cesare Bonesana, Marquis de Beccaria (1733-1781) was educated by the Jesuits and decided on a philosophical career after reading Montesquieu's *Lettres Persans* He wrote "Dei delitti" when he was 25, and at the instigation of his friends who used to find him boring and sluggish. At the time he had read widely, and clear influences were Diderot, Helvetius, Voltaire, D'Alembert, Buffon, and Hume.

5. Beccaria, C., De los delitos y de las penas (translated by Juan Antonio de las Casas). Madrid: Alianza, 1868 (first published in 1764), p. 89.

6. Lanteri-Laura, G., and Del Pistoia, L., Structural analysis of suicidal behavior. *Social Research*, 1970, 37:324-325.

7. Berrios, G.E., Historical aspects of the psychosis. *British Medical Bulletin*, 1987, 43:484-498; ibid., Historical background to abnormal psychology. In Miller, E., and Cooper, P.J. (eds.), *Adult Abnormal Psychology*. Edinburgh: Churchill and Livingstone, 1888.

8. McManners, op. cit.

9. Blondel, C., *Le Suicide*. Strasbourg: Librairie Universitaire D'Alsace, 1933; Ey, H., Le suicide pathologique. In Ey, H., *Etudes Psychiatriques. Aspects Séméiologiques*. Vol. 2. Paris: Desclée de Brouwer, 1950.

10. Diderot and D'Alembert (eds.), *Encyclopédie ou Dictionnaire Raisonné des Sciences, des Arts et des Métieres, par Une Societé de gens de Lettres*, Vol. 14. Neufchâtel: Samuel Faulche, pp. 639-641.

11. Schmitt, J.C., Le suicide au moyen âge. *Annales: Economies, Sociétés, Civilisations*, 1976, 31:3-28.

12. Although of French origin, Dumas worked in Leipzig where he died in 1799. He also published literary criticism and poetry. His main work was: *Traité du Suicide ou du Meurtre Volontaire de Soi-même*, Leipzig, 1773.

13. Burton, E., *Suicide, a Dissertation*. London: Vint, 1790, pp. 15-16.

14. Bayet, A., *Le suicide et la morale*. Paris: Alcan, 1922.

15. Moore, C., *A Full Inquiry into the Subject of Suicide* (2 vols). London: J.F.C. Rivington, 1790, p. 326.

16. Moore, op. cit., p. 329.

17. Blackstone, W., *Commentaries on the Laws of England*. London, 1775-1779 (reference taken from the 15th Edition), p. 326.

18. Rosen, op. cit.

19. Berrios, G.E., and Mohanna, M., Durkheim and French views on suicide during the 19th century: a conceptual history. *British Journal of Psychiatry*, 1990, 156:1-9.

20. Voisin, A., Idées sur le suicide. *Progres Médical*, 1882, 10:614; Krugelstein, J.,

Mémoire sur le suicide. *Annales d'Hygiène Publique et le Médecine Légale*, 1841, 25: 151-182.

21. Saury, H., Etude Clinique sur la Folie Héréditaire (les dégénérés). Paris: Delahaye, 1886, pp. 8-9.

22. These include: Winslow, F., *The Anatomy of Suicide*, London: Henry Renshaw, 1840; Lisle, E., *Du Suicide: Statistique, Médecine, Histoire et Legislation*, Paris: Baillière, 1856; Brierre de Boismont, A., *Du Suicide et de la Folie Suicide*, Paris: Baillière, 1856; Morselli, H., *Suicide: An Essay on Comparative Moral Statistics*, London: C. Kegan Paul, 1881.

23. Esquirol, E., Des maladies mentales considérés sous les rapports médical, hygiènique et médicolégal (2 vols.). Paris: Baillière, 1838, p. 639.

24. Durkheim, E., *Le Suicide*. Paris: Alcan, 1897 (translated by J.A. Spaulding and G. Simpson as *Suicide: A Study in Sociology*, London, Routledge & Kegan Paul, 1952).

25. Halbwachs, M., *Les Causes du Suicide*. Paris: Alcan, 1930.

26. Achille-Delmas, F., *Psychologie Pathologique du Suicide*. Paris: Alcan, 1932.

27. Giddens, A., Introduction to the translation by Goldblatt of Halbwachs, M., *The Causes of Suicide*. London: Routledge & Kegan Paul, 1978.

28. Berrios and Mohanna, op. cit.

29. One of the earliest to recognize this was W. Griesinger in *Die Pathologie und Therapie der psychischen Krankheiten*, 2nd Ed., Stuttgart: Krabbe, 1861. After quoting Esquirol's other well-known lines: "I believe that I have proved that an individual will only put an end to his life when he is deluded, and the suicides are mentally diseased" (Esquirol, 1838, op. cit., p. 183), he writes: "Esquirol expresses himself *less absolutely* in other parts of the book" (Griesinger, op. cit., p. 256, emphasis added).

30. Esquirol, 1821, op. cit., p. 269.

31. Esquirol, op. cit., p. 214.

32. See *History of Mania*, Chapter XX.

33. Esquirol, op. cit., p. 214.

34. Esquirol, 1838, op. cit., p. 655.

35. Blondel, op. cit., pp. 33-56.

36. Blondel, op. cit., p. 55.

37. See footnote 26 in Giddens, A., The suicide problem in French sociology. *British Journal of Sociology*, 1965, 16:3-18: "Esquirol himself did allow that social factors play a certain role in the aetiology of mental disorder and, consequently, suicide." It is arguable whether Esquirol allowed social factors to be relevant to suicide only through their role in mental disorder. The issue here is whether Esquirol felt that all suicides suffered from mental illness. I do not think he did, although he often stated that, during the act, suicidal persons are in an upset state of mind; unfortunately—like all alienists during his period—to refer to this he used terms such as delusion, passion, or transient insanity; this gives the impression that he is talking about real madness.

38. See Cotard J. Folie, in Dechambre, A., and Lereboullet, L. (eds.), *Dictionnaire Encyclopédique des Sciences Médicales,* Vol. 39. Paris: Masson, 1878, pp. 271-306.

39. For this see Esquirol himself: Délire. In Adelon, Alard, Alibert et al. (eds.), *Dictionnaire des Sciences Médicales par une Société de Médecins et de Chirurgiens.* Paris: Panckoucke, 1814, pp. 251-259.

40. Esquirol, 1814, op. cit., p. 255.

41. On the role of the passions in the etiology of mental disease, see Berrios, G.E., The psychopathology of affectivity: conceptual and historical aspects. *Psychological Medicine*, 1985, 15:745-758.

42. Blonde, op. cit., pp. 42-43.

43. Alexandre Jacques François Brierre de Boismont (1797-1881) was a prolific writer who published work on homicidal monomania and hallucinations. In 1840, on account of his political views, he lost the opportunity to replace Esquirol at the Charenton.
44. Brierre de Boismont, op. cit., p. 135.
45. Brierre de Boismont, op. cit., p. 181.
46. Gustave François Etoc-Demazy (1806-1893) trained under Ferrus and Pariset and wrote on stupor (see Berrios, G.E., Stupor: a conceptual history, *Psychological Medicine*, 1981, 11:677-688), monomania, and a number of medicolegal topics.
47. Etoc-Demazy, G.F., *Recherches statistiques sur le Suicide, appliquées à l'hygiène publique et à la médecine légal.* Paris: Baillière, 1844.
48. Bourdin, C.E., *Du suicide considéré comme maladie.* Paris: Batignolles, Hennuyer et Turpin, 1845. Bourdin was a rabid defender of the view that suicide was always a form of mental disease, and fits well into Durkheim's stereotype. However, he was not an alienist, although he also wrote on catalepsy and alcoholism. He claimed that suicide was always a monomania: "frequently, suicide was the earliest manifestation of monomania" (p. 8); thus, the view that suicide was not pathological was based on "incomplete observations" (p. 7.) He also complained that legislators and philosophers attached an idea of criminality, or at least of imputability, to the act of suicide (p. 20): "If I showed that suicide constitutes a real disease, that all its aspects, when considered in themselves and in their relationship and origins, are no different from the array of ordinary symptoms [of mental illness], I would have freed suicidal individuals from all culpability..." (p. 21). Bourdin's book is rambling, sententious, and obsolete in terms of clinical argument.
49. Etoc-Demazy, G.F., Sur la folie dans la production du suicide. *Annales Médico-Psychologiques*, 1846, 7:347.
50. Etoc-Demazy, op. cit., p. 362.
51. Lisle, op. cit.
52. Lisle developed this concept in Falret, J.P., *De l'Hypochondrie et du Suicide. Considérations sur les Causes, sur le Siége et le Traitement de ces Maladies, sur Moyens d'en Arrêter les Progrès et d'en Prévenir le Développement.* Paris: Croullebois, 1822.
53. Monomania was a diagnosis invented by Esquirol, which achieved certain fashion, particularly in the area of forensic psychiatry. It was never fully accepted by those not belonging to Esquirol's school and after severe attack during the 1950s, it gradually disappeared (see Kageyama, J., Sur l'histoire de la monomanie, *L'Evolution Psychiatrique*, 1984, 49:155-162; Debate on Monomanie, *Annales Médico-Psychologiques*, 1854, 6:99-118; 273-298; 464-474; 629-644; Falret, J.P., De la non-existence de la monomanie, in Des Maladies Mentales et des Asiles d'aliénés. *Leçons Cliniques et Considérations Générales*, Paris: Baillière, 1854, pp. 425-455; Linas, A., Monomanie, in Dechambre, A. (ed.), *Dictionnaire Encyclopédique de Sciences Médicales*, Vol. 5, Paris: Asselin, 1871, pp. 146-195.
54. Bertrand, L., *Traité du Suicide considéré dans ses Rapports avec la Philosophie, la Théologie, la Médecine, et la Jurisprudence.* Paris: Baillière, 1857. Bertrand was also well known in the U.S. See Kushner, H.I., American psychiatry and the cause of suicide, 1844-1917. *Bulletin of the History of Medicine*, 1986, 60:36-57.
55. Bertrand, op. cit., p. 56.
56. Esquirol, 1821, op. cit., p. 219.
57. Emmanuel Françoise Fodéré (1764-1835) was a physician in the eighteenth century mould: he held vitalist principles and his views on insanity were an offshoot from his medicolegal preoccupations. He defined *délire* as a "disease in which freedom had been lost."

58. When used by alienists, "moral" meant "psychological," had little moralistic overtones, and carried no implication in regard to duration.
59. Prichard, J.C., in *A Treatise on Insanity*, London: Sherwood, Gilbert & Piper, 1835, pp. 400-401.
60. Griesinger, op. cit., pp. 256-257.
61. Bucknill, J.C., and Tuke, D.H., *A Manual of Psychological Medicine*, London: John Churchill, 1858, pp. 201-203.
62. Cazauvieilh, J.G., *Du Suicide et l'aliénation Mentale et des Crimes contra les Personnes, comparés dans leurs Rapports Reciproques. Recherches sur ce Premier Penchant chez les Habitants des Campagnes.* Paris: Baillière, 1840. A disciple of Esquirol, and organicist au outrance, Cazauvieilh wrote a classical paper on epilepsy (Berrios, G.E., Epilepsy and insanity during the nineteenth century. A conceptual history. *Archives of Neurology*, 1984, 41:978-981). After leaving La Salpêtriere, he worked in various provincial hospitals until he settled in the asylum of Liancourt-Oise. He reported in his book suicide cases from four regions: Gironde, Landes, Seine, and Oise.
63. Cazauvieilh, op. cit., p.v.
64. Cazauvieilh, op. cit., p. 175.
65. See, for example, masterly summaries by Morselli, 1881, op. cit.; Legoyt, A., Suicide, in Dechambre, A. (ed.), *Dictionnaire Encyclopédique de Sciences Médicales*, Vol. 13, Paris: Asselin, 1884, pp. 242-296; Ritti, A., Suicide, in Dechambre, A. (ed.), *Dictionnaire Encyclopédique de Sciences Médicales*, Vol. 13, Paris: Asselin, 1884, pp. 296-347; A discussion on suicide and its psychiatric aspects. *Journal of Mental Science*, 1898, 45:202-203; Strahan, S.A.K., *Suicide and Insanity: a Physiological, Sociological Study.* London, Swan Sonnenschein & Co., 1893.
66. Westcott, W.W., *Suicide: Its History, Literature, Jurisprudence, Causation, and Prevention.* London: H.K. Lewis, 1885.
67. Des Etangs. Du Suicide en France. Etudes sur la mort volontaire depuis 1798 jusqu'a nos jours. *Annales Medico-Psychologiques*, 1857, 3:1-27.
68. Littré, E., *Dictionnaire de la Langue Française, Supplément.* Paris: Hachette, 1881.
69. Guarnieri, P., Between soma and psyche: Morselli and psychiatry in late nineteenth-century Italy. In Bynum, W.F., Porter, R., and Shepherd, M. (eds.), *The Anatomy of Madness*, Vol. 3, London: Tavistock, pp. 102-124.
70. Morselli, op. cit., p. 272.
71. Brouc, M., Considerations sur le suicide de notre époque. *Annales d'Hygiène Publique et le Médecine Légale*, 1836, 6:223-262.
72. Legoyt, A., Suicide. In Dechambre, A. (ed.), *Dictionnaire Encyclopédique de Sciences Médicales*, Vol. 13. Paris: Asselin, 1884, pp. 242-296.
73. Viallon, A., Suicide et folie. *Annales Médico-Psychologiques*, 1901-1902, 59:19-28; 210-234; 60:21-35; 219-229; 379-392; 235-254; 392-403.
74. Pilcz, A., Contribution a l'étude du suicide. *Annales Médico-Psychologiques*, 1908, 7:193-205.
75. Serin, S. Une enquête médico-sociale sur le suicide à Paris. *Annales Médico-Psychologiques*, 1926, 84:358.
76. Durkheim, E., Les règles de la méthode sociologique. *Revue Philosophique*, 1894, 34:466ff.
77. See Parain-Vial, J., *La Nature du Fait dans les Sciences Humaines*, Paris: Presses Universitaires de France, 1966; also Duverger, M., *Méthodes des Sciences Sociales*, Paris: Presses Universitaires de France, 1961, pp. 1-38.
78. Fleury, M., *L'Angoisse Humaine*, Paris: Les Editions de France, 1926.
79. For an account of the process of incorporation of the neurosis, see López Piñero,

J.M., and Morales Meseguer, J.M., *Neurosis y Psicoterapia*. Madrid: Espasa, 1970; also Oppenheim, J., *"Shattered Nerves": Doctors, Patients, and Depression in Victorian England*. Oxford: Oxford University Press, 1991.

80. Achilles-Delmas, op. cit.
81. Deshaies, G., *Psychologie du Suicide*, Paris: Presses Universitaires de France, 1947.
82. Halbwachs, op. cit. This author (1877-1945) died in a Nazi concentration camp.
83. Achille-Delmas, op. cit.
84. Blondel, *La Conscience Morbide: Essai de Psycho-pathologie Générale*, Paris: Alcan, 1914; ibid., *Introduction à la Psychologie Collective*, Paris: Colin, 1964 (first published in 1928). This latter book shows the awareness that Blondel had of the work of Comte, Durkheim, Tarde, and Halbwachs. He had trained both under Lévy-Bruhl and Deny (the latter one of the great French alienists of the early twentieth century).
85. Blondel, op. cit.
86. Blondel, op. cit., p. 132.
87. Blondel, op. cit., p. 3.
88. Blondel, op. cit., p. 4.
89. See, for example, the old paper by H.C. Selvin, Durkheim's *Suicide* and problems of empirical research. *American Journal of Sociology*, 1958, 63:607-619.

12

Bringing Durkheim into the Twenty-First Century: A Network Approach to Unresolved Issues in the Sociology of Suicide

Bernice A. Pescosolido, PhD

As the standard theory lecture goes, when Durkheim wrote *Suicide,* he stood at a unique historical point in the birth and development of a new form of society and the new academic discipline of sociology. The end of the nineteenth century confirmed the triumph of the "modern" age with its transition from an agrarian base to an industrial one, from a rural population to an increasingly urban one, from a collectivity centered culture to an individualistic one, and from legal relations based on status to relations based on contract. This transition was often celebrated (e.g., Webb, 1889; Spencer, 1881; Sumner, 1914). More frequently there was a focus on the human and social costs of change. Many scholars of the time pointed to rising suicide rates as troublesome human markers of the transition, and they struggled to locate the single source of disruption. Masaryk, for example, argued in 1881 that the fundamental root of suicide lay in the unexpected effects of education on the church and the family. For Durkheim, the cause was more complex, pervasive and far-reaching. The transition to the modern era represented a sweeping realignment of society with traditional forms of social organization deteriorating in strength and new ones emerging. Protestantism, as a central case, responded by loosening its hold on members' collective lives and forfeited its ability to restrain self-destructive impulses. The Catholic Church, to the contrary,

I would like to acknowledge financial support from the National Science Foundation (Grant SES 909867).

adopted a stand against "modernity" in all its forms and continued to provide relative protection from new suicidal impulses (Pescosolido and Georgianna, 1989, p. 34).

As new forms of social organization gave rise to new institutions and problems, so it gave rise to new ways of understanding them. Durkheim clearly intended to support the creation of a new discipline and a particular brand of that "sociology" as well as contributing a unique perspective to our understanding of suicide (Smelser and Warner, 1976). His formulation proved to be distinctly successful. Unlike most competing works, *Suicide* as a piece of theoretical, methodological and empirical work continues to hold court among sociologists. And rightly so, for its overall elegance and theoretical power are stunning and durable. And over the last hundred years, Durkheim's theory of suicide has served sociology well. We have relied heavily on its basic propositions, fiddling here, revising there, or updating this hypothesis or that. Scores of studies, sociological and otherwise, have sought to theoretically refine or question its basic insights, but nothing has surfaced to replace or fundamentally discredit the broad scheme of the dual dimensions of integration and regulation in shedding light on the societal quota of suicides. The Durkheimian perspective of sociology, minus its most functional and now out of vogue aspects, continues to present a major way of understanding society in a discipline that prides itself on being nonparadigmatic (see Furniss [1992] on functionalism).

To a certain extent, however, this almost exclusive reliance on Durkheim's early ideas is problematic. There have been major challenges to some of *Suicide's* underlying assumptions. Serious problems have been raised regarding the validity, relevance and utility of Durkheim's original theory for understanding the contemporary pattern of suicides. Such problems, often raised in the debunking tradition of sociology, have been rarely answered or solved. Further, it has been 100 years since Durkheim wrote *Suicide*. There have been 100 years of social change and 100 years of sociological work since then. Durkheim's theory, in its most general form, contends that changing social forms produces shifts in suicide rates. The specifics and examples in *Suicide*, as a sociology of knowledge perspective would dictate, were bound by the context in which they were shaped and constructed. This raises questions about its applicability in times of major social transition. In sum, if Durkheim's theory, so tied to the constraints of extant theoretical and methodological knowledge of a nascent discipline, cannot be improved by 100 years of sociology, both the applicability of the sociological approach to suicide and the legitimacy of the discipline rightly are threatened.

It is not my appointed nor accepted task to inventory our 100-year stock of sociological knowledge on suicide. There are those who have taken on this critical job at various times with greater skill (e.g., Lester, 1972). Rather, I will turn my attention to long-standing problems and new challenges to the sociological study of suicide, so shaped by Durkheim's theory. The purpose of this chapter, then, is twofold. I will lay out the basic theoretical, method-ological and empirical issues that sociologists of suicide must wrestle with over the next century. And I will attempt to advance this effort by offering an overarching theoretical perspective capable of guiding sociological work. This social network perspective represents the essential element uniting the attempt to address the very diverse challenges confronting the sociological study of suicide. This perspective is consistent both with the central thrust of Durkheim's work and its application to "postmodern" society.

To avoid misunderstanding, a social network approach must not be viewed, at this point in its development, as a theory in the usual sense of tightly interconnected propositions deduced from axioms. Rather, it is a set of basic concepts and ideas about how the centrality of social ties or interconnections among individuals both creates social structures and provides an understand-ing of the mechanisms through which these structures influence attitudes, beliefs and behaviors. While drawing its most direct heritage from Simmel (1955), the development of social network theory since has been spotty. At the same time, however, the breadth and range of empirical studies in the last twenty years in which the framework has been fruitfully employed is compel-ling (see, for examples, reviews in Alba [1982] and Granovetter [1983]). Most importantly, this perspective has been brought in fairly successfully to begin the translation of Durkheim's theory for the twenty-first century (Pescosolido, 1990; Pescosolido and Georgianna, 1989; Pescosolido and Wright, 1990).

THE BASIC CHALLENGES TO THE SOCIOLOGICAL
STUDY OF SUICIDE: A BRIEF OVERVIEW

Three broad and cross-cutting criticisms of Durkheim's *Suicide* are my major concern here. For simplicity, I will refer to them as the theoretical, method-ological, and empirical challenges. The *first,* the theoretical challenge, arises from the theoretical literature questioning Durkheim's larger explanatory scheme and from the body of empirical research on the social correlates of suicide. It raises a number of questions. Is the dual and parabolic conceptual-ization valid and viable for present-day studies? Can it be made simultaneously more concrete and more generalizable? To what extent can we rely on Durkheim's *specific* hypotheses in *Suicide* and continue to battle over whether they are correct or not?

From a theoretical point of view, Johnson's (1965) persuasive argument about the logical possibility of only "one cause" of suicide in Durkheim's scheme has yet to be refuted. In any case, the complexity of this overall scheme appears to have led most researchers to abandon its consideration in favor of a focus on specific examples of religion, divorce or economic conditions where we have some but not many consistent and replicable conclusions. Of course, we should not always expect consistent support both because there can be different pathways to the same event, as Tilly's (1991) recent work argues, and because there are scope conditions which can affect the way the same social forces influence individuals in different social and geographic locations, as Ragin (1987) reminds us. But the central challenge is to ask whether inconsistent findings represent a flaw in Durkheim's hypotheses, Durkheim's larger conceptual framework, *or* our applications of them? The answer lies in addressing both gaps in Durkheimian theory and the way we have approached it. Proposing the social mechanism behind Durkheim's general concepts of integration and regulation provides a more concrete hold on how to tailor old hypotheses to new sociocultural locations and to derive new propositions and hypotheses from Durkheim's general theory. I argue that a network perspective offers a way to understand this general framework, providing most importantly, greater clarity and specificity to the meaning of integration and regulation and the viability of the polar states of egoism, altruism, anomie and fatalism.

The second issue I term *methodological*. It is impossible to read any work on suicide without an inevitable mention of the ecological fallacy (Robinson, 1950). Referred to almost continually either as a criticism of empirical attempts or a requisite apology to be made before doing empirical analysis, the ecological fallacy centers on problems in using aggregate suicide data to study individual level phenomena. For example, can we know or discuss whether Protestants or Catholics commit suicide if our data tell us only about the effect of the religious profile of a county, state or country on suicide rates? If this were simply a concern of those who feel that the reliance on aggregate data represents a mismatch with some of the explicit and implicit ideas in *Suicide*, this would be a technical issue solved more or less straightforwardly in one of two ways by the impressive contributions of sociological and social science methodologists over the last 100 years. Hannan (1971), for example, using Durkheim's *Suicide* as a pointed illustration, clarifies that aggregate data are useful where ideas address the larger effects of structure or context, that is, where the theory, operationalization and analysis match in terms of level of aggregation. Durkheim's theory, despite its own slips into individual level analysis and explanation, aims at the level of social facts, social structure and specifically, the societal quota of suicides. These foci make the use of aggregate data quite appropriate and suggest that one potential solution is to increase the precision and consistency of our language, data and tests. Alternatively, if we are "stuck" with aggregate data on suicide but are really interested in individual level phenomena, there have been some convincing analyses that indicate that sound theoretical guidance coupled with precise model specification can produce valid results (e.g., Hanushek, Jackson and Kain, 1974). Another potential solution, then, is provided by employing a sophisticated use of Durkheim's theory in tandem with current analytic techniques.

But I argue that the confusion over whether we say (or, in fact, really mean) for example, that Protestants commit suicide more often than Catholics exists in Durkheim's work and in the work of those that follow because we cannot maintain one or the other level of discourse sociologically. The ecological fallacy has been seen exclusively and inappropriately as a methodological challenge in the small sense of the term. In reality, this issue is fundamentally theoretical in nature, targeting the *sociological method* in the larger sense of the term. We tend to slip between structural and individual metaphors over the effect of religion, for example, because in the sociological study of suicide, starting with Durkheim, we have failed to be clear about how we see individuals linked to social structural contexts and about how we conceptualize the underlying mechanisms or processes through which the two levels of society influence each other. The sociological perspective is fundamentally about the link between individuals and society, between micro-processes and macro-structures, and in Mills' (1959) terms between personal biographies and social histories. Viewed in this way, there are three central questions that simultaneously draw our interest in the methodological challenge. How do the characteristics of individuals affect the suicide rate? Are there larger contextual influences on suicide rates? Do individual and contextual characteristics interact to produce lower or higher aggregate suicide rates?

The central issue in the methodological challenge lies in addressing what is missing from the Durkheimian approach, that is, any sense of how actors and structures reciprocally influence one another. In the context of his times, Durkheim presented the "strong" case for the impact of society on the individual, for his famous society as a reality *sui generis*. But with that now accepted by sociologists and by others outside the field, we can move to a more reciprocal image of individual and society. Network theory provides a way to understand how these levels are linked by looking to the network content, structure and cultural context in which *social interaction* takes place. Because a macro-micro conceptualization based on network theory focuses on social interaction as the most basic form of social life and rejects a reduction to the individual level, it is consistent with Durkheim's most stringent assumptions about sociological explanations (see Pescosolido [1992] for greater detail, Giddens [1976] for a complementary view and Coleman [1990] for a contrary approach).

The third issue is *empirical*, dealing directly with the manner in which researchers attempt to discover the social etiology of suicide. The challenge here is represented by the social constructionists who, quite correctly, see the compilation of suicide rates as a social process in itself, and, at minimum, are skeptical about the validity of using official data in evaluating sociological ideas about suicide. Douglas (1967), Baechler (1973) and Hindess (1973), for example, argue that empirical tests of theoretical ideas using rates may provide erroneous evaluations of sociological theories. Suicide rates do not reflect a valid accounting of who commits suicide but are confounded by a selective reporting of suicide, particularly for the powerless. Cases of suspicious deaths where there are no individuals with the social power and motivation to convince officials to avoid such a stigmatizing and pragmatically recriminating cause of death for their relatives and associates are reported as suicides. In other cases of suspicious death, where influence is exerted on medicolegal officials, a suicide may be "hidden" in other cause-of-death categories such as "undetermined" or "accidental." On his side, Durkheim (1951) found it convenient to ignore "official" data where it met his needs (i.e., dismissing the study of suicide notes, p. 148) and to refute criticism of official information where it did not (p. 50ff).

These criticisms of official data have produced a substantial body of research exploring the process of rate construction, the qualifications and attributes of medicolegal officials, and the comparison of seemingly divergent international rates. Despite these observations, most efforts targeting the etiology of suicide fail to address the criticisms that have plagued the empirical study of suicide and continue to take for granted the use of official aggregate data on suicide. Neither the abandonment of the search for social causes in favor of the study of the social construction of rates nor the luxury of ignoring these problems bring strength to sociology's contributions to understanding suicide. Rather, these two opposing views must be explored simultaneously, that is, in light of the criticisms of social constructionists, can the study of the social causation of suicide be pursued?

The criticisms of the social constructionists are well-taken and convincing, but their general notion of "social pressures" has not resulted in a deductive theory of the social construction of suicide. Furthermore, the empirical study of the social construction of rates has not produced, using an inductive logic, a specific theoretical framework within which to understand the criticisms of the social constructionists. The basic challenge in pursuing the empirical challenge remains the lack of theoretical guidance. In our earlier work, we suggested using a legal and organization framework to collect social constructionist criticisms into an understanding of the discretion available to medicolegal officials in their task of classifying suspicious deaths (Pescosolido and Mendelsohn, 1986). This proved a useful first step, uncovering bias in the suicide rate, supporting the utility of suicide rates for theory testing, and leading to some pointed questions about the mechanisms underlying how science and cross-pressures influence officials making cause-of-death determinations. Following up on this, we have begun the development of a theoretical framework which fleshes out the structure and content of multiple network ties that surround medicolegal officials. This social network theory of the social construction of rates, presented in brief here, provides a way to understand the political, community, and professional "pressures" so central to the social constructionists' criticisms of the process of death determination.

In sum, sociologists must confront theoretical, methodological and empirical challenges facing the study of suicide by incorporating both persistent complaints and recent sociological developments in refining and reworking the dominant sociological theory of suicide. A simultaneous consideration of these challenges has the potential to provide a more useful, albeit more complex, sociological approach to the problem of suicide. The theoretical foundation of Durkheim's theory, the ecological fallacy, and the social construction of rates can be addressed by bringing in what sociologists have learned over the last one hundred years and by reshaping and responding to each issue with an overarching theoretical perspective. Social network theory fits the most crucial criteria. It holds the promise of providing definition to important sociological concepts such as "integration" and "regulation" for the theoretical challenge, "society" and "social structure" for the methodological challenge, and "social pressures" central to the empirical challenge. My task in the following section lies in sketching out the overall network blueprint for the translation of Durkheim's theory and to begin to lay the foundation for theoretical, methodological and empirical avenues of development.

THE THEORETICAL CHALLENGE: THE SOCIAL ETIOLOGY OF SUICIDE AND DURKHEIM'S THEORY, LARGE AND SMALL

The Smaller Issue of Hypothesis Testing: "Underusing" Durkheim's Theory

Durkheim's original conceptualization is a unified theory rather than a set of individual, specific hypotheses, yet this larger theoretical framework is often overlooked in practice. When social structure is disrupted or perverted, Durkheim argued, the ability to constrain the individuals' resort to suicide as a solution to problems is lessened. He conceived of two major dimensions, integration and regulation, each of which is related simultaneously in curvilinear fashion to the suicide rate. These two most general propositions are never stated directly or clearly in *Suicide* as are some of the more specific propositions which focus on one or another pole of the scheme and that break "society" into smaller substantive arenas such as the family and the polity (e.g., see Durkheim, 1951, p. 208). The divorce rate, the never-married rate and the number of Catholics, as indicators of the "state" of social life in these arenas, are the focus of most empirical work. They represent, in classical hypothesis-testing language, select variables which operationalize only parts of the two general propositions and hypotheses for specific propositions.

Sociologists, for the most part, have tended to ignore the logical structure of this theory and concentrate on whether the empirical findings in *Suicide* continue to hold. While this is useful and has built a body of work with some durable conclusions, a key to the continued viability of Durkheim's theory lies in understanding that these hypotheses are time and place bound. The most simple and fundamental point to bring Durkheim into the twenty-first century rests on taking the Durkheimian theory in spirit rather than in literal terms and to reshape theoretical deductions in the context of social, historical and cultural developments in family, religious, economic and political spheres of life.

To be sure, sociologists have approached the empirical examination of

Durkheimian theory to some extent in this way, looking for how changing labor force participation of women or cross-national context affects change in the societal quota of suicides (e.g., see the work of Frank Trovato on Canada and Steven Stack in general). Even here, however, the flavor of research remains at the level of empirical verification or refutation of Durkheim's original hypotheses. Perhaps the issue illustrating this most clearly is the empirical debate over Durkheim's "One Law." As Pope and Danigelis (1981) lay this out, no other sociological idea has taken on the status of a "law" or been subjected to more scrutiny than Durkheim's contention that Protestantism produces more suicides than Catholicism. The empirical debate continues to the present, with findings consistently favoring neither proponents nor skeptics of Durkheim's hypothesis. In 1989, we began to ask whether this was a judicious and fair use of Durkheim's theory of suicide (Pescosolido and Georgianna, 1989). To concentrate on whether deductions derived in one sociohistorical context be directly applied to a different place and era is to obscure the potential theoretical contribution of Durkheim's work.

The large body of work in the sociology of religion provided a base to rethink the translation from Durkheim's original, specific proposition on religious integration to hypotheses about the relative protective or aggravating effects of various religious bodies. In the contemporary U.S., three sociohistorical trends (secularization, ecumenicalism in the 1960s and the post-World War II evangelical revival) realigned the relationship among Protestant denominations, Catholicism and Judaism. The theoretical challenge of integrating 100 years of the sociology of religion in America into Durkheim's theory required a consideration of what these religious realignments implied for the notion of religious integration. Correspondingly, comparing "Protestants" to Catholics (or areas with various profiles of Protestant or Catholic adherents) seemed to hold little meaning either in the context of the Durkheimian theory or late twentieth-century America. Three questions followed. First and most simply, what had changed and how should we operationalize different religious "societies"? Second, what was the meaning of these changes for understanding social integration? And third, was there a way to show in more concrete terms the underlying mechanism that produces more or less integration?

Our investigation was both inductive and deductive. The first question was answered using a deductive logic. Protestantism has changed dramatically in terms of social organization with scores of new denominations (as well as numbers of nondenominational Protestant groups) appearing over the course of the last century in America. These twentieth-century organizational representations, we argued, might differ in their effects on suicide, and we empirically examined the influence of religious organizational representation in county groups using as much detail as possible. Given the limits of available data, we operationalized the religious profile of an area as the percentage of individuals who belonged to 26 different Protestant groups in addition to

Catholicism and Judaism. We found a fairly clean clustering of empirical effects on suicide rates. Those Protestant religions that sociologists of religion call liberal, mainline or institutional (e.g., Episcopal, Congregational) appear to aggravate suicide as Durkheim saw in Western Europe at the turn of the last century. However, those Protestant groups which sociologists of religion call evangelical or conservative (e.g., Seventh-Day Adventists, Southern Baptists) seem to have a protective effect on suicide in the U.S. as do Catholicism and Judaism.

The second question was addressed with an inductive logic. We tried to organize ideas about religious integration from the patterning of the effects of Protestant groups on suicide rates. This required a deeper look into what sociologists of religion knew about these two types of Protestantism. Sociologists of religion have documented that conservative, evangelical Protestants are more likely to participate in religious activities and to name fellow congregation members as best friends (Stark and Glock, 1973). They refer to these churches as strong, primary groups and "some of the most cohesive nonethnic communities in the United States" (Roof and McKinney, 1987, p. 94). To the contrary, they refer to mainline or liberal Protestants as "dormant" because their studies document that adherents to these religious "societies" do not attend church frequently, often do not know one another, and participate in hierarchical church structures that translate into a passive role for members (Kelly, 1972; Quinley, 1974). Clearly there was a strong parallel to what Durkheim saw as the key to religion's protective and aggravating effects on suicide rates and what current sociologists of religion see as differentiating these religious bodies.

The third question was answered using a deductive logic. Could we find a concrete and specific way to flesh out "religious integration" and support the utility of this operationalization? We found social network theory provided a more precise way to conceptualize "integration." For Durkheim, religion was one of many "societies" or, in Simmel's more lucid network imagery, "social circles." These social circles represent personal networks to Fischer (1982), Tilly (1984) and other network theorists. Using crude data from five fairly recent American surveys where we could operationalize both religious networks and denominational membership, we found that variables which measured individuals' levels of participation in their religions (e.g., weekly church attendance and religion-based friendships) helped build the bridge between religious typologies of Protestantism, our findings and a network framework. Religious differences in effects on suicide rates corresponded to whether, on average, the members of those religious bodies actively participated in (i.e., forged a tie into) a religious network. With this, Durkheim's notion of the multiplicity of "societies" becomes both more concrete and more generalizable. The potential protective power of religion depends on the ability of religious networks to provide a source of support on which individuals can draw during difficult times. This is interwoven with the ability of religious groups to draw members to their activities and actually participate in a religious network (Collins, 1982; Pescosolido and Georgianna, 1989).

In his time and given his consideration of countries, Durkheim's deduction from societal integration to religious institutions to the Catholic/Protestant comparison was apt and brilliant. No more stunning changes rode over Europe between the Middle Ages and the Industrial Era than both the loosening of the grip of Catholicism over major societal institutions like the polity and the rise of another religious form providing another worldview connecting the sacred and the secular. America in the late twentieth century was clearly different and called for a different theoretical deduction about the meaning of religious "societies," explicit hypothesis formation, and corresponding variable operationalization. Even if we keep Durkheim's geographical boundaries, the presence of large numbers of Muslims in France, Turks in Germany or Sikhs in England requires us to think seriously within each country about the impact of religious integration on suicide. Network theory allows a more concrete way to deduce from the Durkheim's general proposition *given a particular sociohistorical context* to specific hypotheses about how various religious societies can be expected to affect suicide rates.

In sum, this section cautions against taking Durkheim's specific hypotheses too literally. We tend to overlook the complexity in Durkheim's existing theory. But Durkheim's theory is not without gaps, perhaps not even as complex as it needs to be. Most crucially, the mechanism by which larger structures such as religious society influence such a personal decision remains at an abstract level. It is to this issue that I now turn.

The Larger Issue: Rebuilding a Viable Theory of Suicide Using Social Network Theory

One could read the preceding section as an indictment of suicide researchers who have failed to deal with Durkheim's theory of suicide at its most complex or important level. The implication accompanying this reading would suggest a simple corrective in rethinking the translation of propositions into hypotheses. The problem in such a reading lies with the mistaken assumption that Durkheim provided a clear understanding of the mechanism underlying the meaning of specific arenas of social life or of the larger dual organizing framework of integration and regulation. Late in the nineteenth century, Durkheim lacked the conceptual tools and backing of a body of relevant research to produce a clearer guide to applying his general scheme or to particular mechanisms underlying the "societies" he conceptualized as providing or denying optimal amounts of integration and regulation. A network approach, neither contrary to nor totally distinct from Durkheim's ideas in *Suicide,* incorporates Simmel's and more recent network insights and allows elaboration, not replacement, of Durkheimian theory. Simply translating the theory into network concepts and terms allows greater specificity and cross-fertilization with ideas from the growing body of network and social support literatures. This social network perspective, I argue, offers a way to make the Durkheimian theory of suicide both more concrete and more generalizable.

To advance this argument, two things need to be demonstrated. First, we need to show that network theory provides a reasonable way to translate Durkheim's propositions into hypotheses in a way true to the spirit of Durkheimian theory. Second, we need to convincingly argue that the approach can shed some light on the overall dual and parabolic conceptualization of integration and regulation.

Translating Durkheim's Theory in the Network Metaphor

My major premise is that Durkheimian theory, itself, is consistent with a network theoretical approach and can be updated and refined by integrating the two. As described earlier in this chapter, we began the interpretation of Durkheim's theory along these lines with the investigation of religion and suicide (Pescosolido and Georgianna, 1989). We argued that even Durkheim's original theory, dealing with changes in religion and the suicide rate at the turn of the century, is more fully elaborated when Simmel's ideas about change in the basis of network formation during that period are considered. With the industrial age, the basis of network formation shifted from concentric circles (i.e., little choice, geographic-based, closed structure) to overlapping circles (i.e., greater freedom, interest-based, open structure). While religion was central to the formation and maintenance of social networks in the earlier era, the appearance of diverse organizational forms of religion made its influence less pervasive and uniform. Those who stood with Catholicism had a base of strong and continuing network affiliation located in the church and the wide range of other social institutions (e.g., hospitals and schools) that it controlled. Suicide rates in predominantly Catholic areas continued to be relatively low because of the continued guidance and institutional support the church provided in the "modern" age. Those who sought the more liberal forms were not protected. These more "rational" networks of the "modern" age in which Protestants participated gave rise to tolerance, free inquiry, and diversity but were paid for by less emotional and institutional support, psychological tensions, ambiguity, and ultimately higher suicide rates (Pescosolido and Georgianna, 1986, p. 45).

In general, what differentiates religious groups in their ability to restrain suicidal impulses, then and now, lies in the degree to which religions provide strong support communities. This depends fundamentally on the nature of the religious community and on ties that bind individuals to it. In the social network framework, the focus lies neither in whether individuals formally identify themselves as having a religious affiliation nor in what the formal prohibitions against suicide are. The key is whether they actually become part of the church or temple community. Since beliefs and values are deeply rooted in social networks, these religious networks also serve to reinforce ideas about right and wrong, and about appropriate ways to solve problems (Pescosolido and Georgianna, 1989, p. 40). Already the conceptualization needs to be more complex. Religious networks are, in and of themselves, more or less likely to provide an integrated network of support. And individuals can forge stronger or weaker, single-faceted or multiplex ties with these religious communities. But these two clearly are not independent. Religions that simultaneously demand that members forge stronger ties offer more integrative support.

Durkheim's notion of the centrality of social integration in understanding suicide, then, corresponds to the primary starting point of network theory—the nature of social relations (or the social structure) influences individuals' attitudes, beliefs, and behavior (see White and Boorman, 1976, p. 1442). Churches represent one form of many natural "communities" dependent upon factors such as member participation and socialization of initiates (Gustafson, 1961). But Durkheim's use of the term "society" or even "societies" weakens the power of sociological explanations (Tilly, 1984, pp. 27-28). If we replace "society" with "network," this idea becomes less ambiguous. In network imagery, membership in these "societies" represents one tie in an individual's network which can offer the "constant interchange of ideas and feelings, something like mutual moral support" that Durkheim (1951, p. 210) discusses. Adopting this view requires greater depth in understanding the state of social relations in any formal or informal social network and allows a conceptual wedge into a more generalizable approach to understand, operationalize and examine how integration and regulation influence suicide.

The Larger Framework of Integration and Regulation

If we accept that Durkheim's "societies" are, in reality, the operation of different networks with solidarity coming from the presence (or absence) of strong, interlocking social relationships, as White, Boorman and Breiger (1976) argue, a basic question remains. Do integration and regulation provide a viable basis to conceptualize the major grids along which these networks exist? Perhaps the best known and most elegant critique of the overall system comes from Johnson (1965). His "one cause of suicide" argument suggests that, upon close examination, the two dimensions and four types of suicide that define the ideal-type poles of the cross-cutting dimensions collapse into one and only one "variable." As Johnson points out, Durkheim never explicitly asserts, but only implies, this cross-cutting dual and parabolic scheme, defined at the poles by four ideal types of suicide. Altruistic suicide occurs in social structures with excessive regulation, egoistic suicide where there is too little integration, fatalistic suicide when individuals are so regulated by "oppressive discipline" (p. 276), and anomic suicide where social structure provides only the weakest of controls over the individual. Moderate levels of both integration and regulation are "optimal" in protecting individuals from suicidal impulses.

As a first step, Johnson eliminates consideration of altruistic and fatalistic suicide based on Durkheim's own suggestion that both exist in small, particularly primitive societies and that contemporary cases for fatalistic suicide are not persuasive.* Johnson (pp. 879-880) questions not the possibility of their existence but their applicability to modern society (or what he calls Durkheim's "range of data"). Having eliminated fatalism and altruism, Johnson proceeds to argue that egoism and anomie can be equated into one, "true," underlying dimension because Durkheim rarely considers a group's simultaneous integrative and regulative condition and because he tends to see the two as strong covariates. Anomie, or the absence of regulation, Johnson argues, is by definition one characteristic of egoism—where individuals are not integrated, they cannot, by definition, be expected to be regulated.

Durkheim's theoretical scheme can be imagined in a network perspective. In its most basic form, social structure is a safety net that has different features topographically. One dimension running from left to right represents integration; underintegration is represented by sparse network ties and overintegration by dense or strong network ties. Another dimension, running forward to back and representing regulation, similarly runs from dense to sparse in terms of network ties. When these two are considered simultaneously, the clarity provided by this network depiction is, in itself, useful. When individuals exist in social structures with either too little integration or regulation, the social safety net is "loose" or "open," there is little to "catch" individuals when crisis destabilizes their equilibrium. They fall through the net, and suicides occur. While the multiplicity of meanings that Durkheim attached to polar types confuses their exact meaning (Smelser and Warner, 1976, pp. 173-174), in this conceptualization, we can see why he saw the similarity of egoistic and anomic types. They are diseases of the infinite because they provide no "grip" in the societal safety net that supports people during times of individual or community crises.

When individuals exist in social structures which are too regulated or too integrated, the safety net closes up. There is no flexibility or "give" to the social safety net. When they experience crisis, in essence they hit a wall which shatters rather than supports. It is only in the center of the net, where social networks are balanced and moderate in their provision of integration and/or regulation, in which individuals can be safely "caught" and restrained from their suicidal impulses. As networks become out of balance on the amounts of integration and regulation they provide, the potential for an individual to act successfully on suicidal impulses becomes greater.

Despite the visual power of the network representation of Durkheim's

---

* Durkheim uses the army as a second example where altruistic suicides occur. Johnson claims that this is an exception to the rule rather than another form of suicide. Given issues of how suicide rates may be distorted during military service, particularly in wartime, I choose not to deal with this here.

theory, it cannot be maintained unless we can refute Johnson's two most basic claims: (1) fatalism and altruism are irrelevant, and (2) integration and regulation are, in fact, the same phenomenon. The first error and necessary correction in both Johnson's and even Durkheim's original approach is to equate "social structure" most commonly with geopolitical boundaries such as the nation state. What we know from 100 years of sociology is that people, even in large cities in large modern nations, live their lives in small worlds (see, for example, Fisher's [1982] work on Northern California and Wellman's [1979, 1982] on Toronto). Johnson's objection to Japan or India as "altruistic" societies is irrelevant. The central question is whether or not social networks exist in modern society that can be described as altruistic or fatalistic.

Communities which are overintegrated or overregulated are, by their very nature, not open to free observation by outsiders, but we have caught occasional glimpses. Two of striking importance to the U.S. in the late twentieth century have been written about in detail—the Bhagwan Shree Rajneesh's Rajneeshpuram in Oregon and the Reverend Jim Jones' People's Temple in California and later Guyana (see Fitzgerald [1986] and Coser and Coser [1979], respectively). In these, we have clear evidence that social networks can exist in communities in an imbalanced or even "perverse" fashion. In each of these two cases, there are networks which can legitimately be described as fatalistic, as "choked by oppressive discipline." They are unusual in the sense that they are large but bounded, concentric networks, virtually insular and purposively untouchable by the larger society. In the early stages of their formation, the social networks in these communities appeared to be very integrated, supportive and devoted to creating a utopia in opposition to the perceived crumbling and anomic state of modern society. Given the fidelity of commune members to the larger goal, there appeared to be little need for regulation and, superficially, that may have appeared so. For example, the Bhagwan's doctrine was "extremely permissive in matters of behavior" in order to "simply reduce the coefficient of emotional friction between people" (Fitzgerald, 1986, p. 272). Traditional, regulative social institutions like private property and long-term relationships were discouraged in favor of a "detachment" from the bodily self and a "liquid" family. But a closer look offers a different view. In general, Fitzgerald saw at the Rajneeshpuram "a great deal of hugging" coupled with a "confusion of responsibility" (1986, pp. 320, 399). Travel outside the commune required special permission and all daily tasks were assigned by the commune leadership. And in Jonestown, ties outside of the People's Temple, bonds of marital intimacy, and other traditional sources of integration were disrupted or undermined by Jones. The Reverend Jones explicitly and intentionally used sexual relations with both male and female cult members of the People's Temple to destroy traditional loyalties which could provide an opposing source of integration or regulation. As each commune came under some form of attack by the larger society, instigated in some cases by disgruntled former members, these community networks "clenched up like a muscle, to become rigid, controlling and compulsive" (Fitzgerald, 1986, p. 356) where religious ritual became "baroque" and "elaborate" in the Rajneeshpuram and took on the form of frequent suicide drills in Jonestown. Designated members of each commune wore militaristic uniforms and sported firearms.

These communities were, in essence, what Coser and Coser (1979) call "greedy groups," demanding total commitment to the building of an alternative society and eliminating competing claims to other individuals or groups. Social networks apparently had some integrative strength but were primarily cast in very strong regulative terms, particularly as community crises arose. And their potential for resort to suicide is more than theoretical speculation. In 1978 at the People's Temple in Guyana, almost 1000 adults and children drank cyanide-laced Kool-Aid, whether by choice, ignorance or coercion. They found no support for alternative options in the fatalistic social networks in which they lived. In 1985, prior to the collapse of the commune and arrest of the Bhagwan, investigators feared "a Jonestown-style denouement" (Fitzgerald, 1986, p. 364). In sum, because of the low level of within-group integration, and the nature of the encompassing regulation of social life in Jonestown and the Rajneeshpuram, these communes and the suicides in Jonestown fit squarely into Durkheim's ideas about fatalistic social structures.

Perhaps these are odd, unusual, distorted social networks within the larger society, or even "perverse utopias" in Coser and Coser's (1979) terms. But Fitzgerald (1986) goes further to describe other "cities on a hill," each less extreme than the Rajneeshpuram but all similar in spirit, structure and the search for social networks in opposition to mainstream society. She names many old and new religious or social groups—Scientology, TM, the Tibetan Buddhist community of Trungpa Rimpoche and the Oneida community. Other secular communities exist, she argues, that are not so insular in their social ties but that nonetheless share a "prismatic quality"—essentially certain structural and normative characteristics which stand in opposition to the larger society but illuminate the cultural fractures or stresses within it. The gay community in the Castro area of San Francisco, Sun City Center retirement community in Tampa, and Jerry Falwell's Moral Majority, she contends, all have aspects of social network structures existing within but tightly united against the dominant society.

Community-based social networks are not the only examples of overregulated social structures. On a much smaller scale, there have been scores of sensational descriptions of perverse or severely "dysfunctional" family structures, for example, Lundgren's schismatic Mormon sect in West Virginia and Ohio (Earley, 1991) as well as endless media reports of sexual abuse and incest in families, daycare centers or other social organizations which depend on secrecy and excessive regulation (e.g., Hedda Nusbaum and Joel Steinberg in New York City and the West Point Daycare scandal).

In sum, there exists a good deal of evidence to suggest that in Durkheim's own (1951, p. 276) conclusion that fatalism has "so little contemporary importance that it seems useless to dwell upon it" underestimates the power and utility of the overall conceptualization. In the most extreme contemporary cases, we find to a great degree what Durkheim described in his polar type of fatalism. These accounts dramatically document the existence in modern society of social network characterized by excessive regulation, and in the case of Jonestown, the consequence of fatalistic suicide where individuals confronted an "ineluctable and inflexible nature of a rule against which there is no appeal" (Durkheim, 1951, p. 276).

We do not have to search for such unusual, perverse or isolated social networks to undermine Johnson's second complaint, although these cases do suggest that societal regulation or integration can exist independently. In general, the claim of the invariant, covariate tendency between integration and regulation is also an error. In more commonplace situations in modern society, social networks can offer differing amounts of integration and regulation to its members. For example, those who study families and children of divorce contend that the major problem facing the single-parent family following divorce is not the lack of integration but the lack of regulation (see Furstenberg, 1990). Divorced parents, particularly middle-class families, attend with care to the emotional nurturance of their children in direct response to concerns about the effect of divorce (i.e., an integrative function). More problematic is the consistency with which single parents attend to the setting of limits (i.e., a regulative function), in part out of sheer exhaustion and in part out of a fear of adding additional trauma to their children's lives.

In the social support tradition, derived explicitly in its sociological beginnings from Durkheim's notion of the power of integration (e.g., Myers, et al., 1975), emphasis shifted from a conceptualization of all ties as providing support (and "good" support at that) to a more complex and refined motion of the different types and valences of resources that come from social network ties (Wellman, 1985). Perhaps Umberson's work (1987; Umberson and Greer, 1990) provides the best evidence that social networks can have regulative as well as integrative functions. Her wellness-regulation model explores the link between social relationships and mortality by explicitly conceptualizing and examining the monitoring and regulating function in social networks. In a recent paper, she and her colleague document a gender-specific function of the marriage bond, so crucial to Durkheim's theory and one so dismissed by Johnson. Marital ties produce more regulation for men with a positive effect on health, despite the quality of the marriage (i.e., controlling for the level of integration in the marriage). Further, the loss of the marital bond increases negative health behaviors for everyone, but particularly for men. Men "profit" in marriage, to use Durkheim's terms, at least in part by the regularity with which their wives cajole, coerce or demand that their husbands engage in healthy behavior.

This view of the potential multiple functions of social networks also helps us to resolve the issues of Durkheim's differential explanations of divorce, for example, the "most favored sex" explanation (Smelser and Warner, 1976, p. 176). Gerstel and her colleagues (1985) have documented findings consistent with Durkheim's assumptions about marriage, divorce and gender without resort to Durkheim's biological determinism. They expect and find that for women, the primary negative features of divorce result from financial strain and parental obligations. In addition, women tend to maintain social contacts and intimate ties outside the marriage for emotional support and integration. Greater domestic integration restrains suicide in Durkheim's theory. For men, however, the situation is quite different. Men depend more on spouses for the maintenance of social network ties and less for financial status. As a result, they suffer more devastation of supportive social relations upon divorce. In our earlier work, we found that the effect of divorce rates among similarly aged women had only a negligible effect on women's suicide until old age (65 and over). For men, however, the effect of the divorce rate among similarly aged men is significant and protective for the youngest husbands (18 to 24), is aggravating and increases dramatically through middle age, and approaches zero for elderly men (Pescosolido and Wright, 1990).

Taken together, these studies suggest that, upon divorce, men suffer both more significant losses of social integration and regulation than do women, both of which increase their suicide potential. Women, on the other hand, do not get as much regulative benefit during marriage, do not depend on marriage for their integrative ties, and suffer proportionately less from divorce (except perhaps in old age). Marriage, according to Durkheim's theory and to research by Gerstel and her colleagues (1985, p. 97) "serves men and women in different ways." For women, in and out of marriage, regulation and integration do not covary to the degree it does for men. These "ways," when disrupted, are consistent with conditions that fail to provide men with protection from suicidal impulses.

In sum, the network perspective allows us to maintain the theoretical distinction between integration and regulation by conceptualizing integration and regulation as two of a number of possible functions of social network ties (Pescosolido and Georgianna, 1989, p. 39; Wellman, 1985). While integrative and regulative functions may occur together, they do not always do so. Network structures create the potential to provide members with integrative and regulative benefits. These functions can exist together or out of balance, affecting the ability of individuals and communities to face crises (Pescosolido and Georgianna, 1989, p. 45).

But while these disparate examples of Jonestown, the Rajneeshpuram, children of divorce, families characterized by physical and sexual abuse, or divorced men reveal the importance of integration and regulation as crucial frames for the social safety net, they are not sufficient in themselves to modernize Durkheim's theory. As Erikson (1976, p. 82ff) points out, these "axes of variation" of regulation and integration are basic and important points and counterpoint along which societies are organized. Not only do they organize social life but they are "sources of tension but gradients along which responses to social change are likely to take place." As network theorists contend, networks operate in a larger cultural context that can facilitate or inhibit acceptance of general cultural norms and beliefs (Pescosolido, 1986; White, et al., 1976). Contexts, in turn, constrain the formation of different types of social networks. Three critical aspects of networks—their structure, their function and their operation in larger cultural context—must be simultaneously considered. Our work on the religion-suicide link led us to call for a strong cultural analysis to accompany and frame a network conceptualization of and future work on suicide (Pescosolido and Georgianna, 1989, p. 44). A multilevel conceptualization is required which permits us to see network structures as dynamic and as part of or in opposition to other structures, particularly larger culture-affirming structures. This leads to a consideration of the methodological challenge facing the sociology of suicide.

THE METHODOLOGICAL CHALLENGE: THE SOCIOLOGICAL MEANING OF THE ECOLOGICAL CORRELATION FALLACY

Durkheim (1951, p. 51) argued that cases of individual suicide and the individualistic causes that lead to them are not the concern of the sociologist because they do not depend on the state of social organization and have no social repercussions. He argues that his theory is essentially about the impact of *social structure*. Catholicism creates a more integrated society than Protestantism. But how does this protection work? If Catholics are embedded in personal networks with good levels of integration and regulation, the effect of being Catholic, for example, is a real one. And, if Catholics carry these networks into other parts of their personal or professional lives, the protective effect for Catholic areas is also real, lowering the suicide rate for all members of the geographical area. Still the question remains—who is committing suicide even in these Catholic areas? Are they Catholics who reject or somehow do not profit from this religious integration or Protestants who are not in synchrony with the social protection networks of the Catholics and find themselves either smothered by this level of integration or distraught by their exclusion?

No matter how insistent Durkheim is about the irrelevant nature of individual suicide, the theoretical and methodological problems associated with an exclusive focus on the aggregate level confronts the sociological study of suicide at every turn. Durkheim betrays his own insistence with his shifts in discussion from the overall impact of domestic or economic society to his elaboration of individual cases throughout *Suicide*. It is the very young married man who is prone to suicide (p. 182); it is the man who experiences a financial windfall or bankruptcy who experiences "inextinguishable thirst" as "constantly renewed torture" (p. 247). Implied directly here is the reflection of micro-experience in aggregate phenomena which both seems to set the character of the macro-structure and rebounds on those destabilized by crisis or change.

There is something particularly unsatisfying in reporting that "county groups with higher percentages of Catholics, Evangelical Baptists or Nazarenes report lower suicide rates" (Pescosolido and Georgianna, 1989, p.38). We are naturally drawn as sociologists to wonder how particular acts of suicide, so personal in nature, are shaped so fundamentally by the nature of the social structure in which individuals failed to thrive. We are drawn to ask about the individual-society interaction because, as Mills (1959) so clearly stated, this lies at the heart of the sociological imagination. To understand the private troubles of individuals in light of the public issues that surround them requires us to think past the suicide rate, even while we accept it as a social fact.

But the slips into language describing the experience of individuals when examining aggregate data give rise to one of the most often cited dilemmas in the testing of social theories. Since Robinson's (1950) discussion of the ecological correlation fallacy, sociologists have recognized that inferences about individual behavior derived from aggregate data are not always correct. And, just as quickly, sociological methodologists began to chart how we might proceed (Goodman, 1953, 1959). We now accept that aggregate data can be used to make inferences about the effects of social structure on group behavior as long as theory, hypotheses, data and results are organized at the same level of aggregation (Baron and Reiss, 1985; Hannan, 1971). But as the previously discussed examples illustrate, the ecological fallacy is miscast if it is seen simply as a concern for sociological methodologists. Beginning with Durkheim, we fumble reporting our results and interpreting our findings because the ecological fallacy masks a more fundamental dilemma in casting our theories and providing empirical verification of them. It raises a concern with the sociological method, in the larger sense of the term. Can we realistically maintain a level of discourse on either the individual or the structural level if one of the primary insights of the sociological perspective lies in linking the fate of individuals to the social structures in which they live their lives? This interpretation renders neither individual nor aggregate level meaningless, nor one superior to the other. It pushes us to consider their interconnections in the theories we construct, the data collection protocols we develop, and the analytic tools we bring to bear in the empirical testing. Each of these are discussed in turn below.

The Theoretical Agenda: The Macro-Micro Link

A number of us have suggested that the agenda of sociology, perhaps the social sciences, in the 1990s lies in linking of micro-processes and macro-structures (Coleman, 1990; Collins, 1981; Etzioni, 1989; Giddens, 1989; Ostrom,

1989; Pescosolido, 1992; Stryker, 1980). This movement toward trans-disciplinary, multilevel frameworks may herald a second, more mature stage of social science, appropriate for this, its second century, where syntheses of unique disciplinary insights replaces the early need to establish distinct disciplinary boundaries of knowledge. The beginnings of a synthesis that I offer to this end begins with fundamental sociological principles consistent with a Durkheimian framework. As an explicit attempt to link macro and micro levels of analysis, it offers a way to reconceptualize the theoretical dilemmas that the ecological fallacy brings to the sociology of suicide (Pescosolido, 1992).

What links the lives of individuals to others and to the time and place in which they live is their interaction in social networks. We can conceptualize individuals as actors connected to groups like the family, the church, friendship cliques and the workplace. These groups themselves are characterized by having ties to one another to form some characteristic profile of domestic society, the religious community, the market, and intimate support structures. At even a higher level of consideration, these substantive spheres are tied to each other to form the community and provide the integrative and regulative flavor of the macro-structure. At each level, a unique *sui generis* reality results from the overall nature of the structure of network and individual interactions.

How does this conceptualization help us confront the ecological fallacy? Incorporating the centrality of social networks in a conceptualization of micro-macro linkages demystifies and gives meaning to the idea of social structure as a reality *sui generis* (Pescosolido, 1992, p. 1109). This framework makes it possible to link individuals to one other, to the larger social system and to abstract entities as the state, the economy and the community, so central to Durkheim's theory, and to reconceptualize them as the stable and recurring operation of social networks (see also Laumann and Knoke, 1987; Tilly 1984). Networks, with a preexisting structure and content, are antecedent to any event. Sometimes a problem arises from disruptions or "shocks" to the social network on a small scale (e.g., death of a family member) or on a grand scale (e.g., economic recession). Through interaction in these networks individuals recognize or fail to recognize a problem, find the strengths and limits of social resources available to them, and cope or fail to cope with the difficulties they face. In other words, attempts at coping emerge in the context of a preexisting stream of social life, and any decision or action is embedded in a social process. Networks also link individuals to the structures that shape their lives. Individuals and structures are inextricably intertwined and cannot be understood apart from each other or from the networks that shape them (see Pescosolido, 1992).

We have some preliminary, relevant information to suggest the viability of this conceptualization and to dismiss the suspicion that these different levels of networks are simply summations of the same social phenomena. First, in our early work, we found that the age profile of the county group did not affect suicide in the same way for all groups of individuals who lived there. For young men (25 to 44), a higher average age of the county group significantly increased suicide rates while, for their 65 and older counterparts, this age profile lowered suicide rates (Pescosolido and Mendelsohn, 1986). Second, we have argued that the effects of religious affiliation should be more pronounced in regions of traditional historical strength where the opportunity to construct and maintain strong ties comes from the solid infrastructure grounding of the community, and also in urban or other high-population-density areas where the sheer likelihood of locating co-religionists is greater. And in fact, Catholicism's influence appears to be both large and consistently protective overall, but its effect in the South, a region of relatively few Catholics, is to aggravate suicide potentials. Similarly, in the Northeast, where the presence of Judaism has been historically and numerically strong, its greater strength decreases suicide, but in all other regions of the country, Judaism is associated with an increase in suicide rates (Pescosolido, 1990; see also Bankston, 1983; Kowalski, et al., 1987).

There are, at minimum, two levels at which integration and regulation can be conceptualized in Durkheim's theory—the condition of individuals and the larger social context in which they live. The basic problem for social research becomes interrelating the life-histories of individual suicides with the larger social context (Simpson in Durkheim, 1951, p. 26). It sets three distinctive but interrelated questions for the sociological research agenda. First, how do the network interactions of individuals influence the push to suicide? A crisis that destabilizes individuals can aggravate suicide while membership in social networks that do not provide optimal levels of support or regulation can remove the social cushion that would prevent suicide. So, characteristics of individuals are important in understanding suicide. How does the state or condition of the religious or family life of individuals affect their predisposition to suicide? Given the typical absence of direct network measures, this figure and most of our empirical analyses to date use characteristics of individuals as proxies for micro-interaction profiles. Indicators such as marital status and denominational affiliation will have to do (see White, Boorman and Breiger [1976] on this point). How does divorce affect an individual's probability of suicide? And how do Catholics and Protestants fare in their contribution to the societal quota of suicide?

Second, how do social network structures in which individuals experience crisis aggravate or reduce suicide? The divorce profile of a county or city reveals something about the weakness of the social safety net in general. It may also hint at the opportunity, or lack thereof, for individuals to find other people with similar experiences with whom to commiserate or with whom to form new ties and expectations (in the spirit of Gibbs' theory of status integration [1964] and also Gibbs and Martin [1974]). So, the characteristics of the geographical areas in which individuals live are relevant. The number of Catholic churches or adherents in an area, the divorce rate or the amount of migration proxy the experience of individuals in larger and more formal social structural networks. How do these characteristics of the social structure protect or push people to suicide?

Finally, there is something about the "fit" between individuals and the social circumstances in which they live their lives. Durkheim (1951, p. 156ff) dismisses the role of minority status in this discussion of the protective effects of Judaism, but the inevitable questions arises in this multilevel, network conceptualization—how do the experiences and characteristics of individuals interact with larger social structure to influence suicide rates? How do young divorced men fare in a context of high rates of divorce or in one characterized by low rates of divorce?

A Consideration of Logistics

While Durkheim's work suggests that levels of aggregation larger than individuals are most relevant, the theoretical guide of "the social structure" is of little utility since no direct and/or agreed-upon operationalization exists. Even if it did, the operationalization would be unlikely to match geopolitical boundaries that form the reporting units of major national data collection efforts. Perhaps the most difficult task we face lies, not in understanding how processes operate on different levels, but how we can provide empirical evidence that matches our conceptualizations. There are two basic questions here. What is the proper level of contextual data to employ—the neighborhood, the city, the county, the state, the county group? And, can we hope to include both individual and aggregate data in the same analysis? On the first, currently available data involve an inevitable trade-off. At higher units of aggregation, data are thought to be more accurate (i.e., measured with less error). These "errors in variables" are minimized as the unit of analysis represents greater aggregation, but the homogeneity assumption within aggregation units needs to be evoked (see Johnston, 1972; Hanushek and Jackson, 1977). On the second, even if researchers could agree that individuals and their network interactions (or proxy characteristics) form an important unit of analysis, the practical issue of data availability remains. Given suicide's low probability of occurrence and the inability to locate victims beforehand, we have little opportunity to proceed in a direct fashion. Because of confidentiality protections, information available from the Census Bureau cannot be provided at lower levels of aggregation than the county. Since suicide removes the relevant actors (i.e., in network terms, ego) from networks, we are left with only the possibility of *ad hoc* reconstructions. Further, we might try to collect relevant data, standard sociodemographics or network data no matter how limited, about the cases of suicide *ex post facto*. The stumbling block is that these data would need to be collected not only about the suicides' ties but from the appropriate comparison group—all individuals in the population.

In some ways, this situation is no better than Durkheim (1951, p. 22) faced:

Unless the individual who commits suicide has been under constant and long-time psychiatric examination (either through psychoanalysis or clinical study with full and copious life-history records), an interpretation and classification of his suicide becomes an *ex post facto* reconstruction of his life history. This is extremely difficult, and probably impossible in most cases. Not even the most ardent opinion-poller or attitude-tester can go around interviewing suicides, and representative samples of a population can scarcely be investigated solely on the anticipatory grounds that some of the items in the sample will commit suicide.

Nonetheless, attempts to crack these logistical problems hold the promise to speed both our synthesis of multidisciplinary insights and our simultaneous examination of the influence of complex, layered effects of society on the individual. We must address the need to develop protocols to collect new data that matches theoretical agendas. In the meantime, we must confront issues in the data we routinely use in our studies. This forms the third and final challenge in the sociological study of suicide.

THE EMPIRICAL CHALLENGE: THE SOCIAL CONSTRUCTION OF OFFICIAL RATES

In the 1930s, Zilborg contended that "statistical data on suicide as they are compiled today deserve little if any credence" (quoted in Simpson's introduction to *Suicide* [1951, p.18]). This concern over the utility of the suicide rate as a target for legitimate empirical investigation appears consistently throughout the sociological literature. Comments range from mild consternation over possible error to claims that a dependence on official statistics is irreconcilably flawed (see Pescosolido and Mendelsohn [1986] for a detailed review).

Durkheim refuted these problems despite the fact that he had a very specific definition of suicide which could not possibly match official suicide rates, that he dismissed the utility of suicide notes using a constructivist logic (p. 148), and that he specified different types of suicide which could not be operationalized in overall rates. Considering all of these difficulties, to our credit, we really are providing very conservative estimates of the power of social factors in suicide. The problem lies in whether these estimates are biased as well as underestimated.

Uncertainty does surround a "suspicious" death and raises the potential for error in the classification process. Opponents of the use of official rates speculate that there are "social pressures" on both the victim's significant others and on coroners or medical examiners who bear responsibility for the task of classifying deaths. Despite these observations, as was noted at the beginning of this chapter, the current state of affairs reveals three responses to these long-held objections. First, most sociological efforts continue to take for granted the use of official aggregate data on suicide by noting early problems of official rates but leaving unanswered methodological criticisms that have plagued the study of suicide. In other words, they acknowledge the problem in theory but ignore it in practice. Second, social constructionists, while offering compelling criticisms through a consideration of meaning and method, rely on ambiguous notions of "community pressures" and "family influence" without clearly elaborating how these factors may systematically influence officials' decisions. In other words, they do not provide a testable set of deductions. Third, there has been empirical work, basically of an inductive nature, that indicates that there appears to be universal agreement that rates are underreported with estimates ranging from 10 to 50 percent; that misclassified suicides, though theoretically falling into any other cause of death, tend to be clustered into "obvious" alternatives such as single car fatalities; and that characteristics of personnel and office facilities are correlated systematically with the suicide rate (see Pescosolido and Mendelsohn [1986] for a review). In other words, they uncover problems in the suicide rate but do not relate these problems directly to the attempt to understand the social etiology of suicide.

The lack of an overarching theoretical framework which integrates these different streams of effort and which organizes and gives coherence to the insights of critics of official rates hinders our incorporation of a constructivist framework to understand the mechanism by which meaning and method are established. It also slows our progress on empirical efforts to evaluate official rates, to understand the underlying social mechanisms at work, and to uncover the real nature and magnitude of social factors on suicide.

Using insights from this literature and drawing from sociological theories on organizations in general (e.g., Perrow, 1972) and from those specifically focusing on legal organizations (e.g., Reiss, 1971), we began the development of a theory about the social construction of rates (Pescosolido and Mendelsohn, 1986). We combined this theory with those about the social causes of suicide to provide an integrated evaluation of the potential problems in using suicide rates in empirical analysis. Our results from this preliminary investigation demonstrated the existence of systematic misreporting of American suicide in 1969-1970, on the one hand, but little discernible influence on the social correlates of suicide, on the other. That is, suicides do, in fact, appear to be consistently underreported, and this is related to the legal and organizational character of agencies responsible for classifying deaths. However, that misreporting has little effect on the relationship between suicide rates and indicators of concepts in sociological theories of suicide (Pescosolido and Mendelsohn, 1986, p. 94).

This study did provide a useful starting point for organizing basic ideas which underlie criticisms of the use of official statistics and for bringing in more concrete ideas about the legal and organizational factors that might influence the process of rate construction. But it felt incomplete. It sociologically organized many of the ideas that have been suggested as interfering with the recording of "true" causes of death in suspicious cases, but it presented no overarching theoretical perspective either to outline the social processes and mechanisms at work in classifying official rates or to examine empirically the validity of these claims.

Douglas (1967) and Kitsuse and Cicourel (1963), among others, focus on pressures from local government officials, attempts at concealment by the family and the lack of evidence confounding the recording of cause in suspicious deaths. Pressure requires not only an agent but an opportunity and a mechanism. While coroners and medical examiners acknowledge the subjectivity of rulings on suspicious death, they offer a complex version of how pressures from diverse sources often work at odds. Trade-offs exist between experience and caseload, for example, which influence the ability to "find" a suicide and opposing pressures from interested parties like insurance companies (who will not have to "pay-off" on a suicide) and families (who fear the stigma for themselves and the memory of their relative [see Murphy, 1979]). The process through which this occurs is through interactions in social networks where there is both a structure and a content or culture in which the decision-making process is embedded.

Thus, a network perspective holds potential to guide the specification of how, when and why "pressures" come to influence the decision-making of coroners and medical examiners. Network theory locates individuals in networks where influence, information and resources vary. These networks can be focused on a similar goal (e.g., the quick and efficient disposition of cases) or at cross-purposes (e.g., the discovery of verifiable scientific findings). And the network approach provides a clue to systematizing the ideas of social constructionists in a way that makes them subject to empirical examination. The basic notion that underlies social constructionists' criticisms about social pressures (not those about "meaning") corresponds to the same primary starting point of network theory mentioned earlier. The nature of social relations influences individuals' attitudes, beliefs and behaviors (and specifically in this case, the classification decisions made by coroners and medical examiners [see White and Boorman, 1976, p. 1442]).

Let us consider the network structure that undergirds the social process of death classification. These latent network structures exist to different degrees in different jurisdictions prior to the need to classify any particular case of suspicious death. They are latent structures that may or may not be activated during the process of investigation by medicolegal officials seeking advice or by others in the network seeking to exert social control (i.e., regulation) on the official's methods or conclusions. There are three major types of networks in which coroners and medical examiners do their work.

Organizational Influences

Our earlier work dealt primarily with legal and organizational factors. Coroners and medical examiners face the task of classifying suspicious deaths in an organizational context. Their ability to determine the "facts" of a case depends in part on resources and procedures available to them in their investigations. Because of the absence of standardized and routine organization of medico-legal offices in the U.S., a variety of systems exist with wide-ranging standards on qualifications for officials, access to laboratory facilities, sources of revenue, etc. (Farberow, et al., 1977). As a result, the discretion accorded to officials classifying suspicious deaths also varies considerably. Factors which increase the discretion of officials responsible for classifying suspicious deaths (e.g., coroner system, elected status, ability to call an inquest) or decrease their ability to uncover "proof " (e.g., no easily accessible toxicology or pathology labs, few years of experience) may result in a lower reported suicide rate. These proxy the "tools" which affect the ability of individuals to "find" the proof that a suicide occurred.

The argument to this point, however, is incomplete because it fails (1) to incorporate the social context within which coroners and medical examiners work and (2) to uncover the social processes or mechanisms through which these factors exert influence. The availability of these resources reflects both the "orientation" of the state system (e.g., the tie to political versus "scientific" views) and ties to professional norms that officials bring with them to the decision-making process. Organizational pressures that officials face derive from the actual structural possibility of the work organization to oversee and influence decision-making and to offer and enforce particular norms of death investigation and classification. These orientations and structures are not sterile, invisible forces but come from the actions and attitudes of people who work in the system and policies that are made by them. Co-workers, supervisors and staff can provide more or less guidance and are able to do so depending on the nature and frequency of contact they have with medicolegal officials. Bringing in a network perspective highlights the importance of two contextual factors in operation: the ability of the medicolegal office to exert influence (e.g., the density of the organization's network structure) and the overall content of that network regarding the classification of suspicious deaths. The operation of these two factors is interactive since network structure, in and of itself, is not predictive (White, Boorman and Breiger, 1976). These types of considerations lead to ideas about the structure and meaning of the death classification process for the suicide rate. For example, we might expect that the density of the network in the medicolegal system or the ties of a coroner or medical examiner to it may interact with average organizational predisposition or "attitude" toward suicide to influence the reported suicide rate. Further, the stronger these systems are, the less influential the coroner or medical examiner's personal attitudes will be on the death classification process.

As interactive statements, these propositions suggest that the structure and content of networks in the medicolegal system will affect both the decisions of coroners and medical examiners directly and countervailing pressures from other sources. Specifically, for example, we might expect that medicolegal offices which have dense networks and see suicides as underreported will have higher reported suicide rates.

Professional Networks of Coroners and Medical Examiners

Coroners not only operate in an organizational structure but bring with them differing professional standards of proof and differing social-psychological attitudes and perceptions about the classification process and the social meaning of suicide (e.g., as stigmatizing for the family, as problematic for insurance companies). These factors are particularly important since our earlier work suggested that there may be cross-pressures operating on officials that are built into the system. For example, while "scientific" procedures may increase the ability of a coroner or medical examiner to "find" a suicide in the case of a suspicious death, "scientifically" trained officials may also hold higher standards of proof for classifying a death as a suicide (Murphy, 1979; Warshauer and Monk, 1978). For example, the greater the officials' ties to rigorous standards of proof (e.g., degree in forensics) or direct physical evidence (e.g., suicide notes), the lower the reported suicide rate. The degree to which they are tied to formal professional organizations also provides an indication of the nature of their orientation and consultation contacts.

Community Networks

Finally, coroners and medical examiners are tied to communities and to individuals in the community as well as to professional networks. If we assume, as social constructionists have, that community pressure favors concealing suicides and that an empathy with the people in the community would predispose coroners and medical examiners to "hide" suicides, we might expect that the stronger the officials' tie to the community, the lower the reported suicide rate. For example, by having membership in community organizations or longer residence in the community, the more they may consider the larger community interest.

In addition, medicolegal offices and the officials that work in them are situated in communities which can vary in their ability to influence the processes of classifying death. Again, if we assume that the exertion of community pressure is aimed at concealing suicides, then the ability of the community to do so depends fundamentally on the network strength of the community. Following basic Durkheimian ideas and drawing from more recent network studies of communities (e.g., Fischer, 1982; Wellman, et al., 1987), we might expect that the greater the social "knittedness" of the community, the lower the reported suicide rate. If a community is socially disorganized through high rates of geographical mobility or unemployment, we might expect that little pressure could be mounted to influence the official to conceal suicides. In sum, communities which are not "strong," "integrated" or "tightly knit" are unlikely to marshal efforts or resources to see that the classification of suicides is to be avoided.

CONCLUSIONS

The purpose of this chapter has been to highlight the challenges to the sociological study of suicide that we can no longer afford to ignore. In addressing these challenges, I argue that a network framework is of fundamental utility. As an additional benefit we also are able to reconceptualize Durkheim's theoretical insights. By sketching a blueprint, we have an outline of the translation of the Durkheimian theory into a social network metaphor. At base, the Durkheimian framework remains the standard, it has characteristics that make it both elegant and powerful. It does not formulate one and only one route to suicide. Each of the four polar types represent different pathways by which individuals may find themselves pushed to the brink of social survival. The underlying assumptions are strongly social in nature, relying on the importance of interaction, social structures and the interplay between the two. The scope is broad, encompassing all arenas of social life and providing an explicit view of how society works.

Despite these strengths, the Durkheimian theory has gaps in its articulation of the mechanism underlying the workings of social structural influence and in its guidance on the valid operationalization of concepts. I have attempted to present the most important challenges that face the sociological study of suicide. These involve, first, the theoretical challenges of rethinking the general propositions into specific hypotheses tailored to a particular sociohistorical location and how interaction in social networks helps flesh out the mechanism implicit in Durkheim's theory. Second, I addressed the long-standing problem of the ecological fallacy and restated it as a theoretical issue in linking macro-structures and micro-behaviors. Finally, I outlined a way to concretize the objections of social constructionists regarding the validity of official suicide rates.

These three issues do not encompass all of the theoretical, methodological or empirical challenges that face the study of suicide—sociological or otherwise. But they are basic to moving the field forward. Remaining issues involve the integration of different disciplinary insights to provide a fuller and more nuanced picture of suicide. They span the theoretical spectrum from intrapersonal organization to global or societal organization. At the forefront stand issues of social dynamics. What is the nature of triggers to suicide? How do life-course dynamics change the nature of predispositions to suicide, of triggers, and of social network structures? How do "societies" change in general, and in relation to individual and community crises? What factors may cause them to slide up or around the societal safety net?

Perhaps some of these are issues of psychological or even biological vulnerability, but there are a number of ways in which a sociological orientation can provide guidance. We need to differentiate more clearly between crises of the individual and crises of the community. For example, cults may provide a high degree of integration to members facing *individual* crises, all other things being equal. This does not negate their power in compelling suicides in the presence of *community* crises. While Jonestown and the Rajneeshpuram seemed to provide "optimal" integration and regulation during their early years, they transformed radically during assaults from inside and out. And while both can be described as fatalistic social structures in these ultimate forms, something different occurred—either in the nature of "triggers" or crises, the meaning given them inside the community, or the power of social control agents to prevent it. Further, in the same way that we can conceptualize different levels of social network interactions for individuals, so we can begin to see the importance of different types of events which destabilize structure and the individuals in them. Drawing from the social support literature and the life-course framework, we can begin to explore how different events can take on different meanings for particular people, at different times of their lives, and perhaps when different sequences or combinations of events hit them (Clausen, 1986).

Sociologists must also acknowledge the part that temperament or predisposition plays in conditioning the resort to suicide. This may call for a more explicit role of social psychology in understanding the link between individuals, roles and larger social structures (Stryker, 1980). But perhaps this lies in the realm of the psychobiologist who would provide a conditional probability upon which social factors may wage a more limited suicidal push and pull. And we will need to confront the relationship between mental illness and suicide, dismissed long ago by Durkheim in Book I of *Suicide*, but central to recent debates about the role of depression and alcoholism in suicide. This call for integrating sociological, psychological and psychiatric approaches was issued long ago by sociologists but not pursued in any serious fashion to this point (see, for example, Giddens, 1965; Simpson, 1950).

Finally, we must confront the prescriptive thrust of Durkheim's work. In *Suicide*, Durkheim sought not the bandaging or remolding of old institutions but the creation of newer forms of organization to fill in the supportive void left in the wake of dramatic social change. Durkheim's theory required the implicit conceptualization of the nature of the new social order and an attempt to get at its core structures. Work organizations do not seem to have fulfilled their promise as the source of integration and regulation for which Durkheim hoped. But attempts at praxis necessitate a conceptualization of the essential features of this current postmodern era. To simply refer to it as postmodern defines only a negative state. The central issue lies in what this new era is, not what it is not. To the extent that we do not adjudicate between the discrepant views of this as an accelerated modern era or a new form of social organization, our ability to conceptualize the essence of relevant "societies" and the possible routes of social amelioration are premature. Some postmodernists claim that one dominant culture with social control and integration found in a single set of relations, norms and values is disappearing and being replaced by ambiguity and by multiple, connected communities resigned to and tolerant of normative dissensus. What is the basis of network formation in these communities? Like Durkheim, we need to confront and understand the nature of the new society, its ramifications for social network structure, interaction and culture and, in turn, for suicide potential.

REFERENCES

Alba, R. D. Taking stock of network analysis. *Research in the Sociology of Organizations,* 1981, 1, 39-74.

Baechler, J. *Suicides.* New York: Basic Books, 1975.

Baron, J. N., and Reiss, P. C. Same time, next year. *American Sociological Review,* 1985, 50, 347-332.

Clausen, J. A. *The Life Course.* Englewood Cliffs, NJ: Prentice-Hall, 1986.

Coleman, J. S. *The Foundations of Social Theory.* Cambridge, MA: Belknap, 1990.

Collins, R. On the microfoundations of macrosociology. *American Journal of Sociology,* 1981, 91, 1336-1355.

Collins, R. *Sociological Insight.* New York: Oxford University Press, 1982.

Coser, R. L., and Coser, L. Jonestown as a perverse utopia. *Dissent,* 1979, 26, 158-163.

Douglas, J. *The Social Meanings of Suicide.* Princeton, NJ: Princeton University Press, 1967.

Durkheim, E. *Suicide.* New York: Free Press, 1951.

Earley, P. *Prophet of Death.* New York: William Morrow, 1991.

Erikson, K. T. *Everything in Its Path.* New York: Simon & Schuster, 1976.

Etzioni, A. *The Moral Dimension.* New York: Free Press, 1988.

Farberow, N., MacKinnon, D., and Nelson, F. Suicide. *Public Health Reports,* 1977, 92, 223-232.

Fischer, C. *To Dwell Among Friends.* Chicago: University of Chicago Press, 1982.

FitzGerald, F. *Cities on a Hill.* New York: Simon & Schuster, 1986.

Furniss, N. Functionalism and Policy Studies. In D. Ashford (ed.), *History and Context in Comparative Public Policy.* Pittsburgh: University of Pittsburgh Press, 1992.

Furstenberg, F. F. Divorce and the American family. *Annual Review of Sociology,* 1990, 16, 379-403.

Gerstel, N., Reissman, C. K., and Rosenfield, S. Explaining the symptomatology of separated and divorced women and men. *Social Forces,* 1985, 64, 84-101.

Gibbs, J. *Status Integration and Suicide.* Eugene: University of Oregon Press, 1964.

Gibbs, J., and Martin, W. A problem in testing the theory of status integration. *Social Forces,* 1974, 53, 332-339.

Giddens, A. The suicide problem in French sociology. *British Journal of Sociology,* 1965, 16, 3-15.

Giddens, A. 1976. *New Rules of the Sociological Method.* London: Hutchinson, 1976.

Giddens, A. *The Constitution of Society.* Cambridge: Cambridge University Press, 1984.

Goodman, L. A. Ecological regression and behavior of individuals. *American Sociological Review,* 1953, 18, 663-664.

Goodman, L. A. Some alternatives to ecological correlation. *American Journal of Sociology,* 1959, 64, 610-625.

Granovetter, M. The Strength of Weak Ties. In R. Collins (ed.), *Sociological Theory 1983.* San Francisco: Jossey Bass, 1983.

Gustafson, J. F. *Treasure in Earthen Vessels.* New York: Harper, 1961.

Hannan, M. *Aggregation and Disaggregation in Sociology.* Lexington, MA: Lexington Books, 1971.

Hanushek, E. A., and Jackson, J. E. *Statistical Methods for Social Scientists.* New York: Academic Press, 1977.

Hanushek, E. A., Jackson, J. E., and Kain, J. F. Model specification, use of aggregate data and the ecological correlation fallacy. *Political Methodology,* 1974, 1, 87-107.

Hindess, B. *Official Statistics in Sociology.* London: Macmillan, 1973.

Johnson, B. Durkheim's one cause of suicide. *American Sociological Review,* 1965, 30, 875-886.

Johnston, J. *Econometric Methods.* New York: McGraw-Hill, 1972.

Kelley, D. M. *Why Conservative Churches are Growing.* New York: Harper & Row, 1972.

Kitsuse, J., and Cicourel, A. A note on the uses of official statistics. *Social Problems,* 1963, 11, 131-139.

Kornblum, R., and Fisher, R. A Compendium of State Medico-Legal Investigative Systems. Unpublished manuscript: Maryland Medical-Legal Foundation, 1972.

Kowalski, G. S., Faupel, C. E., and Starr, P. D. Urbanism and suicide. *Social Forces,* 1987, 66, 85-101.

Laumann, E. O., and Knoke, D. 1987. *The Organizational State.* Madison: University of Wisconsin Press, 1987.

Lester, D. *Why People Kill Themselves.* Springfield, IL: Charles C Thomas, 1972.

Masaryk, T. *Suicide and the Meaning of Civilization.* Chicago: University of Chicago Press, 1970 (first published 1881).

Mills, C. W. *The Sociological Imagination.* New York: Oxford University Press, 1959.

Murphy, G. K. The 'undetermined' ruling. *Journal of Forensic Sciences,* 1979, 24, 483-491.

Myers, J. K., Lindenthal, J. J., and Pepper, M. P. Life events, social integration and psychiatric symptomatology. *Journal of Health and Social Behavior,* 1975, 16, 421-427.

Ostrom, E. Microconstitutional change in multiconstitutional political systems. *Rationality and Society,* 1989, 1, 11-49.

Perrow, C. *Complex Organizations.* Glenview, IL: Scott, Foresman, 1972.

Pescosolido, B. A. Migration, medical care preference and the lay referral system. *American Sociological Review,* 1986, 51, 523-540.

Pescosolido, B. A. The social context of religious integration and suicide. *Sociological Quarterly,* 1990, 31, 337-357.

Pescosolido, B. A. Beyond rational choice. *American Journal of Sociology,* 1992, 97, 1096-1138.

Pescosolido, B. A., and Georgianna, S. Durkheim, suicide and religion. *American Sociological Review,* 1989, 54, 33-48.

Pescosolido, B. A., and Mendelsohn, R. Social causation or social construction of suicide? *American Sociological Review,* 1986, 51, 80-100.

Pescosolido, B. A., and Wright, E. R. Suicide and the role of the family over the life course. *Family Perspectives,* 1990, 24, 41-60.

Pope, W., and Danigelis, N. Sociology's 'one law.' *Social Forces,* 1981, 60, 495-516.

Quinley, H. E. *The Prophetic Clergy.* New York: Harper & Row, 1974.

Ragin, C. C. *The Comparative Method.* Berkeley: University of California Press, 1987.

Reiss, A. J. *The Police and the Public.* New Haven, CT: Yale University Press, 1971.

Robinson, W. S. Ecological correlation and the behavior of individuals. *American Sociological Review,* 1950, 15, 351-357.

Roof, W. C., and McKinney, W. *American Mainline Religion.* New Brunswick, NJ: Rutgers University Press, 1987.

Simmel, G. *Conflict and the Web of Group Affiliations.* New York: Free Press, 1955.

Simpson, G. Methodological problems in determining the aetiology of suicide. *American Sociological Review*, 1950, 15, 658-663.

Simpson, G. Editor's Introduction. In E. Durkheim, *Suicide*. New York: Free Press, 1951.

Smelser, N., and Warner, R. S. *Sociological Theory*. Morristown, NJ: General Learning Press, 1976.

Spencer, H. *The Evolution of Society*. Chicago: University of Chicago Press, 1967 (first published 1881).

Stack, S. Suicide. *Deviant Behavior*, 1982, 4, 41-66.

Stark, R., and Glock, C. Y. *American Piety*. Berkeley: University of California Press, 1968.

Sumner, W. G. *The Challenge of Facts and Other Essays*. New Haven, CT: Yale University Press, 1914.

Tilly, C. *Big Structures, Large Processes, Huge Comparisons*. New York: Russell Sage Foundation, 1984.

Tilly, C. Prisoners of the state. Working Paper 129. The Working Paper Series, Center for the Study of Social Change. New School for Social Research, New York, 1991.

Umberson, D. Family status and health behavior. *Journal of Health and Social Behavior*, 1987, 28, 306-315.

Umberson, D., and Greer, M. Social relationships and health behavior. Paper presented at the Annual Meetings of the American Sociological Association, Washington, DC, 1990.

Warshauer, M. E., and Monk, M. Problems in suicide statistics for whites and blacks. *American Journal of Public Health*, 1978, 68, 383-388.

Webb, S. *Fabian Essays*. London: Swann Sonnenschein, 1889.

Wellman, B. The community question. *American Journal of Sociology*, 1979, 84, 1201-1231.

Wellman, B. From Social Support to Social Network. In I. G. Sarason and B. R. Sarason (eds.), *Social Support*. Boston: Martinus Nijhoff, 1985.

White, H., Boorman, S. A., and Breiger, R. Social structure from multiple networks I: blockmodels of roles and positions. *American Journal of Sociology*, 1976, 81, 730-780.

White, H., and Boorman, S. A. Social structure from multiple networks II: role structures. *American Journal of Sociology*, 1976, 81, 1324-1346.

Zilboorg, G. Suicide among civilized and primitive races. *American Journal of Psychiatry*, 1936, 92, 1347-1369.

13

Durkheim's Suicide Theory and Its Applicability to Contemporary American Indians and Alaska Natives

Philip A. May, PhD and Nancy Westlake Van Winkle, PhD

We don't know if Durkheim ever met an American Indian or Alaska Native; neither do we know if he had ever been among a North American tribal group. But we do know that such experience would have been interesting for him as a social scientist. It certainly has been for us over the past several decades. We are sure, however, that the theoretical foundations which Durkheim put forth would have eventually allowed him to understand a great deal of the behavior which he would have observed among Indians. The following will be an elaboration of this theme.

Durkheim's analysis of the importance of social integration to suicide applies quite explicitly to American Indian groups. The fit between Durkheim's theories and the overall phenomenon of suicide among American Indians is quite good. Examples from tribe to tribe have provided evidence of the broad applicability and the timeless nature of Durkheim's work.

THE MAJOR THEORY

"Suicide varies inversely with the degree of integration of the social groups of which the individual forms a part" (Durkheim, 1951, p. 209). This summary statement provides the theoretical base for analyzing suicide patterns and a number of other self-destructive behaviors among American Indians. As a concise axiom it provides an excellent framework for the analysis of Indian tribal and community structures. The genesis of a variety of types of deviant behavior, such as suicide, homicide, alcohol abuse, and child abuse and neglect can be understood by using Durkheim's theory. Suicide alone, however, will be the major focus of this chapter.

In Europe, Durkheim's observations and data led him to the conclusion that suicide varied in social groups by religion,[1] marital status, and political society (Durkheim, 1951, p. 208). This is also the case among American Indian tribes. Variance in suicide rates in particular, and other types of deviance as well, is based on these same variables. Tribes with particular characteristics and patterns of social, political, religious, and familial organization will generally have high rates of suicide, and those with the opposite structural and integrative characteristics will have lower rates of suicide. The independent variables identified by Durkheim are indeed quite universal, and they do influence American Indian communities even though the actual cultural content of these communities is very different from that of Europe in Durkheim's time. Cutting through ethnocentric values and particular cultural traits to analyze basic social structures allows for useful and productive research and a general understanding.

The level of social integration, Durkheim's most broadly encompassing independent variable, is a key diagnostic tool in any society or community. This is quite true among American Indians. There are over 300 federally recognized tribes today and over 500 Indian communities and Alaska Native villages which have independent political and legal status (United States Census, 1991). Furthermore, there is tremendous diversity among American Indian tribes and communities. The specific cultures and lifeways of various groups of Indians and Alaska Natives are highly diverse. The Cherokee of the Southeast woodlands were, and still are, vastly different from the Lakota (Sioux), Cheyenne, Blackfeet, Shoshone, and Arapaho of the Plains. Their language, material culture, and various values and beliefs were very different in the past, and differences persist today. Similarly, the Pueblo, Navajo, and Apache, who all live in the Southwestern United States, are very different from one another in their history, culture, language, lifeways, and even modal personalities and individual characteristics. The lifeways of various groups or bands of Alaska Natives also run the gamut of diversity.

In spite of these differences in culture and content, each tribal and native society contains certain basic elements of social structure which can be identified and analyzed in a consistent and insightful manner. Each has a level of social integration which can be the cornerstone of analysis using social science methods and theories pioneered by Durkheim to understand patterns of behavior and to implement solutions for problems.

Many anthropologists, such as Ruth Benedict (1934), recognized this diversity of lifeways. Yet she also analyzed some of the common and most influential elements of life such as styles of childbearing, conflict resolution, social control, and the integrative importance of custom. More generally, several generations of anthropologists were engaged in the noble enterprise of describing the range of diversity and uniqueness of individual American Indian cultures and aggregating them by common social and cultural types (Josephy, 1968; Hodge, 1981; Spencer and Jennings, 1977).

The focus on the uniqueness of each tribal culture can only go so far in promoting the type of understanding of social behavior which is most useful for proposing practical and transferable solutions in areas such as public health and the prevention of behavioral health problems. The study and understanding of suicide among Indians has had to go beyond the unique patterns among each tribe as they exist in isolation. The common social elements among the different tribal and community groups must be analyzed and utilized for a more general and applied understanding. Durkheim's work, *Suicide,* provides an excellent framework for understanding and a vehicle for intervention and solutions. By beginning with the overall statement with which this section began, that suicide varies inversely with social integration, one can work efficiently and successfully to unravel and analyze the magnitude and patterns of suicide in a tribal community. Such an understanding also applies to many of the personal paths to suicide which are traversed by individual Indians of these groups.

SOCIAL INTEGRATION, SUICIDE AND INDIANS

Traditional Integration

Among American Indian tribes there is a variety of different levels of social integration which ranges from extremely high (tight) to extremely low (loose). Over the years anthropologists have provided the observations, data, and categories necessary for classifying different American Indian tribes into high, medium, and low levels of traditional social integration (Spencer and Jennings, 1977; Hodge, 1981). This facilitates general understanding regarding the pattern of suicide.

In the last three decades of deviance research among Indians, the concept of integration has been utilized by a number of researchers. The most influential proponents have been Jerrold Levy, Steven Kunitz, and their colleagues (see for example Levy, 1965; Levy, et al., 1969; Levy and Kunitz, 1971; Levy and Kunitz, 1974). In these works, social integration refers to the processes which cement a collection of individuals into a large social group. It is also used to refer to the individual's symbolic and structural attachment to larger groups such as the family, religious, and political groups, and also to the overall tribe, ethnic group, state, or nation. This concept is directly from Durkheim, Weber and the early European sociologists (Gould and Kolb, 1964, pp. 656-657, 661-662).

In *low-integration* societies the individual is a member of fewer permanent groups and, in particular, fewer large groups. In such tribal societies the main social units are less likely to place strong and clear mandates of conformity (prescriptions and proscriptions or integration and control) on the individual. The individual has more freedom to define his or her own behavior. Norms are less deterministic. Formal social organization is usually limited to the family or band level in most low-integration tribes, and higher level institutions are weak or nonexistent in their influence and control.

In *high-integration* societies the opposite is true. The individual is expected to conform to the more formal and relatively clear mandates of the entire political organization of the community. In most or all of the social groups to which the individual belongs (e.g., family, religious, and community groups), the contribution to the overall community (tribal) stability is relatively explicit. Norms and mores permeate all parts of society, from dress to gender and occupational roles.

High- and low-integration societies are, essentially, ideal types. That is, Durkheim's work indicates that no society is completely one type or the other. The difference in contemporary social groups is also a matter of degree. For example, Durkheim used the Catholic Church with its hierarchical structure and extensive formal rules and procedures as an example of a high-integration group. Protestant denominations of Europe were used as an example of a lower-integration group. Durkheim obviously set the tone of our research with his general theory of social integration, and we apply it to tribal groups. Different tribal groups approach the ideal types to a degree, and the relative degree of integration becomes a useful independent variable.

In our contemporary Indian studies of suicide, Plains culture tribes of Montana, North and South Dakota, Nebraska, Wyoming, New Mexico, and western Oklahoma, among others, represent low-integration societies. Band-level social structure was generally the most binding form of social control within these low-integration societies. A number of medium-integration groups also exist such as the Navajo, Pima, Tohono O'odam (Papago) of the Southwest. In the medium-integration tribes band level organization is augmented by broader levels of control at the community level (e.g., clan and communal groups organized around larger, rather permanent group-supporting functions). The Pueblo tribes of New Mexico and Arizona represent high-integration societies.

Modernization and Acculturation

In studies of American Indian suicide and deviance, cultural types and tribes can be classified by the *traditional* level of social integration. A rough idea of the level of suicide and other deviance can then be anticipated for the tribe. Traditional in this case refers to the integration characteristics present prior to major and relatively constant contact with peoples from Europe—Hispanic, English, or French society.

But there is another influential and confounding factor. With American Indian tribes social change in the form of modernization has led to variations in the social integration of particular reservations. Some American Indian communities have, and are currently undergoing, rapid change from the effects of modern, western mainstream cultural influences. At the same time, other communities, because of geographic and social isolation (some of it self-im-posed traditionalism), have not changed as rapidly or as radically. Among those tribes where change has been substantial, traditional social control and social integration have generally been weakened.

In the earlier years of contemporary suicide and deviance literature on Indians (see Bynum, 1972; Dizmang, 1967; Minnis, 1963; Resnick and Dizmang, 1971), most articles talked only of social disorganization among Indian cultures as the determining factor of suicide and deviance levels. But later works, such as those by Levy and Kunitz cited above, emphasized the persistence of traditional cultural influences and patterns as well. Later in our own works (May, 1987, 1989a; May and Van Winkle, 1993; Van Winkle and May, 1986, 1993) the dual influences of both traditional culture and modern change and acculturation have been demonstrated and emphasized.

The current understanding of these integrational influences can be capsul-ized as follows. Tribes that have had high traditional social integration and have undergone little disorganization from modernization,[2] have been char-acterized as having very low rates of suicide. On the other hand, tribal communities which had historically high integration and which are experienc-ing rapid change, have rates which are substantially elevated. The same can be said within the other two categories of medium and high traditional integra-tion. An elevation in suicide rates is generally caused by social change and modernization. This elevation can be substantial enough to cause an overlap or overtaking of suicide rates from one category of integration to the next. For example, a high-integration tribe's suicide rate can rise beyond that of a medium-integration tribe when undergoing rapid change.

Some illustrative data from our Southwestern studies are in order. As Table 1 indicates, the rate of suicide between cultural groups in New Mexico does not vary substantially from one group to the next. The low-integration tribes, the Apaches (Southwestern Plains culture), have the highest average suicide rates and the greatest fluctuation over time.[3] In the earlier years of data the pattern of suicide was exactly as Durkheim's work would have predicted. At that time traditional tribal culture was the predominant influence on the rates. In the 3-year-average rates for 1958-59, the low-integration tribal culture (Apache) had the highest suicide death rate. The highest-integration culture (the Pueblo) had the lowest rate, and the medium-integration culture (the Navajo) was intermediate in rate. Thus, the inverse relationship holds exactly in these years as traditional integration is the less affected by modernization.

Later, there are major exceptions, however. In more recent years, the high-integration culture (the Pueblo tribes) had higher suicide rates than the Navajo (medium integration). This deviation in the overall Pueblo rate from the generalized expectation is due to the rather rapid change in integration among a number of the Pueblo tribes which was brought about by the acculturation of individuals and groups and the pressures of modernization.[4] The forces of modernization and acculturation have been influential on

Table 1.

Age-Adjusted[1] Suicide Rates (per 100,000) for the Apache, Navajo and Pueblo Indians in New Mexico for 1957-1968, 1969-1979 and 1980-1987

Cultural Group (level of integration)	Age-Adjusted Rates		
	1957-1968	*1969-1979*	*1980-1987*
Apache (low)	41.3	59.8	48.8
Navajo (medium)	10.2	20.4	18.2
Pueblo (high)	24.0	44.8	32.0
U.S.	12.1[2]	12.2[3]	11.6[4]

[1] Age-adjusted rates based on U.S. 1940 standard population.
[2] Age-adjusted rate for 1963.
[3] Age-adjusted rate for 1974.
[4] Age-adjusted rate for 1984.

American Indian tribes in the Southwest since the late 1950s, but more so on some than others (Van Winkle and May, 1986). The Southwestern data, as illustrated below, show the importance of using both traditional modes of integration and integration changes brought about by acculturation as they affect Indian groups.

Moving to Table 2, the suicide rates of various tribal groups and communities *within* cultural types also show variation. Table 2 illustrates the variation in suicide rates for the eight largest Pueblo tribes. This variation is introduced by the other aspect of social integration mentioned above, change resulting from modernization and acculturation. Pueblos with the highest suicide rates tend to be those who have undergone high levels of change from modernization and acculturation, who are closest to urban areas, and/or who have been less able to shield, buffer, filter, counter, or otherwise stabilize their culture from the introduction of modern, western culture. Within both the Pueblo tribes and the various Navajo communities there is variation in suicide and deviance rates. Generally implicated in the higher rates are greater levels of social change and recent acculturation (Van Winkle and May, 1986, 1993). Among the Apaches, social change and acculturation are very influential as well, but the wide fluctuations in rates is less easily and clearly related to the social integration forces because of their much smaller population size.

Therefore, a single statement that suicide varies inversely with the degree of *traditional tribal social integration* does not hold true in detailed, longitudinal comparisons in the Southwest. With American Indians the correct statement is that *suicide varies inversely with the degree of integration in a tribal group as influenced by both traditional cultural practices and by acculturation and change resulting from modernization*. Thus, the translation of Durkheim's

Table 2.

Crude Suicide Rates (per 100,000) and Level of Acculturation for Pueblo Tribes in New Mexico with Populations over 1000 for 1954-1962, 1957-1965, 1966-1972, 1973-1979, 1980-1987, and 1957-1987

Tribe	1954- 1962[1]	1957- 1965[3]	1966- 1972[3]	1973- 1979[3]	1980- 1987[4]	1957- 1987[4]	Overall Level of Acculturation[2]
Laguna	16.9	27.7	60.5	55.7	56.2	48.6	Acculturated
Isleta	22.2	24.0	57.6	44.8	32.7	38.4	Acculturated
Taos	16.7	19.0	37.8	52.0	10.2	29.0	Transitional
Zuni	2.8	5.6	30.3	53.7	38.4	33.7	Transitional
San Felipe	0.0	0.0	48.1	19.3	12.5	18.1	Traditional
Acoma	5.0	5.5	6.9	33.3	29.2	19.7	Traditional
Jemez	8.3	18.5	11.7	9.2	22.6	16.1	Traditional
Santo Domingo	6.5	0.0	0.0	6.7	10.1	4.9	Traditional

[1] Rates taken from Levy (1965).
[2] Classification originally from Levy; minor adaptations from Van Winkle and May (1993).
[3] Rates originally published in Van Winkle and May (1986).
[4] Rates also found in Van Winkle and May (1993).

ideas to American Indians may have been simplified by both the scholars who have written only of social disorganization and those who have emphasized the singular effect of the traditional culture.

Other Indian Studies with Suicide Rates

The fallout or adverse effect of rapid social change and acculturation on a number of individuals has been documented in other native communities elsewhere in North America. A variety of conditions, from alcohol abuse to all forms of violence, are increased in rate by acculturation in its earliest stages. Many times, all of these social pathologies are manifested simultaneously in one community because of major disruptions and/or dislocations (Shkilnyk, 1985), but also because of more gradual and creeping changes (Braroe, 1973; Bachman, 1992). But the bulk of the literature which implicates rapid social change and acculturation as problematic among Indians and Alaska Natives uses suicide as the dependent variable.

Table 3 presents a summary of a number of North American suicide studies among Indians. These works provide further evidence of the importance of social integration. In the table cultural group/tribal studies are aggregated by the level of traditional social integration of the group studied—low, medium, or high. Therefore, the table only considers one of the two elements of integration mentioned before. For this reason, and possibly others, there is variation within each grouping. For example, the range in rates among the low-integration tribes is from 13 to 267 per 100,000. Similarly, high-integration group rates range from 0 to 74.

The average (mean) suicide rates for the three groupings form a basis for further interpretation. The mean (x) rates for low-, medium-, and high-integration groups produce the exact sequence that Durkheim would have predicted. The rates of suicide per 100,000 are inverse to the level of integration: low social integration = 56.9, medium social integration 31.9 (41.5 excluding the Navajo),[5] and high social integration = 28.3. Furthermore, the standard deviations are higher in the low-integration tribal study results which is also consistent with Durkheim's theories. Lower integration societies allow more variation in human behavior in general and suicide in particular.

A similar pattern emerges when the median suicide rates are compared across tribes. The inverse relationship still holds for suicide and level of integration, but the magnitude of difference between levels is less: high-integration tribes = 18.5, medium = 30.0, and low-integration = 45.0.

A caution in over-interpreting this summary of other studies is necessary. Because these studies were undertaken at different times, there are unaccounted variations in social conditions covered, and various research methods were employed over time. This may be an alternate explanation of the variation in rates. Furthermore, academic studies of suicide, both published and unpublished, are seldom undertaken and pursued to completion in groups which

Table 3.

Suicide Rates of Various Indian Tribes and Alaska Natives
from Selected Studies, 1950s-1980s

Geographic or Cultural Type (Tribe/Group)	Level of Traditional Integration	(Time)	Rate (per 100,000)	Source
1. Plains (Shoshone - Arapaho)	Low	1980s	50	Bechtold, 1988
2. Yukon Indians (all)	Low	1959-64	38	Butler, 1965
3. Basin-Plateau (Shoshone)	Low	1972-76	90 (epidemic year=238)	Berman, 1979
4. Alaska Natives (all)	Low	1970	29	Blackwood,1978
5. Plains (Sioux)	Low	1981-83	66	Claymore, 1988
6. Plateau (Shosone-Bannock)	Low	1963-69	98	Dizmang et al., 1974
7. Alaska Natives (all)	Low	1978-85	1978-32; 1979-36; 1980-45; 1981-45; 1982-37; 1983-43; 1984-35; 1985-69	Forbes & Van der Hyde, 1988
8. Manitoba Indians (all)	Low to Medium	1973-82	40	Garro, 1988
9. Alaska Natives (all)	Low	1961-65 1966-70	13 25	Kraus, 1974
10. S.W. Plains (Apache)	Low	1965-67	20	Levy & Kunitz, 1969
11. Plains (Sioux)	Low	1971-73	73	May, 1973
12. Northern Manitoba Indians (all)	Low to Medium	1981-84	77	Ross & Davis, 1986
13. Canadian Natives (Indian and Inuit)	Low to Medium	1977	41	Seyer, 1979
14. Plains-Woodlands (Ojibway)	Low	1975-82	62	Spaulding, 1985-86
15. Plains (Shoshone-Arapaho)	Low	1985	230 (epidemic period)	Tower, 1989
16. Woodlands (Ojibway)	Low	1971-74 1975	23 267 (epidemic year)	Fox et al., 1984

Table 3. cond.

Geographic or Cultural Type (Tribe/Group)	Level of Traditional Integration	(Time)	Rate (per 100,000)	Source
1. Desert Culture (Papago)	Medium	1969-71	30	Conrad & Kahn, 1974
2. Northwest Coast & & Plateau (various tribes)	Medium	1968	39	Cutler & Morrison, 1971
3. Navajo	Medium	1954-63	8	Levy, 1965
4. Desert Culture (Anonymous)	Medium	1968-70	58	Miller, 1979
5. Northwest Coast & Plateau (various tribes)	Medium	1968-77	30	Nat'l. Native Alcohol Abuse Program, n.d.
6. Northwest Coast	Medium	1969	28	Shore, 1972

Annual average rate = 31.9 (SD = 19.2, n=35) median = 30.0 excluding Navajo mean=41.3 (SD =13.9, n = 25), medium =30.0

Pueblo (Various)	High	1960-62	45	Biernoff, 1969
		1963-65	46	
		1966-68	74	
Woodlands	High	1972-73	12 (Cherokee)	Humphrey & Kupferer, 1982
			8 (Lumbee)	
(Lumbee & Cherokee)	High	1974-76	31 (Cherokee)	
			10 (Lumbee)	
Pueblo (Hopi)	High	1956-65	12	Levy & Kunitz, 1987
		1961-70	28	
		1966-75	29	
		1971-79	39	
Woodlands	High	1982-82		
(Cherokee)		1981-82	0	Thurman et al., 1985

Annual average rate = 28.3 (SD = 16.3, n = 60), median = 28.5

have low rates. Therefore, there are in all probability more studies on the low-integration/high-rate groups than among the others. Lastly, many of the studies in Table 3 are isolated tribal studies. Even compiled in aggregate form as they are here, or in a complete bibliography (May, 1990), they may not be as representative of the actual or true prevalence as are studies of all tribes of different cultures in a geographic region. They represent a selective and possibly biased view of time prevalence. Regional studies of a number of tribes using the same methodologies are more desirable (e.g., Seyer, 1979; Shore, 1972; Van Winkle and May, 1986). Nevertheless, with the above caveats, this review of other studies provides some general and interesting validation of Durkheim's theory of social integration and suicide, and a corroboration of Indian suicide patterns detailed in the Southwestern studies.

OTHER DURKHEIMIAN ISSUES IN SUICIDE AMONG INDIANS

Marriage and Age

In addition to the utility of Durkheim's major thesis for describing the variation of suicide rates of tribal groups, other aspects of his synthesis apply to American Indians. Durkheim suggested that "married persons of both sexes enjoy a coefficient of preservation in comparison with unmarried persons" (Durkheim, 1951, p. 179). As seen in Table 4, the majority of the decedents from the three cultural groups in New Mexico were not married. The Navajo and Pueblo data suggest that being married may be more protective in recent times than was true in the past—or the data might suggest that marriage is occurring later or is less common. But there is a substantial difference between United States and New Mexico Indian patterns in this regard, which is partially evident in Table 4. The vast majority of New Mexico Indian suicide victims in the 1980s has never been married (63 to 71 percent); only 37 to 29 percent have been married. In the general United States population, over twice as many people have been married (72 percent). Those who have been divorced (16.2 percent), separated (9.2 percent), or widowed are a substantial segment of the ever married United States population, far greater than the Indian-only data.

Age and Suicide

Age is an important factor in both Indian suicide and in shaping marital statistics of Indian suicide victims. In Table 4 the average age of suicide is presented. The young age at suicidal death among New Mexico's Indians is evidenced by a median of 24 to 26.5 years compared with 41.6 years for the United States. This is a very typical feature of Indian suicide in virtually all studies (May, 1990). Indians and Alaska Natives commit suicide at a much younger age. Therefore, the significance of youthful suicide is twofold. First,

Table 4.

Marital Status and Age at Suicidal Death for the Apache, Navajo & Pueblo Indians in New Mexico for 1957-1968, 1969-1979 & 1980-1987

	1957-1968	*1969-1979*	*1980-1987*
APACHE			
Married	36.4	11.8	37.5
Not Married	63.6	88.2	62.5
Mean Age at Death	26.0	23.8	26.0
Median Age at Death	23.0	20.0	25.0
NAVAJO			
Married	63.6	44.6	33.3
Not Married	36.4	55.4	66.7
Mean Age at Death	30.6	31.4	30.1
Median Age at Death	26.0	29.0	26.5
PUEBLO			
Married	50.0	32.6	28.8
Not Married	50.0	67.4	71.2
Mean Age at Death	30.5	27.4	26.0
Median Age at Death	28.0	24.0	24.0
U.S. GENERAL POPULATION[1]			
Ever Married	-[2]	-	71.7
Not Married	-	-	28.3
(Divorced)	-	-	(16.2)
(Widowed)	-	-	(9.2)
Mean Age at Death	-	-	41.4
Median Age at Death	-	-	41.6

[1] Source: National Center for Health Statistics. *Vital Statistics of the U.S., 1983, Vol. II, Mortality, Part A*. Washington, DC: U.S. Government Printing Office.
[2] Data not available.

some of the lack of marriage in Indian suicide victims is explained by their young age at suicide. Many have not yet reached an age where the probability of marriage (or divorce, separation, or widowhood) is great. Second, the late teens and early twenties is a period of high stress and low attachment to stable, adult groups (either traditional tribal or modern western) which promote high integration to social systems. The choices of future roles and the lack of integrative forces to carry an individual to social stability and success in a normatively approved, secure, and supportive role present special challenges for youth in most societies today. But they appear to be even greater stressors for young American Indians (May, 1987; Manson, et al., 1988; Lin, 1987; Levy and Kunitz, 1987; LaFromboise and Bigfoot, 1988).

The elevated suicide rates of Indians aged 10 to 29 are consistently higher than those of the general population of the United States. For example, in New Mexico during the period 1957 to 1979 Indian suicide rates were 5.4 times higher than U.S. rates in ages 10 to 29 years, and 3.6 times higher for the same age cohorts in from 1980 to 1987 (Van Winkle and May, 1986; May and Van Winkle, 1993). When considering the specific rates for those under 30 years by 5-year age cohorts, Indian rates are higher in all cohorts. Therefore, the difficulty of acculturation to adult modern or traditional society is probably exacerbated by minority status. One might hypothesize that the marginal level of social integration among youth is probably amplified by the minority status of Indian youth and the challenge of two different sociocultural traditions (McFee, 1968; Bushnell, 1968). This, then, may also be an example or extension of social factors mentioned by Durkheim.

We do not care to or have space to venture into the subtypes of suicide which Durkheim described. But one aside should be noted here in the form of a question. Might it also be said that Indian youth are more likely to experience relatively higher rates of suicide due to fatalism or anomie than other youth groups in America (Breed, 1970; and Davenport and Davenport, 1987)?

Gender and Suicide

Durkheim does not directly address gender or sex except in relation to marital status. He states that marriage is less protective of suicide risk for women. In our American Indian suicide studies, more males who committed suicide were married than females. On face value alone this seems contradictory to Durkheim's work, but it is not. Roles in society are based on gender to a very great degree. Social role is a major influence on suicide among most American Indian tribes.

American Indian suicide is predominantly a male phenomenon. Among all three cultural groups of Indians in New Mexico, the male-to-female ratio is much higher than in the United States general population.

This high rate of male dominance of completed suicide[6] has also been found in virtually all other tribal studies (Butler, 1965; Havighurst, 1972; Garro, 1988; Forbes and Van Der Hyde, 1988; Trott, et al., 1981). Therein lies the relevance to Durkheim's work. The explanatory theme generally put forth in the literature cites an erosion in male roles in traditional tribal culture (Dizmang, 1967; Wills, 1969; Barter and Weist, 1973; Travis, 1984). Indian males are viewed as being less well integrated into overall United States society than Indian women whose roles have changed less in recent decades. The warrior, farmer, hunter, and protector role of the male is no longer as viable in traditional or modern Indian societies, while the childbearer and home-maker role of the female has changed less. Further, Indian females are more likely than males to enter the modern wage work labor system in education, clerical, administrative, social service, and other service sector jobs, jobs which are quite dominant on and around most Indian reservations in the West (Kunitz, 1977; Travis, 1984). Thus, the changing male role and its minimally integrating properties may well predispose a higher number of Indian males to suicide, particularly at a young age when adjustments are being made to life, occupation, and adult male identity.

Methods for Suicide

Durkheim said that "each people has its favorite sort of death" (Durkheim, 1951, p. 290). American Indians in the Southwest tend to use more violent means than others in the United States. Hanging and firearms combined to account for 86 to 100 percent of all Indian deaths compared to 65 to 74 percent in the general United States population.

Furthermore, studies of other forms of mortality indicate that additional means of violent death (parasuicide) are of high prevalence among most tribal groups. Deaths from motor vehicle crashes, homicide, and the overuse of alcohol (both chronic, and most particularly, acute) are quite high (May, 1989a, 1989b). For example, among one tribe, the Navajo, the age-adjusted death rates from motor vehicle crashes, other external injuries, alcoholism (cirrhosis of the liver, alcohol dependence syndrome, and alcoholic psychosis), and homicide were 7.1, 3.4, 21.3 and 2.3 times higher in 1975-77 (Broudy and May, 1983). They have also remained relatively high through the 1980s (Howard, 1990). These patterns are common, and in some cases even higher, among other Indian groups as well (Office of Technology Assessment, 1986).

Methods of suicide among various tribes change with suggestibility, imitation, and fad as Durkheim suggested. On many reservations suicides cluster by time (Ward and Fox, 1977; Fox, et al., 1984; Bechtold, 1988; Tower, 1989) and by method. For example, it is not uncommon for epidemics to occur in a particular season or year as illustrated by several rates in Table 3. Furthermore, methods change by fad. Suicide by hanging when in jail has been popular at various times among Plateau and Plains Indian tribes such as the Shoshone (Dizmang, et al., 1974) and the Sioux (May, 1973). Suicide by rifle shot has been the most common method in the Southwestern tribes over most years (Shuck, et al., 1980; Van Winkle and May, 1986; May and Van Winkle, 1993), although recent trends indicate a substantial increase in suicides by hanging. Popular media (as in Phillips, 1974) and international trends can also influence method choices among Indians as they do other ethnic groups. During the Vietnam War there were a number of reports of suicide by self-immolation on Indian reservations. These were very suggestive of the pattern practiced by Buddhist monks in Southeast Asia frequently portrayed in the media at that time.

Suicide and Homicide

In some American Indian groups, suicide and homicide coexist, a fact which would not surprise Durkheim (1951, pp. 354-360). Some low-integration tribes, such as Plains culture tribes, have consistently high rates of both suicide and homicide. Furthermore, homicide and other violent deaths might also be viewed by Durkheim as expressions of social forces similar to suicide. Durkheim made a case for the common etiology of violence, as have many scholars since (Henry and Short, 1954, 1957; Tabachnick, 1973; Stull, 1973, 1977).

Social Integration, the Family and Suicide

The major translator of social integration to the individual is the family. Durkheim called this concept the family society or conjugal society. He specifically referred to disruption in the family as "domestic anomie" (Durkheim, 1951, pp. 259-276). Disruptions in the social ties through death, divorce, family density (very high birth rates), and other events do not reflect tranquility in marriage.

In addition to the marital status and age influences mentioned previously, a number of Indian studies have implicated the quality of family integration as a factor in suicide. Dizmang and his co-workers (1974), in a controlled study of Shoshone-Bannock adolescent suicides, found three key family problems to be explanatory of suicidal behavior. Families which produced suicidal youth were characterized by more desertion and divorce, the switching of children from one caretaker to the next for long periods of time, and high arrest rates of the primary caretakers. Berlin's (1985, 1986, 1987) writings corroborate the above findings as key etiological variables in suicide. So do the case-control studies of Fox and Ward (1977; Ward and Fox, 1977) among the Ottawa in Ontario, Canada. Furthermore, lack of family integration (familial disruption) has also been linked to child abuse and neglect among Southwestern Indians (Lujan, et al., 1989; DeBruyn, et al., 1992). Much higher rates of violent death, alcohol abuse, and suicide were found in several generations of Indian females who had abused and neglected their children.

Therefore, family disruption as a symptom of poor social integration is a key factor in suicide and other problems among Indians. Durkheim's analysis pointed the way in this area as well.

DISCUSSION

Durkheim's seminal work on suicide has been invaluable in our work among American Indians. This is particularly true of the guiding theory of social integration. How persons, whether Indian or non-Indian, relate to their own social groups is vitally important in all cultures. Furthermore, in behavioral science research, determining the social integration levels of a community or tribe will allow one to roughly estimate the level of suicide (and to some degree parasuicidal behaviors) which one can expect in a community. Two personal experiences of the senior author (P.M.) can illustrate the utility of this approach.

The Suicide of Joe Smith

Years ago when I was early in my career and employed as a commissioned officer in the United States Public Health Service, I was sent to a small, predominantly non-Indian town in the plains of western Nebraska which bordered a large Lakota (also referred to as Sioux) reservation in South Dakota. I was assigned to investigate the recent suicides of several Lakota individuals in the local jail each of which occurred independently over a period of a year. Collecting data on the age, sex, occupation, family status, religion, and statistical variables of the victims, and examining the physical layout and conditions of the jail consumed most of the morning. In the afternoon, while I was completing the data collection and some aggregate information at a desk in the jail office, the non-Indian sheriff approached me in a quizzical manner. He said to me: "I can understand why some of these Indians would kill themselves, for they have very little to live for. However, I can't understand why Joe Smith [fictitious name of local Caucasian] who lived here in town killed himself last week." I then proceeded to have an enlightening conversation with the sheriff, a conversation which proved to be both insightful and entertaining for both of us. I proceeded to ask a whole series of questions, but disguised them as statements about the social situation and social integration of Joe Smith. In other words, I used the statements as vehicles for questioning the sheriff.

I said, "I think that Joe was in trouble financially, for he had recently lost his job."

The sheriff said, "Yes."

"Joe recently got separated or divorced from his wife, didn't he?"

The sheriff said, "Yes."

"Joe was a member of [a Protestant church that I had seen upon entering town], yet he didn't go to church too regularly."

The sheriff said, "You are right."

Continuing on I made other probability statements, and in doing so I asked a whole series of specific questions about Joe's commitment to his occupation, his drinking, children, club affiliations, etc. I even guessed at Joe's age being 44 and only missed it by a year or two. The sheriff was amazed.

Finally after this conversation had gone on for quite a while the sheriff asked me, "You knew Joe, didn't you?" (At that time I lived and worked in a South Dakota town less than 100 miles away.) "You are putting me on," he said.

"No," I explained very humbly, "I just know of hundreds of Joes from the literature."

I then went on to explain the concept of social integration and how it affects virtually every social status and behavior that were the objects of my statements or questions. I also told him about several specific studies which augmented Durkheim's theories in ways that further helped me guess at Joe's presuicidal social situation.

That was in 1971. It was my first major experience that truly convinced me of the utility of Durkheim's theories, particularly as enhanced by the more contemporary literature. Previous discussions with police detectives and public health officials in Washington, D.C., while researching a master's thesis (May, 1970), had merely heightened my curiosity. This discussion and several subsequent ones during field work in the western portion of the United States really began to demonstrate to me the validity and utility of Durkheimian analysis.

Consulting on Suicide Problems

A second example should also be mentioned. The senior author is often asked to consult with various tribes and reservation groups on alcohol abuse, suicide, motor vehicle crashes, fetal alcohol syndrome, and other social problems. Before going to any western reservation or bordertown community, it is quite possible to predict or at least to anticipate a general range of self-destructive behavior which one can expect to find there. Even without exposure to any of the rates of the particular mortality, morbidity, and other problem behaviors for a reservation, knowing the social integration of the traditional tribal culture and the modernization forces which are at play there, one can anticipate what will be found. For example, if going to a Northern Plains reservation characterized by low integration and high social pressure of modernization, I might anticipate that: (1) the suicide rate will be 4 to 10 times the national average (even higher in certain short time clusters), (2) suicide will be predominantly among youth, (3) methods usually will be violent or severe, (4) alcohol involvement generally will relate to binge and flamboyant drinking patterns, (5) problems of self-destruction will be predominantly among the males and among a limited group of multi-problem families, and (6) individual suicide victims will be characterized by marginal levels of social integration regardless of the specific pattern or cultural theme.

Some other dynamics of suicide, however, are less easily discerned because of local fads, cultural trends, or physical conditions. For example, the exact method of suicide or attempt (i.e., caliber of gun, or exact type of drug used to overdose), the place of suicide, the intensity of clusters, and the immediate or crisis-like precursors will frequently vary from one tribe to the next. As some have written, there is a general degree of susceptibility to self-destruction which exists or is generated within a community (Davis and Hardy, 1986).

But specific, temporal, and localized influences will then shape the actual manifestation or specific outcome characteristics. Durkheim's work, however, provides the general framework which helps in understanding the magnitude of the problem that is actually manifested, as well as some of the recurring patterns found in the personal variables. Knowing the general patterns which emanate from social structural forces, allows one to concentrate on the localized specifics of the suicide problem.

Other Behavioral Health Problems

Using similar guidelines when working with behavioral health problems other than suicide, one can further utilize Durkheim's social integration concepts as useful guides. For example, the rate of fetal alcohol syndrome (FAS) and rates of maternal drinking will vary greatly and rather predictably from a low-integration tribe to a high-integration tribe (May, et al., 1983; May, 1991). Low-integration tribes have a higher prevalence of maternal drinking (than do other tribes) which is characterized by rather heavy, sporadic, binge drinking. High-integration tribes have a very low prevalence of women who drink at all, but through ostracism and other forces of social isolation, a pattern of persistent, chronic, and heavy drinking is common among those few who do drink. Thus, variations in social integration produce unique, yet predictable patterns and rates of FAS among the various groups. The FAS rates in the low-integration tribes are generally five to seven times higher than high-integration groups in most time periods studied among Southwestern tribes (May, et al., 1983). Similar patterns seem to hold outside the Southwest as well (May, 1991).

Fetal alcohol syndrome, then, like suicide, is inversely related to social integration. Social integration exerts influence on female drinking behaviors, and consequently on FAS.

Therefore, from Durkheim's theories and the scholarly work of others, a useful and practical understanding emerges. Applied solutions can ultimately be planned for a variety of public health problems. Adult alcohol abuse, motor vehicle crashes, and a number of behavioral health problems other than suicide can all be approached, analyzed, understood, and interventions planned through the use of Durkheimian methods (May, 1986, 1987, 1989a, 1989b, 1992).

CONCLUSION

Durkheimian theory and knowledge, used carefully and sensitively, will many times prompt people from other disciplines or academic training to take note. The utility and ability of Durkheim's general theory and his specific concepts have proven to be valuable tools for predicting specific phenomena in many settings. The general applicability and accurate nature of Durkheim's theories have laid the groundwork for insight which is substantial and many view as impressive in application. When combined with other more recent and complementary literature specific to American Indians, Durkheim's work is extremely useful in applied situations. One must, however, be careful not to overstep one's bounds or assume too much in such situations. Furthermore, the risk of committing the ecological correlation fallacy (Robinson, 1951) is always present. But a knowledge of Durkheim's theory and methodological approach can assure that one will seldom be taken completely by surprise when dealing with suicide or related issues.

Such is the nature of Durkheim's suicide theory. With careful research and elaboration, one can arrive at a broad understanding of the social forces which influence individuals in suicide and in a variety of related behaviors. Many of these behaviors, while seeming to be quite unique, individual, and isolated, are heavily influenced by common and rather universal social and cultural forces. Disciplines which dwell primarily on the individual often miss these broad and very useful insights. Disciplines which deal with the level of the organ, tissue, or cell may never know the joy of the insights which Durkheim discovered and delivered one hundred years ago.

To us, then, Durkheim's *Suicide* and his theory have been amazing tools. In our opinion, *Suicide* is the first major theoretical work in sociology which is of prime applied importance. We continue to use it in our work, and are thankful for it.

NOTES

1. In suicide studies among American Indians and Alaska Natives religion has not been explicitly studied to any degree, nor is it presented in this chapter due to the nature of our data, vital statistics. It is, however, a key variable in understanding suicide among both aggregates and individuals. For this reason our text mentions it as an important topic where appropriate.
2. Modernization is a process of conforming to present-day practices as expressed in mainstream culture and media. Modernization is not by definition a negative force for individuals and cultures, but among Indian tribes it frequently elevates rates of personal tragedy such as suicide.
3. Some of this fluctuation is caused by the small number (<7000) of Apaches in New Mexico.
4. Acculturation refers to the process of cultural change in which contact between two or more distinct groups results in the mixing of elements of the two groups. Usually one group takes on elements of the other group's culture to a greater degree than the other (Gould and Kolb, 1964; see also Linton, 1972; Walker, 1972). Acculturation of Indians to mainstream United States society has been increased or sped up by modernization. The building of new roads, more access to motor vehicles, and the saturation of tribes with new and abundant forms of media (television, radio, movies, videos, and print) have all accelerated change, typically acculturation, of Indians to the mainstream.
5. Many social scientists and others have continually treated the Navajo as a special group, characterizing them as highly unique from most other tribes and somewhat less negatively affected by the forces of modernization, change, and acculturation

than other tribes (Kluckholn and Leighton, 1962; Dutton, 1983). They are the largest tribe in the United States (220,000 members), they are mostly united on one massive reservation in the Southwest, they have been protected from mainstream social intrusion to a much greater degree than other tribes, and they have proven to be very highly adaptable to change over the past centuries. In a sense their minority status has been different. Therefore, they may not be as subject to, nor as likely to conform to, the same social phenomena that affect other tribes, particularly other medium integration groups.

6. Attempted suicide is predominantly a female behavior among Indians as among other groups (May, 1987, 1973).

REFERENCES

Bachman, R. *Death and Violence: On the Reservation.* New York: Auburn House, 1992.

Barter, J. T., and Weist, K. M. Historical and contemporary patterns of Northern Cheyenne suicide. Unpublished paper, University of Montana, Department of Anthropology, 1972.

Bechtold, D. W. Cluster suicide in American Indian adolescents. *American Indian and Alaska Native Mental Health Research,* 1988, 1(3), 26-35.

Benedict, R. *Patterns of Culture.* New York: Mentor, 1934.

Berlin, I. N. Suicide among American Indian adolescents. *Suicide and Life-Threatening Behavior,* 1987, 17, 218-232.

Berlin, I. N. Psychopathology and its antecedents among American Indian adolescents. *Advances in Clinical Child Psychology,* 1986, 9, 125-152.

Berlin, I. N. Prevention of adolescent suicide among some Native American Tribes. In S. C. Feinstein (ed.), *Adolescent Psychiatry: Developmental and Clinical Studies.* Chicago: University of Chicago Press, 1985.

Berman, A. L. Suicide on the Duck Valley Indian reservation. Final Report, grant from the McCormick Foundation, 1979.

Biernoff, M. A report on Pueblo Indian suicide. Unpublished paper, 1969.

Blackwood, L. Health problems of the Alaska Natives: suicide mortality and morbidity. Unpublished manuscript, Alaska Area Native Health Service, Anchorage, 1978.

Braroe, N. W. *Indian and White: Self-Image and Interaction in a Canadian Plains Community.* Palo Alto, CA: Stanford University Press, 1975.

Breed, W. The Negro and fatalistic suicide. *Pacific Sociological Review,* 1970, 13(3), 156-162.

Broudy, D. W., and May, P. A. Demographic and epidemiologic transition among the Navajo Indians. *Social Biology,* 1983, 30, 1-16.

Bushnell, J. H. From American Indian to Indian-American. *American Anthropologist,* 1972, 70, 1108-1116.

Butler, G. C. Incidence of suicide among ethnic groups of the Northwest Territories and Yukon Territory. *Medical Services Journal of Canada,* 1965, 21(4), 252-256.

Bynum, J. Suicide and the American Indian. In H. M. Bahr, B. A. Chadwick, and R. C. Day (eds.), *Native Americans Today.* New York: Harper & Row, 1972.

Claymore, B. J. A public health approach to suicide attempts on a Sioux Reservation. *American Indian and Alaska Native Mental Health Research,* 1988, 1(3), 19-24.

Conrad, R. D., and Kahn, M. An epidemiological study of suicide among the Papago Indians. *American Journal of Psychiatry,* 1974, 131, 69-72.

Cutler, R., and Morrison, N. Sudden death: a study of characteristics of victims and events leading to sudden death in British Columbia with primary emphasis on apparent alcohol involvement and Indian sudden deaths. Vancouver, BC: Alcoholism Foundation of British Columbia, 1971.

Davenport, J. A., and Davenport, J. A. Native American suicide. *Social Casework,* 1987, 68, 533-539.

Davis, B. R., and Hardy, R. J. A suicide epidemic model. *Social Biology,* 1986, 33, 291-300.

DeBruyn, L. M., Lujan, C. C., and May, P. A. A comparative study of abused and neglected American Indian children in the Southwest. *Social Science and Medicine,* 1992, 35, 305-315.

Dizmang, L. H. Suicide among the Cheyenne Indians. *Bulletin of Suicidology,* 1967, 1, 8-11.

Dizmang, L. H., Watson, J., May, P. A., and Bopp, J. Adolescent suicide at an Indian Reservation. *American Journal of Orthopsychiatry,* 1974, 44, 43-49.

Durkheim, E. *Suicide.* New York: Free Press, 1951.

Dutton, B. P. *American Indians of the Southwest.* Albuquerque: University of New Mexico Press, 1983.

Forbes, N., and Van der Hyde, V. Suicide in Alaska from 1978 to 1985. *American Indian and Alaska Native Mental Health Research,* 1988, 1(3), 36-55.

Fox, J., and Ward, J. A. Indian suicide in Northern Ontario. Paper presented at the Annual Meeting of the Canadian Psychiatric Association, Saskatoon, Saskatchewan, 1977.

Fox, J., Manitonabi, D., and Ward, J. A. An Indian community with a high suicide rate. *Canadian Journal of Psychiatry,* 1984, 29, 425-427.

Garro, L. C. Suicides by status Indians in Manitoba. *Arctic Medical Research,* 1988, 47 (Supplement 1), 590-592.

Gould, J., and Kolb, W. *A Dictionary of the Social Sciences.* New York: Free Press, 1964.

Havighurst, R. J. The extent and significance of suicide among American Indians today. *Mental Hygiene,* 1971, 55, 174-177.

Henry, A. F., and Short, J. F. *Suicide and Homicide.* New York: Free Press, 1954.

Henry, A. F., and Short, J. F. The sociology of suicide. In E. S. Shneidman and N. L. Farberow (eds.), *Clues to Suicide.* New York: McGraw-Hill, 1957.

Hodge, W. H. *The First Americans.* New York: Holt, Rinehart & Winston, 1981.

Howard, C. Navajo tribal demography, 1983-1986 in comparative perspective. Unpublished doctoral dissertation, University of New Mexico, 1992.

Humphrey, J. A., and Kupferer, H. J. Homicide and suicide among the Cherokee and Lumbee Indians of North Carolina. *International Journal of Social Psychiatry,* 1982, 28(2), 121-128.

Josephy, A. M. *The Indian Heritage of America.* New York: Bantam Books, 1978.

Kluckholn, C., and Leighton, D. *The Navajo.* Garden City, NY: Doubleday, 1962.

Kraus, R. Suicidal behavior in Alaska Natives. *Alaska Medicine,* 1974, 16(1), 2-6.

Kunitz, S. J. Underdevelopment and social services on the Navajo Reservation. *Human Organization,* 1977, 36, 398-404.

LaFromboise, T. D., and Bigfoot, D. S. Cultural and cognitive considerations in the prevention of American Indian adolescent suicide. *Journal of Adolescence,* 1988, 11, 139-153.

Levy, J. E. Navajo suicide. *Human Organization,* 1965, 24, 308-318.

Levy, J. E., and Kunitz, S. J. Notes on some White Mountain Apache social pathologies. *Plateau,* 1969, 42, 11-19.

Levy, J. E., and Kunitz, S. J. Indian reservations, anomie, and social pathologies. *Southwestern Journal of Anthropology,* 1971, 27(2), 97-128.

Levy, J. E., and Kunitz, S. J. *Indian Drinking.* New York: Wiley Interscience, 1974.

Levy, J. E., and Kunitz, S. J. A suicide prevention program for Hopi youth. *Social Science and Medicine,* 1987, 25, 930-940.

Levy, J. E., Kunitz, S. J., and Everett, M. W. Navajo criminal homicide. *Southwestern Journal of Anthropology,* 1969, 25(2), 124-152.

Lin, R. L. A profile of reservation Indian high school girls. *Journal of American Indian Education,* 1987, 27, 18-28.

Linton, R. The distinctive aspects of acculturation. In D. E. Walker (ed.), *The Emergent Native Americans.* Boston: Little, Brown, 1972.

Lujan, C. C., DeBruyn, L., May, P. A., and Bird, M. Profile of abused and neglected children in the Southwest. *Child Abuse and Neglect,* 1989, 13, 449-461.

Manson, S. J., Beals, J., Dick, R. W., and Duclos, C. Risk factors for suicide among Indian adolescents at a boarding school. *Public Health Reports,* 1988, 104, 609-614.

May, P. A. Suicide in Washington, DC. Unpublished master's thesis, Wake Forest University, 1970.

May, P. A. Suicide and suicide attempts on the Pine Ridge Reservation. Pine Ridge, SD: PHS Community Mental Health Program. Unpublished manuscript, 1973.

May, P. A. Alcohol and drug misuse prevention programs for American Indians. *Journal of Studies on Alcohol,* 1986, 47, 187-195.

May, P. A. Suicide and self-destruction among American Indian youths. *American Indian and Alaska Native Mental Health Research,* 1987, 1(1), 52-69.

May, P. A. Fetal alcohol effects among North American Indians. *Alcohol Health and Research World,* 1988, 15(3), 239-248.

May, P. A. Alcohol abuse and alcoholism among American Indians. In T. D. Watts and R. Wright (eds.), *Alcoholism in Minority Populations.* Springfield, IL: Charles C Thomas, 1989a.

May, P. A. Motor vehicle crashes and alcohol among American Indians and Alaska Natives. Office of the Surgeon General, U.S. Public Health Service. The Surgeon General's Workshop on Drunk Driving, background papers. Washington, DC: U.S. Department of Health and Human Services, 1989b.

May, P. A. A bibliography on suicide and suicide attempts among American Indians and Alaska Natives. *Omega,* 1990, 21, 199-214.

May, P. A. Fetal alcohol syndrome among American Indians. *Alcohol Health and Research World,* 1991, 15(3), 239-248.

May, P. A. Alcohol policy considerations for Indian reservations and bordertown communities. *American Indian and Alaska Native Mental Health Research,* 1992, 4(3), 5-59.

May, P. A., Hymbaugh, K. A., Aase, M., and Samet, J. M. Epidemiology of fetal alcohol syndrome among American Indians of the Southwest. *Social Biology,* 1983, 30, 374-387.

May, P. A., and Van Winkle, N. W. Indian adolescent suicide. *American Indian and Alaska Native Mental Health Research,* 1994, 4.

McFee, M. The 150% man, a product of Blackfeet acculturation. *American Anthropologist,* 1972, 70, 1096-1107.

Minnis, M. S. The relationship of the social structure of an Indian community to adult and juvenile delinquency. *Social Forces,* 1963, 41, 395-403.

Phillips, D. P. The influence of suggestion on suicide. *American Sociology Review,* 1974, 39, 340-354.

Resnick, H. L. P., and Dizmang, L. H. Observations on suicidal behavior among American Indians. *American Journal of Psychiatry,* 1971, 127, 882-887.

Robinson, W. S. The logical structure of analytical induction. *American Sociological Review,* 1951, 16, 812-818.

Ross, C. A., and Davis, B. (1986) Suicide and parasuicide in a Northern Canada Native community. *Canadian Journal of Psychiatry,* 1986, 3, 331-334.

Seyer, D. S. Suicide in the Native Indians of Canada. Paper presented to the 10th International Congress for Suicide Prevention and Crisis Intervention, Ottawa, Ontario, 1979.

Shkilnyk, A. M. *A Poison Stronger Than Love.* New Haven: Yale University Press, 1985.

Shore, J. H. Suicide and suicide attempts among American Indians of the Pacific Northwest. *International Journal of Social Psychiatry,* 1972, 18(2), 91-96.

Shuck, L., Orgel, M. B., and Vogel, A. V. Self-inflicted gunshot wounds to the face. *Journal on Trauma,* 1980, 20, 370-377.

Spaulding, J. M. Recent suicide rates among ten Ojibwa Indian bands in Northwestern Ontario. *Omega,* 1985-1986, 16, 347-354.

Spencer, R. F., and Jennings, J. D. *The Native Americans,* 2nd Ed. New York: Harper & Row, 1977.

Stull, D. D. Modernization and symptoms of stress. Unpublished doctoral dissertation, University of Colorado, 1973.

Stull, D. E. New data on accident victim rates among Papago Indians. *Human Organization,* 1977, 36, 395-398.

Tabachnick, N. L. *Accident or Suicide?* Springfield, IL: Charles C Thomas, 1973.

Thurman, P. J., Martin, D., and Martin, M. An assessment of attempted suicides among adolescent Cherokee Indians. *Journal of Multicultural Counseling and Development,* 1985, 13(4), 176-182.

Tower, M. A suicide epidemic in an American Indian community. *American Indian and Alaska Native Mental Health Research,* 1989, 3(1), 34-44.

Travis, R. Suicide and economic development among the Inupiat Eskimo. *White Cloud Journal,* 1984, 3(3), 14-21.

Trott, L., Barnes, G., and Denmoff, R. Ethnicity and other demographic characteristics as predictors of sudden drug-related deaths. *Journal of Studies on Alcohol,* 1981, 42, 564-578.

U.S. Bureau of the Census. *Statistical Abstract of the United States.* Washington, DC: U.S. Government Printing Office, 1982.

U.S. Bureau of the Census. *Statistical Abstract of the United States.* Washington, DC: U.S. Government Printing Office, 1986.

U.S. Bureau of the Census. *Statistical Abstract of the United States.* Washington, DC: U.S. Government Printing Office, 1990.

U.S. Bureau of the Census. American Indian and Alaska Native Areas: 1990. Washington, DC: unpublished report, 1991.

Van Winkle, N. W., and May, P. A. Native American suicide in New Mexico, 1957-1979. *Human Organization,* 1986, 45, 296-309.

Van Winkle, N. W., and May, P. A. An update on American Indian suicide in New Mexico, 1980-1987. *Human Organization,* 1993, 52 (3), 304-315.

Walker, D. E. *The Emergent Native Americans.* Boston, MA: Little, Brown, 1972.

Ward, J. A., and Fox, J. A suicide epidemic on an Indian Reserve. *Canadian Psychiatric Association Journal,* 1977, 22, 423-426.

Wills, J. E. Psychological problems of the Sioux Indians resulting in the accident phenomena. *Pine Ridge Research Bulletin,* 1969, 8, 49-63.

14

A Random-Walk Hypothesis for the Suicide Rate and Its Implication for Durkheim's Theory of Suicide

Bijou Yang, PhD

Ever since Durkheim's seminal work on suicide was published in 1897, numerous theoretical and empirical works have appeared in the field of suicidology in order to unveil the mystery of the societal suicide rate (e.g., Lester, 1989; Lester and Yang, 1993).[1] However, none of these investigations have looked into the variation of the suicide rate over time itself.[2] This chapter attempts to use econometric techniques in order to explore the characteristics of the time-series suicide rate and to show that the findings are compatible with Durkheim's original data and theoretical framework.

The chapter is organized as follows. The next section will introduce the concept of a random walk and its implications for the suicide rate. Then follows a section discussing the testing procedure involved and test results. The final section summarizes the conclusions and explores their implications for suicide prevention.

A RANDOM-WALK HYPOTHESIS OF THE SUICIDE RATE

If we assume that the suicide rate is a stochastic process, then the time-series suicide rate could be stationary or nonstationary. Stationarity means that the characteristics of the stochastic process do not change over time, whereas nonstationarity means that those characteristics change over time.[3]

Among the nonstationary stochastic processes, the sources of nonstationarity might be due to the underlying stochastic process (difference nonstationarity) or to a linear trend (trend nonstationarity) (Nelson and Plosser, 1982). A good example of the former type of nonstationarity is the movement of stock prices over time, while a good example of the latter type of nonstationarity is a sinusoidal wave along an upward linear trend. The difference between these two types of nonstationary stochastic processes is that the former has a unit root. Any nonstationary stochastic process, if found to have a unit root, is called a *random walk*. Therefore, a random walk refers to a nonstationary stochastic process with a unit root.

By drawing from research in econometrics, two relevant characteristics of a random walk can be identified: (1) the basic characteristics of a time-series are found to change over time, and (2) a portion of any disturbance to the stochastic process of concern will persist through time (Diebold and Nerlove, 1990, p. 37; Rudebusch, 1990).[4] The first property is derived from the fact that a random walk is nonstationary. The second property has interesting and important implications for suicide, that is, major societal events (e.g., a war or an economic recession) which affect the suicide rate will have a permanent effect on the suicide rate. This, in turn, implies that suicide is a chronic process.

It is interesting that we can find traces in Durkheim's writings which are compatible with these two features of a random walk. First, Durkheim called suicide the ransom-money of civilization (Durkheim, 1951, p. 367) because the culturally advanced European countries experienced increases in the suicide rate during the nineteenth century. For example, the suicide rate rose 411 percent in Prussia from 1826 to 1890, 385 percent in France from 1826 to 1888, and 318 percent in German Austria from 1841 to 1877. The extent of the increase in the suicide rate in those days seems to suggest that the basic nature of the suicidal phenomenon changed dramatically in many regions of Europe during the period. This implies that the suicide rate may not be a stationary time series over long periods of time.

Second, social regulation and social integration were the two fundamental concepts proposed by Durkheim (1897) in his theory of the etiology of suicide. Regulation refers to a "spirit of discipline" and integration to "attachment to social groups" (Besnard, 1988). Both concepts are long-term variables because both seem to be the result of interaction among people in the community and because the formation of discipline and social groups involves a process of trial and error over a long period of time.[5] It is interesting to note that, when confronted with both long- and short-term perspectives, Durkheim seemed to emphasize the long-term perspective. For example, in his discussion of anomie, Durkheim was mainly interested in and preoccupied by chronic anomie rather than acute anomie (Besnard, 1988). Anomie, according to Durkheim, results from a lack of social regulation.[6]

Even though detailed annual data were not available for testing the nonstationarity of the European suicide rates in the nineteenth century, it would be interesting to see whether the hypothesis is supported by modern data. We tested for the existence of a unit root in the time-series suicide rate for recent American suicide rates, since a nonstationary stochastic process with a unit root implies that the suicide rate follows a random walk. This, in turn, would support that hypothesis that suicide is a chronic process. Yang (1992) suggested that a possible test procedure for this would involve two steps.

First, the sample autocorrelations of the time-series suicide rate are examined. The sample autocorrelations will indicate whether the time-series follows an autoregressive stochastic process, a moving-average stochastic process, or a mix of the two, namely, an autoregressive moving-average stochastic process. The autocorrelations also indicate whether the time-series is stationary or not. Second, the Dickey-Fuller test (Dickey and Fuller, 1981) is employed to test directly whether the suicide rate has a unit root.

TEST RESULTS

Since the sample autocorrelation functions of all of the suicide rates for the U.S. from 1933 to 1987 examined in Yang's study followed a gradual decay pattern instead of oscillation between consecutive lags, this provided empirical support for the autoregressive model rather than the moving-average model or the autoregressive moving-average model (Box and Jenkins, 1970; Pindyck and Rubinfeld, 1981). Secondly, the sample autocorrelation functions of all of the suicide rates examined took 10 to 20 years to become zero, and this raised doubts about the stationarity of the annual time-series suicide rate. Both conclusions suggested the need for the Dickey-Fuller test.

The results of the Dickey-Fuller test for the total population and for different sociodemographic groups supported the hypothesis that the time-series suicide rates are a second-order autoregressive process with a unit root (without drift). (Yang studied the time-series suicide rates for six age groups and four sex-by-race groups.)

Yang has also applied the same Dickey-Fuller test to the monthly suicide rates for the total population of the United States for the period 1957 to 1986 and obtained evidence for the same conclusion as the results for the annual suicide rate. In order to explore this phenomenon further, the two-step test was applied to the annual Australian suicide rates for the total population, for males, and for females for the time period 1901 to 1985 using data obtained from Hassan and Tan (1989). The results of the tests matched exactly those for the United States data, namely, the autocorrelation functions of those three time-series decayed to zero with a lag of 9 to 20 years, and the time-series appeared to fit a random-walk process. Unfortunately, monthly data for Australian suicides were not available for examination.

CONCLUSIONS

If the annual suicide rate is a random-walk process, then any disturbance to the societal suicide rate will have a permanent impact. As a consequence, the annual suicide rate has the properties of a long-term or chronic process. This random walk hypothesis of the suicide rate is supported by Durkheim's theory of suicide, for Durkheim explicitly mentioned that social regulation tended to take time to have an impact on the societal suicide rate (Durkheim, 1951).[7]

The support for the random-walk hypothesis for the annual suicide rate provided by the annual American and Australian data implies that traumatic events at the societal level will have a permanent long-term effect. It also indicates the importance of chronic processes as a major determinant of the societal suicide rate.

The implication of these results for suicide prevention is that governments should focus on actions which will have a major impact on the society, for disturbances to the societal suicide rate will probably have a permanent impact. Recently, Lester (1992) has shown that American states which instituted programs to prevent youth suicide witnessed a beneficial change in youth suicide rates. These programs included legislation, involvement by governors, commission task forces, manuals and brochures, school curricula, training conferences, direct services and special studies. This study suggests the kinds of government initiatives which may have a long-term impact on suicide rates. Governments should also consider the potential impact of major changes in the social and economic conditions of the society on the suicide rate.

NOTES

1. While Lester (1989) provides a detailed review of the theoretical literature, Lester and Yang (1993) focus more on empirical studies, especially about the relationship between the macroeconomic environment and the suicide rate. Both books review numerous investigations in the field of suicidology.
2. The one exception might be the circadian variation examined by Motohashi (1990) with a spectral analysis using the maximum entropy method and the cosinor method.
3. Most applications of the time-series analyses focus on the nonstationary process, especially in economics. For example, Nelson and Plosser (1982) found that most macroeconomic time-series are better characterized as nonstationary stochastic processes rather than as stationary fluctuations around a deterministic trend. Nonstationary stochastic processes have been applied also to financial market variables such as futures contracts (Samuelson, 1965), stock prices (Samuelson, 1973), dividends (Kleidon, 1986), and spot and forward exchange rates (Meese and Singleton, 1983).
4. One property included in Yang's (1992) paper indicated that individuals use available information rationally. Applied to suicide, this brings up a psychological issue which was, apparently, ignored by Durkheim (1897) since he was concerned only with sociological dimensions of the suicide problem.
5. This does not exclude the observation that some events of a short-term nature may still increase the risk of suicide. It has been documented that the correlation between unemployment and suicide is positive when it is statistically significant (Platt, 1984; Lester and Yang, 1993; Yang, 1992). In addition, suicidologists also acknowledge that publicity of suicide stories by the media is a major cause of an immediate, short-term increase in the suicide rate (Bollen and Phillips, 1982; Phillips, 1974, 1989; Wasserman, 1984).
6. There seems to be a dispute among contemporary sociologists about the meaning of the concept of anomie as used by Durkheim. Merton (1957, 1964), one of the

leading American sociologists, and his followers maintain that anomie results from a disjunction between culturally prescribed goals and socially institutionalized means for achieving these goals. His French counterpart, Besnard (1988) argues, on the other hand, that anomie is a situation characterized by "indeterminate goals and unlimited aspirations...in a context of expansion or increasing upward mobility." It is interesting to note that Merton's definition is more static in nature whereas Besnard's provides a dynamic dimension. Therefore, the two views can be taken as complementary aspects of the same theoretical framework.

7. It is not clear whether Durkheim thought that social integration could also be a chronic process. On the other hand, Durkheim (1951) mentioned that the way in which the Industrial Revolution affected the society clearly illustrated how social regulation could change over a long period.

REFERENCES

Besnard, P. The true nature of anomie. *Sociological Theory,* 1988, 6(1), 91-95.

Bollen, K., and Phillips, D. P. Imitative suicides. *American Sociological Review,* 1982, 47, 802-809.

Box, G. E. P., and Jenkins, G. M. *Time Series Analysis: Forecasting and Control.* San Francisco: Holden-Day, 1970.

Dickey, D. A., and Fuller, W. A. Likelihood ratio statistics for autoregressive time series with a unit root. *Econometrica,* 1981, 49, 1057-1072.

Diebold, F. X., and Nerlove, M. Unit roots in economic time series: a selective survey. In T. B. Fomby and G. F. Rhodes (eds.), *Advances in Econometrics. Vol. 8: Cointegration, Spurious Regressions, and Unit Roots.* Greenwich, CT: JAI Press, 1990.

Durkheim, E. *Le Suicide.* Paris: Felix Alcan, 1897.

Durkheim, E. *Suicide.* (Translated by J. A. Spaulding and G. Simpson.) New York: Free Press, 1951.

Hassan, R., and Tan, G. Suicide trends in Australia, 1901-1985: analysis of sex differentials. *Suicide and Life-Threatening Behavior,* 1989, 19, 362-380.

Kleidon, A. W. Variance bounds tests and stock price valuation models. *Journal of Political Economy,* 1986, 12, 141-153.

Lester, D. *Suicide from a Sociological Perspective.* Springfield, IL: Charles C Thomas, 1989.

Lester, D. State initiatives in addressing youth suicide. *Social Psychiatry and Psychiatric Epidemiology,* 1992, 27, 75-77.

Lester, D., and Yang, B. *Economic Perspectives of Suicide.* New York: AMS Press, 1993.

Meese, R. A., and Singleton, K. J. On unit roots and the empirical modeling of exchange rates. *International Economic Review,* 1983, 24, 1029-1035.

Merton, R. K. *Social Theory and Social Structure.* New York: Free Press, 1957.

Merton, R. K. Anomie, anomia and social interaction. In M. B. Clinard (ed.), *Anomia and Deviant Behavior.* New York: Free Press, 1964.

Motohashi, Y. Circadian variations in suicide attempts in Tokyo from 1978 to 1985. *Suicide and Life-Threatening Behavior,* 1990, 20, 352-361.

Nelson, C. R., and Plosser, C. I. Trends and random walks in macroeconomic time series. *Journal of Monetary Economics,* 1982, 10, 139-162.

Phillips, D. P. Recent advances in suicidology: the study of imitative suicide. In R. F. W. Diekstra, R. Maris, S. Platt, A. Schmidtke, and G. Sonneck (eds.), *Suicide and Its Prevention.* Leiden: E. J. Brill, 1989.

Pindyck, R. S., and Rubinfeld, D. L. *Econometric Models and Economic Forecasts,* 2nd Ed. New York: McGraw-Hill, 1981.

Platt, S. D. Unemployment and suicidal behavior. *Social Science and Medicine*, 1984, 19, 93-115.

Rudebusch, G. D. Trends and random walks in macroeconomic time series: a reexamination. Paper presented at the annual meeting of the American Economic Association, Washington, DC, 1990.

Samuelson, P. A. Proof that properly anticipated prices fluctuate randomly. *Industrial Management Review*, 1965, 6, 41-50.

Samuelson, P. A. Proof that properly discounted present values of assets vibrate randomly. *Bell Journal of Economics and Management Science*, 1973, 4, 369-374.

Wasserman, I. Imitation and suicide. *American Sociological Review*, 1984, 49, 427-436.

Yang, B. Is the time-series suicide rate of the U.S.A. a random walk? Paper presented at the annual meeting of the American Economic Association, New Orleans, 1992.

Index